OF REVELATION AND REVOLUTION

Of

REVELATION

and

REVOLUTION

*Christianity, Colonialism,
and Consciousness in South Africa*

V O L U M E   O N E

Jean Comaroff and John Comaroff

THE UNIVERSITY OF CHICAGO PRESS
Chicago and London

Jean Comaroff and John Comaroff are professors of anthropology at the University of Chicago. She is the author of *Body of Power, Spirit of Resistance*, and has published extensively in medical anthropology and the anthropology of religion. He is the coauthor of *Rules and Processes*, editor of *The Meaning of Marriage Payments* and *The Boer War Diary of Sol T. Plaatje*, and has written numerous papers in social, political, legal, and economic anthropology.

The University of Chicago Press, Chicago 60637
The University of Chicago Press, Ltd., London

© 1991 by The University of Chicago
All rights reserved. Published 1991
Printed in the United States of America
00 99 98 97 96 95 94 93 92 91   5 4 3 2 1

Library of Congress Cataloging-in-Publication Data

Comaroff, Jean.
    Of revelation and revolution : Christianity, colonialism, and consciousness in South Africa / Jean Comaroff and John L. Comaroff.
        p.   cm.
    Includes bibliographical references (p.   ) and index.
    ISBN 0-226-11441-4 (cloth). — ISBN 0-226-11442-2 (paperback)
    1. Tswana (African people)—History.   2. Tswana (African people)—Missions.   3. Tswana (African people)—Social conditions.
    4. London Missionary Society—Missions—South Africa.   5. Wesleyan Methodist Missionary Society—Missions—South Africa.   6. Great Britain—Colonies—Africa.   7. South Africa—History.   I. Comaroff, John L., 1945– .   II. Title.
    DT1058.T78C66   1991
    303.48'241'00899639775—dc20   90-46753
                                                                              CIP

For Josh and Jane

CONTENTS

Volume One

ILLUSTRATIONS

PREFACE

IN 1818 THE DIRECTORS of the London Missionary Society sent a mechanical clock to grace the church at its first station among the Tswana in South Africa. No ordinary clock—its hours were struck by strutting British soldiers carved of wood—it became the measure of a historical process in the making. Clearly meant to proclaim the value of time in Christian, civilized communities, the contraption had an altogether unexpected impact. For the Africans insisted that the "carved ones" were emissaries of a distant king who, with missionary connivance, would place them in a "house of bondage." A disconsolate evangelist had eventually to "take down the fairy-looking strangers, and cut a piece off their painted bodies, to convince the affrighted natives that the objects of their alarm were only bits of coloured wood" (Moffat 1842:339; see below, p. 192). The churchman knew, however, that the timepiece had made visible a fundamental truth. The Tswana had not been reassured by his gesture; indeed, they seem to have concluded that "the motives of the missionary were anything but disinterested." And they were correct, of course. In the face of the clock they had caught their first glimpse of a future time, a time when their colonized world would march to quite different rhythms.

This is a study of the colonization of consciousness and the consciousness of colonization in South Africa. It traces the processes by which Nonconformist Christian missionaries, among the earliest footsoldiers of British colonialism, sought to change the hearts and minds, the signs and practices, of the Southern Tswana. As such, it is a historical anthropology of cultural confrontation—of domination and reaction, struggle and innovation. Its chronological span is approximately a century, between 1820 and 1920, although it is not written according to the strict demands of chronology. But it also casts its eye forward to the present, toward both everyday resistance and historical consciousness in apartheid South Africa. Similarly, while it focuses on a particular people—those made, in the nineteenth century, into an ethnic group called "the" Tswana—its compass extends to the predicament of black South Africans at large.

As this suggests, *Of Revelation and Revolution* is written against a background of what, to us at least, seem the most difficult questions posed by the nature of social experience. How, precisely, is consciousness made and remade? And how is it mediated by such distinctions as class, gender, and ethnicity? How do some meanings and actions, old and new alike, become conventional—either asserted as collective values or just taken for granted—while others become objects of contest and resistance? How, indeed, are we to understand the connections, historical and conceptual, among culture, consciousness, and ideology? In seeking to address some of these issues, our study explores a process which, though situated in South Africa, has echoes throughout the so-called Third World, and probably beyond. It is a process in which the "savages" of colonialism are ushered, by earnest Protestant evangelists, into the revelation of their own misery, are promised salvation through self-discovery and civilization, and are drawn into a conversation with the culture of modern capitalism—only to find themselves enmeshed, willingly or not, in its order of signs and values, interests and passions, wants and needs. Even the established modes of protest open to them speak in ringing Christian terms—terms like civil rights, civilized liberties, freedom of conscience.

And yet, even as they are encompassed by the European capitalist system—consumed, ironically, as they consume its goods and texts—these "natives" of other worlds often seek to seize its symbols, to question their authority and integrity, and to reconstruct them in their own image. Sometimes they do so in open defiance; sometimes through strikingly imaginative acts of cultural subversion and re-presentation; sometimes in silent, sullen resistance. And in so doing, as de Certeau (1984:xiii) would have it, they "escape [the dominant order] without leaving it." In many cases, however, their actions end up contributing to their own subordination. Adorno and Brecht, Lukács and Bloch, among others, have shown how aesthetic works that set out to contest domination often come, by means subtle and diverse, to be implicated in it (see Bloch et al. 1980). So it is with all signification, not least the cultural creations and social reactions of colonized peoples toward those who rule them. Even the most revolutionary consciousness may fail to call into doubt the essential trappings and entrapments of the colonizing culture. And even then, the break with prior structures of power and perception is never as complete as utopian theorists of liberation would have us believe. The difficult road from revelation to revolution, in short, is the continuing epic of black South African history. It is also the route of many others who must walk the byways and backroads of the modern world system.

But *Of Revelation and Revolution* serves also as a metaphor of a more personal kind. It evokes the history of our own engagement with modern South Africa, the land in which we grew up and from which we have taken our reluctant leave. Once caught up in its liberal scholarly orthodoxies, two decades of research and reflection have led us ever further away—toward a concern not with the timeless, and hence mythic, ethnography of indigenous peoples, but with the making of, the struggle for, Southern Africa itself. In this respect we are hardly unique. Many anthropologists have pointed to the dangers, both analytic and political, of treating local cultures as ethnological islands unto themselves, islands without history. To do so in South Africa is especially egregious. For these very islands of culture, of reinvented tradition, have long been an integral part of a brutal system of domination. They are the "ethnic homelands," the notorious "bantustans" that disenfranchise blacks by banishing them from their rightful place both in the land of their birth and in its history. Little wonder that, like other scholars of Southern Africa, our anthropology has been both historicized and radicalized by its encounter with apartheid.

In the same reformist spirit, we also intend *Of Revelation and Revolution* as an affirmation of anthropology itself, an affirmation in the face of persistent political and epistemological critique. We are by now all familiar with the accusing finger pointed at the discipline for its complicity in colonialism, for its alleged part in the creation and domination of the "other." The deprecating ethnographic eye, we have repeatedly been told, has to bear a good deal of the blame for conjuring up the orient and perpetuating the primitive as its own self-serving phantasm. These accusations, often made by "others" who share with us the high bourgeois corridors of academe, are largely correct—although some of them caricature anthropology in order to argue with it. It is all too easy to conflate the analysis of difference with the creation of inequality, and to ignore the role of anthropologists in documenting the capacity of colonized peoples to resist the embrace of the West. Still, the question seems to insist on being asked: Is the act of ethnography *intrinsically* a violation of "the other"? Perhaps, perhaps not. Our own answer, at this point, is to do an anthropology *of* the colonial encounter. We do so on the assumption that, if the discipline has, in the past, been an instrument of a colonizing culture, there is no reason why, in the present, it cannot serve as an instrument of liberation. By revealing the structures and processes by which some people come to dominate others, it may just as well affirm—indeed, chart the way to—revolutionary consciousness. Nor does the point apply only to the study of colonialism. It holds equally in precolonial and postcolonial contexts, in the First as well as the Third World.

Our spirit of affirmation is also directed at the so-called "epistemological hypochondria" found in some anthropological quarters: i.e., the anxiety, fed by diverse forms of radical criticism, that the philosophical bases, intellectual objectives, and analytic methods of the discipline are indefensible. The point also has a political dimension. Our means of describing social reality, it is said, far from being techniques for the production of new knowledge, are merely part of the apparatus through which bourgeois society endlessly reproduces the same old ethnocentric texts. And itself. Assertions of this kind are hardly new, of course. They surface at fairly regular intervals, albeit often phrased as if they had no precedent. At times too they come from outside. Recently, for example, a fine historian, Ken Post (1986), concerned that the ethnographic gaze lacks the breadth to take in macro-social forces, raised the question of whether a historical anthropology is even possible.

Well, is it? Is anthropology really mired in an epistemological fog? Maybe. It certainly confronts as many problems in the production of its knowledge as it faces political issues in its everyday work. Nonetheless, to dwell on the former at the cost of the latter, or to confuse the world of social action with a literary text, is to misunderstand entirely the role of a critical social science. If the discipline can unmask anything unique about the nature of the human condition—of colonialism and consciousness, of domination and resistance, of oppression and liberation—it is both possible and worth-while. And if it can do so self-critically, sensitively, and imaginatively, so much the better. In that light, carefully argued epistemological critique may, and should, sharpen our awareness of our own historical role. But, however finely wrought his or her *angst*, the social scientist has in the end to suspend disbelief and *act*. It is at best a gratuitous indulgence merely to debate epis-temological niceties, or to argue over the impossibility of making "objective" statements about the world, while apartheid and other repressive regimes continue to wreak havoc on human lives, often claiming anthropological alibis as they do so. Our practice may not make perfect, and it demands of us a deep awareness of its inevitable dangers and entanglements. Still, it can make something in the cause of praxis—in South Africa as everywhere else.

It is appropriate that the etymological root of the term "acknowledge-ment" should be "knowledge." We should like to signal our gratitude to a number of people for offering us their wisdom and insight, without which this study would have been all the poorer. Our first teacher, the late Monica Wilson, herself a missionary's daughter, taught us that it is impossible to understand the past or the present in South Africa without taking into ac-count the salience of religion—especially evangelical Christianity. We may have come, all these years later, to differ with her over the precise historical role of Protestant liberalism. But the general point, eschewed by many less percipient scholars, has proven to be absolutely correct.

If anyone has demonstrated the importance of Christianity and the civi-lizing mission in Southern Africa, it is another of our teachers, Isaac Scha-pera. His remarkable *oeuvre* has laid the foundations on which our research is built. Indeed, we regard the present study as a tribute to his pathbreaking work and to his consistent refusal to exclude the impact of colonization from the compass of anthropological concern. In his mature years he continues to amaze us with his command of Tswana history and ethnography, knowledge which he has always made available to us with touching generosity—and with more than a dash of astute criticism.

Our colleagues in the Department of Anthropology at the University of Chicago have been closely and constructively involved in this project from the first. Many of them read all or part of the manuscript, and several gathered each week to discuss earlier drafts, chapter by chapter, hour after hour. It was a rare and invigorating intellectual experience. Our appreciation goes to Bernard Cohn, William Hanks, James Fernandez, Raymond Fogelson, Raymond Smith, Sharon Stephens, and, in particular, Terence Turner and Marshall Sahlins for trying their level best to challenge us into deeper understanding and richer analyses—and for never allowing us to get away with anything less than a *very* good argument. Also, thanks to William Hanks for his acute reading of chapter 1; to Paul Friedrich and Manning Nash for their helpful responses to a version of chapter 5; to our student, Debra Spitulnik, for her valuable suggestions on the topic of colonial linguistics; to Fred Cooper, who read much of this volume with an extraordinarily perceptive eye; and to Shula Marks and Robert Gordon for their spirited and suggestive responses to the project as a whole. We took care to listen to the criticism and advice of these friends and associates. If we did not always hear well enough or, on occasion, have chosen to go our own way, we hope they will forgive us. In any case, we take sole responsibility for the inadequacies of the end product.

The National Science Foundation, the National Endowment for the Humanities, and the Lichtstern Fund of the University of Chicago provided generous funding for the study. We are much obliged to them. Feriale Abdullah, Johanna Schoss, Diana Peterson, and Jan-Lodewijk Grootaers, our research assistants, have been a great source of support during various phases of the study. So, too, have Mark Auslander and Ellen Schattschneider, who, besides preparing the index, gave freely of their insight and imagination throughout. Also along for the ride, but less out of choice than ascription, have been our children, Josh and Jane, teenagers both. They have learned two things from the often obsessional character of our working lives and, in particular, from this project: that they would do almost anything rather than be anthropologists; and that, if you find the right way to humor scholarparents, even they can see the ridiculous in what they do. Of such things are revelations made. Knowing well that they want nothing more to do with it, we dedicate this book to them.

CHRONOLOGY

1652	Van Riebeeck arrives at the Cape of Good Hope. Dutch East India Company station established.
1780	Barolong polity splits into four chiefdoms (Ratlou, Ratshidi, Rapulana, and Seleka) after civil war.
1795	First British administration of the Cape. London Missionary Society (LMS) founded.
1799	LMS begins work in South Africa.
1802	Abortive effort to establish LMS station among the Tlhaping at Dithakong.
1803	Administration of the Cape passes to the Batavian Republic by the Treaty of Amiens.
1806	Second British occupation of the Cape.
1813	Wesleyan Methodist Missionary Society (WMMS) formed.
1816–17	First sustained LMS outreach to the Tlhaping. First WMMS station in South African interior.
1816–28	Rise of the Zulu kingdom under Shaka; period of migration and upheaval throughout southern Africa (*difaqane*).
1821	Moffat founds permanent LMS station among the Tlhaping at Kuruman. Kay travels to Tswana territory to set up first WMMS station.
1822	Broadbent and Hodgson of the WMMS make sustained contact with the Seleka.
1822–23	Southern Tswana polities attacked by Tlokwa and Fokeng.
1823	Griqua and Tlhaping force, under Robert Moffat, defeat Tlokwa.
1832	The Matabele under Mzilikazi settle in Tswana territory; attack surrounding communities.
1833	Thaba 'Nchu founded; WMMS station established there.
1834–38	Emancipation of the slaves at the Cape.
1835–40	Voortrekkers leave the Cape Colony.
1838	Zulu army defeated by Boers at Blood River.

1839	Period of fragmentation and realignment of Tlhaping polities.
1841	Opening of Lovedale Missionary Institution.
1851	WMMS mission established among the Tshidi by Ludorf.
1852	Sand River Convention; Transvaal gains independence.
	Boers attack Kwena and destroy Livingstone's station; also attack Tshidi, forcing Montshiwa into exile at Moshaneng.
1854	Bloemfontein Convention; Britain abandons the Orange River Sovereignty.
1862	MacKenzie founds LMS station among the Ngwato.
1865	Mafikeng established by Molema.
1867	Diamond discovered near Hopetown; diggers pour into Griqualand; disputes break out between Southern Tswana, Griqua, and white settlers over diamondiferous territory.
1870–71	Further diamond discoveries; Kimberley founded; Bloemhof hearing under Lieut.-Governor Keate of Natal.
1871	Britain annexes Griqualand West.
1872	Cape Colony acquires "responsible government."
	Moffat Institution established at Shoshong, later moved to Kuruman.
1877	Shepstone annexes the Transvaal, making it a British colony.
	Montshiwa returns to Tshidi territory, settling at Sehuba.
1878	Griqua Rebellion.
	Outbursts of resistance against state intervention and the mission presence among Southern Tswana; LMS stations attacked.
1880	Transvaal rebels successfully against Britain; "First Anglo-Boer War" breaks out.
1881	Pretoria Convention; retrocession of Transvaal.
1881–84	Sustained hostilities between Southern Tswana chiefdoms and the white settlers of the Transvaal borderland.
1882	Boers proclaim Stellaland and Goshen independent republics on Rolong and Tlhaping land.
	Montshiwa forced into subjection by the Transvaal.
1882–86	Economic depression in southern Africa.

1884	London Convention amends Pretoria Convention. Whitehall agrees to establish a protectorate over the Southern Tswana: British Bechuanaland formerly comes into existence, and MacKenzie is appointed its first Deputy Commissioner.
	Transvaal annexes Goshen.
	Battles between white freebooters and Rolong intensify; Montshiwa made to surrender most of his land.
1885	Warren Expedition sent to Bechuanaland.
	British Bechuanaland made into a Crown Colony.
	Bechuanaland Protectorate proclaimed over northern chiefdoms.
1886	Witwatersrand proclaimed a gold mining area.
	Land Commission established by British administration to settle territorial disputes in Bechuanaland.
	Hut tax introduced in British Bechuanaland.
1889	Charter over (northern) Bechuanaland granted to British South Africa Company (BSAC).
1893	Ndebele (Matabele) War.
1894	Annexation of Pondoland largely completes formal incorporation of blacks into the colonies of the Cape and Natal and into the South African Republic and Orange Free State.
1895	British Bechuanaland incorporated into the Cape Colony.
	Chiefs protest planned transfer of Bechuanaland Protectorate to BSAC governance.
1895–96	Jameson Raid ends BSAC presence in the Protectorate; British government takes administrative control.
1896	Rinderpest cattle pandemic among the Tswana.
1896–97	Construction of Mafeking-Bulawayo railway.
	Tlhaping rebellion in the Langeberg; resistance against the colonial regime spreads to other parts of Southern Tswana territory.
1899–1902	Anglo-Boer War (Siege of Mafeking, 1899–1900).
1900	Founding of first Setswana newspaper in Mafeking.
1903–05	South African Native Affairs Commission.
1904	Tiger Kloof established.

1910   Union of South Africa established.

1912   South African Native National Congress (later the African National Congress) formed.

1913   Natives Land Act no. 27 passed; limits African holdings to "scheduled native areas."

ONE

INTRODUCTION

SOON AFTER DAWN on a steamy February morning in 1960, a group of elders—"tribal headmen," the apartheid government prefers to call them—gathered at the court of Kebalepile, chief of the Barolong boo Ratshidi (Tshidi), a Southern Tswana people. They had been charged by the Bantu Commissioner, the local white administrator, to consider the building of a Dutch Reformed Church in their capital town, Mafikeng. Under the law of the time, the infamous Bantu Authorities Act (1951), "tribes" retained the formal right to ratify or refuse the allocation of sites to religious denominations. But Kebalepile and the Tshidi elders knew well that the DRC, the church of Afrikanerdom and apartheid, would be forced upon them, whether they wanted it or not. Rising slowly from his ceremonial chair, a respected old man, one Rre-Mokaila, spoke out, his body starkly silhouetted above the circular stone wall of the court: [1]

> You must know what it means to accept this church. The Dutch Reformed Church has a motto, a commandment: "There Shall Be No Equality Between Black And White in Church Or In State!" If we allot a site to this church, we know it is as good as [accepting] the Bantu Authorities Act. It does not want educated Africans. . . . It does not want black people to wear shoes. The DRC refuses passports to our children when sympathizers overseas offer them scholarships to further their education. We are afraid of the DRC. Its members are bribed people, people of no intelligence.

He sat down, shaking in mute anger. Then rose Morara Molema, grandson of the first Tshidi royal to become a Christian, a leader among leaders:

> ... the DRC is a state church. One of its representatives said here in *kgotla* (the court) that it will be given a site despite our refusal. That is the way of the Boer government. They want to take our land to put up their Boer church so they can take away our people.

The final speaker, Mhengwa Lecholo, also a headman of great seniority, added, with resignation:

> We all know the attitude of the Afrikaner people toward us. It is bad. . . . The DRC, the Boer church, is today the church of the government. All laws passed in parliament in Cape Town are under its influence and support. Our grandfathers tried to keep this church, this people, away from our country. They were wise. Now we have them trying once more to find their way into our place. No!

The proposed Dutch Reformed Church *was* built. But not in the old Tshidi town. In the face of local opposition, church and government had a yet better idea. As part of the development of the "ethnic homeland" of Bophu-thatswana, then still on the drawing boards, the state established a new township nearby. With its unrelenting files of square houses along wide, eminently policeable thoroughfares, this "location" looked just like Soweto writ small. It was called Montshiwa, after the Tshidi ruling dynasty—in a cynical attempt to appropriate "native" symbols. Among its first buildings, and the most grand by far, was the new DRC, replete with a large, expensively-equipped technical school. In order for education-starved Tswana children to gain entry, it was decreed, their families would have to join the church. The school was hardly opened when it was set on fire. Rebuilt at once, it was to be among the first structures torched in the troubled times of the 1980's, when young blacks throughout the land took to the streets to cry freedom. Their elders, who shun physical conflict at almost any cost, did not much like the violence. They were frightened by the fury in the eyes of their sons and daughters. But, they said, it was not hard to understand.

More recently, on Tuesday, 1 March 1988, the world awoke to read, in its morning newspapers, of a spirited confrontation on the streets of Cape Town.[2] A number of Christian leaders, Archbishop Desmond Tutu among them, had been arraigned by police as they led a solemn march on parliament to hand a petition to the president. They were protesting a ban on the United Democratic Front and the Council of South African Trade Unions, two prominent antiapartheid organizations. Such bannings were not unusual here, as everyone knows. Three years before, on 21 July 1985, the authorities had declared a state of emergency so embracing that it became illegal even for Christian groups to sing Christmas carols, light candles, or hold vigils together. Liberal political cartoonists had seen this as a heaven-sent opportunity to poke fun at the absurdities and excesses of the regime, to subvert it through satire. But the South African government rarely relents in the face of ridicule: it let its resolute silence underscore the enormity of its power over all forms of public discourse.

On this morning, as they knelt to pray in the street, Archbishop Tutu and his reverend colleagues were first threatened with arrest and then fired at with a water cannon. Some of them began to chant *Nkosi Sikelel' iAfrika*, the national anthem of liberation. Usually sung in a capella-style harmony and in two of the major indigenous languages, the manner of its performance speaks of the unity of struggle, of a determination to transcend differences of class and culture, ethnicity and gender, in the quest for freedom. It sounds, for all the world, like a venerable Christian hymn—which is not surprising, since it was composed at Lovedale College, a mission institution, in the 1890's,[3] and was later included in popular books of devotional songs.[4] "God Bless Africa," it intones in a melody more beseeching than belligerent, calling on the Holy Spirit to intervene (*Woza Moya Oyingcwele!*) on the side of *Setshaba sa Jesu!*, the "Nation of Jesus."

At first blush these passing incidents in the battle for South Africa seem merely to reiterate a commonplace: that the church has long been heavily implicated on all sides; that organized religion has played, and continues to play, a complex and contradictory role here (see, e.g., de Gruchy 1979; Hope and Young 1981; Cochrane 1987). Yet there is something remarkable about the fact that those who resist apartheid today—a multiethnic, sometimes secular, and often radical throng of people—can still represent themselves, in the idiom of a Victorian moral army, as a Nation of Jesus. It is significant, too, that the state has tried to appropriate their song of protest, notwithstanding its long association with the liberal tradition and mission Christianity: by Act of Parliament (no. 48 of 1963, section 5), *Nkosi Sikelel'* became the official anthem of the Transkei (Oosthuizen 1973:218), the earliest ethnic "nation" created under the homelands policy. For their part, black South Africans have ignored this Act of symbolic seizure, this political plagiarism. To the masses who sing it, it remains the national hymn of liberation.

It is no less notable that, in the effort to control rural blacks, a seemingly invincible government should go to great lengths to establish the DRC and its schools as instruments of its command. Or that young Tswana, despite their extraordinary hunger for learning, would want to burn these buildings down, just as in the past their great-grandfathers threatened to set fire to mission schools when they became sinister icons of colonial control. Indeed, it is not only the "Boer church" against which many black South Africans feel such resentment, although the DRC *is* marked out for special opprobrium. Take the testimony of Ezekiel Mphahlele, one of the great political poets of the age. Well before anyone in Johannesburg had read Fanon (1967), he argued (1962:192) that Christianity was responsible not merely for the glorification of European "civilization" but also for the "conquest of the [black] mind." So much so that "when Africans [first] began to chafe against mounting oppression, they spoke out . . . in the medium taught by the missionary," despite its inappropriateness and impotence. For their part, the English churchmen with few exceptions "abetted, connived at or stood aloof from" the processes of conquest and conflict (1959:179). Denomination, implies Mphahlele, made little difference to the reality of domination.[5] Nor have the past twenty years of repression and resistance done much to dispel this impression. The youths who tried recently to raze the DRC buildings in Montshiwa Township might as well have been striking a blow at all of white Christianity.

The two incidents, in short, suggest another point: that the making of modern South Africa has involved a long battle for the possession of salient signs and symbols,[6] a bitter, drawn out contest of conscience and consciousness. This is not to deny the coercive, violent bases of class antagonism and racial inequality here—or to underplay their brute material dimensions. As we shall argue, it is never possible simply to pry apart the cultural from the material in such processes; class struggle, Voloshinov (1973) reminds us, is always simultaneously a struggle over the means of signification. In the eyes of the Southern Tswana, to be sure, the past century and half has been dominated by the effort of others to impose upon them a particular way of seeing and being. Whether it be in the name of a "benign," civilizing imperialism or in cynical pursuit of their labor power, the final objective of generations of colonizers has been to colonize their consciousness with the axioms and aesthetics of an alien culture. This culture—the culture of European capitalism, of western modernity—had, and continues to have, enormous historical force—a force at once ideological and economic, semantic and social. In the face of it, some black Africans have succumbed, some have resisted, some have tried to recast its intrusive forms in their own image. And most have done all of these things, at one or another time, in the effort to formulate an awareness of, and to gain a measure of mastery over, their changing world. It is no wonder that, in our attempt to understand the Southern Tswana past and present, we kept being drawn back to the colonization of their consciousness and their consciousness of colonization.

Of course, the dominant motif in the history of the Tswana peoples has been their incorporation into a colonial, and later a postcolonial, state. But

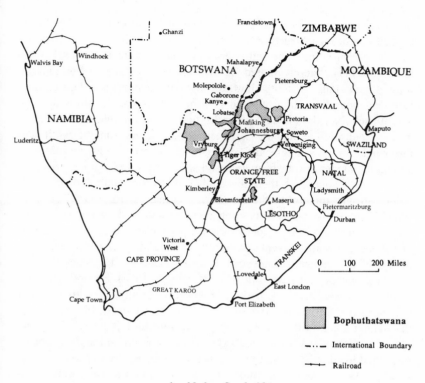

MAP 1   *Modern South Africa*

this is a "state" in both senses of the term: an institutionalized political order *and* a condition of being. Consequently, colonialism has been as much a matter of the politics of perception and experience as it has been an exercise in formal governance. So, too, with Tswana reactions: they have flowed well beyond the domain of the "political" and onto the diffuse terrain of everyday life. Nor is this unusual. Colonizers everywhere try to gain control over the practices through which would-be subjects produce and reproduce the bases of their existence. No habit is too humble, no sign too insignificant to be implicated. And colonization always provokes struggles—albeit often tragically uneven ones—over power and meaning on the frontiers of empire. It is a process of "challenge and riposte" (Harlow 1986:xi, after Bourdieu 1977:12) often much too complex to be captured in simple equations of domination and resistance; or, for that matter, by grand models of the politics of imperialism or the economics of the modern world system.

   Among the Southern Tswana this process began with the entry of mission Christianity onto the historical landscape. Not only were Nonconformist evangelists the vanguard of the British presence in this part of South Africa;

5

they were also the most active cultural agents of empire, being driven by the explicit aim of reconstructing the "native"[7] world in the name of God and European civilization. The settler and the mining magnate, says Etherington (1983:117), "merely wanted the Africans' land and labour. Missionaries wanted their souls." Patently, however, the chronicle of Protestant evangelism does not tell us the whole story of the Tswana past. Nothing does, in and of itself. Nor does it yield generalizations about the role of Christianity in the colonization of the non-European world at large. Nonetheless, it does throw light on the symbolic and material bases of the colonial encounter—and on the modes of transformation and argument to which it gave rise.

Narrowly conceived, then, this study is a historical anthropology of the Nonconformist mission to the Southern Tswana, ca. 1820–1920. But, as stated in the Preface, it sets its sights more broadly in three respects. First, despite its periodization, it looks forward, particularly in the final chapters of volume 2, toward present-day South Africa and specifically toward the modes of consciousness and struggle that have come to characterize its "street sociology and pavement politics" (Bundy 1987). Second, although focused on a small rural population, it is concerned ultimately with processes that occurred throughout the subcontinent—and indeed, in some form, throughout much of the nonwestern world. And third, it speaks to a series of analytic issues that continue to vex many historians and anthropologists interested in colonialism and more generally in the nature of power and resistance. As we asked at the outset (pp. xi–xii): How, precisely, were structures of inequality fashioned during the colonial encounter, often in the absence of more conventional, more coercive, tools of domination? How was consciousness made and remade in this process? And what was the role in it of precolonial economy, society, and culture? How were new hegemonies established and the "ground prepared," in Gramsci's phrase, for formal European political control? How is it that some usages insinuated themselves into the everyday world of the colonized, while others became the object of contest and conflict? Even more fundamentally, how are we to understand the dialectics of culture and power, ideology and consciousness that shape such historical processes?

It is also important to be clear about what we do *not* set out to accomplish. Our account is intended neither as a general anthropology of colonialism among the Tswana nor as an exhaustive social history of the mission, of black resistance, or of religious change in this part of the world. These topics have been covered, in all or part, in the works of others more competent than ourselves. Our horizons are more modest and yet, perhaps, hopelessly ambitious. Let us introduce them in their more general scholarly context.

ANALYTIC THEMES

Missionaries, Motives, and the Motors of History

It is sometimes said that, while the literature on religious transformation in Africa is very large, there are few anthropological analyses of the evangelical encounter itself—analyses, that is, that go beyond detailed, if often sensitive, chronicles of actions and events (e.g., Heise 1967; Beidelman 1982:2f.; Etherington 1983; cf. Shapiro 1981:130).[8] Notwithstanding the fact that Christianity has allegedly been among the more effective agents of change in Africa (e.g., Bohannan 1964:22), the anthropology of missions, we are told, is still in its infancy (Spain 1984:206), and this in spite of some notable efforts to expand its scope.[9] Even the most ambitious attempt to write a historical ethnography of a mission "at the grassroots," Beidelman's *Colonial Evangelism*, has been judged "sadly incomplete" precisely because it fails to bring a systematic—or a novel—anthropological perspective to bear on the subject (Gray 1983: 405; Bourdillon 1983).

This critique also reflects the more general neglect of colonialism—indeed, of history itself—by a discipline mainly interested until very recently in "traditional" African society and culture. Social historians, on the other hand, have long concerned themselves with, even been fascinated by, Christian evangelists. And they have not been alone. In the great awakening of modern Africa, when the colonized began to write their own histories and to reflect upon the technologies of European domination, they too gave a good deal of attention to "the" missionary—if only to excoriate him as an agent of imperialism (Majeke 1952; Ayandele 1966; Zulu 1972). The condemnation was extended also to scholarly apologies that portrayed European churchmen as well-intentioned philanthropists (e.g., Wilson 1969b, 1976; Brookes 1974) or benign imperialists (e.g., Sillery 1971); such accounts being seen by their critics as modern expressions of the same missionizing culture. While this unjoined debate foreshadowed later theoretical disputes over the relative weight of human agency and structural forces in African social change, both arguments were cast with reference to the same tacit question: "Whose side were the Christians really on?"

As a result, complex historical dynamics were reduced to the crude calculus of interest and intention, and colonialism itself to a caricature (Comaroff and Comaroff 1986:1f.; cf. Bundy 1979:36f.; Cochrane 1987:12f.). Stated thus, moreover, the question presupposed an answer in a certain key: the contribution of the evangelists to the modern African predicament, for good or ill, was judged in terms of their political role, narrowly conceived. This is well exemplified by the so-called "missionary imperialist" thesis. Dachs (1972:647f.) for instance, claims that as nineteenth-century Tswana rulers resisted their religious activities, the Christians called increasingly on the "political arm of empire" to erode the chiefship and so make local communities more yielding to their ministrations. As we shall see, this is not wrong. But it is distortingly simplistic.

More recently the study of Christian missions, at least in southern Africa, has been affected by a "historiographic revolution" (Marks 1989: 225). This radical shift has encouraged a greater concern with political economy; that is, with long-term processes of colonial conquest, capitalist expansion, state formation, and proletarianization—and, hence, with the part the evangelists played (1) in reorganizing relations of production in rural communities (Trapido 1980); (2) in abetting the penetration of capital and fostering the rise of peasant agriculture (Bundy 1979; Cochrane 1987); and (3) in encouraging the emergence of classes, the rise of black elites, and the availability of tractable industrial labor (Etherington 1978; Cuthbertson 1987). There has, however, been disagreement over their efficacy. At one extreme Denoon (1973:63f.) declares that they had no historical impact to speak of, certainly not in South Africa; similarly Horton (1971) holds that, in Africa at large, they were never more than incidental catalysts in global processes of rationalization. Elphick (1981), on the other hand, compares them to revolutionaries: their self-conscious elitism and independence, both political and economic, he says, allowed them to dream of transforming all aspects of African life. But this, too, is a minority viewpoint. Cuthbertson (1987:27), who seems to misread Elphick's argument on the autonomy of the churchmen, counters that they were not only "ideological captives" of the imperialist cause but also "important agents of Western capitalism" (1987:23, 28). This rebuttal may itself not draw universal agreement, although the implicit notion that "the" role of "the" mission was unambiguous and homogeneous *is* common enough. Nonetheless, most would now concur with one thing: that, as Strayer (1976:12) once put it, evangelism in Africa can "hardly be regarded as an independent motor of social change" (cf. Cuthbertson 1987:28).

The obvious limitation in all this—especially for anthropology—is the preoccupation with political economy at the expense of culture, symbolism, and ideology. "Most recent historiography of early mission Christianity," notes Ranger (1986:32), referring to east, central, and southern Africa, "has greatly overplayed the manifest political and economic factors in its expansion." This is hardly unique to the study of religious transformation, of course. It stems ultimately from oppositions (between matter and mind, the concrete and the concept, and so on) at the ontological roots of our social thought—oppositions which persist despite growing agreement that the primary processes involved in the production of the everyday world are inseparably material and meaningful. The impact of Protestant evangelists as harbingers of industrial capitalism lay in the fact that their civilizing mission was simultaneously symbolic and practical, theological and temporal. The goods and techniques they brought with them to Africa presupposed the messages and meanings they proclaimed in the pulpit, and vice versa. Both were vehicles of a moral economy that celebrated the global spirit of commerce, the commodity, and the imperial marketplace. Indeed, it is in the signifying role of evangelical practice—often very mundane, material practice—that we begin to find an answer to the most basic, most puzzling question about the historical agency of Christian missionaries: how it is that they, like other colonial functionaries, wrought far-reaching political, social, and economic transformations in the absence of concrete resources of much consequence (cf. Fields 1985).

The question itself raises a much larger methodological issue; namely, the analytic treatment of historical agency *sui generis*. If, as Giddens (1987:60ff.) has remarked, the relation of "structure and agency" has become a crucial problem for modern social theory, it has not been resolved in the study of colonialism in southern Africa. It is true that the rhetorical influence of Thompson's (1978; cf. Giddens 1987:203f.) epic battle to save the humanist subject from structuralist extinction is as plain here as it is elsewhere; thus Marks (1989:225–26) observes approvingly that the new historiography has shown growing interest in "human agency or 'the changing experience of ordinary people.' " Yet, in practice, this seems almost exclusively to involve a concern with (1) the reaction and resistance of blacks to the faceless forces of colonization and control, or (2) the efforts of the "African working class to 'make itself.' " Thompson (e.g., 1975) might have taken care, in the English case, to demonstrate that it is as important to account for the motivations of rulers as it is to understand those of the ruled. With few exceptions (e.g., Ranger 1987), however, comparable attention has not been paid in southern Africa to the consciousness and intentionality of those identified as "agents" of domination. Quite the reverse: their actions continue to be seen largely as a reflex of political and economic processes. An ironic inversion, surely, of the distortions of an earlier liberal historiography!

But there is more than mere irony at stake here. We are challenged to write a historical anthropology of colonialism in southern Africa that takes account of all the players in the game, the motives that drove them, the awareness that informed them, the constraints that limited them. This demands, more generally, that we unravel the dialectics of culture and consciousness, of convention and invention, in this particular part of the world. One consequence of the varied reactions to structuralism over the past decade or so has been to remind us quite how limited our successes have been in just these respects; or, for that matter, in addressing the nature of intentionality, experience, and the imagination (cf. Kapferer 1988:79). Agency, as we implied earlier, is not merely structure in the active voice. Although the latter may generate the former, it does not always contain it. Social practice has effects that sometimes remake the world (cf. Giddens 1987:216); it cannot therefore be dissolved into society or culture. But it is also not an abstract "thing." Human agency is practice invested with subjectivity, meaning, and to a greater or lesser extent power. It is, in short, motivated.

Once the motives, intentions, and imaginings of persons living or dead are allowed to speak from the historical record, it becomes impossible to see them as mere reflections of monolithic cultural structures or social forces. This is especially true of the colonial encounter, and of the civilizing mission in particular. And yet historians and anthropologists may be accused of not having paid sufficient heed to those voices—of not having done justice to the complexities and contradictions on either side of that encounter. Notwithstanding endless programmatic statements urging otherwise, African societies have for the most part been reduced to structural-functionalist islands without history, or to gerontocracies astride "lineage (or tributary) modes of production" (see J. L. Comaroff 1984:572). Either way, they are robbed of any real internal dynamism or agency, any organizational complexity or cultural variation, even as they are drawn into the embrace of the modern world system. And white colonizers, if they are thought worthy of attention at all (cf. Beidelman 1982:1), have more often than not been treated as a homogeneous class—in and for itself. The divisions among them, and the often acute conflicts between them, have been largely ignored in the history of the Third World. At best they are regarded as instances of what Post (1978:35), speaking about Jamaica, terms "non-antagonistic contradictions."

Recent writings at the juncture of history and anthropology (e.g., Cooper and Stoler 1989) have begun to show how important were the divisions within colonizing populations; how they were related to distinctions, at home and abroad, of class, gender, and nation; how, over time, they played across the racial line between ruler and ruled, creating new affinities and alliances that blurred the antinomies of the colonial world (cf. Trapido 1980; Marks 1978). The Christian missions were from the start caught up in these complexities. Not only did the various denominations have diverse and frequently contradictory designs on Africa—designs that sometimes turned out to have unpredictable consequences (cf. Beidelman 1982:214; Strayer 1976:12); their activities also brought them into ambivalent relations with other Europeans on the colonial stage. Some found common cause, and cooperated openly, with administrators and settlers. Others ended up locked in battle with secular forces for—what they took to be—the destiny of the continent (Hallden 1968; Wright 1971:43f.; Guy 1983; J. L. Comaroff 1989).

It follows, then, that the study of Christianity in Africa is more than just an exercise in the analysis of religious change. It is part and parcel of the historical anthropology of colonialism and consciousness, culture and power; of an anthropology concerned at once with the colonizer *and* the colonized, with structure *and* agency. That at least is the assumption behind our portrait of the Nonconformist mission in southern Africa. The substance of our argument, its conception and theoretical texture, lies as much in the form of the account as it does in its content—which is why the latter is not written as a chronology of events or processes. It is just as well, therefore, that we begin by providing a brief synopsis of the analytic path we seek to tread.

The Shape of Things to Come

Our story is woven from two contrapuntal narratives. One speaks of a specific Christian mission and its consequences; the second, of a more general postenlightenment process of colonization in which Europe set out to grasp and subdue the forces of savagery, otherness, and unreason. We also tell it in two parts. In this volume we trace the early phases of the evangelical onslaught on the "Bechuanas," opening with an exploration of the social and cultural roots—and the ideological motivations—of the Nonconformist mission (chapter 2). In particular, we examine the images of Africa that were to shape the British sense of their engagement with the heathen at the frontiers of civilization (chapter 3). Such popular imaginings bore little resemblance to the nature of society and culture in the "dark" interior (chapter 4), a universe fashioned by complex historical dynamics which would in time have their own effect on the evangelical encounter and the process of colonization itself. Especially significant were the initial moments of that encounter (chapter 5). These highly ritualized meetings of Europeans and Africans—endowed alike with their own history, their own culture, their own intentions—set the terms of the "long conversation" to follow. In this exchange of signs and substance, each party was to try to gain some purchase on, some mastery over, the other: the churchmen, to convert the Tswana to Christianity; the Tswana, to divert the potency of the churchmen to themselves (chapter 6). In order to facilitate their work, the Nonconformists attempted to drive a wedge between the realm of the spirit and the temporal affairs of government, both indigenous and imperial (chapter 7). The object was to lay the ground for a new moral economy based on the clear separation of church and state, of sacred authority and secular power—to establish, in short, a state of colonialism in anticipation of the colonial state. Ironically,

11

this effort mired some of the Christians in distinctly secular battles; battles they could not win because of the inherent indeterminacy and impotence of their role in the political arena. It was also to reveal fundamental contradictions between the worldview promised by them and the world wrought by the politics of empire, an earthly dominion in which the mission church was anything but powerful.

It was not only in the fraught space between the realm of the spirit and the politics of the colonial state that contradictions were to surface. They were also to arise at the evangelical workface itself. As the Christians set out to rebuild the Tswana lifeworld, they conjured up one kind of society: a global democracy of material well-being and moral merit, of equality before the law and the Lord. Yet their own actions conduced to something quite different: an empire of inequality, a colonialism of coercion and dispossession. It is here that the second part of our story begins. In volume 2 we go on to show how, once the long conversation had set the terms of the encounter, the Nonconformists sought to remake the Africans both through their everyday activities—dress, agriculture, architecture, and so on—and through "formal" education. The impact of this campaign of reconstruction, and the range of reactions to which it led, was mediated by a process of class formation, a process to which the mission itself contributed a great deal. Thus we shall examine the various ways in which the culture sown by the churchmen took root on the social terrain of the Tswana, some of it to be absorbed silently and seamlessly into a reinvented—or, rather, reified—ethnic "tradition," some to be creatively transformed, some to be redeployed to talk back to the whites. We seek to demonstrate, in other words, how parts of the evangelical message insinuated themselves into the warp and weft of an emerging hegemony, while others gave rise to novel forms of consciousness and action.

It was such novel forms of consciousness that were to spark the earliest reactions—the first, often inchoate and stumbling, expressions of resistance—to the contradictions of the civilizing mission. Later, with the rise of a Christian-educated black bourgeoisie, they would fuel black nationalist politics with both causes of complaint and a rhetoric of protest. These early moments of contestation also foreshadowed other forms of black consciousness and struggle, some of them still part of the fight against apartheid today. But we shall spell that out in the next volume. For now it is enough to restate, summarily, our intention to show that the evangelical encounter took place on an ever expanding subcontinental stage; that it was to have profound, unanticipated effects on both colonizer and colonized; and that, just as colonialism itself was not a coherent monolith, so colonial evangelism was not a simple matter of raw mastery, of British churchmen instilling in passive black South Africans the culture of European modernity or the forms of industrial capitalism. Mission Christianity certainly played an important, subtle part in the reconstruction of Africa; just how subtle—even unexpected—will become clear in the course of this study. But, as we have said, it was enmeshed, from first to last, in a complex dialectic of challenge and riposte, domination and defiance. Nor is this surprising in light of the fact that, while the messages and actions of the churchmen spoke of one ideology, their relations with the Tswana gestured toward another: while they aimed at and in part succeeded in transforming the signs and practices of "native" life, they lacked the capacity to make colonial society conform to their liberal dreams. As in many other theaters of history, the story of the Southern Tswana mission simply would not be contained in the script envisaged for it by any of the players on the stage.

All this raises a number of obvious problems of conception and method, to which we now move on. We are painfully aware that, for some, abstract theoretical discussion is at best less than a pleasure to read. For others, it is an unnecessary diversion. Those who feel thus, be warned: the narrative resumes with an introduction to the dramatis personae on p. 39.

CONCEPTUAL SCHEMES

It is one thing to announce that we have a story to tell, and even, as we have done, to sketch its outlines in advance of the telling. But in an intellectual world beset by postmodernist doubt, where old certainties have been undermined by various forms of deconstruction, it is quite another to establish the terms in which that story is to be told. After all, critical postmodernism[10] has, among other things, called for a "dissolution of linear narrative . . . and a 'revolutionary' break with the (repressive) ideology of storytelling . . ." (Jameson 1984:54). More fundamentally it has thrown up before the social sciences a series of challenges not easily brushed aside: among them, that the coherence and order, the totality and teleology, we typically attribute to society, culture, and history are dangerous illusions; that any form of essentialism in social analysis is an egregious survival of the passing age of naive realism; that ethnography and history alike are merely exercises in the making of texts, no less arbitrary than any other texts and with no greater purchase on the truth. Nor is it sufficient, in the face of such criticism, to acknowledge that the times and places of which we write were, and are, fraught with ambiguities, indeterminacies, incoherencies—and then to add a touch of sensitive inchoateness, of softening disorder, to our accounts. For this in itself cannot remove the logocentric, objectivist biases from our mod-

13

els and narratives of culture and society—not, at least, while they parade as social science in *any* presently recognizable form (Taussig 1987; see Hebdige 1988:185–86).

So how do we respond? Is it sufficient to appeal, as many have done (cf. Ortner 1984), to theories of practice, theories rescued from the early Marx as a panacea for the dehumanizing excesses of structuralism? Or to the so-called "interpretive turn" in the social sciences, in which "cultural order" is seen to subsume both shared meaning and the experiencing subject, both "subjectivity and objectivity" (Rabinow and Sullivan 1987:6f.)? Would these approaches ward off the crusading deconstructionist in search of lingering models of order or totality to discredit? If not, do we simply confess to the nonexistence of social and cultural systems, satisfying ourselves as best we can with descriptions of the particular and the contingent? And does that lead us inexorably to a vision of meaning and action that denies the possibility of any kind of social science? Are we, finally, sliding down the slithery slope, the slippery trope, toward a world in which all life, all history, all society, is really (whatever that may mean) a text? In which all representation is arbitrary? Some time ago, Thompson (1978:220) expressed the fear that the social scientist was condemned to wait forever outside the philosophy department. Our current nightmare has us waiting still. But now we sit, the philosopher at our side, begging an audience with the literary critic.

Our study is, as it inevitably must be, set against this intellectual background, this torrent of questions. Insofar as we seek to address—if not always to answer—these questions, we set out to do so in analytic *practice*. For it is in such practice, we believe, that epistemological and philosophical issues are most effectively decided—not, despite many recent critiques of anthropology (see Preface), in discourses so abstracted from their putative object that their wheels can but spin, solipsistically, on their own axes. Our objective is to understand a particular historical process: an encounter in which a self-elected group of Britons sought, *methodically*, to "make history" for people whom, they thought, lacked it; to induct those people into an *order* of activities and values; to impart *form* to an Africa that was seen as formless; to reduce the chaos of savage life to the *rational* structures and techniques that, for the Europeans, were both the vehicle and the proof of their own civilization. To anticipate one of our usages below, the italics here are ours, but the emphasis was theirs. This colonial encounter was not a contingent set of events, a cosmic coincidence in which some human beings happened arbitrarily into a foreign text. It was, as has been said many times, an integral part of the cultural and social revolution that accompanied the rise of industrial capitalism, an expression of the expansive universalism that marked the dawn of modernity.

It also marked the dawn of modernism: the new age of science and economics; of realism and rationalization; of the "master narrative" and, in both senses of the term, the novel; of heroic, imperious humanism; and of knowledge-as-discovery (cf. Bakhtin 1981). Put them together and they add up to a worldview that bred not only colonialism but also, in the longer run, the social sciences. If our missionaries and their other colonizing compatriots were the self-conscious agents of an heroic imperial history, the social historians and ethnographers who followed them stand accused of having also been unwitting colonialists.[11] De Certeau (1988:72) captures nicely the parallel between the civilizing mission and historiography: "[historians] 'civilize' nature," he says, "which has always meant that they 'colonize' and change it." The point, now commonplace, is that the essence of colonization inheres less in political overrule than in seizing and transforming "others" by the very act of conceptualizing, inscribing, and interacting with them on terms not of their choosing; in making them into the pliant objects and silenced subjects of our scripts and scenarios; in assuming the capacity to "represent" them, the active verb itself conflating politics and poetics. But is it true that the modern historical anthropologist does this in a way no different from the nineteenth-century missionary, military man, merchant, or minister of state? Are we merely manufacturers of texts that convert difference into sameness through the Midas touch of western universalism, just as evangelists sought to convert the savage by removing the differences which excluded him from God's *uni*verse—and from the master narratives of European culture? Some of our interlocutors would certainly answer in the affirmative. And yet there is an obvious irony in the accusation. Anthropologists have long been taken to task for exactly the opposite sin: for fetishizing difference in a global order of political and economic continuities (Said 1978; Fabian 1983a).

But ironies aside, whether we make difference out of sameness or vice versa—each, in any case, is a condition of the other—the underlying point remains. Ethnography and social history are alike, and like nineteenth-century colonial evangelism, the undeniable progeny of modernism. As such they cannot escape the epistemological horizons that continue to enclose mainstream western social thought. Even those "interpretive" anthropologists who eschew most forcefully our positivist heritage appear to be stranded halfway along the road to postmodernism. On the one hand, as Rabinow and Sullivan (1987:9) explain, they reject the existence of a material "reality before and behind the cultural world," a world lacking clarity and characterized by alienation. And they regard the analysis of social action as "analogous to textual interpretation," in which any text is "open to several [if not infinite] readings" (1987:14). And yet, despite being extremely wary of the reification of culture—of totality and teleology, formalism and functionalism—they rarely end up disputing the existence of, say, "Balinese culture." Nor, in analytic practice, do they deny that culture a good deal of closure; and, notwithstanding the language of phenomenology, speak readily of "cultural *systems*" (Geertz 1973). As Evans-Pritchard (1937) long ago realized, the very nature of translation at the core of anthropology—the act of "doing ethnography" itself—makes anything else almost impossible (cf. Leach 1954:chap.1).[12] No wonder, then, as Hebdige (1988:186) reminds us, that postmodernist critiques of the social sciences make

> no real distinctions . . . between positivist/non-positivist; qualitative/quantitative; marxist/pluralist/interpretative/functionalist, etc. sociolog*ies*:[13] all are seen as strategies embedded in institutions themselves irrefragably implicated in and productive of particular configurations of power and knowledge.

If this is true, none of us—not the most reflexive interpretive anthropologist or the most critical humanist Marxist—can be a little bit postmodern. Of course, critical postmodernism is itself largely a western *endo*cultural enterprise. As such it has by and large been able to ignore the task of cultural translation—or the problems of dealing with, for instance, the semantic and material politics of colonialism. Of having, in other words, to be a little bit anthropological.

This is especially apparent in the manner in which those philosophers and literary theorists who live in hyphenated states of ironic detachment—post-structuralism, post-Marxism and so on—cast their cynical gaze upon the nature of meaning and power. Meaning, some of them tell us, is "polymorphously perverse," the polysemic, amorphous solvent of everyday discourses: since we live in a world of unfixed signifiers, meaning cannot inhere in enduring schemes of signs and relations. As this suggests, poststructuralisms, in their various guises, begin with a revisionist reading of the basic principles of structural linguistics—in particular, of the arbitrariness of the sign and of the concept of language as a system of distinctions. Granted the ambiguities of his original formulations (Benveniste 1971:chap.4), Saussure did not, in asserting the arbitrary connection of sign to referent, deny that conventional ties are established between them in culture and history (see Sahlins 1981). But in the poststructuralist reading, the focus is on absences rather than presences. Arbitrariness and difference are taken to imply the fundamental instability of all meaning in the world, its lack of any order or consistent social determination—and, therefore, of any teleology or totality whatsoever in society and history. Negation is the dominant analytic trope here. Anything may turn out to mean anything else and, hence, nothing at all (Hebdige 1988:192). Similarly, in the wake of Foucault, power has long left the formal bounds of "political" institutions and has diffused and proliferated into hitherto uncharted terrains. Inscribed in the mind and on the body of the person—the subject who imagines herself or himself free and who yet bears the terms of subjection within—it saturates all the planes of human existence. Now everywhere, it is nowhere in particular.

It is here that we wish to intervene in the name of a historical anthropology. On the one hand, we believe, some of the lessons of critical postmodernism have to be taken very seriously: among them, (1) the need to address the *in*determinacies of meaning and action, events and processes in history; (2) the admonition to regard culture not as an *over*determining, closed system of signs but as a set of polyvalent practices, texts, and images that may, at any time, be contested; (3) the invitation to see power as a many-sided, often elusive and diffuse force which is always implicated in culture, consciousness, and representation; and (4) the importance of treating the writing of histories as a generic mode of making both the past and the present.

On the other hand, we have our own questions to counterpose. How is it that—if *all* meaning were potentially open to contest, *all* power potentially unfixed—history keeps generating hegemonies that, for long periods, seem able to impose a degree of order and stability on the world? How come relatively small groups of people—class fractions, ethnic minorities, or whatever—often succeed in gaining and sustaining control over large populations and in drawing them into a consensus with dominant values? How do we explain the fact that, at any moment, at any place, some meanings appear meaningless, some practices impracticable, some conceptions of the past and present inconceivable? All histories may or may not be texts; that depends on what we understand by history, what we take to be a text (see e.g., Jameson 1981:296–97, 100f.; Hanks 1989). But nowhere can anything or everything be thought or written or done or told. Most people live in worlds in which many signs, and often the ones that count most, look as though they are eternally fixed.

This is where our particular story, with all its italics and emphases, becomes salient—and why we insist on situating methodological discussion in analytic practice. As we said a few pages back, colonial evangelism in South Africa hinged upon the effort of a few men, with closely shared social origins, to impose an entire worldview upon their would-be subjects; that is, to contrive reality for them as a coherent and closed, uniform and universalistic order. In the long conversation to which this gave rise—a conversation full of arguments of words and images—many of the signifiers of the colonizing culture became unfixed. They were seized by the Africans and, sometimes refashioned, put to symbolic and practical ends previously unforeseen, certainly unintended. Conversely, some of the ways of the Africans interpolated themselves, again detached and transformed, into the habitus of the missionaries. Here, then, was a process in which signifiers were set afloat, fought over, and recaptured on both sides of the colonial encounter. What is more, this encounter led to the objectification of "the" culture of the colonized in opposition to that of the whites. The "natives," that is, began to conceive of their own conventions as an integrated, closed "system" to which they could and did attach an abstract noun (*setswana*). The most curious feature of the process, however, is that, notwithstanding the rejection and transformation of many elements of "the" European worldview, its *forms* became authoritatively inscribed on the African landscape. Not only did colonialism produce reified cultural *orders*; it gave rise to a new hegemony amidst—and despite—cultural contestation. But how can that be?

We shall try to answer this question in the course of our account. For now, the more important implication is this. While signs, social relations, and material practices are constantly open to transformation—and while meaning may indeed *become* unfixed, resisted, and reconstructed—history everywhere is actively made in a dialectic of order and disorder, consensus and contest. At any particular moment, in any marked event, *a* meaning or *a* social arrangement may appear freefloating, underdetermined, ambiguous. But it is often the very attempt to harness that indeterminacy, the seemingly unfixed signifier, that animates both the exercise of power and the resistance to which it may give rise. Such arguments and struggles, though, are seldom equal. They have, *pace* postmodernism, a political sociology that emerges from their place in a system of relations. And so, as the moment gives way to the medium-term, and some people and practices emerge as (or remain) dominant, their authority expresses itself in the apparently established *order* of things—again, in the dual sense of an edifice of command and a condition of being. What might once have seemed eventful and contingent now looks to have been part of a more regular pattern—indeed, of a structured history, a historical structure. As Stuart Hall (1988:44) reminds us, following Gramsci:

> Ruling or dominant conceptions of the world [may] not directly prescribe the mental content of . . . the heads of the dominated classes. But the circle of dominant ideas *does* accumulate the symbolic power to map or classify the world for others; its classifications do acquire not only the constraining power of dominance over other modes of thought but also the inertial authority of habit and instinct. It becomes the horizon of the taken-for-granted: what the world is and how it works, for

all practical purposes. Ruling ideas may dominate other conceptions of the social world by setting the limit to what will appear as rational, reasonable, credible, indeed sayable or thinkable, within the given vocabularies of motive and action available to us.

This would serve well as a description of hegemony *sui generis*, at least as the term has come widely to be understood.[14] Hall is concerned here to account for the rise of the new right in modern Britain. And, finding postmodernist approaches suggestive yet unequal to the task—for the same reasons we do in South Africa—he spins a fine methodological web between the poles of Marxism and structuralism, relying mainly on the concepts of hegemony and ideology. We should also like to appeal to these two concepts, although we locate them in an analytic lexicon broadened to include culture and consciousness, power and representation. Taken together, this array of terms provides a cogent framework within which to capture the story, the history, which we have to tell.

Culture, Hegemony, Ideology

The difficulties of establishing what Gramsci may have meant by hegemony are by now notorious. For reasons to do, perhaps, with the conditions of their production, *The Prison Notebooks* do not help us much. Nowhere in them is there a clear or precise definition (Lears 1985:568). Nowhere do we find, say, the widely cited characterization offered by Williams (1977: 108f.; see n.14): that is, of "the hegemonic" as a dominant system of lived meanings and values, relations and practices, which shapes experienced reality (cf. Hall 1988:44; quoted above). Only in a few places, in fact, does Gramsci come even close to speaking in such terms—and then not about hegemony per se.[15] Moreover, the definition quoted most often in recent commentaries—"the 'spontaneous' consent given by the great masses of the population to the general direction imposed on social life by the dominant fundamental group" (Gramsci 1971:12)—is actually a description of one of "the subaltern functions of social hegemony and political government" exercised by intellectuals. Not only does it raise more problems than it resolves, but it is a far cry from the concept as it has come to be used in much contemporary theoretical writing.

The very fact that Gramsci's notion of hegemony was so unsystematically stated has made it good to think with; as a relatively empty sign, it has been able to serve diverse analytical purposes and positions (see e.g., Genovese 1971; Hebdige 1979; Gaventa 1980; Hall 1986; Laitin 1986). Among poststructuralists its sustained popularity is due in part to the fact that it appears to offer a ready rapprochement between theory and practice, thought and action, ideology and power. But it is also because, as Hebdige

(1988:206) explains, for Gramsci "nothing is anchored to . . . master narratives, to stable (positive) identities, to fixed and certain meanings: all social and semantic relations are contestable, hence mutable." Always uncertain, hegemony is realized through the balancing of competing forces, not the crushing calculus of class domination. Thus Laclau and Mouffe (1985), for example, find it possible to use the term to connote a kind of Foucaultian discourse, cut loose from any objective notion of society or culture—although they have been accused by Geras (1987) of robbing the concept of any principle of historical constraint whatsoever. Among post-Marxists, too, Gramsci has become "the Marxist you can take home to mother" (Romano 1983), providing an appealing escape from vulgar materialism and essentialism by speaking of production as a continuous ideological, social, and economic process (Hall 1988:53f.). And yet, notwithstanding a great deal of discussion and elaboration in recent years,[16] the construct remains underspecified and inadequately situated in its conceptual context. Often used as no more than a trendy buzzword, it is frequently invoked in the name of unreconciled and unreconcilable theoretical approaches.

For our own part, we do not seek to enter into contemporary debates over the notion of hegemony itself, let alone to offer a reading of Gramsci; the textual pursuit of the "real" meaning of an inherently equivocal concept is an exercise in futility. Nonetheless, given suitable specification, the term remains useful for our analytic purposes, since it may be made to illuminate some of the vital connections between power and culture, ideology and consciousness. This having been said, we have no alternative but to spell out our own usage amidst all the ambiguity. We do so, as we have said, by situating it in a more embracing set of analytic terms—and in a particular historical and ethnographic problem.

Some theorists have tried, directly (Williams 1977:108f.) or indirectly (e.g., Lears 1985:572f.), to assert the superiority of the notion of hegemony over culture and/or ideology; as if one might subsume and replace the others. Concealed in this argument is the idea that culture *plus* power *equals* hegemony, an equation that simplifies all three terms. Not that the reasoning behind it is surprising. As we have noted elsewhere (1987), the anthropological conception of culture has long been criticized, especially by Marxists, for overstressing the implicit, systemic, and consensual, for treating symbols and meanings as if they were neutral and above history, and for ignoring their empowering, authoritative dimensions. Conversely, Marxist theories of ideology and consciousness have been taken to task, by anthropologists, for neglecting the complex ways in which meaning inhabits consciousness and ideology. Neither ideology nor consciousness, goes the argument, is merely culture in the active voice. They are alike products of a process in which human beings deploy salient signs and relations to make their lives and worlds; signs and relations drawn from a structured, largely implicit repertoire of forms that lie below the surfaces of everyday experience. If culture seems to require power to make it complete, then, ideology and consciousness seem to require a good dose of semantics. Add all this together and the sum of the parts may appear to be "hegemony." But there is a problem with both the arithmetic of authority and the mathematics of meaning. Since it is possible, indeed inevitable, for some symbols and meanings *not* to be hegemonic—and impossible that any hegemony can claim all the signs in the world for its own—culture cannot be subsumed within hegemony,[17] however the terms may be conceived. Meaning may never be innocent, but it is also not merely reducible to the postures of power.

Gramsci clearly realized this himself. Rather than posit "hegemony" as a replacement for "culture" or "ideology," he treated the three as quite distinct. At times, furthermore, "culture" was described in a manner to which many anthropologists would not object: as an order of values, norms, beliefs, and institutions that, being "reflected in . . . language" and being also profoundly historical, express a "common conception of the world" embodied in a "cultural-social unity" (1971:349). This "common conception" was composed of a stock of shared "dispositions," a "popular 'mentality'," which any hegemony had to capture (1971:348f., 26f.). But there is yet more. Gramsci went on to make an explicit chain of associations in which "common conceptions of the world" were equated with "cultural movements" and, by turn, with "philosophies" (1971:328). Significantly, a few pages before (1971:323), "spontaneous philosophy"—i.e. practical, "everyman" philosophy—was said to be contained in (1) language, itself an order "of determined notions and concepts"; (2) common and good sense; and (3) the "entire system of beliefs, superstitions, ways of seeing things and of acting."

Here, the circle closed, we appear to have Gramsci's image of culture as totality. It is the shared repertoire of practices, symbols, and meanings from which hegemonic forms are cast—and, by extension, resisted. Or, in other words, it is the historically situated field of signifiers, at once material and symbolic, in which occur the dialectics of domination and resistance, the making and breaking of consensus. Of course, not all signifiers are drawn upon at all times in such processes: some may come to be implicated unintentionally; others may become unfixed and remain, at least for a while, freefloating; yet others, more susceptible to the appropriations of authority, may be woven into tightly integrated worldviews, ideologies. We shall have more to say about these things in due course. For now, however, following the *Geist* of Gramsci, let us take culture to be the space of signifying practice, the semantic ground on which human beings seek to construct and represent themselves and others—and, hence, society and history. As this suggests, it is not merely a pot of messages, a repertoire of signs to be flashed across a neutral mental screen. It has form as well as content; is born in action as well as thought; is a product of human creativity as well as mimesis; and, above all, is empowered. But it is not all empowered in the same way, or all of the time.

This is where hegemony and ideology become salient again. They are the two dominant forms in which power enters—or, more accurately, is entailed in—culture. It is through them, therefore, that the relationship between power and culture is finally to be grasped, although a further caveat is necessary: that power itself is Janus-faced. Sometimes it appears as the (relative) capacity of human beings to shape the actions and perceptions of others by exercising control over the production, circulation, and consumption of signs and objects, over the making of both subjectivities and realities. This is power in its *agentive* mode: it refers to the command wielded by human beings in specific historical contexts. But power also presents, or rather hides, itself in the forms of everyday life. Sometimes ascribed to transcendental, suprahistorical forces (gods or ancestors, nature or physics, biological instinct or probability), these forms are not easily questioned. Being "natural" and "ineffable," they seem to be beyond human agency, notwithstanding the fact that the interests they serve may be all too human. This kind of *nonagentive* power proliferates outside the realm of institutional politics, saturating such things as aesthetics and ethics, built form and bodily representation, medical knowledge and mundane usage. What is more, it may not be experienced as power at all, since its effects are rarely wrought by overt compulsion. They are internalized, in their negative guise, as constraints; in their neutral guise, as conventions; and, in their positive guise, as values. Yet the silent power of the sign, the unspoken authority of habit, may be as effective as the most violent coercion in shaping, directing, even dominating social thought and action.

None of this is new, of course: identifying technologies and typologies of power, albeit in very diverse terms, has become a growth industry in modern social theory (see e.g., Lukes 1974; Bourdieu 1977; Wrong 1979; Mann 1986; also Foucault 1978, 1979, 1980a). The point, though, goes back a long way. For Marx, to take one instance, the power of the capitalist was clearly different from the power of the commodity, the contrast corresponding broadly to the way in which ideology is portrayed in *The German Ideology* and *Capital* respectively (see e.g., Larrain 1979, 1983; Lichtheim 1967; Lichtman 1975; J. Comaroff 1985:chap.1). In the former it comes across primarily as a set of ideas that reflect the interests of the ruling class; ideas which, inverted through a camera obscura, are impressed upon the (false) consciousness of the proletariat (Marx and Engels 1970:64f.). It is a function, in other words, of the capacity of the dominant to impose their will and their worldview on others. In *Capital*, by contrast, ideology is not named as such, and it is not said to arise mechanically from the politics of class domination. It is held, instead, to reside unseen in the commodity form itself. For commodity production, the dominant mode of value creation in modern capitalism, makes a whole world of social relations in its own image, a world that appears to be governed by natural laws above and beyond human intervention. Indeed, it is the inversion by which relations between people seem to be determined by relations among objects, and not vice versa, that makes commodity fetishism; and in this ontological moment a historically specific set of inequalities take root in subjective and collective experience, determining the way in which the social order is perceived and acted upon (Marx 1967:71f.; Giddens 1979:183). The contrast between the two images of ideation, in short, goes together with that between the two forms of power. The first is directly supported by, in fact hinges on, the agency of dominant social groups; the second derives, as if naturally, from the very construction of economy and society. As it happens, Marx decided to call the one "ideology." The other, to which he applied no term, lays the ground for a characterization of hegemony.

Until now we also have used both of these terms without specification. Significantly, there is a passage in *The Prison Notebooks* in which Gramsci speaks of "ideology"—in quote marks—in its "highest sense." It is here that he comes closest to defining "hegemony," in the spirit of *Capital*, as Williams and others have characterized it (above, n.15)—and as theorists like Bourdieu (1977) have transposed and redeployed it. In his own words, it is "a conception of the world that is implicitly manifest in art, in law, in economic activity and in all manifestations of individual and collective life" (1971:328). This, however, is not just *any* conception of the world. It is the *dominant* conception, an orthodoxy that has established itself as "historically true" and concretely "universal" (1971:348). Building upon this and upon its conceptual roots, we take hegemony to refer to that order of signs and practices, relations and distinctions, images and epistemologies—drawn from a historically situated cultural field—that come to be taken-for-granted as the natural and received shape of the world and everything that inhabits it. It consists, to paraphrase Bourdieu (1977:167), of things that go without saying because, being axiomatic, they come without saying; things that, being presumptively shared, are not normally the subject of explication or argument (Bourdieu 1977:94). This is why its power has so often been seen to lie in what it silences, what it prevents people from thinking and saying, what it puts beyond the limits of the rational and the credible. In a quite literal sense, hegemony is habit forming. For these reasons, it is rarely contested directly, save perhaps in the roseate dreams of revolutionaries. For once its internal contradictions are revealed, when what seemed natural comes to be negotiable, when the ineffable is put into words—then hegemony becomes something other than itself. It turns into ideology and counterideology, into the "orthodoxy" and "heterodoxy" of Bourdieu's (1977) formulation. More commonly, however, such struggles remain clashes of symbols, the practical iconoclasm that is produced when tensions within the hegemonic—or between the grains of habit and habitat—chafe for immediate resolution.

Ideology in less than the "highest sense," we suggest, is ideology more conventionally understood. Following Raymond Williams (1977:109), who seems here to have *The German Ideology* in mind, we use it to describe "an articulated system of meanings, values, and beliefs of a kind that can be abstracted as [the] 'worldview' " of any social grouping. Borne in explicit manifestos and everyday practices, self-conscious texts and spontaneous images, popular styles and political platforms, this worldview may be more or less internally systematic, more or less assertively coherent in its outward forms. But, as long as it exists, it provides an organizing scheme (a master narrative?) for collective symbolic production. Obviously, to invoke Marx and Engels (1970) once again, the regnant ideology of any period or place will be that of the dominant group. And, while the nature and degree of its preeminence may vary a good deal, it is likely to be protected, even enforced, to the full extent of the power of those who claim it for their own.

But other, subordinate populations, at least those with communal identities, also have ideologies. And, inasmuch as they try to assert themselves against a dominant order or group, perhaps even to reverse existing relations of inequality, they too must call actively upon those ideologies. To be sure, if it is joined in the name of a collective identity, any such struggle, whether or not it is seen to be specifically "political," is an ideological struggle; for it necessarily involves an effort to control the cultural terms in which the world is ordered and, within it, power legitimized. Here, then, is the basic difference between hegemony and ideology. Whereas the first consists of constructs and conventions that have come to be shared and naturalized throughout a political community, the second is the expression and ultimately the possession of a particular social group, although it may be widely peddled beyond. The first is nonnegotiable and therefore beyond direct argument; the second is more susceptible to being perceived as a matter of inimical opinion and interest and therefore is open to contestation. Hegemony homogenizes, ideology articulates. Hegemony, at its most effective, is mute; by contrast, says de Certeau (1984:46), "all the while, ideology babbles on."

There are other differences, to which we shall return in a moment. But first, a more immediate question: What is the relationship between hegemony and ideology, either dominant or dissenting? This is a crucial issue, and one on which we depart from much current—and, we believe, currently confused—thinking. Indeed, the unusual, triangular manner in which we have chosen to define culture, hegemony, and ideology is meant not merely to find a way out of the thicket of ambiguity surrounding these concepts in modern anthropology; it is also to arrive at a set of terms with which to address both this question and the many problems about the nature of power, consciousness, and representation to which it points.

Hegemony, we suggest, exists in reciprocal interdependence with ideology: it is that part of a dominant worldview which has been naturalized and, having hidden itself in orthodoxy, no more appears as ideology at all. Inversely, the ideologies of the subordinate may give expression to discordant but hitherto voiceless experience of contradictions that a prevailing hegemony can no longer conceal. Self-evidently, the hegemonic proportion of any dominant ideology may be greater or lesser. It will never be total, save perhaps in the fanciful dreams of fascists, and only rarely will it shrink away to nothing. The manner in which some of the acts and axioms of a sectarian worldview actually come to be naturalized, or how critical reactions grow from the invisible roots that anchor inequality, is always a historically specific issue; we shall address it in detail in our account. Typically, however, the making of hegemony involves the assertion of control over various modes of symbolic production: over such things as educational and ritual processes, patterns of socialization, political and legal procedures, canons of style and self-representation, public communication, health and bodily discipline, and so on. That control, however—as Foucault understood about the generic nature of surveillance—must be sustained over time and in such a way that it becomes, to all intents and purposes, invisible. For it is only by repetition that signs and practices cease to be perceived or remarked; that they are so habituated, so deeply inscribed in everyday routine, that they may no longer be seen as forms of control—or seen at all. It is then that they come to be (un)spoken of as custom, (dis)regarded as convention—and only disinterred, if at all, on ceremonial occasions, when they are symbolically invoked as eternal verities.

Yet the seeds of hegemony are never scattered on barren ground. They might establish themselves at the expense of prior forms, but they seldom succeed in totally supplanting what was there before. Not only is hegemony never total, as Williams (1977:109) has insisted. It is always threatened by the vitality that remains in the forms of life it thwarts. It follows, then, that the hegemonic is constantly being made—and, by the same token, may be unmade. That is why it has been described as a process as much as a thing: "a process of continuous creation," says Adamson (1980:174), which "is bound to be uneven . . . and to leave some room for antagonistic cultural expressions. . . ." Nor is its perpetuation a mechanical consequence of politicoeconomic control: ruling regimes can never rest on their material laurels. Even the most repressive ones tend to be highly evangelical, constantly "seek[ing] to win the consent of subordinate groups to the existing social order" (Lears 1985:569). As we have said, the more successful they are, the more of their ideology will disappear into the domain of the hegemonic; the less successful, the more that unremarked truths and unspoken conventions will become remarked, reopened for debate. This, as we shall see, is ever more likely to occur as the contradictions between the world as represented and the world as experienced become ever more palpable, ever more insupportable; although the human capacity to tolerate and rationalize cognitive dissonance is notoriously variable. It is this form of dissonance that Gramsci (1971:333) himself, again following Marx and Engels (1970:51ff.), took to be the basis of "contradictory consciousness"; that is, the discontinuity between (1) the world as hegemonically constituted and (2) the world as practically apprehended, and ideologically represented, by subordinated people (the "man-in-the-mass").[18]

It is also with reference to this form of contradictory consciousness that some historians—most notably, perhaps, Genovese (1974)—have accounted for the reactions of oppressed peoples to their experience of subordination and dehumanization (see Lears 1985:569f.). Those reactions, it is said, consisted in a complex admixture of tacit (even uncomprehending) accommodation to the hegemonic order at one level and diverse expressions of symbolic and practical resistance at another, although the latter might have reinforced the former by displacing attention away from, or by actively reproducing, the hidden signs and structures of domination. The point may be extended to colonialism at large: a critical feature of the colonization of consciousness among the Tswana, and others like them, was the process by which they were drawn unwittingly into the dominion of European "civilization" while at the same time often contesting its presence and the explicit content of its worldview. A new hegemonic order, as we said earlier, was established amidst ideological struggle along an expanding, imploding cultural frontier. However, there is also a counterpoint to be anticipated here. "Contradictory consciousness" may be one key to the creation and perpetuation of relations of domination. But as it gives way to an ever more acute, articulate consciousness of contradictions, it may also be a source of ever more acute, articulate resistance. Of course, dominant groups usually seek to paper over such contradictions and to suppress their revelation by means both symbolic and violent; it is, more often than not, a very long road from the dawning of an antihegemonic consciousness to an ideological struggle won. That is why the history of colonialism, even in the most remote backwaters of the modern world, is such a drawn out affair, such an intricate fugue of challenge and riposte, mastery and misery.

Hegemony, then, is always intrinsically unstable, always vulnerable. For Gramsci (1971:12, 168) the ascendancy of a particular group, class, or whatever, was founded on its "position and function in the world of production," with the qualification that "production" ought not to be understood in narrow economistic terms. Quite the opposite: its material bases notwithstanding, effective domination was held to depend on cultural imperialism—on the ceaseless effort to forge alliances never simply given by existing structures of class and society (cf. Hall 1988:53–54), on the constant attempt to convert sectarian ideas into universal truths. Even in the face of such exertions, though, changes in the content and extent of hegemonies can occur fairly rapidly.

In the societies of the modern West, for instance, there have been significant shifts, in the late twentieth century, in the degree to which discrimination based on gender and race is naturalized. Distinctions of sex and color are obviously still inscribed in common linguistic usage, in aesthetic values and scientific knowledge; they continue to be a matter of widespread consensus and silent complicity; they also remain inscribed in everyday activity. Yet ever more articulate political and social protest has forced these issues on the collective conscience and into ideological debate. Formerly taken-for-granted discriminatory usages have been thrust before the public eye. As a result, the premises of racial and sexual inequality are no longer acceptable, at least in the official rhetoric of most modern states—although, in the world of mundane practice, the battle to control key signs and ostensibly neutral values rages on. This follows a very common pattern: once something leaves the domain of the hegemonic, it frequently becomes a major site of ideological struggle. Even when there is no well-formed opposing ideology, no clearly articulated collective consciousness among subordinate populations, such struggles may still occur. But they are liable to be heard in the genre of negation—refusal, reversal, the smashing of idols and icons—and not in the narrative voice of political argument. Which, finally, brings us to the relationship between culture, hegemony, and ideology and their human vehicles, consciousness and representation.

Consciousness and Representation

Thus far we have portrayed hegemony and ideology as two modalities, each associated with a characteristic form of empowerment, within any cultural field. We use "cultural field" here for two reasons: first, to reiterate that, far from being reducible to a closed system of signs and relations, the meaningful world always presents itself as a fluid, often contested, and only partially integrated mosaic of narratives, images, and signifying practices; and, second, to mark the fact that, in colonial (and many other) contexts, the seman-

27

tic scape contains a plurality of "cultures"—that is, of "systems" of symbols, values, and meanings which are reified and objectified in the course of colonization itself (see chapter 6; Comaroff and Comaroff 1989). In these circumstances ideological struggles come often to be clothed in the rhetoric of cultural difference, although the field of signifiers in which they occur necessarily expands to take in the very possibility of "intercultural" discourse and its primary textual act, translation.

If hegemony and ideology are two modalities within a cultural field—two tendencies whose relative proportions and substance are constantly liable to shift—it follows that they are best visualized as the ends of a continuum. So too are the forms of power associated with them. Indeed, just as the hegemonic and the ideological may alter in relation to one another, so may the nature of empowerment inscribed in any regime of signs and values. Take the case of modern South Africa, for example: between 1950 and 1990, black campaigns of defiance repeatedly contested the everyday vehicles—such things as segregated trains and buses, hospitals and schools—that naturalized racial inequality. The hidden bases of domination were repeatedly brought into the light of scrutiny. With each crack in, each diminution of, the axiomatic foundations of apartheid, the resort to state power in its brute, agentive form became more palpable, more pervasive. Conversely, as hegemonies insinuate themselves into a political community and spread, the perceived need to protect them by the visible exercise of force recedes; their authority is internalized through habitual practice, suffusing everyday life and the conventions that regulate it.

But this continuum is still missing a crucial element. For what differentiates hegemony from ideology, one face of power from the other, is not some existential essence. It is, as we have implied throughout, the factor of human consciousness and the modes of representation that bear it. The postenlightenment western tradition has left the human sciences—except maybe psychology—with a binary image of social consciousness. This is not merely an extension into the collective realm of theories of the individual psyche. The founders of modern sociology and anthropology were vehemently opposed, in principle if not always in practice, to psychological reductionism and to any idea of a collective unconscious; recall Malinowski's (1954) denunciation of what he misread as the notion of a "group mind" in Durkheim's writings on religion (see 1947). It is rather a matter of the unspecified Cartesian assumptions about personhood, cognition, and social being that persist in mainstream western thought, both orthodox and critical. In this tradition consciousness is all or none, true or false, present or absent. It is moreover the stuff of contemplative rather than practical understanding—though, as we have noted, theorists in the Gramscian tradition have long challenged the dichotomy. Whether it be seen as the mere reflection of social facts or the actual source of common action, consciousness itself is rarely treated as a problem. It is understood as content not form, as knowledge not modes of knowing. For all our sophisticated analyses of subjectivity and experience, we social scientists continue to speak as if it stands in a simple opposition to *un*consciousness, as if these were the only collective states of mind and being in the world.

Yet few anthropologists should be able to accept this; it runs counter to much of what we presume when we interpret cultures and the meaningful practices that animate them. Much more plausible is the notion that social knowledge and experience situate themselves along a *chain of consciousness*— once again a continuum whose two extremes are the unseen and the seen, the submerged and the apprehended, the unrecognized and the cognized. It hardly needs pointing out that the one extreme corresponds to the hegemonic pole of culture, the other to the ideological. And just as hegemonies and ideologies shift over time and space, so the contents of consciousness are not fixed. On the one hand, the submerged, the unseen, the unrecognized may under certain conditions be called to awareness; on the other, things once perceived and explicitly marked may slip below the level of discourse into the unremarked recesses of the collective unconscious. The latter is emphatically *not* some form of group mind. It is the implicit structure of shared meaning that human beings absorb as they learn to be members of particular social worlds.

Between the conscious and the unconscious lies the most critical domain of all for historical anthropology and especially for the analysis of colonialism and resistance. It is the realm of partial recognition, of inchoate awareness, of ambiguous perception, and, sometimes, of creative tension: that liminal space of human experience in which people discern acts and facts but cannot or do not order them into narrative descriptions or even into articulate conceptions of the world; in which signs and events are observed, but in a hazy, translucent light; in which individuals or groups know that something is happening to them but find it difficult to put their fingers on quite what it is. It is from this realm, we suggest, that silent signifiers and unmarked practices may rise to the level of explicit consciousness, of ideological assertion, and become the subject of overt political and social contestation—or from which they may recede into the hegemonic, to languish there unremarked for the time being. As we shall see, it is also the realm from which emanate the poetics of history, the innovative impulses of the bricoleur and the organic intellectual, the novel imagery called upon to bear the content of symbolic struggles.

The space between consciousness and unconsciousness is significant for another reason. In the course of our account we shall argue that hegemony stands to ideology, broadly speaking, as form to content—with the qualification that the distinction is self-evidently one of degree. The hegemonic, in short, is inscribed largely in what we take to be enduring forms (or "structures")—the commodity form, linguistic forms, epistemological forms, and so on—in relation to which substantive differences of social value and political ideology are given voice (*form*ulated?). As long as they last, these forms lay down the implicit ground—the authoritative frame of reference—within which the content of the meaningful world may be subjectively constructed, negotiated, actively empowered. The obvious analogy here is with language, which is commonly described, like culture, in such a way as to suggest that it plies the chain of consciousness between the unsaid and the said, code and message, grammatical form and the content of speech. The journey along the chain, patently, is envisaged as dialectical (Barthes 1967:15ff.): if grammatical forms were not a ("deeper" structural) distillate of substance, they could not generate meaningful new utterances, new moments of content; conversely, if the latter were not expressions of those underlying grammatical forms, it would be difficult to account for their production, let alone their comprehensibility. So it is with culture, hegemony, and ideology: hegemony is a product of the dialectic whereby the content of dominant ideologies is distilled into the shared forms that seem to have such historical longevity as to be above history—and, hence, to have the capacity to generate new substantive practices along the surfaces of economy and society. Like formal semantic oppositions in culture—with their putative arbitrariness—they do not themselves appear to have any ideological content. They belong to the domain of fact, not value. They are just there, ineffably.

Because the liminal space between the hegemonic and the ideological, consciousness and unconsciousness, is also an area in which new relations are forged between form and content, it is likely to be the source of the poetic imagination, the creative, the innovative. The latter, after all, *depend* on the play of form and content, on experimentations in expressive technique, on conjuring with ambiguity. Ideology may, of course, take many guises, narrative and nonnarrative, realistic or whimsical; it may be heavily symbolic, deeply coded; but at root its messages must be communicable. Hegemony, as we have said, represents itself everywhere in its saturating silences or its ritual repetitions. It is on the middle ground between such silences and repetitions that human beings often seek new ways to test out and give voice to their evolving perceptions of, and dispositions toward, the world. The analytic implication is both clear and complex: modes of representation, and the diverse forms they take, are *part* of culture and consciousness, hegemony and ideology, not merely their vehicles. "Reading" them, then, is the primary methodological act of any historical anthropology. Consequently, we shall return to this topic in the discussion of methodology in the following section.

One last, closely related issue remains: the nature of protest and symbolic struggle. It is taken up in the Introduction to volume 2. To anticipate our argument there, we believe that the present debate among historians and anthropologists over the conception and definition of resistance boils down to the problem of consciousness and motivation. As we put it in a recent paper (Comaroff and Comaroff 1989), much of that debate hinges on two matters: Does an act require *explicit* consciousness and articulation to be properly called "resistance?" Should the term apply only to the intentions behind social and political acts, or may it refer equally to their consequences? When a people can be shown to express some measure of awareness of their predicament as victims of domination—and, better yet, can state the terms of their response—the matter is clear. Where they do not, characterizing their reactions becomes an altogether more murky business. We will suggest, however, that there is an analytic lesson to be taken from the evident fact that most historical situations *are* extremely murky in just this respect.

Just as technologies of control run the gamut from overt coercion to implicit persuasion, so modes of resistance may extend across a similarly wide spectrum. At one end is organized protest, explicit moments and movements of dissent that are easily recognizable as "political" by western lights. At the other are gestures of tacit refusal and iconoclasm, gestures that sullenly and silently contest the forms of an existing hegemony. For the most part, however, the ripostes of the colonized hover in the space between the tacit and the articulate, the direct and the indirect. And far from being a mere reflection—or a reflex expression—of historical consciousness, these acts are a practical means of *producing* it. If anything will become evident in our study, it is that much of the Tswana response to the mission encounter was an effort to fashion an understanding of, and gain conceptual mastery over, a changing world. This, it seems, is a very general phenomenon. Early on in the colonizing process, wherever it occurs, the assault on local societies and cultures is the subject of neither "consciousness" nor "unconsciousness" on the part of the victim, but of recognition—recognition that occurs with varying degrees of inchoateness and clarity. Out of that recognition, and the creative tensions to which it may lead, there typically arise forms of *experimental practice* that are at once techniques of empowerment and the signs of collective representation.

Through such reactions "native peoples" seek to plumb the depths of the colonizing process. They search for the coherence—and, sometimes, the *deus ex machina*—that lies behind its visible face. For the recently colonized, or those who feel the vibrations of the imperial presence just over the horizon, generally believe that there *is* something invisible, something profound, happening to them—and that their future may well depend on gaining control over its "magic." Thus, for instance, many "Christianized" peoples the world over are, or once were, convinced that whites have a second, secret bible or set of rites (cricket? telegraphs? tea parties?) on which their power depends. The whimsical "unreason" of such movements as cargo cults stems from precisely this conviction. These movements, as is now well known, are early efforts to capture and redeploy the colonialist's ability to produce value. And they are often seen as enough of a threat to elicit a punitive response.

With time and historical experience, the colonized show greater discrimination, greater subtlety in interpreting the European embrace and its implications. Attempts to come to terms with the latter grow more diverse and are ever more closely tied to processes of social stratification. Among those drawn most fully into the forms of "modernity"—the petite bourgeoisies and "new elites" scattered across the Third World—there occurs a gradual appropriation of the images, ideologies, and aesthetics of the postenlightenment West, and, not least, its orthodox styles of political discourse and protest. But for the rest modernity and its modes of resistance are by no means the inevitable or even the likely consequences of the colonization of consciousness— or of the consciousness of colonization that follows. Indeed, as we have said several times already, the dynamics of cultural imperialism are such that, while the power structure of colonialism is everywhere clearly drawn, the colonizing process itself is rarely a simple dialectic of domination and resistance. That is why the manner in which we interrogate that process in general, and the part of the civilizing mission in particular, raises major methodological issues. We now turn to these issues, a shift of focus that requires a change of voice.

MEMORIES, MATERIALS, AND METHODS

Though we did not know it at the time, it was a pilgrimage. We had driven northward on the road to Mafeking, north over endless miles of gleaming highway to our first field site among the Tshidi Barolong in the borderland between Botswana and South Africa. It was an August afternoon in 1969, and the unflinching sunlight fell on the name of a deserted railway siding. Tiger Kloof! A name to be conjured with in the history of black South Africa. From our reading we already knew that, while Tiger Kloof was now a physical ruin, for the Tswana it was anything but a discarded sign. It had been the crowning achievement of the London Missionary Society in one of its finest hours; a "Native Institution" founded in 1904, it was to train teachers and craftsmen, upstanding members a black petite bourgeoisie. This elite had been meant to take a prominent place in the multiracial Christian commonwealth of missionary fantasy. As we drove through its fine gates—lofty, desolate portals giving clear evidence of dashed ideals—we were enveloped in a world of nineteenth-century proportion and order, a settlement whose solid stone features had been mocked and desecrated by a capricious but powerful hand. Tiger Kloof had been a testimony to civilization in the veld, a model of European enlightenment whose firm foundations and noble clock tower declared the lasting improvement it would make in the destiny of those it served. The school had been closed by the South African government in 1956. It was one of the sites where a newly triumphant Afrikaner regime had settled old scores with the British evangelists. The mounds of torn paper, the moldy blackboards on which Afrikaans obscenities had been scrawled recalled an episode in the nineteenth century, when enraged Boers had burned the books and broken the windows of mission schools in which they thought the Tswana had learned to defy white authority.

Reading these deserted, windswept buildings—for, as Darnton (1984:5) puts it, one can "read a city" just as one can read a folktale—we gained new insight into a history whose battles had been fought on diverse planes of the human imagination. We would soon learn more of the ambiguous status of Tiger Kloof on the mental map of the Southern Tswana, a place where many community leaders of a generation past had been made into "natives with moral backbone" (Willoughby 1912:70). Although its clock had stopped, the school embodied a past alive in the present. It was a feature in a landscape often still traversed, its signs saturated with meanings that remained— in an era of escalating apartheid and Bantu education—the objects of bitter struggle.

The point of this reminiscence is not merely to give words to the mute irony of that scene in the veld, the deserted battleground of whites at war over their place in a history so utterly dependent upon the black presence. It is more to raise an issue of method. What we first realized, as we walked the contours of that abandoned dream, was something of the infinite variety of historical texts, of the enduring signs of consciousness past. There were things to be learned from the concrete reality of those buildings—the forms of life they encouraged and proscribed, the affront they became to the Afrikaner self-image—that had not been legible in conventional histories. The design of the mission school had done more than express a cogent vision of subject and society. It had actually created it. In the sturdiness of its structures and the refined ornamental finish of its public buildings, in its spartan student accommodations and its overall plan, it had made real and natural the forms of a would-be hegemony. Nowhere in the loquacious accounts of the Institution left by its planners and founders was the cogency of this fact, the logic of its internal relations and inequalities, as plain. As yet we had no vocabulary with which to speak of the sort of three-dimensional texts that Tiger Kloof presented us. As anthropologists trained in the classic British tradition, we assumed that social relations were the primary features of any analytic field. Culture had no determining force in itself; it was distinct and epiphenomenal, an idiom in which more basic realities were represented. Concepts such as "hegemony" or "habitus" had not yet entered the universe of anthropological discourse. But we were fascinated and perplexed by the brutal "social facts" before us, facts that were so evidently both images and instruments in the making of a particular human world.

We were soon to discover that it was this sense of the making of a world that the Tswana themselves understood by "history." Elsewhere (Comaroff and Comaroff 1987:193) we have argued that this history is seldom spontaneously told in narrative style, as a linear account of events. Neither can it be readily reduced from its various expressive forms into an "objective" chronicle. For it resides less in propositions than in dispositions, in a dynamic, open-ended order of distinctions (*setswana/sekgoa*; work/labor; cattle/money) which are sometimes acted out, sometimes spoken out, but which are always vested in everyday things and activities.

This patently is at odds with the popular western notion of history as an account of "actual" persons and processes—a notion based on the distinction between "reality," the material occurrence of events, and "representation," the terms in which the story is told and acted on. A similar division underlies the contrast between society and culture, the concrete and the concept (Comaroff and Comaroff 1987:193). But representation, in the lay imagination, is also widely assumed to have two distinct modes: realism, where images aim to be undistorted reflections of the world; and rhetoric, whose images by their nature evaluate the world as they portray it. The first is seen as the medium of factual historical narratives and documentary accounts; the second, of poetic interpretation and artistic expression (cf. Mitchell 1986). Philosophers, semioticians, and social scientists have often called this distinction into question; few, probably, would still defend it, least of all those for whom the postmodern world has become a jungle of "wild signifiers" (Hebdige 1988:195). But it remains implicit in the weave of our everyday culture and still has profound effects upon our ways of seeing, especially in the empirically grounded social sciences (cf. Friedrich 1979: 442). Most relevant to our concerns here is that it leads to the assumption that poetic representation[19] is less true, more manipulative, than realistic narrative. While the latter is the stuff of verbal signs, the former is more frequently associated, in our own recent history, with graphic images (Mitchell 1986); it is seen to belong to the separate realms of aesthetics and ideology, refracting collective consciousness through the prism of social interest. Inasmuch as this distinction separates representations from real facts, "advertisements" from "documentaries," it leaves no place for a poetics of history (Comaroff and Comaroff 1987:193; Hebdige 1988:19).

Yet the beam of narrative history casts only a weak light on our particular scene, showing us little that we did not already know. In the early records of the encounter between the Tswana and the Nonconformists, only the Europeans spoke audibly in the genre of narrative realism. And even they did so for only part of the time. Of course, the missionaries were especially diligent providers of stories about their own intentions, projects, and achievements; in fact, we argue that they were the prototypical subjects of a modern "history as biography," producing a range of heroic texts whose linear progression gave putatively sufficient account of human motives, actions, and consequences. Such folk histories are indeed testimonies of agency, and of the pulse of the vital imagination. But they do not yield a sufficient analytic account of the complex social forces of which they themselves are products. Nor can the "true confessions" of letter or journal reveal the chain of collective consciousness in which it is but one link. Read for its story line, the most self-scrutinizing description of an evangelist's calling gives us only limited insight into how—in Althusser's terms—he was interpellated as colonizing subject and how he set about enacting this role.

Narrative realism, as we have already noted, was even less relevant to the African participants in our drama, although some of them soon began to talk to the whites in their own terms and a few, members of the new petite bourgeoisie, even became masters of the genre. Not only were there hardly any Tswana narratives in the nineteenth-century sources, but our own research elicited few chronicles of indigenous events, except those left by the self-conscious, literate elite (Comaroff and Comaroff 1987:193). We found rural people more prone to commenting on their past and present by drawing upon a range of graphic verbal and gestural tropes to construct the distinctions and contrasts—the "here" and "there," "black" and "white," "country" and "city"—that capture the contradictions of their world. Poetics (in the form of praise poems, initiation songs, and the like) had been the medium of collective representation in precolonial Tswana politics. But in the modern context such poetic practice was most tangible in the everyday actions of the illiterate majority, who spoke of their history with their bodies and their homes, in their puns, jokes, and irreverencies.[20] This convinced us that historical consciousness is not confined to one expressive mode, that it may be created and conveyed, with great subtlety and no less "truth," in a variety of genres. If we listen only to narratives of events or past relations, we may be led to conclude that people who are reluctant to offer them lack historical awareness—even that they live in a "cold" society. But history and its representations are not nicely distinguishable. To the contrary: history lies in its representations, for representation is as much the making of history as it is consciousness speaking out (Comaroff and Comaroff 1987: 205). What is more, realism and rhetoric do not stand opposed. Just as the latter is not a mere aesthetic embellishment of a truth that lies elsewhere, the former is but one among many modes of constructing the past and present, with no greater claim on authenticity, no less attention to aesthetics.

Thus, while our missionaries recount their stories in a clear narrative voice—and other "objective" sources exist with which to compare them—it is often the telling that is as significant as the tale itself. The profound forces that motivated them, and the varied vehicles of their awareness, emerge not so much from the content of those stories as from their poetics; that is, from their unselfconscious play on signs and symbols, their structures and silences, their implicit references. Furthermore, the actions of the churchmen often speak as poetically as their words, for practice is never shaped by utility alone; its form always exceeds its function. To take one example: the evangelists had to feed themselves in the field, but it was not mere necessity that persuaded them to make their agricultural labors into an exercise in moral instruction, their gestures into metonyms of a mode of production (chapter 6). What they were sowing was a new hegemony. And sometimes their acts conflicted with their professions for, as we have insisted, consciousness is never free from contradiction. Thus we discovered that, while Nonconformist ideology denied the salience of the flesh, its bearers betrayed, in their mundane behavior and uncensored thoughts, a preoccupation with the unclothed black body and with the power of corporeal politics.

As this suggests, in our concern to push beyond too simple a view of consciousness and agency, meaning and power, we found ourselves with an embarrassing richness of data. Indeed, not only did our perspective yield an alarming proliferation of "texts," but it made reading them a complicated task. For as well as the usual forms of written documents—which in the case of the missionaries were plentiful—we also had to deal with a wide array of unconventional evidence. The form as much as the content of verbal and visual accounts became relevant. So too did the whole range of "trivial" aesthetics through which the colonizing culture let down its hair—the fashions and fictions, the seemingly innocent trinkets and trifles, with which its hegemony was actually built.

We had initially chosen to work among the Tshidi-Barolong, a Southern Tswana people, because there existed a wealth of documentation about them dating back to the beginning of the nineteenth century (J. Comaroff 1985:13). The earliest accounts were written by the vanguards of imperialism: explorers, traders, and missionaries. They were soon followed by Boer settlers and yet others who ventured into the South African interior. Each party had its distinct reasons for producing detailed, if partial accounts of Tswana life, accounts of various kinds. The evangelists, for example, had been exposed to conventions of African reportage well before they left Britain. Their writing became part of a long-established tale that postenlightenment Europeans told each other about the march of civilization into the dark places on earth. Dispatches from the field assumed a stylized form, diligently probing virgin vistas of self and landscape to satisfy a hungry readership at home (chapter 5). These communications varied in their intent and formality: the subjects and degrees of disclosure permitted in letters to relatives were not appropriate for the ever-vigilant evangelical authorities, for carefully crafted appeals to philanthropists, or for dissemination to "the great British public." The same material was strategically re-presented for each of these audiences, yielding layers of text that made visible diverse purposes and constraints. Once addressed to the missionary societies, letters and reports became their property, to be widely recycled as local propaganda. The red ink of censorship reveals how such fragments were rationalized into journals and memoirs as mission testimony became a veritable industry. In the field, the churchmen were also avid propagators of the "word." Their printing presses soon poured forth a stream of texts: lessons, hymnals, vernacular Bibles—and most of all newspapers, which were to bear the fruits of their campaign to produce black literati. Thus the first letters from Tswana school children that appeared in the latter half of the nineteenth century were soon followed by the more public writings of vernacular journalists and historians. The African petite bourgeoisie was to be as obsessed with leaving its signature on the world as its teachers had been.

What of those who did not acquire such cultural capital? And what of that important range of representations that is not consciously articulated in the first place? The flood of writings by colonizing whites conveys much that was unintended; even the most tightly rationalized texts are polyvalent and convey far more than they mean to say. In subtexts that disrupt their major themes, the voice of the silent other is audible through disconcerted accounts of his "irrational" behavior, his mockery, or his resistance (chapter 5). Thus, while we have relatively few examples of direct Tswana speech in the archives, we do have ample indirect evidence of their reactions and conversations with the mission—of the ways in which they chose to express themselves, often using the poetically intensified language of action, gesture, and the concrete sign (chapter 6). There is also a great deal of detailed description of "native" products and practices, detail for its own sake being the stuff of colonizing surveillance. Such data were enhanced by the more self-consciously "ethnographic" materials gathered by later evangelists and early social scientists, once African culture had been safely marginalized and reified as "tradition." As heirs to this legacy, we ourselves collected contemporary and historical materials, some of the latter from Tshidi-Barolong elders whose grandparents had experience of the mission before the formal imposition of overrule. It goes almost without saying that our reading of the nineteenth-century sources was profoundly affected by this experience, just as our first perceptions in the field were prefaced by forays into the records. This interplay of images, past and present, heightened our awareness of longer durations and continuities and also impressed upon us the difficulty of discerning the complex shifts that lay beneath superficial similarities.

In all these cases, of course, the Tswana speak through the European text; to the extent that "the other" is a construction of an imperializing imagination, s/he will always dwell in the shadows of its dominant discourse. In this sense we anthropologists are still explorers who tell ourselves stories about savagery and civilization. Not pejorative or racist stories, we hope, but stories nevertheless. At the same time modern anthropology hardly goes without challenge or contradiction. Nonwestern peoples have an objective existence in the world and, happily, they impose themselves increasingly on our narratives, affecting their substance, disrupting their harmony, and refusing to acknowledge their self-appointed sovereignty. In the postmodern age, the empire strikes back. Such tensions, incidentally, are not absent from the accounts of Tswana history and society produced by indigenous writers (e.g., Plaatje n.d.; Molema 1920, 1951, 1966; Matthews 1940, 1945; Tlou 1970, 1973, 1974; Setiloane 1976; Silitshena 1979, 1983). For many of these writers have been able students of western scholarly forms—forms that today distinguish elite consciousness in an ever more stratified postcolonial society.

We have tried as much as possible to recognize these tensions, to allow the productive discord we have found within and between our sources to have play in our own text. Yet we have also tried to keep a clear focus on the forces that shaped the colonial encounter and on the modes of power and knowledge to which it gave rise. For while there are always many histories, many refractions of a process such as this, there is little that is arbitrary about its brute inequalities or about the reality of its repression. Thus our aim is to do more than merely "read for the meaning" inscribed by the participants in the relics of these moments (Darnton 1984:5). We wish to explore how meanings of different kinds were actually produced in their material contexts; how they engaged each other in accommodation and struggle, domination and defiance; how they fed the human imagination, yet also limited its flight. We have tried, in the preceding section, to lay out the scheme of concepts which orients the exercise. This is a history in the anthropological mode, an attempt to account for the making of a social and cultural world, both in time and at a particular time. It explores the relationship of matter and meaning, reproduction and change. Finally, this is a history of events, not an event history. Because we explore those events within a multidimensional process, an engagement of ever increasing scale and complexity, we cannot construct a single-stranded chronology in which to fit them. The problem of how best to represent such a process is not easily resolved: as Goody (1977) notes, orthodox structuralism is more susceptible to the reductions of the two dimensional page. We attempt to describe the meshing of two social worlds themselves in motion, two worlds of power and meaning whose interplay was only partly predictable. In such a history, for all its obvious causes and effects, there is no single determination, no bottom line for a linear narrative to run along. Thus we have presented our account by dealing with its distinct levels and phases, identifying sequences of acts and events, each with its own logic, integrity, and significance in the embracing drama. By disentangling these strands, it becomes possible to scrutinize the fibre of each—so that, when they are entwined again, we may understand how the Tswana past came to yield a continuous history of particular texture and hue.

THE CAST OF CHARACTERS

The Southern Tswana

Our subject is born of the fateful meeting, in the early nineteenth century, between the Southern Tswana and British Nonconformist missionaries. At this stage we do no more than introduce the dramatis personae; sustained discussion of their respective origins and motivations will follow in the chapters below. The category "Southern Tswana"—even, as we have already noted, that of the "Tswana"—had no real indigenous significance at the time. But as a classification of the peoples living between the Vaal and Molopo rivers (the Tlhaping, Tlharo, and Rolong), it was to be made a reality by colonial history.[21] The annexation of the Crown Colonies of Griqualand West (1871), and then of British Bechuanaland (1885), embraced these peoples in a unified constitutional fate that would eventually make them part of the Cape Colony (1895) and the Union of South Africa (1910)—in contrast to the Tswana of the north, most of whom would be absorbed into the Bechuanaland Protectorate, now Botswana. In our study we have been mindful that these events imposed rigid political boundaries on what remained in many respects a continuous social terrain. Thus, while we focus centrally on the communities of this region, we follow them as they migrate in and out of its compass on the waves of historical necessity. We also pursue processes that originated in this arena but had consequences beyond it—like the founding of the first missions among the Tlhaping and Rolong, the effects of which were soon felt by northerly peoples such as the Kwena and Ngwaketse.

Of all the Tswana polities, those farthest south were to be most affected by their location in the direct path of European traffic beyond the borders of the Cape Colony. Their interactions with the whites had a cumulative impact upon the ecological, social, and cultural forms they shared with other Tswana peoples (see Shillington 1985). Conventionally classified as part of the more inclusive Sotho-Tswana cluster of southern Bantu speakers,[22] the geographical genesis of these peoples is hard to pin down. Some years ago Inskeep (1969:32) noted a general agreement among archaeologists that they "derived in a vague way from regions to the north" (cf. Schapera 1953:14). More recent research has added further speculation but little certainty: Hall (1987:21f.), reviewing existing linguistic and archeological knowledge of the peopling of the subcontinent, says of the Bantu language group that "there is no longer any consensus about routes of dispersal [or] methods of spread" (1987:31). The same, he adds, is true of the origins of farming communities.

There is less disagreement over the movement of Tswana into their present territory, however. Inskeep (1979:138f.) claims that they reached its southernmost fringe by the fifteenth century; Maggs (1976a:287), regarding the archeological record more conservatively, speaks of "the seventeenth century or earlier" but points to historical data which prove that they had arrived by the sixteenth. In fact, genealogies from some chiefdoms suggest yet earlier beginnings: the ruling dynasty of the Rolong, for one, dates itself back to the fourteen hundreds (cf. Legassick 1969b:115; Wilson 1969a:135). Nor is this impossible, as we now know of iron age settlement in eastern Botswana by the eighth century (Maggs 1980:340). Even by the most circumspect reading, the available evidence flies in the face of the political mythology of apartheid, which echoes the progenitors of Afrikaner historiography (Theal 1910:chap.5; Stow 1905:chap.21) in claiming that "the Bantu" moved into the region much later: to wit, at roughly the same time as European settlers.

A recurrent and consequential feature of precolonial Sotho-Tswana history was the fragmentation of polities in the wake of competition for the chiefship among the members of polygynous royal houses (J. L. Comaroff 1973). Many of the chiefdoms that existed at the time of first contact with the evangelists traced their origins to such internecine strife; the Rolong, for example, had broken into four chiefdoms (the Ratlou, Tshidi, Seleka, and Rapulana) in the late eighteenth century as a result of a protracted series of succession disputes and civil wars (Molema 1966). In fact, the ruling lines of most Southern Tswana communities recognized ranked genealogical

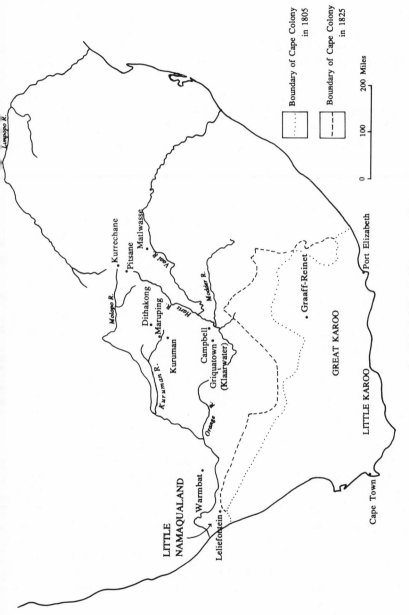

MAP 2 *Colonial South Africa, circa 1820*

Boundary of Cape Colony
in 1805

Boundary of Cape Colony
in 1825

0   100   200 Miles

Limpopo R.

Kurrechane
Pitsane
Matlwasse
Vaal R.
Molopo R.
Dithakong
Maruping
Harts R.
Modder R.
Kuruman R.
Kuruman
Campbell
Griquatown
(Klaarwater)
Orange R.
Graaff-Reinet
GREAT KAROO
Port Elizabeth
LITTLE KAROO
LITTLE
NAMAQUALAND
Warmbat.
Leliefontein
Cape Town

links with one another, links that went back to the putative co-membership of parent groups (see Breutz 1956, 1959). This fissile tendency, which seems to have commenced around 1500 (below, p.127), played itself out in an arid environment that placed limits upon sustained large-scale settlement. By the eighteenth century, however, it had partially reversed itself, giving way to a period of amalgamation and consolidation, facilitated by chiefly control over trade with northerly Tswana groups and with the Kora and Griqua on the colonial border (Legassick 1969b).

By the early nineteenth century, when the Nonconformists met with Chief Mothibi of the Tlhaping, the process of expansion and growth had ground to a halt and the larger polities were beginning to fracture. Patterns of exchange and power had shifted, to the disadvantage of the Southern Tswana sovereigns, as the Kora and Griqua became increasingly well armed and belligerent (Legassick 1989:395f.). This was exacerbated by *difaqane*, a period of destructive warfare and raiding, in the 1820's and early 1830's; long associated by historians with the rise of the Zulu state under Shaka (but cf. Cobbing 1988; below, p. 168), the widespread turmoil dramatically destabilized many peoples in the interior (see e.g., Lye 1969). So deeply affected were some polities that the early evangelists, used to European monarchies, had difficulty in discerning their structures of authority. The problem was to be compounded by their own effect—and by the global political and economic forces they represented—upon the power of local chiefs.

The People of the Cape Colony

The early nineteenth-century Tswana chiefdoms, being part of a complex network of regional relations, were subjected increasingly to material influences from the south. These were indirect at first, mediated by the "mixed" populations of the borderlands, peoples who were themselves the social, cultural, and physical offspring of the frontier. The missionaries were to establish a more direct link between the Southern Tswana and the colonial political economy. Indeed, the Cape Colony figures as the ever-more visible horizon in the background of our account. As any standard history of South Africa tells us, the Colony was founded by the Dutch East India Company in 1652. It was seized by the British in 1795 as a consequence of their war with France, only to be returned to the New Batavian Republic in 1803 under the Treaty of Amiens (see chapter 3). Taken again by Britain in 1806 with the resumption of the Napoleonic Wars, the Cape remained in her possession until 1910.

These simple facts had complex social consequences. While the first evangelists pictured southern Africa as an empty land, they were to find it a force field of tension and conflict. It presented them with a settler population made up of three major sets of characters: (1) His Majesty's administrators and officers, most of them gentlemen of high birth and rank, the rest, members of the garrison at the Cape; (2) British settlers, largely respectable middle-class burghers of Cape Town and growing numbers of farmers in the colony; and (3) Boers (lit. "farmers") of Dutch, German, and French descent, a population that had sedimented over a century and a half of colonial settlement and that was regarded by the British, the missionaries among them, as "rude" (J. L. Comaroff 1989). These discordant strands, to which the churchmen added—by virtue of class and interests—a fourth, were never really knit into a single social fabric. If anything, the Nonconformists exacerbated the tension and tumult, which finally culminated in the late 1830's, when many Boers trekked beyond the colonial frontier and the sovereignty of the Crown. As is so frequently the case in modern European history, the black other served here as an objective correlative in white conflicts over values and resources: the Great Trek was precipitated in large part by the emancipation of slaves and by the liberal policies of the British administration toward "natives." These policies, actively encouraged by the evangelists, threatened the material interests of the Boers, offended their segregationist ideology, and promised to overturn their "traditional" way of life (Peires 1989:499f.).

The Missionaries

Ironically, the black African served a similar ideological role in the history that brought the Nonconformist missionaries into this colonial cauldron in the first place. The great eighteenth-century evangelical movements out of which they came were both causes and consequences of the rise of European modernity, a process that turned, as we have said and will demonstrate below, upon newly salient differences between civilization and savagery. The heathen "other" of the dark continent provided a language for talking about (and a standard of comparison for) the rising working classes, the "dark satanic" populations at home—and this well before the "natives" of Africa seemed to beckon pious Britons to save them from themselves.

1. The London Missionary Society

The London Missionary Society took the first British initiative in the South African field and was the earliest to develop a network of stations in the interior. Although it was founded in 1795 to "consist of evangelical ministers and lay brethren of all denominations,"[23] the Society was predominantly Congregationalist, especially once the Presbyterians and Episcopalians withdrew to found their own evangelical societies (du Plessis 1911:99).

Since the first attacks on the papacy in England, secret assemblies of men and women had met together for common worship and mutual Christian instruction beyond consecrated walls and priestly authority (Dale 1907:59). Such assemblies anticipated the principles of Congregationalism, a denomination born of sixteenth-century Puritan resistance against the rites, episcopal authority, and "idolatrous gear" of the Church of England (Dale 1907:89f.). It is worth noting, given the significance of dress in our account of domination and defiance, that Elizabethan Nonconformity expressed its deep-seated dissent in an irreconcilable debate with the Queen over ritual vestments. The Congregationalist churches drew on the Calvinist tradition. They were founded in a covenant relationship with God and one another, giving absolute obedience to none but the sovereign Spirit. This autonomy, along with the sure knowledge that they were members of the elect, strengthened their resolve to stand firm as divine witnesses (Davies 1961:114). A creed that encouraged self-reliance, it would be well suited, in its modern form, to the isolation and uncertainties of the mission frontier. Like the rest of their Puritan brethren, the early Congregationalists suffered repression for their challenge to established ecclesiastical dominion. But they pursued their struggle for what they took to be the truth, righteousness, and vigor of a lost "communion of the saints." Cromwell's Commonwealth ushered in an era of theological tolerance, and the Independents[24] grew to be a notable "religious aristocracy," active in parliament, the army, and the city (Dale 1907:364). While the restoration brought renewed repression—Nonconformists were debarred from serving King or corporation, and from attending Oxford or Cambridge (Watts 1978:361)—the state was now more limited in its ability to put down dissent. Indeed, the nature of its sovereignty had altered and, with it, the forms of religious division. Puritan separatism had become increasingly reconciled with authority, turning the doctrine of election into an elitism that showed little sympathy with the ungodly multitude (Collinson 1986:6).

During the early decades of the eighteenth century there was an awareness of decline in the Dissenting ranks and a sense that a pervasive rationalism was "chilling faith"—"freezing the emotions and . . . public devotions," as Davies (1961:96) puts it. In a world newly persuaded of the value of statistics, Nonconformists began to measure the malaise of their own institutions. Dissenters had long been "middling sort of people" (Hurwich, as quoted by Watts 1978:352), religious Independency being associated with freedom from economic need or political patronage. Now there appeared to be a growing opulence among urban congregations (Davies 1961:98), but there was also a noticeable drift of wealthy families—those in commerce and the professions—to the established church. This seemed especially the case among the Congregationalists. Presbyterians, by comparison, gave more continuing evidence of "hereditary wealth and education" (Dale 1907:541).

By the latter half of the eighteenth century, however, a "second reformation" was afoot (Vaughan 1862:469). The Wesleyan revival, a direct response to the travails of the industrial workplace, began to attract large numbers from the newly formed laboring and managerial classes and to breath fresh life into Nonconformism in general. The Old Dissenters were now "caught between the 'enthusiasm' of the Methodists and the rational and moral emphasis of the Establishment" (Davies 1961:99). From a "decorous distance" they began to imbibe the evangelical spirit and imitate vital Wesleyan innovations (Davies 1961:113). A tangible product of this process was the founding of foreign mission societies like the LMS.

The earliest directors of the LMS had been captivated by visions of "multitudes of Hindoos flying to Christ as doves to their windows" (Lovett 1899,1:21) and by Captain Cook's descriptions of the South Seas. But Britain had taken possession of the Cape in 1795, and the Society soon turned its attention to the prospects offered by the new Colony. These prospects crystallized in the person of Johannes van der Kemp, a Dutchman with a medical degree, who offered himself for work in South Africa (du Plessis 1911:100). In 1798 four missionaries, two Dutch and two British, sailed to the Cape, where they were warmly received by both settler populations. Van der Kemp and an English colleague set off for the eastern border, while the others traveled north to found the first station among so-called Bushmen. While the latter was not to be a success, it did provide a stepping-stone to the peoples of the interior. During the first decade of the nineteenth century, the LMS managed to set up a viable mission among the Griqua at Klaarwater, just beyond the Orange River and not much more than a hundred miles south of the Tlhaping capital, Dithakong (Lovett 1899,1:525f.). In fact, an attempt was made to gain access to the latter but was abandoned in 1802. A second station, somewhat more precarious, was established to the west at Warmbat, in Little Namaqualand.

But, as we have suggested, the evangelists were not to escape the social and political tensions of the Colony. From very early on the African communities along the frontier became the object of struggle among white colonists with designs on their land and labor, and the Dutch Reformed Church had long opposed mission work among the slaves at the Cape. Not unexpectedly, then, the Nonconformists entered this troubled arena as marked men and were soon drawn into the thick of the dispute. For they too were competitors in the battle to gain control over black populations. Fresh from an abolitionist climate, they tried to force the issue of "native" social and legal rights upon the administration. In the eyes of the Boers, their presence emboldened the "Hottentots" (Khoi) to resist efforts to press them into service, undermining the very basis of the colonial mode of production; this, as we said, was one of the factors that sparked the Great Trek. But the churchmen also accused the Cape government of tacit connivance with

45

Boer exploitation (Philip 1828:passim), and they seem actively to have frustrated attempts to conscript Africans into the armed forces (Macmillan 1936b:282f.). The evangelists had already assumed the interstitial social role they would occupy for the rest of the century. By virtue of their championing of the interests of indigenous peoples, they alienated other European fractions. Yet by virtue of being white, they were always open to the suspicion of being colonial agents. Their mediating position between colonizers and colonized was inherently contradictory, invariably difficult. And it had complex historical implications.

The LMS was a society without a strongly uniform ideology, and it was torn by internal dissent when strong antimissionary feeling developed at the Cape. As the antipathy deepened, the government tightened its control over those wishing to establish stations beyond the colonial frontier (Mears 1970:2). In 1812 the directors thought it necessary to send one of their number, the Rev. John Campbell, on a prolonged tour of inspection of its South African outposts (Lovett 1899:533). It was he who first visited the Tlhaping, gaining an ostensible mandate from Chief Mothibi to set up a mission in his domain (below, p. 179). On Campbell's return the directors wrote to reassure Lord Somerset, Governor of the Colony:[25]

> [We] have no other object in view in sending, at great expense, missions to various parts of the heathen world than the ultimate good of the barbarous and unenlightened countries. . . . The Directors humbly entreat your Lordship's continued protection to the missionaries.

When Robert Moffat and four colleagues arrived at the Cape in 1817, however, Somerset refused them permission to proceed beyond the border. The "English establishments" over the frontier, he declared, ignored colonial law and served as a refuge for runaway slaves (du Plessis 1911:155). It was not until 1821 that Moffat gained formal access to the Tswana peoples to the north. Even then, the missionaries had to contend with the continuing hostility of the Boers, who resented their intrusion into the established order of white-black relations and persistently disrupted their efforts. The journey to the interior—on what was to become the Missionary Road—was a passage across a highly conflicted social landscape, one not at all anticipated in the evangelists' dreams.

2. The Methodists

From the perspective of the Tlhaping peoples, the churchmen of the LMS were the dominant evangelical influence in the region during the nineteenth century (Shillington 1985:17). They were the first in the field, gained epic status in the British imagination, and mediated most directly the formal forces of colonization from the south. But from the standpoint of the more northerly Barolong, the other great cluster of Southern Tswana polities, it was the Wesleyan Methodist Missionary Society that predominated (Molema 1966). Methodist evangelical technique—its stress upon a self-propagating African leadership, for example, and its organizational genius—ensured that its cultural forms made a deep impression on black consciousness at a time of unprecedented social upheaval. Their influence reached way beyond the confines of the mission church. The effect of Wesleyan rhetorical and administrative style, for instance, would be palpable in the independent churches and the rising black nationalist movement in South Africa in the early twentieth century.

Methodism, which had originated as a revival within the established Church of England half a century or so earlier, was a missionary movement from the start; no institutional separation was made, in the field, between pastor and evangelist (du Plessis 1911:294). John Wesley had aimed to "awaken the masses" dispirited by the effects of industrialization (Troeltsch 1949,2:721). Hence, where Congregationalism had its strongholds in the agricultural South Midlands and among the merchants and weavers of the old clothing towns (Bradley 1978:142; Watts 1978:353), Methodism was directed mainly at the growing working and middle classes in the industrial valleys of the north and southwest. But its effects were by no means limited to these areas (Obelkevich 1976). Denounced by the ecclesiastic authorities, Wesleyan preachers took to the streets and fields, drawing thousands to hear impromptu sermons. Their message of salvation, we are told, transported audiences from despair to bliss (Halévy 1971:36f.). Addressed to the multitudes overlooked by the Old Dissent, this message was specifically tailored to the experience of urbanization and wage labor.

Wesleyan techniques would soon be imitated by other Nonconformists, but their threat was not easily allayed. By the early nineteenth century Methodists were taking over many of the deserted meeting houses of the Old Dissenters (Bradley 1978:100). When the WMMS was officially formed in 1813, it was as the "overseas" extension of a vibrant movement that had long ministered to what Lecky (1892:101) called the "most brutal and neglected portions of the population" (below, chapter 2). This was the other "nation," living—so went the phraseology of the time—in the "unknown continents," "jungles," and "Africas" of the city slums (Hebdige 1988:20). The association is highly significant. As we shall see, the identification of the oppressed classes of Europe with heathen Africa allowed each to discredit the other in a two-faced politics of colonization that operated both at home and abroad.

It should not surprise us, then, that the WMMS was regarded as an anomaly in British colonial society. When the first Methodist preacher arrived in Cape Town in 1814, he found the Anglican Church established as the regnant denomination; alongside it, Dutch Reformism ministered to the

Boer population. The governor at the Cape, fearful of disturbing these delicately poised interests, refused him permission to preach to blacks—or to whites (du Plessis 1911:167). The Wesleyans were thus forced almost immediately to concentrate their hopes and energies beyond the frontier. In 1816 they were allowed to set up a station at Leliefontein in Namaqualand, across the northwest border of the Colony. Here they soon learned of the numerous "Bechuana" peoples in the hinterland who, rumor had it, were hospitable to evangelism.

And so it is that in 1821 we find Rev. Kay, one of two Methodist evangelists posted to Bechuanaland, traveling north with a large party of Griqua and Tswana who were on their way back from a trading expedition to the borders of the colony (Mears 1970:1). He is met en route by Robert Moffat and taken to the LMS station at Kuruman. This settlement is near Maruping, the seat of the Tlhaping chief, Mothibi, who had moved there just a few years before from his old capital at Dithakong.[26] Here Kay begins to survey the surrounding countryside, seeking a site for the Wesleyan "Bechuana" mission. And here we leave him for the while; for, having introduced our main cast of characters, we move to the task of setting the scene for their first encounter.

T W O

BRITISH
BEGINNINGS

Spirits of an Age, Signs of the Times

T HE BRITISH APPETITE for accounts of overseas missionaries goes back a long way—at least as far, observed Reverend
Wickham in 1912, as the later volumes of *Robinson Crusoe*
([1719] 1927). Added the good reverend (1912:181ff.), somewhat dismissively, Daniel Defoe was a journalist with a keen sense of public
tastes; aware that mission societies were being formed in the late 1600's and
early 1700's, he anticipated a growing interest in the exploits of evangelists
abroad. Defoe, Wickham goes on to note, was always a man ahead of his
time. This was certainly true in another sense, unremarked by the literary
cleric. Unlike those pre–nineteenth-century poets and historians—Milton,
Gibbon, and their contemporaries[1]—who celebrated the spread of Christianity, he cast a distinctly skeptical eye on some of its emissaries (e.g.,
1927,3:13f.). In that respect he foreshadowed a literary trend which was to
arise with the Victorian age, when the foreign missions came to be drawn in
an altogether more equivocal light—most unforgettably, perhaps, in the person of St. John Rivers, Jane Eyre's "ecclesiastical cousin."

Charlotte Brontë sketches the missionary,[2] in deft strokes, through
Jane's increasingly self-conscious musings. Jane's early impressions speak
of Rivers' abstracted, coldly brooding nature, his lack of the "mental
serenity . . . which should be the reward of every sincere Christian and practical philanthropist" (1969:448).[3] This view is strengthened by his unfeeling

49

proposal of marriage: "You are formed for labour, not for love," he tells her. "A missionary's wife you must—shall be. I claim you—not for my pleasure, but for my Sovereign's service" (1969:514). Likening the prospect to suicide (1969:526), Jane scorns St. John's offer. Above all, she abhors the kind of humanity for which he stands: driven by pitiless fanaticism, he turns away from those who most need him back home, preferring the heroism of his "own large views" to "the feelings and claims of little people" in England (1969:531). Despite her strong commitment to Christianity, Miss Eyre clearly entertains serious doubts about the missionary project. So, too, does the thinly-veiled authorial voice hovering behind her.

Nonetheless, Brontë does not merely ridicule the evangelist. To the contrary, her ambivalence toward him is unmistakable. Rivers may be blinded by his own ambition, yet he is "a good man" (1969:501) and every bit the Christian martyr (Spivak 1985:249); he may be unyielding in his "twisted heroism" (Eagleton 1975:19), yet he is the very essence of such positive attributes as endurance and industry, talent and reason; his autocratic hauteur may be stifling, yet his sincere zeal has its attractions. This ambivalence is especially interesting in that it was founded on considerable exposure to the missionary enterprise. Brontë was the daughter of an Anglican vicar. A "Low Church Evangelical" with increasingly conservative political and religious views, Patrick Brontë had come from Irish peasant stock and, by turns an artisan and a teacher, had entered the ministry by way of Cambridge.[4] He raised his children in the vicarage at Haworth, Yorkshire, where their small circle was made up largely of clergy and their families, and where much of their reading matter was church literature then full of discussion of mission work abroad. Even more significantly, Haworth was in the West Riding, one of the regions of England most affected by the industrial revolution. It was also an area in which Christian revivalism gained a firm hold and from which many Protestants departed for Africa to extend the Empire of Christ and, no less, of Great Britain. Both the evangelical wing of the Church of England and a large number of Nonconformist denominations were very active here—at times (as in the abolitionist movement; see chapter 3) in cooperation, at times in competition. This tension seems to have reached into the Brontë household itself, since, by all accounts, its members felt deeply divided about Nonconformism. Haworth, in short, was not far from the center of the social, economic, and religious upheavals of the age. By coincidence, too, it was the home of one James Broadbent, the brother of the first Methodist evangelist among the Tswana. Samuel Broadbent wrote from Bechuanaland to the Yorkshire village during the 1820's, when Charlotte was a young girl.[5]

For all her doubts about the missionary enterprise, Charlotte Brontë was less damning than many writers of the period. It has become almost a commonplace, in accounts of Victorian representations of "the Other," to cite Dickens (see e.g., Curtin 1964:343f., 422f., 470; Lorimer 1978:120; Brantlinger 1985:175): in particular, his acutely critical essay (1908a), published just a year after *Jane Eyre*, on the disastrous Niger Expedition,[6] and his biting characterization of Mrs. Jellyby, the absurd evangelist in *Bleak House*. In the first piece Dickens called upon all his powers of polemic and sarcasm to attack the very idea of missionary philanthropy, and he dismissed Africa as irredeemably unfit for civilization. The second, though, was probably even more effective: here he relied on satire to vent his spleen against evangelists and the "ignoble savages" themselves. (In the same year, after seeing an exhibition of "extremely ugly . . . rather picturesque" Zulus at the St. George's Gallery, Hyde Park Corner, Dickens wrote his biting essay on "The Noble Savage," whom he wished "off the face of the earth" [1853:337, repr. 1908b:229; see also chapter 3].) To an even greater extent than Charlotte Brontë, he was convinced that the work to be done at home was far more urgent and important; to him, the call for missionization overseas, or for grand colonial schemes, simply distracted attention from the dire social and political problems that beset England.

Notwithstanding the literary brilliance with which it was stated, Dickens's argument—like Brontë's more muted misgivings—had been rehearsed before, perhaps most vividly in the *Edinburgh Review* of 1808. Written by the founder of the *Review*, Sydney Smith, this article appeared in the wake of an uprising in the Indian town of Vellore (near Madras) of two battalions of sepoys. These "dread . . . native troops" (1808:153) had fallen upon four companies of the 69th regiment of the British army as they slept, killing hundreds of men. Smith ascribed this massacre and other attacks on Christians by Muslims and Hindus to the defensive religious fervor incited by European missionaries (1808:171). Hindus, he went on to say, cling tenaciously to "their religious prejudices" (1808:174) and hence resent the activities of the evangelists. Under such conditions the latter were not merely destined to be unsuccessful but were quite liable to spark off a major insurrection. Smith then went on to deliver a stinging personal attack on the missionaries who had worked in South India, directing his invective at the Baptists in particular. Blinded by their own zeal, they were, he claimed, woefully injudicious and incompetent (1808:171):

> If the management [of the missions] was in the hands of men who
> were discrete and wise, . . . the desire of putting an end to [them]
> might be premature, and indecorous. But, the misfortune is, the men
> who wield the instrument, ought not, in common sense and propriety,

to be trusted with it for a single instant. Upon this subject they are quite insane, and ungovernable; they would deliberately, piously, and conscientiously expose our whole Eastern empire to destruction, for the sake of converting half a dozen Brahmans, who, after stuffing themselves with rum and rice, and borrowing money from the missionaries, would run away, and cover the gospel and its professors with every species of impious ridicule and abuse.

Upon the whole, it appears to us hardly possible to push the business of proselytism in India to any length, without incurring the utmost risk of losing our empire.

Smith was unmoved by the vision of Christian colonization that had taken shape in the abolitionist debate (below, pp.118f). Even more condescendingly than Dickens, he tells these men what they might do with their energies (1808:171):

Methodism at home is no unprofitable game to play.

The essay drew a spirited reply from Robert Southey in the *Quarterly Review* of February 1809.[7] The Nonconformist evangelists could not be blamed for the political troubles in India, he asserted. Quite the opposite: they were sincere, well-intentioned men who, if not faultless, had shown admirable perseverance and had performed a real service to the nation. The object of Empire, concluded Southey, was to gain adherents not subjects, and this could only be done by bringing the heathen into a Christian commonwealth—in Asia as elsewhere. Smith responded[8] by hurling yet further abuse at the "consecrated cobblers" who purveyed "debased mummery and nonsense," the "drunken declarations of Methodism." Regardless of whoever had the better of this particular argument, the spirit of skepticism and ambivalence evident in the writings of Brontë, Dickens, and many others had suffused widely through British public consciousness by the 1840's.

There were many dissenters, of course: those who celebrated the missionary as hero. Indeed hero worship, as Houghton (1957:305ff.) long ago pointed out, was to become so central a feature of early Victorian England that Carlyle was to call it "the basis of all possible good, religious or social, for mankind."[9] Some evangelists—most notably David Livingstone—were to become idols in the heroic imagination of Britain and to find their way into the ultimate repository of myth in the era of "print capitalism" (Anderson 1983), the children's adventure book. Wordsworth's sonnet "Missions and Travels"[10] might have been written in the style of an earlier age, and it might have spoken of an epoch past; but it evoked just the hybrid imagery that would appear again and again in nineteenth-century missionary apologia and books for young boys—that of the lonely gardener

scattering seeds on barbarous soil, of the itinerant merchant dealing in the
moral economy of the spirit, of the armored knight laying bare all before his
triumphal march:

> Not sedentary all: there are who roam
> To scatter seeds of life on barbarous shores;
> Or quit with zealous step their knee-worn floors
> To seek the general mart of Christendom;
> Whence they, like richly-laden merchants, come
> To their beloved cells:—or shall we say
> That, like the Red-cross Knight, they urge their way,
> To lead in memorable triumph home
> Truth, their immortal Una? Babylon,
> Learned and wise, hath perished utterly,
> Nor leaves her Speech one word to aid the sigh
> That would lament her;—Memphis, Tyre, are gone
> With all their Arts,—but classic lore glides on
> By these Religious saved for all posterity.

Wordsworth wrote his *Ecclesiastical Sonnets* in 1821–22 as a "hymn in defence of the established church" (Purkis 1970:89). Notwithstanding the
complexity of his political and religious views, which changed a good deal
during his life (Purkis 1970:68–94; Chandler 1984), he became a strong
protagonist of the union of church and state. Both the Church of England
and the national interest would be endangered, he believed, by either Catholic Emancipation or concessions to Nonconformism (Ellis 1967:336). No
wonder that merchant, knight, and missionary—heroism past and heroism
present—are drawn together in a paean to the eternal value of the evangelical crusade. It was a vision that the mission societies themselves were to
struggle hard, and with increasingly erratic success, to sustain for the rest of
the century.

It is striking how far a cry it was from Wordsworth's idyll to the dark
worlds sketched a decade before by Sydney Smith; how distant were the
poet's barbarous shores and Christian knights from the journalist's incorrigi-
ble, wily savages and perilously inept missionaries. These contrasts mark
out the spectrum of views and images that pervaded literary and public discourse in Britain between 1810 and 1850, the period during which the first
generation of Nonconformists took themselves to work among the Southern
Tswana. As we shall see in the next chapter, this discourse had its origins in
eighteenth-century debates among Europeans about the nature of man, civilization, and savagery. Nor is it surprising that the emerging universe of

opinion was so broad—broad enough both in style and content to embrace Wordsworth's romantic idealism, Defoe's gentle skepticism, and Smith's editorial cynicism; Southey's polemical imperialism, Brontë's fictional ambivalence, and Dickens's populist criticism. For the Britain from which the missionaries came was a society in the throes of profound structural change, a society in which elevated literary works, recurrent political controversies, and everyday public consciousness were alike caught up in a great, if not always audible, debate. Under discussion, sometimes openly, sometimes unknowingly, were the dominant (or, more accurately, the dominating) ideological categories of a new era, the very spirit of an age.

ECONOMY AND SOCIETY, 1810–1850

Several critics have argued that, in dealing with the encounter between Christian missionaries and African peoples, anthropological analyses have often been hopelessly one-sided. While minute attention is paid to the social and cultural orders of the Africans, the Europeans are seldom placed under the same scrutiny (see e.g., Beidelman 1974:234, 1981:74f., 1982:9; cf. Shapiro 1981:130); this being taken as an instance of the more general tendency to "study down," endowing others with esoteric cultures and ourselves with practical reason (Sahlins 1976). As a result, we persist in treating the evangelists not as individuals possessed of socially conditioned biographies that make a difference (Welbourn 1961:ch.9, 1965:204; Beidelman 1982:9f.) but as a taken-for-granted, faceless presence on the colonial stage. And this in spite of our being well aware that their actions and interactions are—and always were—deeply influenced by their backgrounds, their cultures, and their ideologies. Further, while many ethnographies discuss the effect of evangelization on local communities, few explore the impact of the encounter on the consciousness of the Europeans or their societies. Consequently, even our best analyses lack subtlety and depth. At worst, they reduce complex processes to caricatures in which *the* missionary becomes an anonymous agent of "social change" or "colonial domination."

The point, though hardly new, is well taken. It has two methodological implications. The first, which we addressed in the Introduction, suffuses every aspect of the present study. It is that the missionary encounter must be regarded as a *two*-sided historical process; as a dialectic that takes into account the social and cultural endowments of, and the consequences for, *all* the actors—missionaries no less than Africans. Second, as this suggests, a comprehensive study of that encounter, and of its place in the past and present of Third World peoples, ought to begin in Europe (see Beidelman 1982:22). The rest of this chapter, then, returns us to England, ca. 1810–50, the context in terms of which we may read the biographies of the early Non-

conformist missionaries to the Tswana—and from which we may disinter
the social heritage, the cultural categories, and the ideological baggage that
they were to take with them into the unfamiliar reaches beyond the frontiers
of the Cape Colony.

The Spirit of the Age

Eric Hobsbawm (1962:xvi) is not the first to observe that the "age of revolution" between 1789 and 1848 was an epoch so complex, "its mass of print
so vast, as to be beyond the knowledge of any individual." How indeed are
we to grasp its essence if, as Hobsbawm rightly warns, "the web of history
cannot be unravelled into separate threads without destroying it?" The answer, it would seem, is to try to write not a history but a social archeology:
that is, to identify some of the more significant planes and contours of the
age—especially those that were to underlie the development of nineteenth
and twentieth-century colonialism and in particular the Nonconformist
mission to Africa.

The industrial revolution was well under way by the turn of the nineteenth century (Clapham 1926; Hill 1969:282), and by 1810 it had already
made a deep impression on the social, cultural, and physical landscape of
Britain.[11] The very term "*industrial* revolution," as Ashton (1948:2) implies,
tends to direct our gaze toward its productive ecology and its technological
aspects. The machine, after all, was the dominant metaphor of the age
(Briggs 1979:33f.). As Carlyle (repr. 1970:6–7) observed—and lamented—
in 1829:

> Were we required to characterise this age of ours by any single epithet,
> we should be tempted to call it . . . the Mechanical Age. It is the Age
> of Machinery, in every outward and inward sense of that word; the age
> which . . . practises the great art of adapting means to ends. Nothing
> is now done directly, or by hand; all is by rule and calculated contriv-
> ance. . . . On every hand, the living artisan is driven from his work-
> shop, to make room for a speedier, inanimate one. . . . For all earthly,
> and for some unearthly purposes, we have machines and mechanic
> furtherances; for mincing our cabbages; for casting us into magnetic
> sleep. We remove mountains, and make seas our smooth highway;
> nothing can resist us. We war with rude Nature; and, by our resistless
> engines, come off always victorious. . . .

Such, for Carlyle, were the "Signs of the Times." And few would take issue
with him: there is no doubting the importance of the technical bases of the
Industrial Revolution, or their thoroughgoing impact on the texture of social
life and science, mathematics and morality, intellectual pursuits and the arts
(Bowden 1925:5). Yet it is difficult to disagree with Marx (1967), Engels

(1968), Thompson (1963), and a host of other scholars from both right and left[12] that the essence of the revolution lay in the transformation of relations of production and, concomitantly, relations among classes—understanding, of course, that this process, far from simply altering the demography of stratification, contained all the cultural and material elements of a New Society, a new Age of Modernity.

The stress on radical social reconstruction in this historical epoch, common both in contemporary and in later writings, does not deny that the industrial revolution had economic, political, and social roots in earlier times. Not only is there a good deal of testimony to the depth of those roots, but there has long been debate over their precise weight in determining the onset and direction of the great transformation after 1780.[13] Similarly, it can hardly be claimed that industrial capitalist relations were not foreshadowed in the development of eighteenth-century commerce and agriculture, or that an antinomy between employers and workers sprung into existence for the first time as the factory system gained dominance over domestic production. Still, the revolution hinged upon a metamorphosis in the division of labor and, with it, the restructuring of classes and their relations.

From this perspective the industrial revolution has been portrayed as the triumph of a "conquering bourgeoisie" (Hobsbawm 1962:19) over a proletariat vanquished in the very process of its making (Thompson 1963; cf. Hill 1969:282, 288).[14] Certainly, its polarizing effect on British society was abundantly clear to people of the time (Hammond and Hammond 1928:275, 278; see Thomis 1974:184)—as it has been to generations of both Whig and Marxist historians ever since (see n. 12). It could not have been otherwise: the brute fact of class consciousness and antagonism was everywhere visible, from the passing of the Combination Acts to the outbreak of machine-wrecking Luddism.[15] Moreover, as we might imagine, there arose a drawn-out, often bitter controversy over the social effects of industrialization, a controversy between "pessimists" and "optimists" that found its way into artistic and literary expression as well as into scholarly debate (see chapter 3).[16] Nevertheless, for all the vital imagery that cast common "Men of England" against lordly "tyrants" (Shelley [1819] 1882:164), "vulgar rich" against "ill-used" worker (Dodd 1847), or benign captains of industry against the ungrateful, improving masses (Ashton 1948), it would be simplifying matters to characterize the emerging social structure purely in terms of two opposed classes locked in agonistic embrace (*pace* Marx and Engels 1968:36).

This point—the irreducibility of British Society to two antagonistic classes—will turn out to be crucial for us. Interestingly, it seems to have been appreciated by a rather remarkable man of the period, one William Dodd. Dodd, whose family was impoverished when he was a boy, had no schooling and was forced into twenty-five years of mill work, during which he lost an arm but acquired the wherewithal to write movingly of his experiences. A number of his letters to an unnamed interlocutor in America were published anonymously in 1847. These letters are extraordinary enough, but more astonishing still is his Introduction to them. In it he gives account of social and economic divisions in contemporary England, telling us that there existed eight "classes." The first four—(1) royalty, (2) nobility, (3) capitalists, and (4) gentlemen of trade, the professions and the clergy—were "the privileged." They made the law and profited from the toils and privations of others (1847:11f.). The latter—(5) skilled laborers, (6) common laborers, (7) honorable paupers, and the (8) dishonorable poor—composed the non-privileged masses, from which upward ascent was "attended with difficulty," but into whose ranks "descent [was] accomplished much easier." Others had spoken of class in broadly similar terms before;[17] most notable was Charles Hall (1805), who described civil society as consisting of different orders but, in respect of material wealth, as being divisible "into two classes, viz. the rich and the poor" (1805:3–4). Dodd, however, made a pair of observations of particular salience here: first, that neither of the social strata, the privileged nor the poor, was homogeneous or united, each being caught up in its own affinities and animosities; and second, that the "humbler . . . of the clergy" (1847:3), as the most poorly paid members of the privileged ranks, occupied their lowest, least secure reaches.

The first of these observations calls to mind Marx's classic characterization, in *The Eighteenth Brumaire* ([1852] 1963), of France in the first half of the nineteenth century. Here "the hereditary . . . lords of the soil" were caught up in a factional struggle with "bourgeois *parvenus*," a struggle based not on differences of principle but on a contest between "town and country, . . . capital and landed property" (1963:47). Later historians, including those who were less concerned with class relations per se, were to confirm that Dodd's point was correct. Bowden (1925:ch.3), for example, long ago pointed to the complex relations among the upper orders between an ever more powerful industrial bourgeoisie, with its urban base, and the landed aristocracy (see also Eagleton 1975:5f.). At times these two groups came into open conflict, while at other times they were enmeshed in such a close alliance of interests that they might well be seen as two fractions of a single ruling class. In some contexts there was a palpable osmotic process, with landed gentry becoming captains of industry and, albeit to a lesser extent, industrialists looking to establish a foothold in the countryside. And, of course, there was increasing social (if not quite as immediate nuptial) intercourse across the divide. This set of relations was yet further complicated, early on, by a growing cleavage between north and south. Apart from all else, where the cotton millionaires and other new rich of London might be absorbed into "official" society and upper-crust political circles, the "hard-faced" businessmen of Manchester were an altogether different matter (Hobsbawm 1962:221–22). Nor was it just a question of style, important as this was. The capitalists of the north appear to have been more anxious to "impose [their] terms on the capital" than to gain access to its hallowed social circles (Hobsbawm 1962:222).

Likewise, for all its identity of interests in opposition to the upper orders, the lower class was internally divided along several axes (Thompson 1963)—as early political activists often found out to their cost. Thus in purely sociological terms the urban and agrarian poor were caught up in starkly dissimilar situations, the yawning gap between them not easily bridged. More generally, the "non-privileged" were differentiated according to their positions in the division of labor (by such things as gender and age, type of industry and religious affiliation)—differences that fragmented the work force and were invoked to exercise control over it. Of course the dominant ideology of the age also distinguished sharply between diligent laborers and the undeserving poor, those shameless parasites and paupers later immortalized by Alfred Doolittle in Shaw's *Pygmalion*. Where the just deserts of the former would one day be recognized by the great accountant in the sky, the destiny of the latter was eternal damnation to a satanic hell that looked for all the world like a Mancunian foundry.

One significant corollary of the internal fragmentation of the classes was that upward mobility presented itself as a possibility for those who "improved" themselves. There was little to stop a common laborer from seeking to become a craftsman, a young ploughman from setting his sights on the clergy, the son of a skilled worker from dreaming of being a clerk in the lower levels of the privileged orders. That much the poor were told incessantly from the pulpit and in the press. Without such gradations within and across the major lines of class, this would have been less plausible: a pauper could not easily envision becoming a prince, and only the most star-struck chimney sweep aspired to be a captain of industry. Again, the actual incidence of social mobility has long been debated, but that is not our immediate concern. William Dodd's lay impression—that ascent was difficult, descent much easier—is probably as accurate as any. The point, rather, is that those who did make their way up the social ladder often found themselves not secure members of a more elevated class, but the bearers of anomalous, contradictory social positions: neither of the rich nor the poor, of the ruling nor the ruled. For, caught in the fissures of the class structure, they were suspended uneasily between the privileged, whose values they shared, and the impoverished, from among whom they came—and to whom, if their fortunes did not prosper, they would be compelled to return.

This is precisely where William Dodd's second observation becomes relevant. Low churchmen were not merely the lowest-paid members of the privileged orders; many of them, especially in rural northern parishes, were former artisans who had climbed rather unsteadily into the ranks of the middle class. Interestingly, Eagleton (1975:9) argues that this was just the situation of Patrick Brontë, Charlotte's father, and ascribes to it the ambiguity of his social and political views—on some issues highly radical, on others archly conservative. Recall that Brontë, a low church evangelical, came from a peasant background, entered the "respectable classes" through the clergy, and passed most his life as a poor vicar in the troubled West Riding. Rather than fitting easily into the emerging class structure, he was one of those who inhabited its uncomfortable interstices. Significantly, as we shall see, Patrick Brontë could have been the social archetype of the Nonconformist missionary to southern Africa—give or take some minor theological differences.

The industrial revolution, then, forged the particular sociological context from which arose the clerical army of Nonconformist missionaries to the colonies. Their position as the "dominated fraction of a dominant class" within British society (Bourdieu 1984:421) was to have a profound effect on the role of these men in the imperial scheme of things (see chapter 7; J.L. Comaroff 1989). But more pervasively, the fact that they came from this context, from a social niche wrought by the process of class formation and by an ethos of upward mobility, was also to affect their everyday dealings with "the Other." Their biographies, built on an unremitting commitment to rational self-improvement, were the very embodiment of the spirit of capitalism, a living testimonial to its moral and material workings. To the degree that they sought to evangelize and civilize by personal example (itself an expression of bourgeois ideology), the pathway along which they were to lead the heathen was to retrace their own journey through contemporary British society—or, rather, toward an image of that society as they wished to see it. And what they wished to see was a neat fusion of three idealized worlds: the scientific, capitalist age in its most ideologically roseate form, wherein individuals were free to better themselves and to aspire to ever greater heights; an idyllic countryside in which, alongside agrarian estates, hardworking peasants, equipped with suitable tools, might produce gainfully for the market; and a sovereign Empire of God, whose temporal affairs would remain securely under the eye, if not the daily management, of divine authority.

Let us examine each of these three elements in turn. Not only do they give us yet further insight into the spirit of the age; they also bring us a step closer to the missionary encounter itself.

Imagined Worlds: (1) The Individual and Civilized Society

The first element—the ideological scaffolding of industrial capitalism—is at once utterly familiar and yet easy to oversimplify. Much has been made, quite correctly, of the rise of utilitarian individualism: in particular, its celebration of the virtues of the disciplined, self-made man; of private property and status as signs of personal success, poverty as a fitting sanction for human failure; of enlightened self-interest and the free market, with its "invisible hand," as the mechanism for arriving at the greatest public good; of reason and method, science and technology, as the proper means for achieving an ever more educated and elevated, civilized and cultivated mankind.

But these values and virtues did not go uncontested. Nor were they merely handed down by the privileged to the malleable, waiting masses. For all the philosophical support they enjoyed in the classical liberalism of Bentham and Mill, they were freely challenged in the literary and artistic works of the likes of Shelley and Blake; for all their backing in the influential political economy of Adam Smith and Ricardo, they were subject to ever more outspoken socialist critique and to the vocal objection of a fraction of the working population. Indeed, the entire history of the British labor movement from the late eighteenth century to the present has been a discourse on precisely this ideology. On a rather different plane, moreover, the "counter-enlightenment" (Berlin 1980:1ff.) had, from the first, questioned the pursuit of pure reason and rational individualism. In various ways and from a wide range of perspectives (Berlin 1980:20), it had also fought against the disenchantment of the world and the eclipse of the human imagination, repudiating the idea that civil society ought to be built on the "calculating intellect," on the methods of the natural sciences, or on the bloodless laws of the marketplace. Nonetheless, the triumph of the bourgeoisie, to recall Hobsbawm's epigram for the era (above, p.55), might be measured by the degree to which its worldview became hegemonic. Never absolutely, of course—as we noted in chapter 1 (cf. Williams 1977:113), no hegemony is ever complete—but clearly dominant. To wit, the proletarian revolution confidently forecast by Engels (1968:ch.9, 332ff.) in the 1840's never did arise out of the squalor of Manchester; just as the voice of protest, albeit often heroic and sometimes clamorous, did not call forth political action strong enough to discomfort the ruling classes. As Matthew Arnold (1903:viii) was to reflect in 1865, even such popular organs as the *Saturday Review* had decided that "the British nation [had] finally anchored itself, in the fulness of perfected knowledge, on Benthamism." This statement, albeit an exaggeration,[18] troubled Arnold. But he took consolation from the "fact" that "our class," the middle class, had "done all the great things . . . ever done in England" (1903:ix). The ascendancy of its ethics, aesthetics, and economics seemed unquestionable.

There has long been a tendency, fed as much by *The German Ideology* as *The Protestant Ethic*, to find explanation for the ideology of the period, and for its tacit conventions, in the demands of capitalist production. Thus it is, for instance, that the stress on self-discipline—expressed in such things as punctuality, cleanliness, and a preparedness for arduous toil—is attributed to the inability of the factory system to function without "regular and disciplined work" (Briggs 1959:61; cf. Mantoux 1928:384; Thompson 1967). The political quiescence preached by Protestantism has often been put down to much the same thing, as if there were open complicity between the cloth and the capitalist in ensuring a smooth control of labor power. Ruling classes everywhere might have a nice appreciation of their own interests and might encourage popular attitudes accordingly. But the reduction of ideology to a form of crude utilitarian consciousness, a kind of folk functionalism, is plainly unsatisfactory (see e.g., Lichtheim 1967; Larrain 1979). More subtly, and more to the point here, the rise of capitalist economy and society entailed in its very development the reconstruction of a set of signs, practices, and images of the world.

Among these signs and concepts, perhaps the most far-reaching concerned the nature of the person. Classic liberalism at its most general posited a world consisting of self-contained, right-bearing individuals who, in seeking to maximize their own well-being, created society by the sum of their actions and interactions. "Universal History," declaimed Carlyle (1842:1), is the history of what men—and especially great men—have accomplished. That "history" was also the narrative frame within which modern imperialism was to be enacted, an enterprise that united a specific concept of self-determining, generative personhood with a heroic vision of making the universe.[19] As Russell (1961:623–24) was to observe, philosophical individualism and the cult of the hero went easily together. In its popular form, this philosophy saw the person less as a product of a social environment than as an autonomous being[20] with the innate capacity to construct himself—at least, to the extent that he put his energies and powers of reason to the task. Note too, here, the gendering of the imagery: in the stereotypic representation of the age, the universal person was always Man (see below, p. 68f).

That this bourgeois subject is often termed "Promethean" should alert us to the fact that he was not cut of wholly new cloth; he had a thoroughly classical Judeo-Christian ancestry. Similarly, the distinction in medieval Christian culture between "soul" and "estate" ought to caution us against seeing the "divided self" as an entirely modern creation. As Sahlins (n.d.)

reminds us, *homo economicus* did not emerge *de novo* from the ferment of the Enlightenment. A direct descendant of Augustinian man, his "natural" pursuit of self-interest was a reformulation of the original sin of self-love and greed (Sahlins n.d.:1). Yet the rise of capitalism did stress, as never before, the radical individuation of the person—or so it appeared to those who spoke authoritatively for contemporary society, fashioning its optimistic self-imagery in an ever more assertive popular culture. That person seemed to have been cut free at last from enchanted entanglements, his soul transformed into an inward probing consciousness with the potential for knowing the world—and for making a place within it for himself.

The modern imagining of this radically individuated, divided self has become very familiar, its construction the subject of much recent writing in the history of consciousness and representation (e.g., Foucault 1975:197; Rzepka 1986:18f.). On the one hand, that self was the core of human subjectivity: the "I," the center from which a person looked out upon, and acted on, the world. On the other, it was also an object: "me, my-self," something of which "I" could become (self-) conscious and subject to (self-) restraint or (self-) indulgence (see e.g., Briggs and Sellers 1973:13–15). Reed (1975:289f.) makes the point that this divided self was to become a ubiquitous presence in early Victorian literature (cf. Miyoshi 1969; Keppler 1972); he analyzes the use of disguise—by, for example, Lancelot in Tennyson's *Idylls of the King*, Rochester in *Jane Eyre* and, later, John Jasper in Dickens' *Edwin Drood*—as reflections on its essence. The radically freed "I" of Descartes may have vexed an entire genealogy of philosophers, from Kant through James and Husserl to Merleau-Ponty (Mathur 1971:18). But it colonized the popular consciousness through such vehicles as the novel, the theatrical, the moral tract, and the diary (Barker 1984:9f.).

One immediate corollary of the reconstructed self was that the social values of bourgeois ideology could be internalized as human qualities. Hence discipline, generosity, respect, loyalty, and ownership, to name but a few, became the virtues of individual personality embodied in self-control, self-denial, self-esteem, self-sacrifice, and self-possession. Once again, this had its foreshadowings. Hirschman (1977:16) recalls that there were already signs in the seventeenth century of a thesis later to be advanced by Vico and Mandeville: that man's passions had to be harnessed by society if they were to work toward the general welfare. The conversion of "private vices" into "public benefits" was effected when passions were subsumed by interests—in the eighteenth century sense of rational economic advantage (1977:39). "Interests," in short, were the "passion of self-love upgraded and contained by reason." In the Gospel according to the *Wealth of Nations*, they held the key to the good of society at large, to the production of its commonweal. That, to return to Sahlins' point, was how Augustinian man could, over time, mutate into the creature of neoclassical ontology; how unreconstructed greed, once pure sin, could be transformed into constructive self-interest, (literally) an enlightened ideal. Not surprisingly, by the early nineteenth century a noble and notable archetype of the literary success story had become the "self-made man" who, often enough, turned out to be a manufacturer.[21] The regnant mythology of the age echoed the Marxian dictum that, in making things, humans made themselves and their social relations—save that the heroic producer of wealth fêted here was the industrialist, not the expropriated worker.

This image of the person was cogently expressed in the doctrine of self-improvement; in the notion that, by virtue of rigorously methodical practice and the avoidance of overindulgence, one might better oneself—the ultimate reward being upward mobility for men, upward nubility for women. The outer shell of the individual was taken to be a gauge of his or her inner essence: neat dress, personal cleanliness, and a healthy body spoke of a worthy heart and an alert mind (Haley 1978:4, 17, 21 et passim); melioration, therefore, ought to be visible in everyday comportment. In this respect, too, the subjective self, "I," was in a position to observe and analyze the condition of the objective self, and so to direct its progress. Witness, again, the struggle Dickens puts Bradley Headstone through, in *Our Mutual Friend*, to show that true restraint and self-realization require "a courageous recognition of all features of the self" (Reed 1975:228–29).

Nothing captured these values more comprehensively than the link between self-improvement and literacy. Notwithstanding the debate in some upper class circles as to whether the laboring poor should be educated (Bowden 1925:278f.; Hill 1969:278), the act of reading had a doubly positive connotation. Not only did it represent a tangible effort to develop the mind, but it also was held to engage the divided self in a particularly profound manner: in addressing the written word, readers internalized it, reflected upon it in the deepest recesses of their being, and entered into silent conversation with it. And in the process they came to know both the outer world and their inner selves all the better (cf. Barker 1984). The extraordinary rise of literacy in the late eighteenth and early nineteenth centuries (see e.g., Altick 1957) might have been encouraged by a complex set of technological and economic factors (Hill 1969:208f.), by the politicization of public opinion (ibid:278), and by the commoditization of the printed word (Halévy 1924:440f.; Anderson 1983:38f.). But its social impact was closely tied to the ascendance of the reflective, inner-directed self: a self, long enshrined in Protestant personhood, now secularized and generalized as bourgeois ideology. As we shall see later, the Nonconformist missions to the Tswana were to put great faith and effort into the spread of literacy. As bearers of the religion of the book, they believed that, by teaching the natives to read, they would set them on the path of self-improvement and salvation, revelation and refinement, civilization and, finally, conversion.

The partibility of the self—which was to be elevated from cultural principle to "scientific" theory in such diverse intellectual traditions as Freudian psychology and the symbolic interactionist sociology of G.H. Mead[22]—was also expressed in other, less tangible ways. It manifested itself, for example, in the "natural" oppositions of mind and body, spirit and essence, consciousness and being; oppositions which, though they had pervaded Western thought since Plato, came to assume a particularly "modern" form in post-enlightenment philosophy (Spicker 1970). Even more significantly for the development of industrial capitalism, this image of the partible self underlay the possibility that individuals could separate from the rest of their being, and sell, their labor (Marx 1967:2,ch.6). The alienation of human energy for cash payment in turn placed an altogether new weight on the value of time. For, inasmuch as commodity production involved the exchange of labor power between worker and capitalist, that exchange required a standardized measure of quantity (for effort) and a universal medium of remuneration (for pay). The former, in short, was time; the latter, money.

Under the terms of this well-worn equation, without which commodity production would not have been possible, time appeared, in essence, to be money (Marx 1967:2,ch.6, ch.10). It could be spent or used, wasted or owned. And so it became both a measure and a means for dividing the self and for mediating the rhythms of everyday life, separating labor(-time) from leisure(-time), workplace from the home, wage labor from unpaid domestic toil, production from consumption. By implication, too, money—or, more grandly, wealth—seemed to be the just and due reward for gainful effort. John Wesley, in fact, had spoken of its "precious talents" (Warner 1930:155) and saw it as a true measure, at once spiritual, moral, and material, of human worth. (There were, however, those who argued that, far from being well paid for their exertions, the poor should be kept hungry to compel them to continue working [Briggs 1959:16].) That time and money were explicitly equated in the early nineteenth century is nicely demonstrated by Thompson (1967:87), who goes on to confirm that the growing salience of the clock resonated with both secular and Protestant notions of discipline and self-improvement.[23]

For all the value placed on time and money, the accumulation of wealth was not seen to excuse intemperate consumption or, heaven forbid, vulgar display. To the contrary: with its moralistic abhorrence of self-indulgence, particularly in the north, the respectable middle-class set out to make money for its own sake. And, having given generously to philanthropic causes and civic projects, they tended to reinvest it in production. Although they built ample homes in secluded suburbs, they did not, like rich country proprietors, show off their fortunes in ostentatious estates, ornamental gardens, or collections of precious objects (Briggs 1959:38). To be sure, the march of the bourgeoisie, however triumphal, was a rather gaunt, joyless affair. Halévy (1924: 428–29), surveying English history from over the Channel, could not hide his disgust at the ascetic unloveliness of the period. True, he admits, it may be unfair to blame bourgeois pietism for the "worthlessness of British music," but it is undeniable that the combination of capitalism and Puritanism produced architecture of "uniform ugliness ... which boasted no style."[24] Among the grimy, deformed buildings, those that most offended Halévy seem to have been the "hideous meeting-houses" of the Nonconformists.

Halévy chose to make the point in aesthetic terms, but he was not alone in highlighting the close connections, at once ideological and symbolic, between industrial capitalism and Protestantism, bourgeois culture and religious individualism.[25] Many studies echo the monumental works of Weber (1958) and Tawney (1926) in showing that Nonconformist Christianity in its early modern form, the last great revival of European Puritanism, expressed its liberal individualism in its strong commitment to self-construction through rational, self-willed duty. Notwithstanding doctrinal differences over such questions as predestination and election, sin and salvation, Protestant theology[26] envisaged the human career as a cumulative moral voyage, unrelieved by the possibility of confession, atonement, or absolution (Troelstch 1912; see also below). The person, as a self-determining being, laid up treasures for her or himself in heaven in the same way as he or she did on earth—by means of devoted labor, neighborly duty, and charitable deeds. Even in Calvinism, with its stress on predestination, the "improvement" of the self became an important spiritual propriety. Thus Davies (1961:99f.) detects a new "subjectivity in the worship" of the Congregationalists and Presbyterians in the eighteenth century. For example, "whereas objectivity had characterized the metrical psalmody of the previous century," the hymns of the influential Watts now sing "When *I* survey the wondrous Cross" or "Give *me* the wings of faith to rise ..." (Davies 1961:100; original emphases).

But Nonconformism did more than make instrumental reason into a faith, practical rationality into a fetish. Nor did it merely reverse the signs of early Christianity, transforming self-interest (and, in time, consumption) from an abomination into a virtue.[27] It went as far as to regard the entire physical world as providentially-given so that ordinary mortals might use its resources to redeem their innate sinfulness. To the ethic of practical reason, in short, was added ontology of spiritual functionalism. This was particularly visible in Methodism, although it also spread to the other denominations of the "Old Dissent," including Congregationalism. Wesleyanism, founded on the thoroughgoing dichotomy of church and state, drew from Lutheranism a democratizing belief in the redeeming power of good works. In its view, the humble sinner could attain glory—if not in this world then in the next—through patient, perpetual duty.

Medieval Christians might have lived "ethically from hand to mouth" (Weber 1958:116); nineteenth century Nonconformists, by contrast, were heir to an ideal of spiritual and material accumulation that demanded careful management and that prized "method" above all else. This ideal expressed itself easily in modern idioms of commerce and commodities, manufacture and money, but it also evoked older, more "traditional" images of agricultural toil, cultivation, and husbandry (Weber 1958:124). So avid was Nonconformism in disseminating these ideals and images—the "Good News" of a revived Christianity—that its "congregations [came to be] called 'schools of capitalism.'"[28] As another French historian, Taine, remarked with some disdain (de Riencourt 1983:303): "A preacher [in England] is nothing but an economist in priest's clothing who treats conscience like flour, and fights vices as if they were prohibitions on imports." Not that this metaphorical link between economy and theology was altogether new. The older covenant theology of Congregationalism and Presbyterianism had long represented the bond of the Elect to God in the image of the debtor-creditor relationship (Hill 1989:171).

Of course, Nonconformism was not alone in lending support to the structures of capitalist society or in cultivating the forms of selfhood and subjectivity on which it rested. However, the individualistic moral and material *Weltanshauung* of the age, and of modern Protestantism in particular, was especially transparent in Methodism—which is not surprising, since the latter had grown up in response to the radical social reconstruction of contemporary Britain. Tailored to the brutalizing experience of urbanization and wage labor (Troeltsch 1949,2:721), its churches conjured up a world of spiritual opportunity, a free market of the soul in which everyone had the right to pursue her or his own moral salvation. From the start its objective was to reconcile evangelical fervor with solemn Calvinist discipline, emotionalism with self-control, democratism with authority—and to chart a methodical course of self-improvement for its adherents. Religious revival, it was hoped, would give a sense of worth and purpose to the depersonalized, troubled masses and would draw them into secure social and spiritual communities. By its own lights the movement was successful in channelling the enthusiasm that it inspired; that is, at harnessing, through respectable routine, the power and passion sparked by its sensuous ritual. Its special genius lay in its ability to address conflict and degradation suffered at the workplace, but to do so in a way that seldom challenged existing economic or political arrangements. Once aroused, the vitality of the sufferer was directed toward individual self-realization through diligent toil and virtuous acceptance of his or her lot in life.

Indeed, in speaking of self-realization through work and the discharge of duty, Methodist clergy were very quick to exhort the poor to make peace with their predicament. Take, for example, a remarkably blunt column that appeared in *The Evangelical Magazine and Missionary Chronicle* of March 1834 under the heading "Important Hints to Domestic Servants":

> While you evince your thankfulness to God for placing you [in service], show also, by practising all good fidelity, by the strictest honesty and most respectful obedience, your gratitude to your employers. As our Lord said to the soldiers, "Be content with your wages, and meddle not with those who are given to change.

It goes on to warn that

> The nature of that compact which exists between masters and servants sufficiently proves that the *time* of domestics is not their own, but the actual property of their masters, who have purchased it at a stipulated price. I have seen many a servant diligent, even to bustle, in the presence of a mistress or master, who could relax to absolute idleness and sleep when a convenient opportunity offers. This is to be guilty of [a] sin . . . against the *omniscience* of God [original italics].

It has long been noted that Nonconformism did not hesitate to affirm the premises of a patently unequal society. The Methodist position in this regard was expressed in John Wesley's well-known theological axiom: that "the labor relationship [is] an ethical one" in which employee and master have different functions by virtue of divine calling (Warner 1930:146–47). Each was to be industrious, respectful, and reliable in their own way; a person's spiritual status depended ultimately on the manner in which he or she fulfilled his or her appointed role. As this implies, "a diversity of ranks" was regarded as perfectly natural and was confidently predicted to "subsist to the end of the world" (Warner 1930:125). At a stroke the alienating experience of wage labor became the necessary cost of salvation, and inequality— measured, in large part, in monetary terms—was elevated into a sacred instrument of moral sanction (J. Comaroff 1985:133). Although he advocated fair pay and prices, Wesley was as vociferous as any industrialist in decrying agitation by workers: "meddling" on the part of "those who are given to change" might threaten the providential market and, even worse, encourage sloth on the part of the poor. The threat was not taken lightly. As Hill (1969:264) notes, early Methodists condoned child labor "because they were convinced of the dangers of idleness to the originally sinful."

But it was not only the disparity of master and worker, rich and poor, the well-born and the commoner, that was sanctioned by Protestantism. Inequality of male and female was also taken to be a fact of life, a natural feature of the social world. Along with the rest of the Nonconformist movement, Methodism and Congregationalism were unreceptive to the demand for sexual equality becoming audible in the late eighteenth century (Schnorrenberg 1979:199); just as they were implicated in the making of the modern individual, so they reinforced the gendered images of self and society that lay at the core of bourgeois ideology. These images were cogently contained in the idealized domestic group, a household based on the nuclear family with its sexual division of labor. The latter, like so many other social features of the period (see above), had its roots prior to the Age of Revolution; some (e.g., Rowbotham 1976:3) have even argued that it had played a vital part in the genesis of capitalist production. But it was during the eighteenth century that this family-household took on the status of a "natural atom," the God-given foundation, of civil society. Its enshrinement in the social canon of Protestantism was to assure that it would become a vital part of the civilizing mission to "undomesticated" savages abroad. As we shall see, few things were to excite evangelists in southern Africa more than the "need" to remove all vestiges of heathen kinship and family life.

The modern engendering of self and society was tangibly inscribed in the social architecture of the capitalist order itself. Under the factory system the workplace was seen increasingly as a distinctly male domain; females, by contrast, belonged in (and to) the home. Economic production and "public life" became associated primarily with men; consumption, reproduction, and "private (domestic) life," with women (cf. Sacks 1975; Reiter 1975; T. Turner 1980). As Rybczynski (1986:51ff.) has remarked, the spatial separation of "work" from "family" had in fact long preceded the industrial revolution; in some Western European cities it was already visible in the early 1600's. But this separation had not entailed the exclusion of women from primary production: in England, the wives of journeymen and masters continued to toil alongside their husbands; moreover, many females were involved in producing and distributing food and clothing, some being active in the brewing trade, for instance, until the end of the seventeenth century (Rowbotham 1976:1–2; Tilly and Scott 1978:49). Between the sixteenth and eighteenth centuries, however, the growth of commerce and manufacture had a palpable impact on local British communities. Where women and children had been essential to peasant agriculture (Jordanova 1981:43), among richer yeomen they gradually withdrew from cultivation (Rowbotham 1976:1); where, before, female leisure was an exclusive mark of nobility, now it became a sign of middle class gentility, urban and rural alike. Indeed, as bourgeois wealth accumulated, "ladies" of that class were ever more narrowly restricted to the roles of wife and mother. So much so that one observer has described the 'Victorian' version of the 'good woman' as the "parallel of monasticism for men" (de Riencourt 1983:306). This in due course was also to be invoked as a rationale for debarring females from better paid jobs in the new industrial economy (Jordanova 1981:50).

The sharpening of middle class gender distinctions appears, among other things, to have focused a great deal of attention on the so-called problem of "female nature." In an intellectual environment as obsessed with human difference as it was with selfhood (see chapter 3), eighteenth-century philosophers, theologians, and literati—almost all males, of course—felt compelled to address the "woman question." It seemed crucial to them both to comment on the qualities of "character and conduct" that befitted wives and daughters for domesticity (Fordyce 1776; Thomas 1773) and to teach them their appropriate "duty" (Kenrick 1753; Moore 1744). The woman's natural habitat was the home, many of them said, as it was only there that, sheltered from temptation, she could nurture childish innocents and regenerate men whose moral resources had been "spent" in the (public) world (Schnorrenberg 1979:185). No wonder that the first stirrings of modern feminism were couched as a complaint against the way in which women were forced to "remain immured in their families groping in the dark" (Wollstonecraft 1967:Dedication). But these stirrings had little immediate impact on an androcentric society, least of all on its religious authorities. Although females had always outnumbered males in the churches of the Old Dissent, biblical authority had long been used to debar them from preaching. Well into the eighteenth century, in fact, they sat apart during worship, could not lead prayer, and were forbidden to voice an opinion in business meetings, the organizational heart of Congregationalism (Watts 1978:320).

Methodism, once again, was especially vocal in perpetrating a narrow, Pauline view of the social and spiritual role of women (Schnorrenberg 1979:200), its clergy often speaking on the subject in their sermons. For example, Whitefield (1772:185), in "Christ the Believer's Husband," asserts quite plainly that "the husband is head of the wife, even as Christ is the head of the church." Here and elsewhere, Wesleyans portrayed female insubordination as a "fountain of domestic evil" (1772:183), synonymous with disrespect for the Lord Himself. While there were a few women of influence among high church evangelicals at the time—most notably, the educated and prolific Hannah More of the Clapham Sect—they too encouraged pious compliance with the established order.

The neatly gendered separation of home from work, of reproduction from production, was part bourgeois ideal, part bourgeois myth. The consequences of industrial and agrarian capitalism alike were very different for the poor. As early as 1739 a rural washerwoman gave rare and remarkable witness to the lot of female agricultural wage laborers in Britain. Her poem, *The Women's Labour*, leaves no doubt that the worlds of work and domestic nurture were often promiscuously conjoined (Rowbotham 1976:25):

> . . . Our tender babes into the field we bear,
> And wrap them in our Cloaths to keep them warm,
> While round about we gather up the Corn.

In the towns and cities too the wives and children of the poor were made to provide cheap, docile labor. Given the association, within the rising middle class, between females and clothes of fashion, it may not be coincidence that most working women were employed in textile mills and the garment industry (Tilly and Scott 1978:75). The ideal of leisure and domestic confinement was as remote from the experience of these women as it was to be from their African sisters—whom the missions hoped to recast in the same gendered mold of the modern bourgeois worldview.

In due course there was to be angry reaction, especially amongst the poor, to the contradictions and quiescence of Nonconformism in general and of Wesleyanism in particular (Hobsbawm 1957). But in the short term its positive appeal was striking. Despite its preachy sobriety and its preoccupation with the evils of sensuality, the sheer ardor of Methodist revivalism possessed great allure, in a depleted emotional landscape, for laboring men and women (Thompson 1963:368f.). We stress again that its assertion of spiritual democracy—the right of everyone to seek redemption from original sin and ultimate damnation—gave cheer to the hopeless and the hopeful alike. For the latter it sanctified the moral currency of the market economy and, with it, the earthly pursuit of money. To the former it promised another, transcendent form of wealth. To both it offered a world built on values simultaneously spiritual and secular, a world in which civilization and progress were synonymous with the arrival of industrial and agrarian capitalism—and the social order they implied.

The Nonconformist evangelists were to take these images from the factory and the foundry, the mine and the mill, and transpose them onto African soil. Born by the earnest metaphors of the mission, the signs and practices of European economy and society were to be among the first exports of an expansive new imperialism.

Imagined Worlds: (2) The City and the Countryside

The extent to which the industrial revolution altered the contours of British society is unmistakably reflected in images of a changing landscape. For those who spoke—in words, pictures, or actions—of a paradise lost, the idealized past was situated in a pristine countryside. This rural idyll, cast timelessly somewhere in the early eighteenth century, was inhabited by three estates: (1) the feudal establishment, in which lord and tenant, master and servant, were bound together in a web of mutually beneficial obligations; (2) the yeomanry, independent peasants who "[produced] for the market, themselves employing wage-labour, and shared the outlook and interests of gentlemen and merchants rather than of landless labourers and subsistence husbandmen" (Hill 1969:70); and (3) a mass of poor, honest smallholders engaged in both agriculture and domestic industry. In the public perception, and in many literary works, these last two categories were often lumped together as one (e.g., Clapham 1926:99) and romanticized as the "perfect Republic of Shepherds and Agriculturists" (Wordsworth 1948:54).

More than anything else perhaps, the transformation of the countryside was associated in the British collective consciousness with the disappearance of the yeomanry. Typically attributed to the enclosure movement and the agrarian revolution that preceded and enabled industrialization,[29] its passing was dramatized by the large-scale movement of population to the bleak northern cities, "those vast abodes of wretchedness and guilt."[30] Along with the privatization of the commons and the commoditization of agriculture, the fall of the yeomanry was widely deplored precisely because it signaled the unravelling of the social fabric at large. Take, for example, the utterly unsentimental inquiry into agricultural conditions in the 1770's by "a Farmer," one John Arbuthnot (1773). Appealing to a mass of facts and calculations, Arbuthnot argued the case for large-scale farming but commented (1773: 139), in a decidedly less clinical tone:

> As to the circumstances of the ranks of men being altered, . . . I most truly lament the loss of our yeomanry, that set of men who really kept up the independence of this nation; and sorry I am to see their lands now in the hands of monopolizing Lords.

Some years later John Stuart Mill ([1848] 1929,1:256) added his condolences at the demise of those "who were vaunted as the glory of England while they existed, and have been so much mourned over since they disappeared."[31]

In the eye of contemporary beholders, the disappearing yeomanry became the mythical embodiment of a "traditional" lifestyle in which the family, with its customary division of labor, was the unit of production and consumption; in which the domestic unit was embedded, securely and comfortably, in an enduring community of kin and neighbors; and in which its private estate, like its social position, was the guarantor of its sturdy independence. Wordsworth's (1948) ethnographic sketch of this Eden, written for "tourists and residents," describes the Lake District. But as an elegy for a disappearing world, it would have done as well for counties further south (cf. Toynbee 1969:182). Here

> the plough of each man was confined to the maintenance of his own family, or to the occasional accommodation of his neighbour. [Wordsworth adds, in a note, that a "pleasing characteristic of . . . thinly-peopled districts, is . . . the degree in which human happiness and comfort are dependent on the contingency of neighbourhood."] Two or three cows furnished each family with milk and cheese. The chapel was the only edifice that presided over these dwellings, the supreme head of this pure Commonwealth; the members of which existed in the midst of a powerful empire, like an ideal society or an organized community, whose constitution had been imposed and regulated by the mountains which protected it. Neither high-born nobleman, knight, nor esquire, was here; but many of these humble sons of the hills had a consciousness that the land, which they walked over and tilled, had for more than five hundred years been possessed by men of their name and blood.[32]

The powerful appeal of this dream, however slim its basis in history (Briggs 1959:40), is attested by the fact that the nineteenth-century social reformers who most seized the public imagination were those who undertook to stitch back together the torn social fabric. Thus Thomis (1974:148) argues that Robert Owen's popularity among workers lay, first, in his attempt "to reconcile the mechanization of industry with domestic employment" and, second, in his promise of "a return to the rural existence [with its] family and community life." Likewise,

> William Cobbett made a similar kind of appeal to them in seeking somehow to undo the whole process of industrialisation and return to the unspoilt countryside. Similarly, the land scheme of Feargus O'Connor, the anti-industrialisation limb of the next stage of the Parliamentary Reform movement, Chartism, was to provide a rural Utopia of peasant proprietors where the ills of industrial society did not extend.

Christopher Hill has suggested by implication that the transformation of the countryside subsumed, in a nutshell, the antagonism between the new bourgeoisie and the working class. The bitterness of the poor, he observes (1969:272), flowed as much from a feeling that they had been swindled out of their land as from their resentment at being forced into factories. But that bitterness was directed at more than just larceny, however grand its scale. It was fanned, as we have said, by the death throes of an epoch.

Some, of course, found no cause to mourn. But for many of those who did—whether or not they had themselves been dispossessed—the most tragic symptom of the demise of the ancien régime lay in the scarring of the earth itself, the defacing of England-as-garden.[33] There is, for instance, a lithograph by Henry Alken, done in ca. 1841–45, which is memorable for its sheer ordinariness (plate 1). The picture is of a smallholding in which barnyard animals stand around the detritus of an age past—the torn metal corpse of a Midlands stagecoach—while a passenger train edges across an open rural background dominated by a massive railway station. Asa Briggs (1979:6), who has reproduced the drawing, interprets it as an optimistic representation of nineteenth-century industrial progress, and he may well be correct. But the littered, impoverished farmyard, uninhabited except for its relict animals, also tells another story. It is the story of a landscape made ugly by the discordant presence of things unfamiliar, machines and buildings that dwarf its proper scale.

There is plenty of evidence to show that the physical remaking of the landscape deeply troubled much of the British public—and provoked an especially outraged reaction, with consequences for the British sense of Africa, from the romantic naturalist movement, which we shall encounter again in chapter 3. Of more immediate salience, however, is the fact that the industrial revolution had a *contradictory* impact on popular conceptions of the relationship between country and city.[34] On one hand, the chasm between them appeared to widen. As Marx and Engels (1970:69f.) suggest, the rise of capitalism might have intensified their productive interdependence, but it also heightened the sheer antagonism between urban and rural interests. For members of village communities drawn into the growing towns, the contrast between the two environments had roots in direct experience. But for the population at large, too, it took on renewed cultural force. Thompson (1963: 231) notes, for example, that it was industrial, not agrarian, workers who agitated most loudly for a return to the land, a mythical world of contented labor, village cricket, and county entertainments. As this implies, the opposition between the rural and the urban was more than just a description of observed sociospatial realities. It became the ideological pivot of a broad fan of symbolic associations—and sentimental outpourings (Thomas 1984:250f.)— in British historical consciousness. In both poetry and popular imagery, the country stood to the city as nature to worldliness, innocence to corruption, a harmonious past to the disjunctive present (Williams 1973:ch.5 et passim; cf. Comaroff and Comaroff 1987).

On the other hand, the industrial revolution was seen also to have dissolved the distinction between country and city. Apart from all else, the mill and the mine, the quintessence of urban capitalist production, had made their noisy entry into the rural northern valleys. Thompson (1963:189) quotes an anxious aristocrat who, traveling in remotest Yorkshire in the last years of the eighteenth century, happened upon a "great flaring mill." Not only had

PLATE 1   *Chromolithograph by Henry Alken, circa 1841–45. Elton Collection, Iron-bridge Gorge Museum Trust.*

the monstrosity disturbed the pastoral vale, but its clamor threatened to toll rebellion; the horror of nature defiled by industry, it seemed, could lead nowhere but to innocence lost, tradition violated, and the established order overturned. In a quite different voice, a noted economic historian, Sir John Clapham (1926:36), also speaks of the dissolving boundary. Possessed of assured hindsight rather than the alarmed foresight of Thompson's peripatetic aristocrat, he remarks that

> Rural labour and town labour, country house and town house, were divided by no clear line. In one sense there was no line at all. Very many of the industrial workpeople were countrymen, though their countryside might be fouling and blackening, their cottages creeping together and adhering into rows, courts, formless towns.

Others have confirmed the general point. Far from there ever having been a mass movement to the city or an abrupt redistribution of labor, says Ashton (1948:125), mixed agriculture and cottage industry gave way slowly to full time work at the loom or coalface—especially where the latter came to be situated nearby. In other words the contrast between the country and the city seemed, paradoxically, to be sharpening and disappearing at the same time. But the paradox is more apparent than real, for it describes two levels of a single process. As the ecological, social, and economic separation between the rural and the urban dissolved—itself a function of the expansion of industrial capitalism—the resulting dislocation was acutely felt throughout Britain, leaving fragmented and discontented working populations in its wake (Briggs 1959:42). Some had been compelled to move to the city, while others found that the city had moved to them; either way, the sense of having crossed boundaries both old and new was unavoidable and often painful. This in turn could not but underscore the contrast, in popular consciousness, between the worlds separated by those boundaries—even if, measured in physical distance, they were barely apart at all (cf. Williams 1973).

The significance of the perceived opposition between the country and the city, then, grew in rough proportion to the breakdown of the ecological and social division between them. And as it did, it came to stand symbolically for the radical change of British society, picking out the counterpoint between mythic past and present reality. In this respect too the idealized countryside represented not only innocence lost, nature defiled; it also stood for the possibility of paradise regained, Jerusalem rebuilt, a Utopian rhapsody for the future. That, as we said earlier, is why the dreams of Owen and Cobbett were paid so much attention. In practice these dreams could not be realized in a greatly transformed England. But the open vistas of the non-European world seemed to offer limitless possibilities. The Nonconformist missionaries to southern Africa were to resuscitate the mythic rural domain as a model of the British past, a model for the African future; many of them, as we shall see, came from the rural communities most disturbed by the changing structure of British society. Their optimistic pursuit of a new Eden in the wilderness fused old ecclesiastical imagery—the reversal of the fall of Society and its Church (Hill 1989:91; see below)—with a then popular presumption: that, somehow, there was greater holiness in the countryside than in the city, greater moral purity in the sprawl of fields than in the jostle of factories (Thomas 1984:294).[35]

Imagined Worlds: (3) The Empire of God

The strength and vibrancy of the Protestant revival during the industrial revolution might give the impression that the early nineteenth-century English church was in an unusually strong position. After all, the correspondence between its ideology and the spirit of the age was clear enough. And in spite of the Duchess of Buckingham—who earlier had found the Methodists' teaching to be "tinctured with impertinence . . . towards their superiors"[36]—the concerns of both orthodox and Nonconformist denominations coincided closely with those of the politically and economically powerful. Chadwick (1966:1), a somewhat Panglossian church historian, goes farthest in asserting the ascendancy of contemporary Christianity. Victorian England (which, for the purposes of his account, extended back into our period), we are told, was profoundly religious:

> Its churches thrived and multiplied, its best minds brooded over divine metaphysic and argued about moral principle, its authors and painters and architects and poets seldom forgot that art and literature shadowed eternal truth or beauty, its legislators professed outward and often accepted inward allegiance to divine law, its men of empire ascribed national greatness to the providence of God and Protestant faith.

Perhaps. But there is another side to the story. It speaks less of fervent displays of spiritual enthusiasm than of the diminishing suzerainty of the church in a secularizing world (see e.g., Toynbee 1969:235f.; Anderson 1983:20f.). At the time of the Reformation, to paraphrase Hill (1969:34f., 109f.), religious authority had two aspects: first, and most obviously, church and state were not merely united but were deeply entailed in one another; and, second, the parish church was the epicenter of political and social life for nine out of ten Britons. To these two we may add a third: that the signs and concepts of Christianity were integral, taken-for-granted features of everyday existence, an unspoken condition of seeing and being. This third aspect was perhaps most crucial to ecclesiastical hegemony. For it followed that, if Christianity was ineffable and all-encompassing, temporal authority could only be one facet of spiritual sovereignty. In these circumstances religion and politics, the sacred and the secular, *lex Dei* (the law of God) and *lex naturae* (the law of nature), were hard to distinguish at all; indeed, James I had not only identified kingly power with divine command but had equated sedition with blasphemy (Mill [1824] 1982,6:10–11). No wonder that "the reformed Church of England . . . [became] inseparable from national consciousness" (Chadwick 1966:3).

 With the profound economic turmoil of the mid-sixteenth century, however, all of Europe suffered a spiritual crisis and witnessed a protracted struggle for control over religious life. Among the longer-term consequences of this process were the steady increase of Christian Dissent and, especially salient here, the growth of Congregationalism, most notably among lower-class groups, after the collapse of ecclesiastical dominion in the 1640's (Hill 1969:111; Dale 1907:360f.). The credo of this movement reflected with particular clarity its birth in an age of anti-establishment, anti-authoritarian ferment. Recall its most basic tenet: that every congregation ought to have its own autonomous government, free from the stifling hierarchy or theological orthodoxy of a national church. Congregations might join together in fellowship—as they were later to do in the creation of mission societies (Jeal 1973:12f.)—but their joint undertakings were always to be conducted on a voluntary, egalitarian basis.

The breakdown of ecclesiastical authority in the 1640's, Hill (1969:190) suggests, was a critical turning point:

> Bishops and church courts ceased to function, church lands were sold. Ecclesiastical censorship ceased to exist, as did ecclesiastical control over education. Burning for heresy was abolished. . . . The attempt after 1660 to reimpose a narrow Anglican uniformity failed, and henceforth it could never again be pretended that all Englishmen belonged to a single church.

The Kingdom and God, and hence the Kingdom of God, would no longer exist in the same seamless unity or enjoy the same peerless hegemony. The gradual decrease of religious dominion would continue, despite some dramatic ups and downs, for a long while to come. Catholic Emancipation, a crescendo of sectarian Dissent, and the clamor for disestablishment in the early nineteenth century were just three symptoms of the same process more than a hundred and fifty years on; recall that the *Ecclesiastical Sonnets*, written in response to that clamor, were Wordsworth's contribution to the defence of a beleaguered Anglican Church (above, p. 53). Whatever the degree of religiosity in England ca.1810–50—and such things are, *pace* Chadwick, impossible to measure—the position of the church was being assailed from within as well as from without.

This is not to say that organized religion had ceded its influence in the political process or that Protestant doctrine had ceased to loom large in public discourse. As the vast literature on nineteenth-century ecclesiastical history proves, the matter is much too complex to be captured in such general terms. Our point, rather, is that spiritual sovereignty, *sui generis*, had lost its supreme ineffability. Far from being an unquestioned order of signs and symbols through which nature and society were apprehended, Christianity had itself become an object of debate and political struggle. The growing disunity of the English church was an element in this process. So too was the steady breakdown of doctrinal homogeneity among Nonconformists after 1800 (Briggs and Sellers 1973:6). But the first and most telling portent of hegemony undermined was the fact that the role of the church—and the relationship between sacred and secular authority—could be questioned at all; any ideology is powerful to the extent that it hides itself in the unmarked reflexes of everyday life, and vulnerable to the degree that it becomes open to scrutiny and argument (see chapter 1). No longer was reality constructed by autonomic reference to the moral language of Christendom.

In short, from the moment that the church had, like other human agencies, to negotiate its position in the world, its absolutist spiritual dominion began to melt away. For, as we suggested a moment ago, that dominion had been built on the capacity of Christianity-as-culture to dissolve any distinction between the law of God and the law of the land, the divine and the mundane. That is why, although Protestantism was a vital part of the industrial revolution, it cannot be held, as Weber and Tawney well knew (above, p.65f), to account for the rise of bourgeois ideology, let alone for the development of the new social order. Having lost its hegemony, it too was transformed by the forces that drove the age of revolution. Like most other things, the Protestant spirit was refashioned in the ethical mould of capitalism.[37]

There was, however, no reason why the Kingdom of God could not be re-created elsewhere, and nowhere seemed more suitable than the fringes of the European world. The coincidence of two historical factors made this especially plausible at the time. The first grew out of the extremely delicate condition of English colonial interests abroad. The loss of the American colonies in the late eighteenth century had sparked a crisis in foreign policy and national identity. The collapse of the Old British Empire, as Knorr (1944:211) describes this moment, had rendered "colonial expansion so distasteful to the English that they had even abolished the Secretaryship of State 'for the Colonies'" (Halévy 1924:87). This is not to imply that the ideology of imperialism had died or had receded into insignificance. Quite the opposite. In the years between the end of the "old" and the rise of the "new" colonialism, there was bitter debate, both scholarly and political, over the virtues and costs of empire—a debate fueled by, among other things, Adam Smith's well-known and cogently stated hostility toward a dominion of anything but free trade.[38]

But in the meantime the relative inactivity of the British overseas left an uncontested space for the Kingdom of God. In addition, the enactment of abolition by parliament implied a moral responsibility to right "the wrongs of Africa" (see below, p.115), a responsibility that weighed heavily on the mission societies. To the Nonconformists, the call to evangelize in an imperial vacuum was particularly appealing. Being "intrinsically suspicious of Empire" (Briggs and Sellers 1973:143) and strongly in favor of the separation of church and state, they were always ambivalent about the presence of a colonial government. While the latter might give support and security to missionaries, it also curbed their freedom to minister to an unfettered spiritual sovereignty. It is noteworthy, for example, that the early Congregationalists in southern Africa invariably tried to reach beyond the colonial frontier, well away from the secular authorities (see chapter 5); in some cases too those authorities, like Lord Somerset at the Cape (Marrat 1894: 39; above, p. 48), barred the Protestants from working within their jurisdiction.[39] Neill (1964:285) confirms that this fits a more general pattern. Many Nonconformists, he says, went out into the world determined "to preach the pure Gospel without tying it to any western form of organization or polity" (cf. Knorr 1944:381; Warren 1965:72). By contrast, the more established Anglican evangelicals advocated a colonial government for West Africa (Curtin 1964:109f.).

As time passed and circumstances changed, of course, the Kingdom of God would pave the way for the Empire of Britain. Some missionaries, in fact, were to be active protagonists in the process. In England itself Bloomsbury Chapel would one day hear panegyrics, spoken by the Reverend J.G. Greenough, to their role in transforming the fairly modest realm of Elizabeth into the glorious imperium of Victoria.[40] But, in the first light of the nineteenth century, the hiatus in colonial expansion enabled English Christians to dream of their own spiritual imperium. Not surprisingly, several evangelical associations—most notably for us the London Missionary Society (1795) and the Wesleyan Methodist Missionary Society (1813)—either were formed or renewed their activity abroad during this period (Neill 1964:252; du Plessis 1911:165). When in 1803 the Rev. Richard Cecil began a sermon to the Church Missionary Society with the words "Thy Kingdom come!" he meant exactly what he said.[41]

The second historical factor behind the dream of a Kingdom of God, a spiritual sovereignty at the edge of the realm, returns us to the ethos of the period itself. The latter, as we have said, was founded on a moral economy that celebrated, among other things, commerce and manufacture, methodical self-construction and the practical arts of life, reason and good works; therein, to parody Marx,[42] lay the rational spirit of a spirited age. Put this together with (1) the nostalgia evoked by the passing of the yeomanry and the despoliation of the countryside, (2) a strong commitment to philanthropy, and (3) a generous measure of ethnocentrism, and the predictable result is a mission to bring a "light unto the nations." The light, it goes without saying, was "civilization" and "cultivation," the twin terms of European ideology clothed in the assertive language of universalism.

As Warren (1965:17f.), a mission apologist, has noted, Christianity, commerce, and civilization were always inseparable clauses of the same vision. At home they came together in the fight against slavery (see chapter 3), a political struggle that in the short-run strengthened the position of the church in English public life and extended its alliances with secular humanist interests. But the debate over abolition had another effect. It brought into focus the envisioned character of the Kingdom of God itself. For in the heat of the argument the mission societies could not but portray their idyll, to themselves and others, by contrast to popular images of the enslaved heathen purgatory. The Kingdom of God, not surprisingly, would be governed by precisely the opposite principles; that is, by the moral economy of the "free" (industrial capitalist) world. Like all utopian dreams, it promised a future that fused the values of the present with the myths of the past. The savage would, by careful tending, be elevated into something like the late British yeomanry; many of the evangelists whom we shall encounter spoke quite openly of creating a society of independent peasants. What is more, in speaking thus they relied heavily on horticultural metaphors, evoking the recreation of the spoiled English garden in Africa's "vast moral wastes" (Moffat 1842:614). The countryside, in other words, would be tilled and planted anew—cultivating the heathen workers as they cultivated the soil. The poetic bridge between cultivation and civilization was not coincidental.

But the African garden was to be part of the imperial marketplace. After all, commerce, like money, was an integral—even sanctified—aspect of civilization. For many, in fact, commercial agriculture was the panacea that would establish both the material and the moral infrastructure of the Kingdom of God. On the one hand, most Christians seem to have believed that it would put an end to the traffic in slaves; David Livingstone (1857:34), as we shall see, was to give influential backing to the cause of emancipation through commerce. More fundamentally, however, this imagined world brought together all the positive elements of the Benthamite vision of liberation through free exchange, the Protestant notion of self-construction through rational improvement, and the bourgeois ideal of accumulation through hard work. From small seeds there grew large dreams; from modest biographies, heroic visions of deeds to be done.

MISSIONARY ORIGINS

Earlier on we noted that many of the Nonconformist missionaries to southern Africa were part of "the dominated fraction of the dominant class." The majority were men who had made their way from laboring, peasant, and artisan backgrounds to the lower reaches of the bourgeoisie, often through the church: men who, more than most, were caught up in the social contradictions of the age (above, p. 59f). Few of the Congregationalists or Wesleyans had any university education—some had virtually no schooling at all—and many "would probably have spent their lives as artisans had they not been invited to enter the ministry" (Etherington 1978:28). Indeed, the London Missionary Society (LMS) *Rules for the Examination of Missionaries*, laid down in 1795, stressed that candidates did *not* have to be learned. Godly men who knew "mechanic arts" were also of great use as evangelists.[43] The Rev. John Campbell was to reinforce this view in an early dispatch from the South African interior:[44]

> . . . it is not at all necessary that all of [the missionaries] should come from that school of the prophets [the seminary]—if you can find simple hearted men, who know the worth of souls, who understand and love the gospel, they will do well for this people. . . .

After all, as Bunyan had said many years before (Hill 1989:347), " . . . the soul of religion is in the practic part."

The Nonconformist evangelical societies concurred. For a long time they stressed the need for men with practical skills, humble horticulturalists and craftsmen rather than elevated scholar-priests or saintly ascetics. This, as we shall see, was to give a notably pragmatic cast to the Southern Tswana mission, most of whose clergy were men of action rather than contemplation. Having had little theological training, their concerns were flatly quotidian. This is not to say that their labors did not bear the imprint of a puritan worldview or Nonconformist doctrine. Nor is it to deny that they were driven by a deep desire to teach Christian conduct and to save souls. But even in their most meditative moments, when they reflected upon their place in the encounter between savagery and civilization, these men spoke of their task in distinctly practical terms.

Beidelman (1982:50) has reiterated that "the missionary movement in Britain cannot be separated from the Industrial Revolution and the rise of the lower middle classes" (see also Neill 1964; Chadwick 1966,1:37; Etherington 1978). Not only was it primarily from this social niche that the evangelists came; many of their personal biographies, marked by modest upward mobility and the acquisition of respectability, echoed the rise of the class itself. Methodism and Congregationalism, like Nonconformism in general, may have drawn its following from all strata (Briggs 1959:69; Thompson 1963:355f.), but the foreign missionaries came from a notably narrow band of the social spectrum. Hobsbawm's (1962:270) description of the "new sects," whatever its other merits, would stand as an excellent summary of the origins of these men:

> [The sects] spread most readily among those who stood between the rich and powerful on one side, the masses of the traditional society on the other: i.e., among those who were about to rise into the new middle class, those about to decline into a new proletariat, and the indiscriminate mass of small and independent men in between.

Brantlinger (1985:181) in fact suggests that these Europeans found Africa attractive *because* of their humble roots.[45] Here "their subordinate status . . . was reversed": a factory boy might be a great white leader, a pauper could blaze a trail for civilization.

But it is not only the restructuring of class relations and divisions that weaves missionary biography into the social history of the age. Also significant were the other major transformations of which we have spoken: the growing distance between north and south, with the brunt of dislocation and devastation falling upon the former; the social, ecological, and aesthetic despoliation of the countryside; and the ascendancy of the new moral economy.

The most heroic British figures in the early history of the southern African mission, with one possible exception,[46] were Robert Moffat and his son-in-law, David Livingstone. They are the only two who appear regularly in the innumerable compendia of national biography to be found in any English reference library, and they are enshrined in even the most obscure of mission memorabilia.[47] The backgrounds of these two men, if not the course of their later lives, were fairly typical of the first generation of Nonconformist evangelists to the region.

Moffat was the son of a ploughman, Robert, Sr., who bettered his position by becoming a petty official in a Scottish Salt Tax Office.[48] The elder Moffat's life bore testimony to an ideology of disciplined, self-sacrificing improvement: he died leaving £2,351 and a freehold dwelling, great wealth in light of his origins. In 1795, when Robert, Jr. was born, his parental home, like that of his mother's father, was at Ormiston, some 26 miles from Edinburgh. His maternal grandparents' cottage still stands in the Ormiston public garden, while the remains of his own natal home are now enclosed in the yard of a National Coal Board property. The one faces rural, horticultural Scotland, the other industrialized Britain. Furthermore, Ormiston itself had been rebuilt by the reform-minded John Cockburn, a capitalist and planner, who erected a distillery, introduced flax production, and revivified local agriculture around the town. The young Robert, in short, witnessed the age of revolution at close quarters. He saw the countryside and town begin to merge, and the peasantry, of which his father had been a member, become an agrarian and industrial workforce. The dislocation of northern Britain reached to his own doorstep.

Moffat himself had a strict Calvinist upbringing in a pious United Presbyterian household, a household for which improvement meant not only industry and thrift, but also good works for those less fortunate. Apparently this sense of philanthropy included a "lively evangelical interest in foreign parts" (Northcott 1961:17). For all the familial emphasis on improvement, however, Robert, Jr., had almost no formal schooling, although evening reading, as well as sewing and knitting for both sons and daughters, was a regular activity. At fourteen he became an apprentice gardener, and he later moved to Cheshire, where he happened on a group of Independent Methodists whose style of worship and theological views appealed to him. From this intimate cottage prayer circle, via the good offices of a Congregationalist minister in nearby Manchester, Moffat's path led to the LMS, ordination, and a long and celebrated sojourn among the Tswana. He had little theological instruction along the way, his education consisting in reading and copying out the lectures of William Roby, the Mancunian clergyman who acted as his patron. Roby also gave Moffat some weekend lessons in which he seems to have spoken primarily of the need to obey the Lord in all things (Northcott 1969:v–vi; Bradlow 1987:5–7).

Just as Robert Moffat's youth was dominated by the currents of the age—hardening class divisions, the transformation of the countryside and the peasantry, the widening gap between north and south, and the absorption of the poor into the bourgeois moral economy—so his evangelical career was dedicated to the reenactment of his own life amidst those currents. The African was to be guided along similar paths, learning to read and reflect, to master the practical arts of civilization, to cultivate and to sell his labor, and to see the value of industry and charity. In that way he too might better himself. Mission biography, more often than not, was mission ideology personified. And mission ideology echoed the spirit of Carlyle (above p.61): history was a moral progress to be led by the heroic individual—in this case, the priest-hero.

The early life of David Livingstone, on whose career there is an enormous literature,[49] bears close resemblance to that of Robert Moffat (Davies 1951:68), although the former was to eke out a medical school education. Livingstone also grew up in the fissures of the emerging class structure; his childhood too was spent at the intersection of the country and the city. Blantyre, where he was born, was on the banks of the River Clyde some eight miles from Glasgow, and it boasted a major textile industry. It was here that he sold his labor as a child: at the age of ten, family circumstances made it necessary for him to become a piecer in the local cotton mill. His grandfather, Neil, Sr., like Robert Moffat, Sr., had been a rural man. Formerly a tenant farmer on the Scottish isle of Ulva, he was evicted in 1792 when the landowner converted the estate into a commercial sheep farm, and he had no option but to migrate to the industrial periphery of Glasgow. By means of slow, hard-earned promotions and modest savings, he raised enough to allow his son, Neil, Jr., to leave mill work and become a tailor's apprentice. After qualifying and marrying the tailor's daughter, however, David's father became a traveling tea salesman, a more respectable if less lucrative job. And so his children were raised in a tenement on Shuttle Row, in a property owned by Blantyre Mill. The village of which it was a part, like Ormiston, was planned by the owner of the textile works (Ransford 1978:8–9). It also abutted a park, the private garden of the mill manager's large residence—thereby underscoring the contrast between the stark tenement and the verdant countryside, the laboring poor and the new rich. From the Livingstone home, says Sir Harry Johnston (n.d.:501), it was possible to see "a peep of Glasgow, with its thousand-and-one furnace chimneys dimly discernible through [an] iridescent mist of smoke, sunshine, and rain." Between Blantyre and Glasgow, he goes on, lay clearly visible "strips of murdered country, fields of rye alternating with fields of baking bricks."

Like the Moffats, the Livingstones were deeply religious and devoted themselves energetically to education and self-improvement; the atmosphere and daily routine in the two households seem to have been similar. Most accounts tell how David, who was taught to read by his father, spent two hours each evening in the company school and then came home to read—all this after a twelve-and-a-half hour working day (Jeal 1973:9). His family were also staunch members of the established church until the 1830's, when Neil, affected by Nonconformist preaching, began to move toward Congregationalism. Eventually he joined the independent Hamilton Church and from there brought home a pamphlet on medical missionaries in China. David had long shown an interest in medicine (as well as in rural flora and fauna) and was immediately attracted by the prospect.

The rest is well known. After carefully saving the necessary funds, David Livingstone went to study in Glasgow and from there found his way, like Robert Moffat, to the LMS and Bechuanaland. He had a bit more formal religious instruction en route than did Moffat, but not much. Although he read some theology at university, it was not enough even for the undemanding Society, and he was sent for three months to the noted Rev. Richard Cecil of Essex (above, p. 79), who set about teaching him Latin, Hebrew, and Greek. Even after this, however, the Directors were unconvinced of his fitness to be a missionary. Apparently he lacked fluency in prayer and the conduct of worship, and it is unclear how well he knew the Bible. Only after a further three months of learning and revision did he scrape through the LMS examination (Johnston n.d.:60–1). But what he lacked in education and wealth, his hagiographers are fond of pointing out, he certainly made up for in sheer energy and zeal.

The general pattern will be clear. Of the seventeen LMS and Methodist missionaries who began work among the Southern Tswana before 1860, and for whom sufficient information is available, twelve came from Scotland or the north of England, two from rural Wales, and only three from the south of England; thirteen of them were from either the industrializing river valleys, the urban peripheries, or proletarianized villages. And most of them had very little formal education, theological or secular. Sixteen of the seventeen, moreover, would fit Hobsbawm's description (above, p.81)—that is, of persons caught between the rich and the poor, either indeterminate in their class affiliation or struggling hard to make their way over the invisible boundary into the bourgeoisie. Five came from peasant stock, five were from artisan backgrounds or had been artisans themselves, three had been petty clerks or traders, and three had emerged directly from the ranks of the laboring poor. Many, like Moffat and Livingstone, were from families displaced from the countryside. For all these men, the church conferred respectability and a measure of security in their social position, even though it did not enrich them materially. A few took the Protestant ethic somewhat further than the mission. For example, James Archbell, a Yorkshireman from the West Riding, withdrew from the Methodist ministry after a long evangelical career in southern Africa and took up farming in Natal. A successful entrepreneur, he went on to found a bank and later became mayor of Pietermaritzburg, the capital of the province (Mears n.d.). In so doing, he managed to recapture his own rural roots, to realize the highest ideals of commerce, and, perhaps, to store up much treasure in both this and the next world.

This social pattern confirms the extent to which the Nonconformist evangelists were creatures of their age and its contradictions. It also indicates why they, of all people, should have been so caught up in its moral economy and its particular imagery. In due course we shall see how their ideological categories and symbolic practices, born of the refashioned culture of industrializing Britain, were to direct their civilizing mission—how these categories, both implicitly and explicitly, wittingly and unwittingly, were to give meaning to their encounter with the Southern Tswana. But first it is necessary to consider how, in the throes of their changing world, they and their compatriots perceived the Africa to which they were about to bear both the Protestant ethic and the spirit of capitalism.

THREE

AFRICA OBSERVED

Discourses of the Imperial Imagination

> *Let us . . . contrast piety with atheism, the philosopher with the rude*
> *savage, the monarch with the Chief, luxury with want, philanthropy*
> *with lawless rapine: let us set before us in one view, the lofty cathedral*
> *and the straw-hut, the flowery garden and the stony waste, the ver-*
> *dant meadow and the arid sands. And when our imagination shall*
> *have completed the picture, and placed it in a light which may invite*
> *contemplation, it will, I think, be impossible not to derive from it in-*
> *struction of the highest class.*
>
> William Burchell (1824:2,444)

THE IMAGINED LANDSCAPE of Africa was greatly elaborated in late eighteenth-century Britain, albeit less as an end
in itself than as a byproduct of the making of modern European self-consciousness (cf. Said 1978; Asad 1973; Gates
1986). Its features were formed in the context of vigorous arguments about
humanity, reason, and civilization—debates that were driven by the social
and cultural upheavals that accompanied the rise of capitalism and that
forced the nations of Europe to refashion their sense of themselves as polities on a world map. Africa became an indispensable term, a negative trope,
in the language of modernity; it provided a rhetorical ground on which a
new sense of heroic history could be acted out (cf. Godzich 1987).

More than anything else, perhaps, abolitionism subsumed the great debates and discourses of the age. For it raised all the crucial issues involved in the contested relationship between European and Other, savagery and civilization, free labor and servitude, man and commodity; the ideological stuff, that is, from which a liberal hegemony was being made. As Davis (1975:350) has noted, the antislavery movement replayed Adam Smith's message in another key, making of it a program for global social transformation: that all classes of society should be recognized as sharing a natural identity of interest; that the common wealth depended on the liberty of everyone to pursue their own ends in an unfettered material and moral economy (above, p.60f.).

Abolitionism, as some have claimed, might have been a pragmatic attempt to resolve contradictions in the culture of postenlightenment Britain. And it clearly was a dispute about the merits and morals of different modes of colonial production. But it was also an exercise in mobilizing new forms of representation and communication (see Anderson 1983) to arouse the middle and laboring classes to a passion for epic reform; the controversy was widely aired in mass-circulating pamphlets, newspapers, and religious tracts, as well as in the discriminating columns of the literary reviews. And it drew upon a number of related discourses which alike had become sites for the formulation of a coherent bourgeois awareness. These discourses arose out of a number of distinct but related fields of exploration. Each aimed to construct what Heidegger (1977:115f.; see Godzich 1987:xiv) has identified as a mechanism of mastery, an explanatory scheme capable of objectifying nature and representing it to the knowing, synthesizing human subject. Most significant among them—at least in shaping the consciousness of our evangelists— were the discoveries of the geographical mission to Africa; the investigations into human essence and difference within the emerging life sciences; and the mythology of the noble savage celebrated by the romantic movement (Curtin 1964:34), which explored otherness in a variety of aesthetic genres. Each of these discourses had its own institutional context and expressive forms. But each played off the others—often in productive discord—and conduced to an increasingly rationalized debate about the nature of civilization, the civilization of nature. And together, by virtue of *both* their form and their content, they established the dark continent as a metaphysical stage on which various white crusaders struck moral postures (Achebe 1978:9).[1]

The symbolic terrain of a rarely-seen Africa, then, was being shaped by a cascade of narratives that strung together motley "scientific facts" and poetic images—facts and images surveyed by an ever more roving European eye. As this suggests, the rhetoric of light and dark, of color and culture, was already palpable in contemporary Europe, though it had not yet taken on the full fan of connotations it was to bear in Victorian thought. Hume (1854: 3,228n), after all, had argued that "there scarcely ever was a civilized nation of [Negro] complexion," and Rousseau had echoed his sentiment that blacks were mentally inferior by nature.[2] Those who opposed abolition argued that slavery was the "natural law" of Africa, as much part of the condition of savagery as the cannibalism and wanton bloodshed so luridly described by some observers (Dalzel [1793] 1799; Norris [1789] 1968). Abolitionists tended to respond by blaming the slave trade itself for deforming the normal progress of civilization (Austen and Smith 1969:79). Either way, Africa was degraded and debased.

It was also inextricably entangled in a western embrace. Romantic poets might have envisaged Africans living lives free of Europe (Brantlinger 1985: 170), but the weight of public opinion at the turn of the nineteenth century suggested the opposite. So, too, did the sheer weight of evidence. Whether as purveyors or reformers of the "evil traffic," white men had written themselves into the present and future of the continent. Whatever else it might have entailed, abolitionism did not argue for European withdrawal from Africa. It made the case for the replacement of one mode of colonial extraction with another. Once emancipated, his humanity established, the savage would become a fit subject of Empire and Christendom.

In this chapter we examine each of the discourses through which Africa came to be imagined, tracing their confluence to the argument over slavery itself. In so doing, we witness the rise of a more and more elaborate model of the relationship of Europe to the "dark continent": a relationship of both complementary opposition and inequality, in which the former stood to the latter as civilization to nature, savior to victim, actor to subject. It was a relationship whose very creation implied a historical imperative, a process of intervention through which the wild would be cultivated, the suffering saved. Life would imitate the masterful gestures of art and science. The "native" would be brought into the European world, but as the recipient of a gift he could never return—except by acknowledging, gratefully, his own subordination. And in this colonizing project the Christian missionary would play a special role as agent, scribe, and moral alibi.

At least in South Africa. Patently, these discourses—given that they were evolving, highly complex, and only partially articulated—did not have the same relevance everywhere during the age of revolution. We are reminded,[3] for example, of the very different influences that played upon Protestant missionaries in the British West Indies, who began their work as early as 1754. In the late eighteenth century these evangelists were openly allied with plantation owners and showed little apparent concern for abolition, although once emancipation became an inescapable issue some decades later, the alliance gave way to hostility (Goveia 1965). Our "reading" of the discourses of the age, however, center specifically on Africa and take as their frame of reference the perspectives of the Nonconformist missions to the Tswana.

THE GEOGRAPHICAL MISSION

As Curtin (1964:9) has noted, the slave trade had provided Britain with quite detailed descriptions of coastal Africa. So too had earlier Arab geographers and more recent European voyagers of "discovery" (cf. Sinclair 1977:80f.). While many of these accounts had long been available—some authoritative Arab texts dated back to the tenth century—it was the rationalizing vision of the Enlightenment that collated them, seeking to make of them a coherent body of knowledge. Such compendia as *A New General Collection of Voyages and Travels* (1745–47) and syntheses as *Universal History* (1736, 1765)[4] were founded on what Heidegger (1977: 128f.) was to call a "world picture" (*Weltbild*); a systematic grasp of the universe as a map on which spaces could be identified as challenges to a conquering human intelligence. As we shall see, this vision also implied a "moral geography" (Park 1816:xxix) which animated missionary consciousness.

Into Africa: a "liberal spirit of curiosity"[5]

The fact that the African interior remained a terra incognita in the late eighteenth century[6] appears to have worried certain "men of letters," men not driven in the first instance by any direct material or political interests in the region. The *Monthly Review* of May 1790 (1790:60), for example, carried an extensive, anonymous review of the *Proceedings of the Association for Promoting the Discovery of the Interior Parts of Africa* (1790), a work printed not for sale but for the use of the ninety-five members of the recently-formed African Association:

> Europeans know very little, if any thing, of the *interior districts of Africa*; we are happy to find that a number of learned and opulent individuals have formed themselves into a society for the purpose of exploring them [original emphasis].

The African Association was an "organization of gentlemen." For several decades it was to coordinate geographical and ethnographic investigation and to exert influence on British foreign policy. Addressing itself to the "ardour of research so visible in our countrymen," the Association speedily set about finding suitable persons to pursue its geographical mission (1790: 60). The tone of its *Proceedings* suggests that such adventures in exploration were almost a moral imperative. Notwithstanding the use of such terms as "science" and "research," these were heroic quests pursued by men of daring before such investigations were subdivided among the different scientific disciplines.

To "penetrate the *terra incognita* of the globe," the Association chose two seasoned explorers and amateur ethnographers (1790:60). John Ledyard was an American who had lived among Indians and traveled with Captain Cook; William Lucas, a Briton, had been captured and made to serve as a royal slave in Morocco, subsequently escaping to serve as Oriental Interpreter to the British Court. The first of these colorful cosmopolitans died in Cairo before setting out for the interior; the second failed to cross the Sahara, reaching Murzuk in the Fezzan and then retreating to the coast. As a result, the Society had to content itself with a memoir based largely on the accounts of Islamic informants encountered en route. And while its members professed themselves skeptical of "Mohammedan exaggeration," they publicized the material all the same: information on architecture, production, and government in Fez, and descriptions of the idolatry—as well, yes, as of the cannibalism—of its "Negro neighbours." Tellingly, what the gentlemen seem to have found least credible was the assertion that the African interior contained diverse black races and could be "divided into regular, civilized states." Despite its disclaimers, the report concluded (1790:68):

> . . . the prospect which this narrative opens to us, of the interior of Africa, (the greater part of which we have been accustomed to consider as consigned, by nature, to perpetual sterility and desolation,) must afford great pleasure. . . . [It] ought to induce Europeans, without delay, actually to explore the central provinces of the African continent.

While this account might have hinted at the pragmatic advantage of "opening" the fertile heartland, its message was to be found elsewhere. For, by portraying the real Africa as a dark recess, much akin to a bodily interior, it suggested that there was intrinsic value in laying it bare to the probing eye of the European observer. Foucault (1975) points out that the birth of clinical pathology at this time was a touchstone for the developing language of empiricism. To know was to raise to the light of scrutiny the dark secrets of life lurking in the body's interior. The terms of this biological discourse would soon be extended to the African person as well.

The African Association was to support a number of other investigative assaults on the continent. These were to be linked ever more closely to the prospect of lucrative commerce, their objectives typically being described as the pursuit of "*useful* knowledge and scientific discovery" (Park 1816:ix; our emphasis). One such foray in particular demonstrates well the emerging image of knowledge as cartography. It involved the integration of previous information into a series of maps and commentaries, executed under the synthesizing eye of James Rennell, former Surveyor-General of Bengal. Regarded as a founder of modern British geography (Markham 1895), Rennell was a draughtsman whose spatial sense had been sharpened by the practical experience of imperialism. His special skill was the translation of varied descriptions of journeys and explorations—the natural and historical features of the landscape as lived—into the two-dimensional conventions of "astronomical observations."[7] Such mapmaking, through its labeling and specification, converted diverse representations of human existence into an essential spatial uniformity, a ground upon which an expanding European sense of history could take shape.

Mungo Park, the Association's most successful emissary, set off in 1795 to follow the course of the River Niger from the Gambian coast.[8] A former ship's surgeon and amateur naturalist, Park stood between an earlier age of enlightened travelers and the nineteenth-century explorers proper (Curtin 1964:207). His return from the first two-and-a-half year mission in Africa was hailed as a triumph by the public at large; the account of his *Travels* (1799) rapidly sold out its first two printings and went on to become a classic of the European travel genre. The book was intended as a "plain, unvarnished tale" (1799:vii), and its style neither aggrandized nor effaced the narrator, pretending to no interpretation other than apparently reasoned conclusions drawn from a host of factual observations. European readers were given their first glimpse of the fabled Niger, the mighty African "artery" whose nature had been disputed since the writings of Herodotus. The interior was presented in terms of identifiable, human features: populous agricultural villages, where diligent weavers worked on looms "existing upon the same principles as [those] of Europe" (1799:275); where life was regulated by "laws and manners, trade and government" (1799:303). While whites on the coast might have thought of Africans as indolent, Park suggested that "few people work harder, when the occasion requires, than the Mandingoes" (1799:273).

By its very detailed ordinariness, its prosaic narrative order, this account demystified the fanciful rhetoric of the scattered sixteenth and seventeenth-century accounts of Africa (George 1958). Even when the savage seemed at his most bestial, Park rendered him tame by such devices as comparison with his own biblical forebears. Under duress he might sell himself into slavery, but Esau had long ago realized that, on the point of death, a birthright was of limited value (1799:287). Curtin (1964:144) has argued correctly that this work opened the West African Sudan to European penetration, both imaginative and material. But Park also wove a muted romance of his own. Nor were its contents fortuitous. As the anonymous editor of a later edition put it (1816:xxix), his "moral geography" presented an "affecting" picture of the disposition of the natives of the interior. Their lyricism and compassion were contrasted with the brutality of the coastal inhabitants, peoples (often Islamic) who mediated between the natural innocence of the savage and European corruption. With plainspoken sentimentality, he personified Africa in the "soft and amiable nature" of its women, who on several occasions made winsome overtures and showed him kindness. The potential of such material was soon to be seized by romantic naturalists and champions of the "noble savage." It was also grist for the abolitionists' mill. Most captivating of Park's statements to this audience was one which he attributed to some African women singers (1799:198):

> The air was sweet and plaintive, and the words, literally translated, were these.—"The winds roared, and the rains fell.—The poor white man, faint and weary, came and sat under our tree.—He has no mother to bring him milk; no wife to grind his corn. *Chorus*. Let us pity the poor white man; no mother has he, etc. etc."

This image of an Africa eager to play mother nature to the orphaned white man far from home was to be recycled by several contemporary humanist poets. It was given even wider currency in a popular song, written by the Duchess of Devonshire and promoted by well-connected opponents of the slave trade (Fairchild 1928:488f.).[9] As this suggests, the geographical mission became closely interwoven with the debate over abolition. Indeed, both sides of the argument found support in Mungo Park's account and others like it.

For Park's narrative did not speak in a single voice. While unquestionably sharing our humanity, the African in his text remains fundamentally other. In the *Travels* (1799:284), for instance, much is made of the "poor Negro"; "poor," that is, because slavery had long been "the condition of [his] life" (1799:280). The traffic in humans, it is true, was a product of duress; otherwise the natives would surely not have sold each other into bondage. But their duress was itself inherent in the uncivil state of the continent. This was why Park was skeptical about abolition, an opinion widely touted by the proslavery lobby (1799:298):[10]

> If my sentiments should be required concerning the effect which a discontinuance of that commerce would produce on the manners of the natives, I should have no hesitation in observing, that in the present unenlightened state of their minds, my opinion is, the effect would neither be so extensive nor beneficial, as many wise and worthy persons fondly expect.

Park's text betrays, in its modest use of the subjunctive, a sense of the distinction between facts and values. But his construction of "the Negro" infuses the former with the latter, presenting him as human, suffering, and devoid of light. This opinion is affirmed by other statements, direct and oblique, which together assert native violence and savagery—and hence subvert the basic identity established between the European and Africa. It is left to Park's faithful guide, whose word we have learned to trust, to deliver the final coup de grace: "Black men," he says, "are nothing" (1799:349). Part of our moral universe they might be, but they are dark inversions of ourselves, standing to us as does rudeness to refinement. In a climate of technical optimism and rational idealism, the stage is set for humane imperialism (1799:303):

> It was not possible to me . . . [not to lament] that a country, so abundantly gifted and favoured by nature, should remain in its present savage and neglected state. Much more did I lament that a people of manners and disposition so gentle and benevolent, should . . . be left as they now are, immersed in the gross and uncomfortable blindness of pagan superstition. . . .

The charter is clear. It was taken up by the African Association which in 1799 passed a resolution in favor of British occupation of the territory between the Gambia valley and upper Niger (Curtin 1964:148). It also reinforced the vision of the rising evangelical movement, for it saw the spiritual cultivation of Africa as a moral, almost sacred duty, an essential part of colonizing the land. Park himself was to be a sacrificial victim for the cause, put to death by those whose enlightenment he advocated. An illustration on the title page of a later edition of his *Travels* (1860; see plate 2) affirms this image: he kneels Christ-like, back to a tree and bare head bowed, as savage-looking Africans retreat into the bush.[11] Significantly, it was the African Institution, an evangelical and humanitarian organization founded in 1807, that took charge of Park's papers after his death and prepared them for publication.

Into South Africa: Of Maps and Morals

In Britain ca. 1800, West Africa served as stereotype for the continent as a whole. The Cape of Good Hope was a secondary focus of European concern. A small colony administered since 1652 by the Dutch East India Company, it had generated little travel literature, especially in English.[12] In 1795, however, the Cape was taken over by Britain as a consequence of her war with the French (see chapter 1), who had invaded Holland and were thought likely to seize the Dutch outpost on the sea route to the East (Harlow 1936: 171f.). John Barrow, founder of the Royal Geographical Society (which was to absorb the African Association), was appointed personal secretary to

TRAVELS

IN

THE INTERIOR OF AFRICA

BY MUNGO PARK.

EDINBURGH:

ADAM AND CHARLES BLACK, NORTH BRIDGE.

MDCCCLX.

PLATE 2 *Mungo Park: The Author Abandoned. Reproduced from Park,* Travels *(1860: title page)*

Macartney, the new governor of the Colony.[13] As Macartney's protege he had accompanied the latter to China in 1792, serving officially as comptroller to the embassy but acting also as observer of Chinese civilization (Lloyd 1970:24). Now he was sent on a tour of the South African interior to represent His Majesty and to investigate the discontents of frontier farmers, whose long-standing resistance to the Dutch Company had been transferred to the new administration.[14]

Barrow's *Account of Travels into the Interior of Southern Africa in the Years 1797 and 1798* (1801–04) was self-evidently a colonial document. A legitimation of the British annexation of the Cape, it also gave eyewitness account of the degradation of the Dutch frontiersmen, who, lacking a European "spirit of improvement and experiment," had regressed to take on the qualities of their rugged and soporific surrounds (1801–04:1,67; see also Streak 1974:5f.; Coetzee 1988:29f.). The very landscape conveyed this unrefined state to Barrow's eye, schooled as he was on nicely-demarcated European vistas of private ownership (1801–04:1,57):

> As none of the [extensive lands] are enclosed there is a general appearance of nakedness in the country . . . which . . . if divided by fences, would become sufficiently beautiful, as nature in drawing the outline has performed her part.

The Dutch had not investigated the interior systematically and, perhaps most diagnostic for Barrow, had "no kind of chart or survey, save of such districts as were contiguous to the Cape" (1801–04:1,8). This was taken to indicate lax colonial control, something that the British "spirit of commerce and adventurous industry" would remedy. The frontispiece of Barrow's book has a comprehensive map of the Cape Colony, constructed from bearings, distances, and latitudes observed during his travels. The map presents this land to Britain for the taking, its virgin scapes laid tantalizingly bare, its routes of access picked out in red.

Barrow's *Account* was also a moral geography of the interior of the Cape, one which not so much emptied the landscape of its human inhabitants (Pratt 1985) as denied them any legitimate claim to it. The text cleared the ethical ground for British colonialism by depicting the territory as a polarized human universe of unregenerate natives and degenerate Dutchmen. The dualistic vision of nature in postenlightenment imagery, to which we alluded above and shall return, speaks out here. The Dutch had negated their own humanity by treating the blacks as objects, prey to be "hunted" (1801–04:1,273); they sought to validate a "monstrous" manhood (1801–04:1,145) by exterminating nature's innocents—rather than by elevating them, and all African humanity, through forceful cultivation. Their brutal bravado was founded on a myth of savagery that Barrow feels called upon to dispel (1801–04:1,196):

> It is a common idea, industriously kept up in the colony, that the Kaffers[15] are a savage, treacherous, and cruel people, a character as false as it is unmerited. . . .

Likewise, speaking of the Khoisan, he adds that the "Hottentots" (Khoi) were "mild, quiet, and timid people, perfectly harmless, honest, faithful," their timeless customary existence destroyed by Dutch abuse (180104:1,151); and the "Bushmen" (San) were "like frightened children" mowed down by Boer bullets as they played with bows and arrows (1801–04:1,273).

These observations were grounded in the very real fact of genocide; there is plenty of collateral evidence to prove that a war of extermination had been waged along the frontier against the Khoisan (see e.g., Marais 1944; Marks 1972; Elphick and Malherbe 1989). Nor is there any doubt that Barrow believed himself to be writing a *historical* account of both Boer and Bushman, explaining how each had been affected by the violent encounter with the other. Nonetheless, there is in this historiography another process at work. In building his stereotypic contrasts, Barrow, intentionally or not, was also fleshing out an imaginative structure, a set of oppositions which came to be shared by many of his contemporaries (see Coetzee 1988:29f.). The Dutch farmer was European civilization grown rotten in the African sun— his "nature" made yet more degenerate, his "indolence of body and low groveling mind" corrupted yet further by being an owner and master of slaves (Barrow 1801–04 quoted by Coetzee 1988:29; see also Philip 1828,1: 367f.; Moodie 1835:1,176). He was the very antithesis of Protestant enlightenment, having wilfully permitted his own debasement. The "savage tribes," made so brutish by seventeenth-century Dutch reports (see Willem ten Rhyne in Schapera 1933), were really innocent and ignorant. They might dance and sing when moved by their childish passions, and slept in beds "like the nest of an ostrich" (1801–04:1,148, 275). While "low on the scale of humanity," they were raw material for the civilizing project. For, notwithstanding their common predicament as "miserable savages" (1801–04: 1,287) in opposition to the British, peoples such as the "Hottentots" had their own nobility. This *Account*, in short, validated the moral scheme of the first LMS and WMMS missionaries to South Africa, coloring their view of the white perverts and would-be black converts who peopled the interior.

Barrow's social position guaranteed him a wide readership among scholars, politicians, and the literate public. The natural historian Lichtenstein ([1815] 1930,2:12) noted at the time that in his native Germany the "journals and almanacks" vied to publish the British author's accounts of the "ignorance, the brutality, the filthiness" of the Dutch colonists. Lichtenstein himself had traveled in the interior of South Africa between 1803 and 1806 in the employ of the Dutch government. His own two volume narrative appeared in German in 1810 and 1812 and in English in 1812 [repr. 1928] and 1815 [repr. 1930]. It was highly critical of Barrow's portrayal of the Dutch farmers and their brutal domination of the "Caffres" (1928:1,59):

> I was led almost daily to ask myself whether these were really the same African colonists which the celebrated Mr. Barrow represented as such barbarians, as such more than half-savages—so much did I find the reality in contradiction to his description.

Again we are reminded that images of Africa are born of European arguments about their own essential nature.[16] Barrow was accused of betraying his own kind; of failing, as an educated European, to credit the effects of the African climate and hence to understand the "rough Cape peasantry" and their relation to the blacks (1930:2,6–13). Yet, lying beneath the surfaces of the debate, is a set of shared constructs that makes the dispute possible in the first place. Lichtenstein does not really take issue with Barrow's portrayal of Africans, although his own descriptions lack the Englishman's stress on their innocence and vulnerability. For him, "Bushmen" are miserable and voracious: "no class of savages . . . lead lives so near those of brutes" or are so low on the "scale of existence" (1930:2,244). But, he adds (1930:2,65):[17]

> The rude rough man, left entirely in a state of nature, is not in himself evil and wicked. . . . [He] follows blindly the impulse of his passions, which lead him to acts, that to us, in the high point of civilization we have attained, appear as crimes. . . .

Africa might have become a moral battlefield, but its representation in late eighteenth-century Europe also reflected a conceptual order fast spreading among persons "of reason," an essential humanism in terms of which man became his own measure (Foucault 1975). No longer satisfied with a notion of himself as God's passive creature, he sought to define his "place in nature" (Thomas 1984:243 et passim); that is, to assess his position on a scale of humanity rather than on a ladder to heaven. A new narrative of human types was being written, and the African was to have a definite niche in it. As a foil to the enlightened European, he was doubly devalued: human yet ignorant of salvation to begin with, he had now lost his innocence at the hands of civilization's most depraved elements, slavers and the degenerate white men of the tropics.[18] Here, as we have said, the texts of travelers and explorers became entangled in the debate over abolition (see Barrow 1801–04:1,46). But the discourse also informed, and was informed by, arguments within the related field of natural history and the emerging science of biology.

THE NEW BIOLOGY AND THE
GREAT CHAIN OF BEING

In the early nineteenth century the life sciences were preoccupied with the "great chain of being"—and especially with its lower half. As Figlio (1976: 25) observes, contemporary debates about man's place in nature hinged upon the relationship of the human species to the rest of the living world:

> There was a focusing upon the multi-faceted idea of animality, as opposed to an insistence upon a scalar, uni-dimensional hierarchy, with man at the top of the visible, and God at the top of the invisible, realm.

Rooted in the contrast between the animate and the inanimate, this focus on animality implied a concern with the properties of "life" common to all beings. And it fixed on man as the embodiment of perfection, since he alone had distinguished himself by using reason to discover his own essence. This in turn led inexorably to the concept of "generic human nature" (Stocking 1987:17), a notion that separated man from beast, people from objects, and rendered anomalous anything—like the slave trade—that confused them. But "human nature" was a highly abstract category. Once put to work in the world it was immediately subject to internal differentiation. This is where the chain of being served as a powerful metaphor, for it conjured up a hierarchy of distinct varieties within (a single) humankind.

In the epistemology of the time, then, the key to knowledge seemed to lie increasingly within man himself. The essence of life was in the unplumbed depths of organic being, to be grasped through the invasive thrust, the looking and naming, of the new biology (Foucault 1975). Its interior truth, merely signified in outer bodily form, gave rise to meaningful differences in the faculties and function of living beings.

African Bodies, African Nature

We have already encountered traces of this epistemology in the geographical mission, where the thrust into the African interior likened the continent to a female body. Bernhard Fabian (quoted in Nerlich 1987:179) reminds us that, in the late eighteenth century, the qualities of the scientific "spirit" were identified with the heroic "spirit" of the adventurer: the natural scientist's penetration into hitherto unknown realms had become one with the advance into regions unknown. The newly charted surfaces of the African landscape were to have a direct connection with the universe opening up within the person, for the geographical mission expanded European knowledge of the global biology of mankind. In investigating the savage, the West set up a mirror in which it might find a tangible, if inverted, self-image. Non-Europeans filled out the nether reaches of the scale of being, providing the contrast against which cultivated man might distinguish himself. On this scale, moreover, the African was assigned a particularly base position: he marked the point at which humanity gave way to animality. In treating him as the very embodiment of savagery, of deviance from a racially-defined ideal (Gould 1981:38), the travel and adventure literature gave ostensibly objective, precise descriptions of both his bodily form and his "manners and customs." In such popular accounts, in other words, African "nature" was grounded in the color, shape, and substance of the black physique.

With the rise of comparative anatomy and biology as formal sciences, the organic reduction of African society and culture took on ever greater authority. For much of the eighteenth century it had been civilization that separated savage man from his white counterpart—moral and politico-economic circumstance rather than physical endowment (Stocking 1987: 18). But the vocabulary of natural science was to strengthen and legiti-mize the association of dark continents with black bodies and dim minds. Comparative anatomical schemes typically presented Africans as the most extreme contrast with Europeans—in the new technical argot, the "link" between man and beast (Curtin 1964:42). Linnaeus' *Systema Naturae*, first published in 1735, laid out in initial form what would soon become a con-vention of biological classification: a chromatic scale of white, yellow, red, and black races, each native to one of the four major continents (Gould 1981: 35; Curtin 1964:37). As in the popular literature of travel and adventure, Africans were invariably placed at the bottom of the ladder of enlighten-ment, below such paler peoples as Asians or American Indians (Buffon 1791; Blumenbach 1775, 1795; White 1799). By 1778 Buffon, who had added such features as hair, stature, and physiognomy to his scheme, declared that white was the "real and natural colour of man" (quoted in West 1982:56).[19] Blumenbach took this yet further, to the shape of the skull, thereby introduc-ing one of the more pervasive and enduring elements in the annals of racial taxonomy. He went on to claim, on this basis, that the Ethiopian was the low-liest deviation from the "most beautiful" Caucasian type (Street 1975:52ff.). The great chain of being, a vertical scale, had been set on its side, becoming also a linear history of human progress from the peripheral regions of the earth to its north European core. The hard facts of organic form, it seemed, could now explain and determine the place of men in the world.

Science, Aesthetics, and Selfhood

The life sciences, then, were part of a broader discourse about the human condition—a discourse closely tied to Europe's encounter with the non-European world. Raised to a new level of self-consciousness and authority, their "value free" knowledge found a natural validation for cultural imperial-ism in the inner secrets of existence. "Natural" scientists read off the degree of animality and the perfection of life from the external features of different "organisms"; for these were taken to be a function of the relative complexity, symmetry, and refinement of the faculties within. Take, for example, the influential Dutch scholar Camper, who, in a manner similar to Blumenbach (see above), devised a scale that correlated the shape of the skull with aesthetic appearance and mental capacity: his "facial angle" measured the projection of the jaw, a protruding profile being linked with the long snouts, low brows, and sensory-bound state of animals. Applied to an eclectic array of "evidence"— including African traveler's accounts—this measurement defined and ranked national character, giving physical shape to the current philosophical concern with the relationship of race, nationality, and civilization (cf. Hume 1854).

Camper's scale extended from dog through ape to Negro, then through the European peoples to the ideal beauty of form epitomized in Greek sculpture (1821:x; see Figlio 1976:28f.). And it was rapidly publicized well beyond the scientific community, as were his more general pronouncements. Thus the preface to an English translation of his popular lectures addressed an artistic audience on the moral and aesthetic implications of the science of comparative anatomy (1821:x):

> [The] grand object was to shew, that national differences may be
> reduced to rules; of which the different directions of the facial line
> form a fundamental norma or canon . . . the knowledge of which will
> prevent the artist from blending the features of different nations in the
> same individual. . . .

Nationality, physical type, and aesthetic value are condensed here into an iconography that would in due course become part of the language of scientific racism. With his apartheid of the sketchpad, Camper imprinted the bodily contours of stereotypic others on the European imagination—and with them, a host of qualitative associations. His sample African profile, for instance, a distinctly bestial representation, was to become standard in nineteenth-century texts on racial difference; significantly, these texts gave prominence to images of black South Africans (see plates 3a and 3b).

Georges Cuvier, the prestigious Swiss comparative anatomist of the early nineteenth century, took the facial angle and the biological reduction of culture to new levels of sophistication. He developed a scale to evaluate the perfection not only of the intellect but also of the introspective self, the moral core of the person. By gauging the proportion of the mid-cranial area to that of the face, he sought to reveal the degree of dependence of an organism upon external sensations; the size of the cranium itself was taken to reflect the development of reason and self-control. On this count, the "negro" stood between the "most ferocious apes" and the Europeans, who were themselves superseded by the men and deities of ancient Greek sculpture (Figlio 1976:28). But it was the neurological dimension of Cuvier's scheme (1827:1,49f.) that raised most explicitly the spiritual and moral capacity of man. For the nervous system was the site of internal animation, and its complexity determined the higher faculties of life—intelligence and volition. The latter were expressions of a "soul or sentient principle," whose source of vitality remained, at the time, a matter of serious debate. Scientists, however, were more concerned with the physical organization of this system, which was centered on a compact inner core that reached its most perfect form in the complicated brain of man. As Figlio (1976:24) explains:

> . . . this compactness [was associated] quite explicitly with the higher faculties, indeed with the sense of the 'self.' Just as the nervous system coalesced into a centre from which dependent nerves arose, so too was the sense of self increasingly solidified and distinct. Thus, a grading of this . . . concentrating of the nervous system was simultaneously a grading of animal sentience and selfhood.

And so the bourgeois subject of the new Age of Capitalism, already secure in the Protestant ethic and rational philosophy, was given incontestable grounding in biological nature. Needless to say, the inner density and refinement associated by Cuvier with self-awareness and control were held to be underdeveloped among non-Europeans. This was especially true of blacks, who were bound by the animal reflexes of survival (1827:1,97; see Curtin 1964:231):

> The negro race is confined to the south of Mount Atlas. Its characters are, black complexion, woolly hair, compressed cranium, and flattish nose. In the prominence of the lower part of the face, and the thickness of the lips, it manifestly approaches to the monkey tribe. The hordes of which this variety is composed have always remained in a state of complete barbarism.

Cuvier's writings were summarized in the British biomedical press within months of their publication and were assiduously discussed by scientists, theologians, and men of letters (Figlio 1976:35). In an age when specialist knowledge was not yet set apart by technical language, work such as this— and that of Camper—was rapidly directed to a receptive, almost insatiable public. Often, as in one widely read translation of Cuvier's *Animal Kingdom*, some "popular and entertaining matter" was added on the instincts and habits of animals and primitive man (1827:1,i–ii). The editors in this particular instance included a description of the "unhappy races" of South Africa, a telling bricolage of current European curiosity, with substantiating

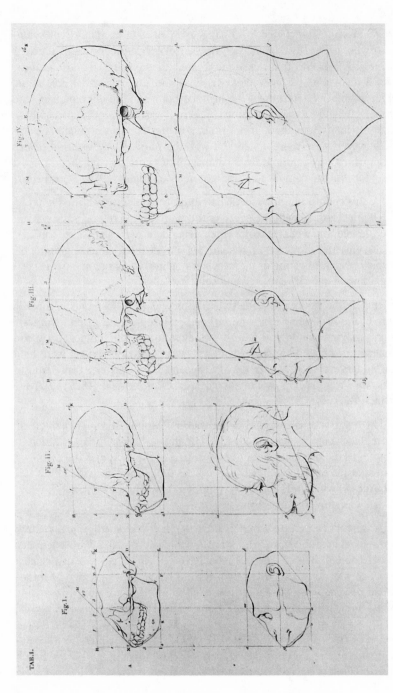

TAB. I.

Fig. I.   Fig. II.   Fig. III.   Fig. IV.

PLATE 3a   *Petrus Camper: Facial Lines and Angles. Left to right: ape; orang-utang; negro; calmuck. Reproduced from Camper (1821:119).*

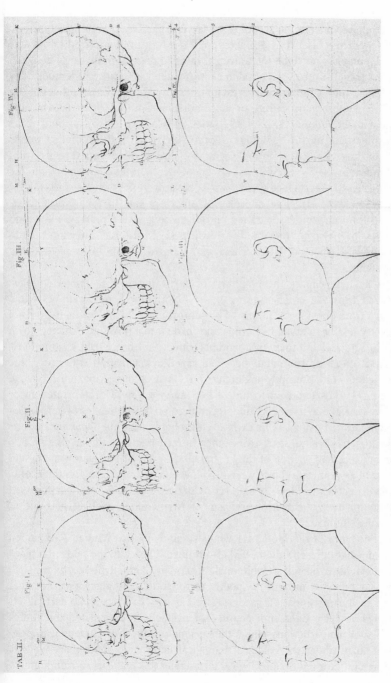

PLATE 3b   *Petrus Camper: Facial Lines and Angles. Europeans (first three); "antique" (fourth). Reproduced from Camper (1821:119).*

material drawn from the accounts of travelers like Barrow and Lichtenstein. Thus were the discoveries of geographical adventure converted into a scientific currency in which the universal value of man might be reckoned.

As these travel tales and salon exotica gained scientific credentials, they hardened into stereotypic representations of Africa. Their influence on the eye of subsequent European observations in South Africa was to be tangible. Cuvier's editors (1827:1,197), for example, provided an account of the "Bushmen" as pygmy "plunderers" who "lurk[ed]" in the complicit woods and bushes. This description seems to have been drawn directly from Lichtenstein (1928:1,68n), yet we encounter it, metaphor intact, in the "eyewitness" report given many years afterwards by the Rev. Edwards (1886: 66; below, p. 174). The interplay of other epithets in the *Animal Kingdom*—"Hottentots" as degraded and disgusting, or as swarthy, filthy, and greasy—may also be traced to Lichtenstein (1928:1,69).[20] They too were to flow from the pens of later writers who claimed the authority of firsthand experience.

One item among the potpourri of curiosities in the *Animal Kingdom* (1827:1,196) was a description of the "Hottentot Venus," an "essential black" from the Cape Colony. This unfortunate "wild" woman of Khoi ancestry had been taken to Europe and made into a traveling exhibit, shown first in England and then, by an animal trainer, in France. She died in Paris in 1815 after European audiences had gazed in fascination at her for some five years—and promptly ended up on Cuvier's dissecting table (Gould 1985:294). His famous account of her autopsy was to be reprinted twice within a decade of its publication; it centered on the anomalies of her "organ of generation," which, in its excessive development of the *labia minora*, was held to set her kind apart from other human beings (Gilman 1985:212). Barrow, too, had written of the genital aberrations of Khoisan women, and a host of anatomical reports were to follow Cuvier in focusing on the exotic, simian qualities of black female reproductive organs. A barely suppressed infatuation with the torrid eroticism of Africa made itself respectable as biological inquiry.

The story of the Hottentot Venus reminds us that Mungo Park, albeit in somewhat different idiom, had also reduced Africa to the body of a black female yielding herself to white male discovery. This mytheme, as we shall see, was repeated in both the poetry of romantic naturalists and the sober prose of our missionary crusaders. But Cuvier's writings show particularly plainly how early nineteenth-century science actually articulated and authorized such constructions—how the various products of current European fancy sailed under the colors of biological knowledge about man, woman, and nature. Nor did the ideological message of this material remain implicit.

Supplementary details on African peoples in the *Animal Kingdom* (1827: 1, 196) were summarized with the confident statement that "a physical obstacle to their progress seemed to be a more natural solution to [the] problem [of their lack of development] than any political or local circumstances."

The Nature of Gender

As all this suggests, the "signifying economy" (Godzich 1987:xi) of otherness took in gender as well as race. That "economy" has a long history, of course. But we need only break into it at the dawn of modernism. "Sometime in the late eighteenth century," Lacquer (1986:1) observes, "human sexual nature changed." It certainly did. With the reorganization of production and perception in the age of revolution, novel distinctions arose in the construction of gender. And they raised the problematic "nature of woman" to consciousness in Europe as never before (above, chapter 2).

Given the epistemology of the time, it was inevitable that this new consciousness should find the source of gender relations in the bodies of men and women—and that biology should be invoked to explain a division of labor already established in economy and society. The ideology of the enlightened free market might celebrate equality and a generic humanity. But its material practices sanctioned the exploitation of whole categories of people, usually on the basis of "natural" distinctions like race and sex. Such stigmatizing signs often come to imply each other: in late eighteenth-century images of Africa, the feminization of the black "other" was a potent trope of devaluation. The non-European was to be made as peripheral to the global axes of reason and production as women had become at home. Both were vital to the material and imaginative order of modern Europe. Yet both were deprived of access to its highest values. Biology again provided the authoritative terms for this simultaneous process of inclusion and disqualification.

In sum, the manner in which Africa was portrayed as woman—with reference in particular to the organs of procreation—was an extension of a gender ideology fast taking root in late eighteenth-century Europe. Here "the female body in its reproductive capacity and in its distinction from that of the male, [had come] to occupy a critical place in a whole range of political discourses" (Lacquer 1986:1). As the biology of childbearing became the essence of womanhood, it also seemed to prescribe an increasingly radical, physically-derived contrast between male and female. For centuries prior to this time, both medical and commonsense knowledge appear to have assumed that women had the same reproductive organs as men; that they were "men turned outside in" (Lacquer 1986:1). Moreover, gender identity had not been vested in the anatomy of procreation alone but in more general features of moral and social disposition. In this respect too there was a continuity between male and female: far from "a total division of mental properties between the sexes," as Jordanova (1980:63) puts it, there had been "a continuum according to which reason dominated. . . ."

Reason and intelligence were male properties, of course; men and women had thus been arrayed along a single axis whose telos was masculine (Lacquer 1986:3). But the struggle between the two qualities had occurred within rather than between individuals, each person's temperament being the product of both. Here Foucault's insight into changing perceptions of hermaphrodites throws light on the emergence of modern gender identity. In his introduction to the memoirs of Herculine Barbin (1980b:viif.), he notes that medieval canon and civil law defined them as people in whom the two sexes were juxtaposed in variable proportions. By the nineteenth century, however, it had become the task of the medical expert to "find the one true sex of the so-called hermaphrodite" (Davidson 1987), to reveal the unambiguous biological reality that underlay uncertain appearances.

The premodern language of gender had also integrated physical, mental, and social qualities, making the body an icon of moral as much as of procreative status. Jordanova (1980:49) notes that medical and philosophical writings in the eighteenth century focused on the breast as a symbol of the valued role of women in domestic nurture. The shift of attention to the uterus in nineteenth-century biology marked a retreat into the hidden recesses of gynecological anatomy, whence female nature now seemed to emanate.

The new biology of difference and incommensurability, then, shackled women to their sexual nature as resolutely as it freed men—or at least European men—from the constraints of instinct and bodily function. "It was," one physician explained, "as if the Almighty, in creating the female sex, had taken the uterus and built up a woman around it" (Holbrook 1882; quoted in Smith-Rosenberg and Rosenberg 1973:335). Here the ideology of gender cut across contemporary models of the nervous system and became implicated in the more general definition of modern selfhood. For, by implication, women's reproductive physiology rerouted their neurological pathways, diffusing the compact density of the rational, male self. As opponents of female education were to argue, the brain and the reproductive organs simply could not develop at the same time. The uterus was assumed to be connected directly to the central nervous system, shaping its constitution and in return being affected by it (Smith-Rosenberg and Rosenberg 1973:335).

Women's sensibility was both greater and more labile than that of men, and their nervous systems lacked focus; their "fibres" were "mobile," especially "those in the uterus" (Macquart 1799; quoted in Jordanova 1980:48).

Like the "low brow" non-European, the European female was played upon by strong and frequent sensations from the external environment. Her constitution was passionate and intuitive, susceptible to nervous disorders, and responsive to control by males—particularly men of science (Stocking 1987:199). A privileged relationship of sex and selfhood had been born: with the emergence of the "psyche" in later nineteenth-century thought, sexuality would become the "externalization of the hidden, inner essence of personality" (Davidson 1987:47). This development was prefigured in the vision of missionaries earlier in the century, which placed great diagnostic weight upon sexual propriety as a symptom of "moral fiber." After all, as Davidson reminds us, moral theology had once used "pervert"—a person wilfully turning to evil from good—as an antonym of "convert." There is evidence of this connotation, and of the more modern sense of "sexual deviance," in the evangelists' use of the term.

It has been pointed out (Smith-Rosenberg and Rosenberg 1973:338; Stocking 1987:199; Jordanova 1980:49) that contemporary discourses on female nature were neither unanimous nor free of contradiction. Women were held at once to be sensitive and delicate, yet hardy and longer-lived; passionate and quintessentially sexual, yet innocent and intuitively moral. Given the political load that the anatomy of woman had come to bear, such ambiguities were bound to fuel angry dispute; it is not surprising that her body soon became an ideological battleground (Lacquer 1986:24). Feminists and antifeminists both exploited these contradictions, albeit in contrasting ways—the former being no less quick than the latter to appeal to natural differences in making their case. Anna Wheeler and William Thompson (1825; quoted in Lacquer 1986:23), for example, argued that women deserved greater political participation on grounds of their innate moral aptitude and their undesiring, even passionless dispositions. And Fuller (1855), in her manifesto, *Woman in the Nineteenth Century*, described male and female as "two sides of the great radical dualism," the female system being "electrical in movement" and "intuitive in function" (quoted in Ayala 1977:263). Thus, while the debate raged over social values, its terms reinforced the hegemony of biological determinism and ineluctable gender distinction.

The new biology, in short, gave legitimacy to an idealized image of rational man. Unlike women and non-Europeans, he was a self-contained individual and was driven by inner reason, not by sensory stimuli from the social and material environment. This image of selfhood appeared simultaneously in a wide range of late eighteenth-century moral and technical discourses; biomedical science was just one voice in a richly redundant chorus, its concern with the inner body drawing attention away from man's dialectical relation with his context. But the reduction did not go unchecked. It was countered by the social reformism of mainstream enlightenment religion and philosophy, which stressed the reconstruction of persons and, through them, the world. Humanitarian and evangelical rhetoric alike had it that the possession of a soul and the capacity to reason made every human being capable of improvement. The self could be "cultured,"[21] the will strengthened by implanting spiritual truth and by "uplifting" physical and social conditions.

Thus the biological determinism of the age was usually qualified by some attention to the effects of environment; conversely, the optimism of philanthropists and evangelists was often tempered by a suspicion that nature placed limits on the ability of some human beings to develop. Nor were scientists undivided on the issues: Gould (1981:31ff.) has distinguished "hard-" from "softliners" among significant eighteenth and nineteenth-century thinkers on the question of the African's potential for civilization.[22] While this distinction may be too rigidly drawn, there certainly were loud and lengthy arguments about the origin and implications of racial difference. Witness the debate over the role of climate in the origin of human diversity, in which some early naturalists (e.g., Buffon 1791) and biologists (e.g., Blumenbach [1775, 1795] 1969) claimed that negro physical characteristics grew out of life in the tropics (Curtin 1964:40). Here again scientific thought evoked European notions of ecology that went back at least a hundred years—in particular, the humoral theory that "as the air is, so are the inhabitants" (cf. Hodgen 1964:283). In this legacy "southern climes" were repeatedly associated with heat and fecundity, sensuality and decay. For instance, in his defense of Cape Dutchmen against Barrow's attacks (see above), Lichtenstein (1928:1,58) attributed their "phlegm" to the African environment. And for comparative support he quoted Goethe's similar observations of the indolent Neapolitans.

The writings of the South African missionaries suggest that they too perceived a complex connection between African bodies and landscapes. Moreover, their efforts to reform the benighted blacks were to express an unresolved conflict between the incorrigibility of natural endowment and the possibility of human improvement. Visible in the conflict, and in the entire European discourse about savagery, was an increasingly sharp—and gendered—contrast between "nature" (all that exists prior to civil society) and "civilization" or "culture" (collectively wrought existence, though not yet the modern anthropological idea of a distinct, meaningful lifeworld; see Stocking 1987:19; also note 21 above). This dichotomy was elaborated most extensively, perhaps, in the debate over the "noble savage," a chimera which relied heavily on images of Africa already in popular European circulation.

THE NOBLE SAVAGE AND THE NATURAL UTOPIA

In speaking of the enhanced significance of nature in eighteenth-century European thought, the Blochs (1980:27; cf. Thomas 1984) remind us that the concept played upon a dynamic ambiguity. While the term itself had acquired new meaning—as the innocent, fecund source of new material from which civil society could be formed and replenished—it also retained a longer-standing association with degeneracy, savagery, and the Fall. Either way, it was a cultural construct, the product of an endless effort by human-kind to conceive of itself by envisaging its obverse—now in an ever more disenchanted world. If degenerate nature was the foil to postenlightenment European self-confidence, idealized nature was the trope of its critics and visionaries. We have seen how the savage, the wild man of the human realm, became the counter-image of an assertive Western civilization. It remains to explore his role in the social criticism that, challenging the ethos of rational progress, presented him as the embodiment of a lost utopia. As this implies, the African had been reinvented as a creature with two faces (cf. Sinclair 1977:55).[23] And sometimes both faces appeared in a single discourse. For example, the missionaries to South Africa would aim to establish him first as degenerate other; then they would take hold of him in a transforming grasp that would harness his brute potential, making him into a lowlier, artless version of themselves. As it turned out, the ambiguity of savage nature—the threat that accompanied its vital promise—was not that easily contained. It was to confound the churchmen from the very start, and it is discernible in early representations of their adventures in the African garden. Two commonly depicted scenes, to which we shall return, capture this ambiguity well. The first, "The Abandoned Mother," ostensibly an incident in the life of Robert Moffat, presents Africa as suffering innocent, awaiting the regenerative attentions of the white hero and his black disciple (plates 4a and 4b). The second, an encounter between missionary and serpent—here a cobra—shows Africa clasping God's emissary in a satanic embrace as he valiantly holds aloft the divine text (plates 5a and 5b).

Fairchild (1928:2ff.) has claimed that the noble savage stood to the (early) modern world as the golden age did to the ancient. Both looked "yearningly back from the corruptions of civilization to an imaginary primeval inno-cence." Thus Erasmus had praised nature and instinct above "artificial training"; Montaigne had extolled the American Indian, sitting "all naked, simply-pure, in Nature's lap"; Diderot (1972) had published a fictitious travel narrative that presented a native artfully tailored to his philosophical needs; and Rousseau, for all the debate over his primitivism, was widely read as exalting man in a "state of nature" (Cook 1936; Lovejoy 1923). The noble

PLATE 4a   *The Abandoned Mother (i). Engraving by George Baxter. Reproduced from Moffat, Missionary Labours (1842:135).*

savage, at least in English writing, had his heyday between 1750 and 1830, precisely the period when the geographical mission was yielding increasingly "scientific" observations of human diversity and development.

English romantic writers drew on the same travel and exploratory literature to paint a picture of a non-European Eden, a picture that challenged those for whom enlightened Europe was the yardstick of perfection. Craftsmen of the imaginary, they built the savage world as a stage on which to rehearse their largely domestic concerns, often making explicit the fact that their Eden was an illusory device (Curtin 1964:51). A cynical Dickens (1853:337; above, p. 51) might later pour scorn on the "ignoble savage," dubbing him "a prodigious nuisance and an enormous superstition." But for many romantic naturalists of an earlier generation, he took his place—along with children, yeomen, and the virgin landscape—as an indictment of the "jarring and dissonant thing" that civilization had made of man (Coleridge, "The Dungeon," [1798] 1912:185). Humanists and abolitionists also invoked him to personify the tragic figure of the slave—an innocent witness

110

PLATE 4b *The Abandoned Mother (ii). Reproduced from* The Life and Explorations of Dr. Livingstone *(n.d.).*

PLATE 5a *In Jeopardy. Reproduced from Thomas,* Eleven Years in Central Africa *(1873:125)*

to, and victim of, European debauchery. As we shall see from the writings of Wesley, the rising evangelical movement was somewhat ambivalent about such imagery. Ignorance of salvation clearly tainted the primitive paradise. But the critique of European worldliness appealed to Puritan sensibilities, and missionaries were hopeful that the savage wilderness might be made to yield a new Christian Arcadia (Moorhouse 1973:37–39).

Summoned up as an alibi for European discontents, then, the wild man was not intended as a vehicle for purveying knowledge about the non-European world. But neither was he a mere romantic fantasy. What Sypher (1942:103) calls the "jargon of primitivism" in eighteenth-century human-ist literature fed fitfully off the writings of philosophers and explorers, bor-rowing signs and figures to suit its poetic needs. The original prototype of the noble savage himself was the American Indian; this being the legacy of Spanish travel and missionary narratives in the new world—especially the often appreciative portrayals of Columbus and Las Casas—combined with the British colonial experience. But Cook's voyages also brought South Sea Islanders into the gaze of the European, where they were to remain long into the age of French impressionism (see Gauguin 1985). And the British

PLATE 5b *Dr. Moffat and the Cobra. Reproduced from* The Life and Explorations of Dr. Livingstone *(n.d.).*

humanitarian movement added black Africans to the consciousness and conscience of "civilized" man (Fairchild 1928:10). As literary device, however, all that was required of the native was his otherness and "natural" nobility, embellished with authenticating details gleaned from the likes of Mungo Park.

The savage of English belles lettres was usually a syncretism, a careless composite of non-European colors and customs; hence the confusion of Indian and African features in Moore's *Mangora* or in Colman's *Inkle and Yarico* (Sypher 1942:105). Yet this sort of primitivist pastiche was an important source of popular images of Africa. That much is evident in missionary accounts of "native custom," which fabricate a synthetic savagery drawn from a standardized myth. In fact, as the abolitionist campaign became more audible, this savage most often had a black face and an African identity, but he remained an impressionistic blend of circumstantial ethnographic detail. And, with predictable irony, his noblest features had a distinctly European shape.

Most historians regard Aphra Behn's novelette, *Oroonoko*, as the founding myth of the noble negro (1915:5). A "gallant Moor" and African aristocrat, Oroonoko had an Indian name, a Roman nose, and a Caribbean destiny, and was more reminiscent of Othello than the suffering black everyman of later abolitionist poetics. Indeed, Behn's preoccupation with this courtly "Narcissus in ebony" has been castigated by literary historians as sentimental primitivism rather than authentic humanism.[24] But her text was unambiguous in its use of the royal slave to reveal—if with a rather romantic randomness—the decadence of European civilization. And in its many eighteenth-century editions in English, French, and German, its chapbook circulation and its dramatic renditions, this seems to have been its most appealing theme (Fairchild 1928:40).

It is in the romanticism of the mid–eighteenth century—with its reaction to urban bourgeois society, its espousal of rural simplicity, and its abolitionist sympathies—that a more conventional savage innocent steps forth. Joseph Warton's "The Enthusiast; or the Love of Nature" (1811:39), written in 1740, captures the mood well:

> Happy is the first of men ere yet confin'd
> To smoky cities; who in sheltering groves,
> Warm caves, and deep-sunk valleys liv'd and lov'd,
> By cares unwounded; what the sun and showers,
> And genial earth untillag'd could produce,
> They gather'd grateful.

But paradise had been blighted by those who, having tasted the fruit of knowledge, could no longer remember simple virtues. By 1750 Warton (1811:52) had put the following words into the mouth of an Andean Indian, a generic savage with a keen appreciation of the corrupting impact of European materialism:

> I see all Europe's children curs'd
> With lucre's universal thirst;
> The rage that sweeps my sons away
> My baneful gold shall well repay.

Africa's gold was its manpower, and by the closing years of the eighteenth century the rising strain of abolitionist sympathy had blended with romantic naturalism to depict a vanquished African Eden and an exiled native son. Thus William Roscoe, in *The Wrongs of Africa* (1787:10), writes of the blissful state from which the royal Cymbello, a latter-day Oroonoko, is snatched by slave traders:

> Lord of his time, the healthful native rose,
> And seiz'd his faithful bow, and took his way
> Midst tangled woods, or over distant plains,
> To pierce the murd'rous Pard; when glowing noon
> Pour'd its meridian fervours, in cool shades
> He slept away th'uncounted hours. . . .

The portrayal of the idyllic African landscape, however phantasmic, coincided with the rise of a practical, all-too-real interest in the continent. Roscoe's paradise was indeed overtaken by a "foul plague" from Europe: slavery. And so "Nature recoiled, and tore with frantic hands her own immortal features" (1787:12). Poetic critiques of this sort provided a mandate for humanists and evangelists of a more pragmatic bent. *The Wrongs of Africa* served as a moral call to arms, an appeal to those who would heal the ills of the afflicted savage.

Robert Southey's (1815:39) well-publicized invocation of the "Genius of Africa" had similar ideological implications. First, the continent is made into an enchanted landscape:

> O Thou, who from the mountain's height
> Roll'st down thy clouds with all their weight
> Of waters to old Nile's majestic tide;
> Or o'er the dark sepulchral plain
> Recallest Carthage in her ancient pride,
> The Mistress of the Main. . . .

Then comes the violation. Maternal Africa is despoiled by Europe's polluting embrace, her offspring torn from her breast by slavery. Although the poet calls upon her to summon up her spent spirit to redress the wrong, it is really white heroism that he seeks to rouse:

> Arise, thy children's wrong's redress
> Ah heed the mother's wretchedness
> When in the hot infectious air
> O'er her sick babe she bows opprest,
> Ah hear her when the Traders tear
> The drooping infant from her breast!

Note the theme that links the romantic poetry of the period to the accounts of travelers like Park. It is a theme that was to warrant, and to shape, the Protestant mission to Africa: the tragedy of a continent robbed of its masculinity, exiled from Eden, awaiting the restorative attentions the valiant white man (see, again, plates 4a and 4b). The seductively helpless Africa cultivated in such romantic poetry, especially in the cause of abolition, was fertile ground for an ideology of crusading colonialism—a colonialism whose founding charter fixed contemporary images of nature and gender, race and reason, savagery and civility, into a compelling mythological mosaic.

The popular literature that told of "the sad Negro" at the turn of the nineteenth century was replete with motifs of poignant romance, from the slave-prince banished from his court and love[25] to the thwarted liaison of white and black.[26] In these texts, as in the missionary writings to follow, the erotic allure of Africa is betrayed less by the stories themselves than by their submerged sexual metaphors of encounter and conquest, of the voluptuous and accessible landscapes with their carefree, sensuous inhabitants. This conceit, and its salience to the early colonizing impulse, are all the more noteworthy when we recall how representations of the continent were to change under the impact of the colonial encounter. Hammond and Jablow (1977: 149), for example, have shown that, in the creative literature of twentieth-century Europe, "Africa is never gentle or cherishing." In a striking reversal of the signs of times past, her once irresistible charms were to become "a snare and an enticement to destruction" (1977: 148).

But all that was still far into the future. During an earlier age, when the ideals of humane imperialism were first finding public voice, it is no wonder that the most congenial passage in Park's *Travels* seems to have been the "African women's song," with its charming embrace of the European male hero. The song was widely invoked by contemporary writers (Fairchild 1928: 488f.): James Montgomery's "The West Indies" (1860: 60), commissioned in 1807 to celebrate the parliamentary approval of abolition, paraphrased it to prove the negro's innate lyricism. And Crabbe's "Woman!" (1855: 515), quoting the lines about the sympathy shown to the traveler by

Africa's fairer sex, opines that such feminine compassion for white male wanderers is universal. Indeed, because woman was generic nature, Park's dark damsels had appeal far beyond their own context. The once influential William Lisle Bowles (1813:71, 135) acknowledged the *Travels* as the source for verses sung by a Chilean Indian woman who, in "The Missionary," consoles a captive "poor white maid." The poem goes on to suggest that by his simple piety the evangelist can yet perfect the natural goodness of the savage. In the same spirit Robert Moffat (1842:619) ends his *Missionary Labours and Scenes* by remembering how, when wandering famished in the heathen interior, he was given succor by an African Christian woman of compassion.

If romantic pity made the dark continent into a woman despoiled, it also infantilized it (cf. Street 1975:68); African men were almost invariably portrayed as childlike. The natural "other," after all, was afflicted by an absence, a *lack* of the qualities that characterized the adult white male ideal of European civilization (Mason 1987:165). This ensured that the attitude toward him remained condescending, even at its most sympathetic (Curtin 1964:50). As nature personified, we reiterate, he was at once pure and less than fully human. This is particularly clear in the narrative techniques by which the puerile savage was made into a figure of the English nursery. When Blake's innocent "Little Black Boy" tells "little English boy" that, despite his skin, his soul is white, his inability to speak the master language confirms his true inferiority (1966:125). Likewise, the naive simplicity and playfulness of many other "negro" portrayals was conveyed through the caricature of black speech forms. Thus, for example, in Amelia Opie's poem "The Negro Boy's Tale," the protagonist hails his "missa" in broken English probably laughable even in its time (Opie 1802:61; cf. Fairchild 1928:475). And so he was consigned to the juvenile bookshelf, although such hardly appears to have been his author's intention. Significantly, an 1826 edition of Opie's *Black Man's Lament* had an endpaper advertising six children's volumes on related themes, including *Samboe; or the African Boy* and *Prejudice Reproved; or the History of the Negro Toy-seller.*

By the time our missionaries encountered the Tswana and began to write their own texts, the infantilization of Africans was firmly established. Adult black males were the "boys" whom the civilizing mission hoped one day to usher into "moral manhood." And "boys" they would remain well into the age of apartheid, whether or not they actually became Christian. Even at their most subtle and well meaning, the various discourses on the nature of the savage pressed his immaturity upon European consciousness, adding to his race and symbolic gender yet a third trope of devaluation. This was no less true of the abolitionist movement, the most self-consciously compassionate voice of the age.

AFRICANS, APES, AND ABOLITION

Throughout this and the previous chapters we have been at pains to stress the tensions and contradictions in the maturing liberal vision of civilization, nature, and mankind—and hence to elucidate the arguments through which bourgeois consciousness took shape and conceived its global designs. Thus we have seen how disputes over the nature of woman and the savage, among other things, flowed from ambiguities in the definition of humanity itself: inclusive and homogeneous for some purposes, selective and differentiated for others. Abolitionism brought these discontinuities into sharp relief. In seeking to reconcile them—if not always to obliterate them—the movement helped replace the chains of slavery with the bonds of an imperialism based on the free market. A plea for generic humanism was gathering momentum. But it was being made in terms that also gave voice to Eurocentric racism in its modern form.

The "Commerce of the Human Species"[27]

The consensus emerging in the writings of eighteenth-century travelers, scientists, poets, and philosophers—that mankind was a single species sharing a common humanity—was affirmed in Wesley's (1835:6,263) resounding statement on religious liberty:

> Every man living, as man, has a right to [liberty], as he is a rational creature. The Creator gave him this right when he endowed him with understanding. And every man must judge for himself, because every man must give an account of himself to God.

As European thinkers debated the social contract, the concept of natural rights, and the principles of economy, it became ever more difficult to deny the fundamental unity of mankind. Or to blur the distinctions among men, goods, and brute nature. An Elizabethan slave trader might have sported a coat of arms bearing a "demi-Moor, bound and captive" (Sypher 1942:11). But in the mood of enlightenment, the "traffic in the human species" was increasingly condemned as "impious," an anomalous trade in "human flesh as a normal commodity" (Austen and Smith 1969:79; see also Drescher 1987:15). Wesley (1835:6,292) again: "It cannot be, that either war, or contract, can give any man such a property in another as he has in his sheep or oxen." Slavery began to seem as offensive to the libertarian principles of free trade and rational improvement as it was to the egalitarian individualism of the Protestant church.

By virtue of its anomalous character, then, slavery underscored the unity of interest of all mankind, accentuating the contrast between man and raw nature, human subjects and inanimate objects. The trade also confused the two, antithetical senses of nature—as generative and degenerate, fecund and fetid—that had come to coexist in postenlightenment culture (above, p. 109). For the innocent potential of the African had been harnessed to the most debased impulse of European civilization, making it brutal and depraved. It was the call to resolve these contradictions that was to animate both abolitionism and the evangelical mission.

Roscoe's *The Wrongs of Africa* shows clearly how the "unnatural trade" looked through the lens of Europe's enlightened libertarianism (1787:31):

> Nations of Europe! o'er whose favour'd lands
> Philosophy hath rais'd her light divine,
> (A brighter sun than that which rules the day)
> Beneath whose piercing beam, the spectre forms
> Of slavish superstition slow retire!
> Who greatly struggling with degrading chains,
> Have freed your limbs from bondage! felt the charms
> Of property! beyond a tyrant's lust
> Have plac'd domestic bliss! and soon shall own
> That noblest freedom, freedom of the mind,
> Secure from priestly craft and papal claims!

This self-satisfied bourgeois vision of reason, private enterprise, and "the charms of property" was advanced as a charter for universal human rights, to be extended "from the centre of this island to the extremities of the earth" (Roscoe 1787:iii). As abolitionism grew from its Quaker roots into a popular cause, it disseminated an image of individual liberty conceived as much in the shadow of the factory as the church; as we noted in chapter 2, the moral economy of Protestant rhetoric fell increasingly into line with the ethic of disciplined work (see also J. Comaroff 1985:134). As a result, the pamphlets and preachings of humanists and evangelists resonated with the basic principles of laissez faire economics; both laid stress on a self-regulating, unfettered market of goods and labor. To wit, Adam Smith (1937:365) had argued cogently that slave labor was costlier than free, since persons debarred from acquiring property had no incentive to work. His argument was to find its way directly into the South African colonial context: the Rev. John Philip (1828:1,367), LMS Superintendent at the Cape, evoked Smith to legitimize the civilizing mission, its struggle against "vassalage," and its commitment to the values of liberal individualism (J.L. Comaroff 1989).

Nor is this surprising. Smith's thesis had been echoed by Wesley, who lent it the weighty support of the Methodist church, with its hold over the lower classes of the mushrooming cities (Fogel 1989:212). In fitting commercial idiom, he asserted in his influential *Thoughts Upon Slavery* (Wesley

1835:2,293) that the trade was contrary to the law of nature: the purchase of the slave, as of any human being, could be made by Christ's blood alone. He also hinted that abolition might stimulate the white capacity to work and would not, as its opponents claimed, threaten the common wealth.

Following Davis (1975:347), we interpret the rise of abolitionism not as a simple function of capitalist self-interest (cf. Williams 1961) but as one element in a complex process; namely, the thoroughgoing reconstruction of culture and consciousness entailed in the industrial revolution. Above all, antislavery rhetoric gave voice to the notions of value and interest, humanity and society, civility and nature—in short, the ontology—integral to the triumph of capitalism. Davis (1975:349) argues that the movement was more than just the vehicle for a new hegemony. It was a major site for the symbolic production of that hegemony; part of a general revolution in meaning that cannot be tied neatly to the deliberate actions of particular interest groups or to nice calculations of the unprofitability of plantation production (cf. Anstey 1968). Neither was it, at least in origin, a direct expression of class interest. Aristocratic statesmen were prominent among its leadership, even though the latter would later come to label as retrogressive both the landed nobility and the mercantalist system. Like other formulations of popular ideology at the time, abolitionism arose in the context of a vigorous argument about productivity, property, human rights, and national interest. And from this perspective its liberal values appeared contradictory in one vital respect: the call for universal liberty and self-determination was not easily reconciled, in a world haunted by the specter of inequality and revolution, with the demands of social order and authority.

In due course the antislavery campaign would become ever more bourgeois in its spirit and substance; indeed, one of its tangible effects was to be the growing identification of British middle-class concerns with those of the nation state (Davis 1975:361). For us, however, the significant point is that the movement was to forge a new charter for empire, replacing slavery with a mode of colonial production that celebrated the material utility and moral virtue of free labor. Thus Clarkson (1816:vii), the leading researcher, ideologue, and activist of the London Abolition Committee, contrasted the "tyranny" of the Caribbean slave economy, which flouted the rights of man and the revelations of God, with "honorable, advantageous" commerce based on self-possessed labor, peasant farming, and the "inexhaustible mine of wealth . . . neglected in Africa." This vision clearly owed something to the popular romantic trope of the wasted garden. Like Roscoe's poem, it pitted archaic inequality against liberal enlightenment, superstitious parochialism against rational universalism. And it implied two quite distinct models of imperial relations: on the one hand, the domination and brutality of the New World plantation, a system destined to founder in its own wanton wastefulness and impious oppression; and on the other, the flourishing new colonial garden, whose virtuous trade, based on the "natural right to liberty," would increase British revenues and naval strength (1816:vii, 174).

The appeal of this humane colonialism was enhanced by the loss of the American possessions and by the geographical mission of the African Association, which presented West Africa as a site for a new and nobler empire (above, pp. 91–93). Wilberforce, parliamentarian and leader of the evangelical Clapham Sect, was also a forceful proponent of "legitimate commerce" and free labor as the route both to African reconstruction and to good, honest profit (Curtin 1964:69). He joined Clarkson, Granville Sharp (then chairman of the Abolition Committee), and other wealthy philanthropists in the founding of Sierra Leone, a humanitarian colony largely for destitute ex-slaves; in this pragmatic age, there was a strong drive to implement utopian ideals. For Wilberforce (1807:247), reformist politics merged with revivalist Christianity, yielding a utilitarian charter for moral imperialism and missionary effort:

> . . . I must once more raise my voice against that gross misconception of the character of the Negroes (an impeachment of the wisdom and goodness of their Creator no less than of our own), which represents them as a race of such natural baseness and brutality as to be incapable of religious impressions and improvements. Encourage marriage and the rearing of children in the only proper way; by settling the Slaves in family life, with their cottage and gardens, and with such other immunities and comforts and distinctions as will make them be respected by others and teach them to respect themselves.

We shall return to this horticultural idyll when we consider the imagery conjured up by the Nonconformists as they set about cultivating the heathen. More immediately, the conviction that social ills should be remedied by changing the individual and his domestic life—rather than the politico-economic structures that contained him—bespoke the essential conservatism of the Protestant revival. For John Wesley, after all, the French Revolution was "the work of Satan" (Fogel 1989:212).

Amongst the religious reformers, moreover, there was little faith that Africa could be civilized by the introduction of agriculture or trade alone. As Clarkson (1839:2, 12) put it, the "dreadful marks left upon her would be effaced only by the establishment of improving *Christian* communities." The italics are ours, the emphasis his. Nor was this view limited to evangelicals. Park also had noted that those who would tend the "savage and neglected lands" of Africa would have to combat the "blindness of pagan superstition" (above, p. 93). For most Christian humanists, of course, the charge to free the slave had, from the first, included his redemption through Christ. Wesley's *Thoughts Upon Slavery* ended with the exhortation (1835:6,293):

> The servile progeny of Ham
> Seize as the purchase of thy blood!
> Let all the Heathens know thy name:
> From idols to the living God
> The dark Americans convert
> And shine in every pagan heart!

As we have already noted, much of the impetus for the antislavery movement came from the assertive Protestantism of the late eighteenth century, which taught that salvation was attained through the use of personal talents for "the extirpation of private and public misery" at home and abroad (Clarkson 1839:36). This evangelism, an unmistakable creature of its age, echoed the presumption that society and history were driven by human agency, intentional and individual. The mission societies would provide the heroes, the benign agents of empire who would save the heathen and reverse the effects of the evil traffic. By 1807, when the latter was abolished, the dual commitment to trade and missionization was securely in place, with important implications for British dealings with Africa in the nineteenth century (Austen and Smith 1969:82). The impact of this commitment is palpable in evangelists like Livingstone (1857:34), who seldom let slip an opportunity to contrast legitimate commerce with slavery and to advocate it as a means of introducing "the Negro family into the body of [Christian] corporate nations."

Abolition did not end slavery, as we well know. Neither had its triumph been a foregone conclusion. The institution had been accepted without question for much of the history of mankind. It was still a vital part of the European economic system (Drescher 1977) and was vigorously defended by those with interests in it, especially merchants, naval men, and West Indian planters. Each side tried to mobilize support among parliamentarians and the concerned public, invoking the aid of rhetoricians and the evidence of scientists, philosophers, and travelers. For, while the new humanist hegemony was in formation, it was not yet securely in place, and strong, countervailing voices were still to be heard. The public debate focused on matters of morality and national revenue (Austen and Smith 1969:76), but it implied a more profound deliberation about the essence of humankind, the commodity, personhood, private property, and the production of wealth. Abolitionists had to refute claims that blacks were natural slaves, that Africa would present hopeless obstacles to the civilizing mission, and that no "legitimate" trade could ever replace the profits of bondage.

Of these proslavery voices, that of the Jamaican historian Edward Long was perhaps the most vociferous. The sort of case he made, like contemporary polygenetic arguments, ran counter to the dominant humanism of the age; Africans, he claimed, were a different, inferior species of the human genus. While his reasoning was never developed into a coherent, proslavery ideology, it clearly had an audience and was not "totally unrepresentative of [its] time" (Davis 1966; Drescher 1987). It has even been suggested that Long had a wide and enduring following (Curtin 1964:44). He could assert the authority of having lived in the West Indies for twelve years, and his *History of Jamaica* (1774) effected a tone of careful empiricism, mobilizing all the conventions of current scholarship (and citing the likes of Hume and Buffon) in support of its unremitting racism. He argued for an essential African nature by stipulating tangible physical "particulars"—the "very dark skin," the "wool, like bestial fleece, instead of hair," the "thick lips," "black lice," and "fetid smell"—that together comprised the generic black body (1774:2,351). In order to undermine further the human status of blacks, he picked up on the efforts of those who had reworked the chain of being, making such peoples as the "Hottentots" into the link between Europeans and the great primates (Stocking 1987:18). Having "established" the protohuman character of the "orangoutang race"—on the grounds of its capacity for elemental language and for forming a "kind of society" (1774: 2,363, 370)—he delivered his coup de grace. The orangoutang, he wrote (1774:2,364), had

> a passion for Negroe women, and hence must be supposed to covet their embraces from a natural impulse of desire, such as inclines one animal towards another of the same species, or which has conformity in the organs of generation.

Here, then, was definitive proof of the affinity of Ape and African.

We should no longer be surprised to find Africa represented by the genitalia of its women. This, after all, was the opening through which animality was held to enter into black being. "An orangoutang husband," Long assured his readers, "would [not] be any dishonour to an Hottentot female" (1774:2,355); note that a major criterion for defining a species at the time was successful mating within, but not beyond, its boundaries (Street 1975:94). Bestiality, however, was only one face of the coin that devalued black nature. For, if generic human beings were held to mate within the species, they ate outside it. Cannibalism, a potent symbol of savagery, appears often in postenlightenment constructions of the exotic other (Taussig 1984). Long's anthropology was no exception. Africans, we learn, were witless "devourers of human flesh, and quaffers of human blood" (1774:2,354). Their brains, like those of the orangoutang, were mere "senseless icons" of the human. The Great Fabricator had destined blacks, as other inferior animals, to be slaves to their superiors (1774:2,366). Long was doubtful that such debased creatures might be susceptible to moral reform. "Experience" in Africa and the French Caribbean suggested that Christianity made little headway among them, except in corrupted form. Catholicism, because it was content to "strike the eye" rather than touch the heart, might be more appealing. So might "those systems which are set off with abundance of outlandish rant and gesticulation," like Quakerism, Methodism, or Moravianism. But the established Church of England, being "founded on the principles of reason," was obviously inappropriate to the superstitious and sensual negro (1774:2,430).

Notwithstanding such extreme opinions, the debate over abolition reinforced a number of assumptions *shared* by both sides—tacit axioms about savages that went far deeper than the issue of slavery itself. Indicative here were the writings of John Stedman (1988:xxi), a former soldier who spent several years in Surinam assisting local troops against marauding bands of escaped slaves. His *Narrative of a Five Years' Expedition against the Revolted Negroes of Surinam* was ostensibly the eyewitness account of a military man of middle-of-the-road political opinions. Although no abolitionist, his sense of the common humanity of Africans and Europeans and his unvarnished description of planter cruelty ensured that his book was put to work in the antislavery cause as soon as it appeared. We are told, in fact, that the editor of the second edition felt moved to temper its cultural relativism, his deft excisions making the tone of the account almost indistinguishable from Long's proslavery apologetics (1988:lxii). But Stedman's unexpurgated writing still included passages like the following (1988:172):

> [I]f we really wish to keep our remaining . . . possessions that lay between the Tropicks, I . . . maintain, that they can never be cultivated but by Negroes alone. Neither the fair European, or the American Indian, being adequate to the task—then the Grand Question that remains to be solved is—are these Negroes to be Slaves or a free People—to which I answer without hesitation—*dependent*, & under proper restrictions/ a very few individuals only excepted [/]—not so much for the Sake of the European as for that of the African himself, with whose passions, debauchery and indolence, I am perfectly acquainted, and who like a Spirited Horse, when unbridled often Gallops to destruction himself . . . they would indeed in time provide for their *immediate* Subsistence but would no more think . . . of amassing Wealth by industry than their Countrymen the *Orangoutang*. . . .

Even in abolitionist circles there was continuing debate as to whether emancipation alone would bring out the desired industry and acquisitiveness in ex-slaves. As we have noted, the question was closely tied to the future of the West Indian plantations (Holt 1982:288f.) and in particular to anxieties about the labor discipline to be expected of freed men. These anxieties only served to underline further the axiom that, as far as South Africa was concerned, the civilizing mission and moral reform were a *sine qua non* of any productive intercourse between savages and Europeans.

Neither party in the abolitionist debate seems to have doubted that the history of Africa and its peoples was a European responsibility. Both seem also to have agreed that the first principle of the British stewardship of Africa was national self-interest. Stedman (1988:173), for instance, urged the passage of laws that would protect the rights of enslaved Africans as human beings, making them "perfectly happy"—and, hence, of increased benefit to "this *glorious Island*." Abolitionists, as we would expect, countered by stressing the gain to Britain of colonial production based upon free labor. Their explicit rationale was the axiom—by now all too familiar—shared by Protestant evangelism and classical economics alike: that the pursuit of enlightened self-interest contributed to the moral and material benefit of all. Antislavery rhetoric might have equated colonial advantage with the economic and ethical virtues of universal free labor. But it never questioned the opposition between white civility and black savagery, adult reason and childlike passion, the saved and the fallen, the heroic, active male and the passive female. Once woven together, these signs composed a tightly-knit cultural cloth, its internal pattern seldom unravelled. From this fabric were cut the models of benign domination to be carried by the first generation of missionaries to South Africa.

FOUR

AFRICAN WORLDS

Economy, Culture, and Society, circa 1800–1830

J UST AS IT would be misleading to reduce nineteenth-century British culture and society to a homogeneous "order," so too with "the" Tswana. We use the ethnological term, at this point, purely for convenience; it describes a loose congeries of peoples who occupied a mutually intelligible universe and a contiguous space on a terrain yet to be mapped.[1] Indeed, their very existence as "Bechuana," a collective noun, was yet to be dreamed up, their "tradition" to be invented. Tswana culture, so to speak, had still to be customized and objectified. This would occur during the colonial period, and the missions would have a lot to do with it. In the meantime, however, far from living in an unproductive desert or a hellish spiritual void—that is, in the "dark," prehistorical abyss of contemporary European imaginings—these peoples appear to have inhabited a world of dynamic communities: a lively world of open polities, changing societies. *Pace* "classical" anthropological models of later vintage, their chiefdoms were not islands unto themselves. Nor did they suffer from "closed predicaments" (Horton 1967), have "cold" cultures (Lévi-Strauss 1966:233f.), or occupy the timeless *Lebenswelt* that social scientists would, in the tradition of postenlightenment thinking, attribute to them by contrast to ourselves (Goody 1977:1). Quite the opposite: the Tswana, and others like them, were caught up in complex regional relations, subtle political and material processes, and vital cultural discourses; in short, in processes that gave historical motion to the construction of economy and society—just as they did in Europe.

Elsewhere we have described in detail the Southern Tswana world and its transformations from the early nineteenth century onward.[2] Here we are less concerned to provide a full account of their social order, their culture, or their political economy. Rather, we direct our attention, selectively, to those aspects of Tswana life that were to inform the colonial encounter in general and the engagement with the missionaries in particular.[3]

Legassick (1969b:98f.) has suggested that, whatever their origins (above, p. 39f.), there were several major Tswana chiefdoms in the present-day Transvaal by ca. 1500, when two began to fragment. This, he argues, set in motion a lengthy process of fission that spread small "lineage clusters" across the central heartland of southern Africa; later, in the eighteenth century, there followed a counter-process of amalgamation, in which many of the clusters were absorbed into political "confederations" (1969b:106–07; see below, p. 161). While there is little definite evidence from recent archeological and ethnohistorical research to confirm this scenario, there is nothing to contradict it either.[4] In any case, by the early nineteenth century the transformations visible within and among Tswana polities were truly striking.

At one extreme, Moffat (1842:388; cf. A. Smith 1939:1,278; Philip 1828:2,133f.) describes the Tshidi chiefdom, ca. 1824, as a large, densely centralized city-state under a ruler who wielded great power and monopolized external relations. And just to the north, Campbell (1822:1,253ff.) tells us, the Hurutse lived in an even more elaborately structured "nation," its "principal town" containing some 16,000 people (1822:1,277). Similarly, Barrow (1806:404) saw Rolong settlements "so extensive that it required a whole day" to walk from one end to the other. The Tlhaping capital, with its 10,000–15,000 souls, he says, was "as large as Cape Town" (1806:309f.). It had a well-developed administrative order (cf. Burchell 1824:2,511), and a strong "king" who owned large herds and regulated trade, supervised rainmaking and other rites, controlled the allocation of land and public meetings, and derived considerable wealth from tributary labor and the spoils of the hunt (Campbell 1822:1,249, 268, 314f.; 2,194ff.; Burchell 1824:2,532f.; Lichtenstein 1930:2,414; Stow 1905:440). Yet within thirty years his realm had divided into three small communities, each under the weak leadership of a man whose authority was no greater than that of a colonial Central African village headman (Gluckman, Mitchell, and Barnes 1949). Even more notably, Barrow (1806:412) and A. Smith (1939:1,240f.), among others, came across Southern Tswana living in autonomous political communities made up of a single village with no more than forty scattered huts. And Bain (in Steedman 1835:2,233; cf. Harris 1838:66) gives eyewitness account of small acephalous populations peppered along the Molopo River and the fringes of the Kalahari Desert in the 1820's. Some of these populations had, until not long before, been part of large centralized chiefdoms. Fifty years after *African Political Systems* (Fortes and Evans-Pritchard 1940), it is evident that, far from being taxonomic types, such centralized and acephalous "systems," state and stateless "societies," were the historical transformations of a dynamic social world.

The source of these dynamic fluctuations, their historical motor, lay partly in the internal workings of Tswana culture and society at the time, partly in the external relations among local chiefdoms and the other occupants of their environment. And they played themselves out in a variety of forms and registers: in, among other things, the spatial anatomy of the settlement, mythic and ritual representations of the cosmos, interaction with the nonhuman realm, the division of labor and the social ecology of production, structures of power and dominance, family organization and gender relations, kinship ties and marriage arrangements. In order to make our way into these complex African worlds, then, we begin by exploring the interior of contemporary Southern Tswana polities; thereafter, we shall locate them within the broader regional context.

THE UNIVERSE WITHIN

The most notable feature of "the ordinary life of a Bechuana community," it seems, was its dualistic quality: structured yet negotiable, regulated by conventional rules and practices yet enigmatical, fluid, and full of "internal strifes" (Mackenzie 1871:410–11). This dualism is clearly expressed in what a later observer was to dub "the sinuosity of native thought."[5] For example, in talking of the chief, Tswana accentuated his role in sustaining order—in its economic and spiritual, social and cosmological aspects, since these were indivisible (Mackenzie 1871:371)—and regarded his office as the epicenter of an elaborate administrative hierarchy. Thus, in the context of male initiation, a periodic rite involving the recreation of the chiefdom itself (J. Comaroff 1985:ch.4), he was known as *setlhaba-molao*, a compelling image that elided his personification of the law (*molao*) with his situation (*setlhaba*, "flat place atop a hill") at the apex of the polity.[6] And yet despite this, his legitimacy, indeed all relations and statuses throughout the *morafe* ("polity"), were often contested (see e.g., Moffat 1842:389; Solomon 1855: 47; Mackenzie 1871:410, 1883:231f.; J.L. Comaroff 1978). Even the law embodied by the ruler was impermanent. A Setswana proverb, also uttered in initiation rituals, declared that *molao sekhutlo, moelwa o ya*, "the law has an end, it can be left behind" (Brown 1926:87; *moelwa*, "left behind," derived from *go ela*, which also meant "to flow"). Or, as Brown (1926:87) put it, "The law is evanescent, temporary." One corollary of the shifting character of this world was that personal identities and positions, relationships and rank, groups and alliances, appeared to be the object of ongoing "work" (*tiro*), the active fabrication and negotiation of everyday life. These processes were given their meaning by a set of conventions that, later in the colonial era, would be rationalized as *mekgwa le melao ya Setswana*, "Tswana law and custom." As we shall see, the strong emphasis on the active construction of the social and material world had profound implications for prevailing notions of time, person, and practice.

A Southern Tswana polity of the early nineteenth century might be described from a number of contrasting perspectives. Not only was it capable of great variation over space and time, but no single folk model could have grasped it in its entirety. Depending on their positions in the social division of labor, some would have perceived it from the "bottom up" or the periphery inward, others from the "top down" or the center outward. Nonetheless, the dominant imagery of the period—inscribed in the spatial anatomy of the community, in mythico-historical representation, and so on—portrayed society as an hierarchical order; an order into which all citizens were integrated as members of a pyramid of residential and administrative units under the chiefship (Molema 1920:113; cf. Livingstone 1857:17; Burchell 1824: 2,513–14; Solomon 1855:46). All, that is, except for serfs. These people—mainly Sarwa ("bushmen"), Kgalagadi, and destitute Tswana—were regarded as less than fully social beings, "dogs" (Moffat 1842:383) who ought properly to inhabit the undomesticated reaches beyond human settlement (Moffat 1842:8; Holub 1881:1,258, 345f.; Mackenzie 1883:57f, 1871: 128f, 368). It was this centralized order that the missionaries and other early white observers understood to compose Tswana "tribes."

The Anatomy of the Polity

According to the dominant Tswana worldview of the time, then, the administrative hierarchy, with the chiefship (*bokgosi*) at its core, was a necessary condition for the persistence of civil society (*botho*, "socialized humanity"; cf. Setiloane 1976:32f.); whenever a community moved, its forms were laid out anew and the anatomy of the chiefdom was thereby recreated (Mackenzie 1871:370). In fact, the large town classically associated with "traditional" Tswana society (e.g., Schapera 1938; cf. Okihiro 1976:ch.2) was no more than this hierarchy in its architectural aspect. As the *axis mundi* of the polity, moreover, it loomed large in symbolic representations of space. Among other things, the town (*motse*) evoked the triumph of social order over the wild beyond the settlement—over the threateningly fecund, chaotic realm of nature unconfined. Being the nucleus about which the *motse* grew up, and without which it would instantly dissolve, the chiefship seemed to be the fountainhead of this triumph. At the same time it was a tenuous victory, one that had to be jealously protected, by politico-ritual means, under the aegis of a vigilant ruler. Of course, the authority of that ruler was potentiated by his control of just these means of symbolic production. Skillfully deployed, they could give him the wherewithal to wield a good deal of power.

Motse, in sum, did not merely translate as "town," its given definition in mission dictionaries.[7] It also connoted a "nucleus," the epicenter of the surrounding world. As both Barrow (1806:391) and Burchell (1824:2,517) noticed early on, circles and arcs were the primary motifs in Tswana architecture (see also Philip 1828:2,133). At the core of the precolonial *motse* was the chief's court which was ringed, concentrically, by (1) the residential quarters that composed the settlement; (2) a belt of fields and gardens, to which families took annually to cultivate their crops; (3) a band of pasturage dotted about by rude cattleposts (*meraka*); and (4) the bush beyond.[8] From the ruler's place (*kgosing*) to the fringe of the wild there radiated a number of pathways, the spines along which moved people and products, cattle and commerce, the traffic of everyday life (Campbell 1822:1,229). So intricate were these spatial arrangements that Campbell (1822:1,255) likened them, in one town, to the maze "at Hampton-court Palace."

Significantly, the plural form of *motse* (*metse*) also meant "water" (see Brown 1931:194), a critical source of life in this context and, not surprisingly, the symbol par excellence of growth and transformation. There is even some hint of a linguistic link between "town" and "semen" (*motsé*), whose metaphoric referents were equally wide (J. Comaroff 1985:ch.4). Water, in the form of rain (*pula*; also "wellbeing"), featured prominently in public ceremonial: for example, when a chief entered the court or closed a gathering, he greeted his people "*ka* [with] *pula!*" (Campbell 1822:2,157f.; Solomon 1855:47). The ruler was responsible for bringing the rain, either by his own effort or with the aid of rainmakers (Campbell 1822:2,197; Schapera 1971); to be sure, his success in this sphere was intimately connected to his legitimacy and his ability to keep the *motse* together. It was to be over rainmaking that chiefs and missionaries would have some of their most bitter confrontations (Comaroff and Comaroff 1986).

The administrative hierarchy itself consisted of four nesting levels: domestic units, local agnatic segments, wards, and the chiefdom.[9] Each marked out, at once, a domain of authority, a species of social group, and a set of habitual practices (*ka mekgwa,* "by convention")—practices at once political, economic, and social, for Tswana culture did not divide the work of daily life into discrete parts. At the base of the hierarchy a number of adjacent, agnatically-linked households formed a local segment. And two or more agnatically-related segments in turn made up the core of the ward (*kgotla*),[10] the most significant administrative constituency in the polity (Campbell 1813:187; see Schapera 1935). While a *kgotla* was seldom composed purely of patrikin, its headmanship—a position best conceived as the chiefship writ small—devolved within the agnatic core. Ostensibly, its succession was regulated by strict genealogical seniority;[11] in practice, the rules were ambiguous enough to make competition for the office an everyday occurrence (Moffat 1842:389; Mackenzie 1871:400; J.L. Comaroff 1978). The ward was an aggressively self-contained circle of earthen homesteads, whose labyrinthine rear courtyards formed a dense patchwork of domestic spaces—all of which was to be taken by the Protestants as proof that the Tswana lived in a state of primitive communism (see e.g., Mackenzie, in Dachs 1972: 652). Their impression was reinforced by the fact that there lay, at the ward center, a communal cattle-byre and a public enclosure, the court of its headman and the venue of all collective activities.

The sociopolitical units that made up a chiefdom, we stress, were not segmentary lineages or corporate descent groups—even though office depended on genealogical reckoning, and patrikin cooperated (and competed) with one another. Above the level of the household, it seems, agnation served mainly to order rank and access to positions within the administrative hierarchy—positions that carried with them a good deal of control over people and property, land and labor, communal action and court cases (see e.g., Philip 1828,2:132). As this suggests, agnation laid down the cultural terms for the exercise of power and the legitimation of material inequality. Here as in other places relations of gender and generation within the domestic family provided a "natural" model of social dominance and subordination. But kinship was not the basis of collective activity on the part of bounded groups.

Agnatic politics, then, was the stuff of the public domain, from the household to the chiefship. The documentary record is full of accounts of royal patrikin plotting against one another; of men fighting with their paternal uncles and patrilateral cousins—even killing their fathers (e.g., Campbell 1822:1,314–16)—in struggles for power and position. It was the context in which males sought to "eat" each other by means as diverse as the creation of economic debt and clientage, the resort to sorcery, and litigation.[12] These processes, however, involved more than just the passing effort of rivals to best one another in games of wealth and influence. For reasons that lay deep in the structure of the Tswana world of the period (see below), men were compelled to construct their own identities, often by "overshadowing" the viability of others (Brown 1926:137f.). Agnatic conflict might superficially have had the familiar ring of politics everywhere. But as we shall see shortly, it ran to the existential core of personhood and social identity. For now, though, the point is that, being the medium through which relations of power and production were worked out, it animated the polity and its centralized administrative order.

And yet, at the same time, the Tswana world appears to have contained within it other, centrifugal forces that encouraged the disaggregation of the community. In order to understand these, however, we must turn from the anatomy of the chiefdom as a whole to the atoms of culture and society on which it was founded. These lay, first, in the household at the base of the polity and, second, in marriage. For households bore within them all the raw materials, the signs and relations, from which the social fabric was woven. And marriage, it seems clear in retrospect, was the mechanism whereby these units were brought into being and drawn into sundry kinds of linkages with others; it was the vehicle, in other words, by means of which the social and symbolic division of labor was made tangible.

Atoms of Culture, Elements of Society
1. The House and Beyond

In the early nineteenth-century Tswana imagination, the quintessential domestic unit was a polygynous household (Lichtenstein 1973:76), although polygamy was in fact the preserve of the rich and powerful (Lichtenstein 1973:77; Campbell 1822:1,66). This compound unit subsumed all the elements of rank and relationship, gender and generation, persons and property, from which arose the segmentary structure of the *morafe*.[13] As a contemporary idiom put it, *motse o lwapeng*, "the town [administrative hierarchy] is [rooted] in the domestic courtyard" (Brown 1926:201). Not only did the polygamous household form the base of the polity; it also underpinned the symbolic construction of the social world. Indeed, when the Nonconformists later tried, as did most missionaries, to banish the "barbarism" of plural marriage, they had scant idea what was at issue. Some, it is true, understood that the worldly authority of chiefs and royals would suffer. But none were aware quite how profoundly they were tampering with the invisible scaffolding of the sociocultural order.

Polygamous families were themselves made up of uterine houses—the "atoms" of the social system, so to speak—each of which consisted of a wife and her children (Brown 1926:48). These houses and their offspring were ranked, but the *mekgwa* governing seniority seem to have been ambiguous, and they were further complicated by the practice of the levirate and sororate (see e.g., Campbell 1822:1,226). Hence it was possible, in principle at least, to dispute their relative standing. Nor was this a trivial matter. Since property and position depended on it, houses often contested their rank, the interests of "children of one womb" (*setsalò*; also "allies") being inimical to those of their half-siblings—and, in the next generation, to those of their paternal uncles and cousins. This is why, for Southern Tswana, the courtly politics of agnatic rivalry, and the effort of men to "eat" one another, were born in the household. What Mackenzie (1871:410) saw as "casuistic difficulties as to relationship and property arising out of polygamy" were regarded as a lamentable but inevitable feature of everyday existence. These "difficulties," as he notes (1871:411, 1883:227), were heightened by the tendency of mothers to guard tenaciously over the fortunes of their progeny. It is interesting that the Setswana word for polygyny, *lefufa*, was also the generic term for "jealousy"; that the vernacular for "cowife" (*mogadikane*) derived from *go gadika*, "to rival, to annoy," or, even more vividly, "to cause a pain in the stomach" (J.L. Comaroff n.d.:ch.2).

The integrity of the house (*ntlo*) was expressed in the most taken-for-granted of social forms. Not only did the everyday politics of rank and status underscore its uniqueness and indivisibility;[14] the only term in the kinship lexicon for a discrete, impermeable group of agnatic peers was *setsalò* (from *tsala*; "womb"), a singular noun which implied the merged social identity of those born of one mother. The same symbolic point was made by prevailing leviratic and sororatic arrangements (Campbell 1822:1,212; A. Smith 1939: 1,272), whose stated object was to ensure that a house never died. Thus a woman who gave birth on behalf of a barren (or deceased) sister or cousin was known as *seantlo*, the personification of a *ntlo*. Similarly, a levir, taking his agnate's widow to "raise seed" for the dead man (Campbell 1822:1,226; Mackenzie 1871:364), did so in order to "enter [his] house" (*go tsena mo tlung*; *tlung* is the locative form of *ntlo*). Yet more remarkable, perhaps, was the resemblance between the architecture of the house and the female reproductive anatomy, a resemblance faithfully (if unintentionally) captured in Burchell's careful sketchplan of a Tlhaping dwelling (1824:2,plate 5; cf. Barrow 1806:390–91).

The cultural point also had an economic aspect: houses were the primary units of production and property. Just as every wife had a hut and a courtyard of her own, so each was allotted a field to till (e.g., Bain 1949:55; Lichtenstein 1973:76; Campbell 1813:184). Its yield was inalienably hers to use in nurturing her *loumo*, the "fruit of her womb." In addition, while a woman might also feed her spouse and contribute to the cooking pot on the communal hearth, her grain was always kept in separate storage and could not be taken without her permission. The individuation of houses—their simultaneous symbolic and economic integrity, productive and reproductive fertility—was signaled in a phatic voice at the annual firstfruit rites. According to the missionary-ethnographer Willoughby (1928:231), himself an eye-witness to part of the proceedings among northern Tswana later in the century:

Nothing is more remarkable in the Becwana [Tswana] usage for this festival than its linking of sexual congress between husband and wife with the fruitfulness of the fields which they sow. It is a hard and fast rule that every man should sleep with his chief wife on the night of the

festival, and that he should sleep on successive nights with his secondary wives in the order of their standing in his family—for each of these
wives sows her own field.

Many women took pains to ensure that the perimeters of their productive land, like those of the dwelling-place and the body, were medicinally
"pegged out" (Brown 1926:132, 136)—a symbolic act which at once for-
tified the house against intrusive outsiders and declared its unyielding
boundedness.

In its social aspect the integrity of the house was most clearly marked
out by its exclusive set of matrilateral ties. Of all the things bestowed collectively on members of a uterine group, the only one that they had neither to
share nor to contest was their access to their maternal kin. The bond between a mother's brother (*malome*) and his sister's children, unaffected by
considerations of property and status, was characterized by practical support, moral solidarity, and ritual exchange.[15] Unlike agnatic relations, which
were always ranked and potentially antagonistic, matrilateral ties were un-
ranked and privileged; they bore not the slightest hint of enmity or duplicity.
Where patrikin "ate" (*ja*) each other, often by means of the malevolent
victuals of sorcery (*sejeso*), matrikin nourished one another (J. Comaroff
1985:48). "A man and his mother's brother never fight," we were told repeatedly by Tshidi in the 1970's; and, while we cannot be sure that precisely
this formula was uttered in the rather different Tswana world of a century
and a half ago, the social convention to which it attests is known to have
extended far back into the past (Mackenzie 1871:410f, 1883:226f.).

As all this suggests, the opposition between agnation and matrilaterality
ran to the very heart of Tswana society and culture and was closely connected to the contrast between male and female. Here we offer just two
instances of the opposition, instances that will later turn out to be salient.
The first concerns the symbolic construction of space. It is notable that,
while the activities characteristic of agnatic relations centered on the communal arenas monopolized by men (the open front yard of the homestead,
the ward meeting-place, the royal court), the inviolable backyard (*segotlo*) of a
mother, a sister, or a maternal relative connoted sanctuary, privacy, and support (Solomon 1855:42). It was where females and the males linked through
them might confer in secret, where a man might entrust his most personal
possessions and communications. The famed Ngwato chief Sekgoma, it is
told, always took to his mother's *segotlo* at times of trial: on her premises he
stored his effects, held secret conclaves with his political intimates, and hid
when his office and life appeared threatened (Mackenzie 1871:410f, 1883:
250, 232). Indeed, a person found guilty of a serious misdeed by the chief's
court—itself the pinnacle of the male-centric world of agnatic politics—

might try to flee to the yard of the ruler's mother. Those who were successful went free. For she was *mohumagadi* ("great woman"), the mother of all; her *segotlo*, courtyard of the nation, could give sanctuary to anyone.

The second instance involves relations of production, which were informed by the same sociospatial symbolism. As we shall see, cattle, the most valued of all possessions, were the preserve of males, and they mediated agnatic bonds even though they regularly flowed through sisters and wives (see below). In the form of loans (*mahisa*), they were a means by which their owners might extend themselves and their social influence over others. As bridewealth, they traced out complex patterns of alliance among men. Within the town, beasts were kept in pens, at the center of the ward, from which women were debarred (Mackenzie 1871:499; cf. Campbell 1822:2,254); outside, they were ranched at posts tended by the sons, male clients, or servants of their holders. By contrast, the less valued labor of cultivation rested on females and on relations articulated through them. At her fields during the arable season a woman cooperated less with her husband's agnates than with her own kin. Furthermore, it was in her *segotlo*, her private space, that she processed and distributed her grain. Little wonder, as Willougby (1928:57) reports, that a "patriarch" was interred inside his byre "so that he may hear the tramp of his cattle as they go out to graze in the morning and return for safety at sundown." Or that his wife was buried, watched by her maternal uncle, beneath the threshing-floor "that she may hear the thud of the flails, threshing out each new crop." All this was a far cry from the division of labor, the images of gender, or for that matter the iconography of death, to which the missionaries would introduce the unsuspecting Tswana.

The roots of the opposition between agnation and matrilaterality, as we have said, lay in the house itself, and specifically in the contrast between fraternal relations and the brother-sister bond. This is clearly evident when the unit is placed within its developmental cycle. Notwithstanding its integrity, the uterine group had to divide as it matured. For when brothers reached adulthood, they had no option but to establish their own conjugal households. Otherwise they remained incompletely socialized beings—in Setswana, *makgope* (v. *kgopa*, "offend" or "vex"), a synonym for "large yellow locusts," the rapacious parasites that laid waste the productive efforts of others as they ate (Brown 1931:129). But the moment these men married, their concerns became separate and antithetical. At roughly the same time too their sisters were removed, with their possessions, to the homes created for them by their spouses.[16] Thus fields and beasts that had quite literally been "husbanded" together—whose fortunes had been united in common purpose, prosperity, or adversity—were finally split up, each to go their own ways.

As the figures around whom a house divided into units of inimical interest and unequal rank, men were cast as the "natural" protagonists of their own children against their brothers, brothers' children, and other patrikin.[17] Thus it was that the germ of antagonism and asymmetry born in the fraternal bond spread throughout the agnatic domain. Or so the Tswana told each other in folk homilies, some of them much like the Cain and Abel story (Brown 1926:169f.). Nor were such conflicts of interest a matter of personal volition. "The internal strifes . . . which characterize the ordinary life of a Bechuana community," observed by Mackenzie (1871:411; above, p. 128), flowed unavoidably from "this system." In contradistinction, the brother-sister tie lay at the core of the domain of matrilateral relations, and it signified all the social values, the moral certainties, and material complicities associated with those relations. The privileged status of the bond was symbolically called into being when a father "cattle-linked" the children of a house into mixed pairs. Once tied to a particular woman, her brother was obliged to represent her and look after her wellbeing. Reciprocally, she cooked and cared for him before he married and continued to support him throughout his life. When she had children, moreover, he became their "special" uncle: he would counsel them in their most intimate affairs and take the initiative in protecting them from their agnates.

The defining feature of cattle-linkage was the fact that a brother became the recipient of his sister's bridewealth (A. Smith 1939:1,345). These beasts, it was said, were to succour her in times of need. They might also be put to just one other purpose: to secure *his* union. This seems rarely to have happened, as far as we can tell,[18] but the *mokgwa* itself marked the social and moral complementarity of the two siblings, the merging of their interests and identities. Recall that marriage elevated man from a hapless "locust" to an active subject in the world. The cosmogonic theme of females giving to males the raw materials with which to engage in the social process was common in Tswana metaphorical discourses. Not only did the role of marriage prestations (*bogadi*, lit. "womanhood"; Brown 1926:61) in linked siblingship make the point with archetypal clarity; it also tied it to the antinomy between matrilaterality and agnation. For these cattle established the brother-sister bond—and hence the matrilateral domain—as the guarantor of a man's social capital and his distinct persona. It ensured that, whatever his circumstances, he would not lack the currency with which to enter the public arena and negotiate his place in the agnatic scheme of things. That the beasts were termed "womanhood" underscored the link between matrilateral ties and femaleness; it was on the back of both, so to speak, that a man might participate in the political domain.[19]

The social anatomy of the house, then, held the symbolic key to Tswana economy and society (Bourdieu 1977:89). Its constituent signs and relations lay behind the opposition between agnation and matrilaterality and gave form to the architecture of the chiefdom, its everyday social and productive processes, its discourses of property and power, its gender relations, and its division of labor. However, while great weight was placed on the distinction between agnation and matrilaterality, this was not posited as an opposition of equals. To the contrary, agnation took clear priority in authoritative representations of the world. Being the principle by which persons and groupings were integrated into the hierarchical polity, from the household to the chiefship, it encompassed all other forms of relationship. We have seen that the matricentric house was incorporated within and regulated by the agnatically ranked, male-centric household; so too the *segotlo* of a woman, her domestic sanctuary and the point of contact with her matrikin, was enclosed by the front yard of the homestead and by the *kgotla* and cattle-byre beyond, all quintessentially agnatic arenas. Indeed, an incessant stream of political, social, and ritual acts reiterated the precedence of agnation over matrilaterality, of males over females, of pastoral production over cultivation, of the dictates of the public arena over those of the domestic sphere.

This pattern of hierarchical encompassment had many applications. For example, capital towns like Dithakong (Lattakoo) were ordered along an axis marked out by the royal court at its hub and the houses along its perimeter. From the vantage of the former, *kaha ntlè* (the "core") was the place, even the body, of the ruler; *ha gare* (outside) was the domestic periphery and the arable belt beyond. Leaving their houses, women moved out seasonally to the fields, bringing back the harvest, while men moved daily inward to the ward and chiefly courts—an arrangement which, as we shall see, the missionaries took to be "most unnatural." These movements retraced the flow of value that animated the chiefdom itself, spelling out the connection between the communal center and the domestic periphery. Thus males could only enter the public arena as heads of households that produced their own subsistence and, better yet, surpluses with which to feed retainers and clients—and to pay tribute. In this, they drew upon the agricultural and domestic work of their womenfolk, whose labors were thereby appropriated to subsidize the political exchanges on which the *morafe* ("polity") was built. Nevertheless, it was the sovereign, as the embodiment of the agnatic principle and maleness, who was seen as the *fons et origo* of the productive process. He alone was the guarantor of the rain, "owner" of the land, intercessor with his ancestors, and "giver of the seed-time" (see p. 146).

The general point was dramatized in firstfruits ceremonies, which acted out, anew each year, the dependency and subordination of women to men, domestic units to the royal center. Similarly, the origin myth of the male initiation, a rite in which boys were removed from the household and inducted into the public domain, told how the social order was born when the raw fertility of women was harnessed by men and put to collective ends (J. Comaroff 1985:85). The same theme was also played out in another key. The productive and reproductive labors of females, vital though they were, were often laid waste by sorcery, the byproduct of agnatic politics. This, it is said, was an unavoidable cost of communal life. On the other hand, because (male) political and ritual enterprises could be jeopardized by the polluting heat carried within their bodies, females were excluded from public spaces, especially the royal court. They were also debarred from the management of cattle, the major repository of wealth and currency of power.

2. Marriage and the Paradoxes of Social Life

We said earlier that marriage was the mechanism whereby houses, and the households of which they were part, were drawn into relations with others. It was also fundamental to the social and symbolic construction of the Tswana world at large. Of course, matrimony and family were every bit as crucial to the Protestant view of the sacred human estate (above, chapter 2). But the manner in which they were regarded could hardly have been more different. That this would become a site of enduring cultural struggle between the Europeans and the Africans seems to have been overdetermined from the start. In conventional anthropological terms Tswana were "endogamous."[20] More precisely, they preferred to marry cousins of all types, including father's brother's daughters [FBDs]. It has long been noted that the coexistence of such endogamous arrangements with an agnatic "ideology"—i.e., a stress on agnation in ordering sociopolitical and material relations—tends to produce a field of contradictory and ambiguous ties.[21] Typically, this is explained by the fact that close kin unions create multiple bonds, bonds which are *at once* agnatic, matrilateral, and affinal. Repeat such unions over the generations and a myriad of overlapping ties, often of astonishing complexity, is the outcome. What is more, the various strands of these multiple ties may entail incompatible canons of behavior, as they do, say, in cultures where agnation and matrilaterality have diametrically opposed attributes. This, as we already know, was the case among the early nineteenth-century Southern Tswana, for whom the antinomy was especially acute—so much so that they seem to have had no kinship term for a "multiply linked relative." Indeed, the very notion of a bond being both agnatic and matrilateral offended the semantic basis of their universe. A relationship simply could not be simultaneously hostile and supportive, politically negotiable and morally absolute—any more than it was plausible for the bush and the town to occupy the same space. And yet by marrying as they did, Tswana created just such relations.

How, then, did they reconcile this apparent paradox? The answer was that they could not. Social relations had, of need, to be managed, reduced, and defined in the practical contexts of everyday life. Significant others had to be construed as one thing or another: senior or junior agnates, matrilaterals, affines or outsiders. It follows that these terms came to reflect the negotiated content of relations; negotiated, that is, in the course of transactions over property and rank. Thus, when kinsmen were caught up in competitive relations, actively or potentially, the agnatic tie between them was emphasized. However else they were connected, in other words, that tie took precedence as long as they were sufficiently equal in status and wealth to try and "eat" each other. Conversely, when a household emerged as clearly subordinate or superordinate to another—where the bond between their heads was so *un*equal as to preclude rivalry—a matrilateral label was applied. For here the bond lost its competitive content, often as a result of one agnate having "eaten" another, and became one of complementarity—the senior partner exchanging social, ritual, and material patronage for the political loyalty and clientage of the junior. By contrast to both agnation and matrilaterality, affinity described a partnership of easy cooperation and mutual interest between two households. It appears that affinal terms were also used when "in-laws" wished to sustain the ambiguity of their tie.

All this returns us to the dualistic nature of Tswana society—to the fact that, from within, it appeared highly ordered yet fluid, governed by *mekgwa* yet eminently negotiable. Insofar as existing marriage arrangements yielded an ambiguous, contradictory field of relations, they threw the onus on men (and by extension on their households) for building networks of linkages and thereby constructing their social identities. Individuals had no choice but to act upon the world—even inertia took on the character of interested activity. No wonder that this world seemed to be driven by practical activity; that groups and alliances were seen to be a product of coincident interest; that individuated households were regarded as the critical social units; that the community was thought to be redolent with intrigue, sorcery, and nefarious secret deeds; that social reality was perceived to be shifting and enigmatical. No wonder, too, that early European visitors should find these Africans recognizably "political"; that is, strategic, clever, and self-interested in their dealings among themselves and with outsiders (see e.g., Burchell 1824:2,554f.; Moffat 1842:254, 309; Livingstone 1857:21f.; Mackenzie 1871:371f.; J. Comaroff 1985:27). At the same time, because social rank and political relations were always indexed in the given categories of Setswana, they never failed to measure up to expectation. It is absolutely true, for instance, that men did not compete or fight with their matrilateral kin (above, p. 134); if they had, the latter would have been agnates. Similarly, seniors invariably did take precedence over their juniors in matters of succession, inheritance, and authority; it was power that decided rank, not the other way around. And so, by virtue of a cultural tautology, the social field was at once a structured order of relations *and* a fluid environment in which persons and identities had actively to be constructed.

Another dimension of Tswana conjugal arrangements is also salient here. If the contrivance of relations was the key to the creation and transaction of social value, marriage was seen to offer a ready context in which such relations could be negotiated. With hindsight it is clear that the structure of conjugal choice reflected the major avenues of social management open to men. Three options seem to have presented themselves, and, because affinity involved a tie between households, each had different connotations: (1) unions between unrelated spouses spoke of the effort to forge alliances beyond the field of close kin; (2) those with matrilaterals entailed the continuation of existing bonds of complementarity; and (3) agnatic marriages opened the way for males to try to "eat" each other and so reduce rivals to (matrilateral) clientage. While such managerial activity was not confined to the sphere of marriage, this range of choice indicates that it took three primary forms: the creation of new alliances among equals; the perpetuation of inequalities; and the attempt to transform ties of relative equality into unequal ones. For individuals, these forms charted the practical navigation of the social universe, which is why ruling cadres were so quick to object when missions sought to meddle with "marriage customs" (see below). From a structural perspective, they implanted within the Southern Tswana world countervailing tendencies toward inequality and egalitarianism.[22]

We shall come across these tendencies again when we turn to the political economy of the period. For now it is enough to note that they were realized, in ever changing proportion to each other, in the course of everyday activity; that much was assured by the structured fluidity of the social field. And, in the process, the observable contours of Tswana economy and society took their dynamic shape. Translating this into indigenous categories, social practice, itself given meaning by the signs and relations rooted in the house, was the "work" (*tiro*) by which persons made themselves and, in so doing, made and remade their world.

Work and Social Being

In Setswana, *go dira* has long meant "to make," "to do," or "to cause to happen." It includes a wide range of acts, from cultivation, cooking, and creating a family to pastoralism, politics, and ritual performance. By extension, *tiro* has usually been translated as "[a] work" and emphasizes the *act* of fabrication (Brown 1931:308). It yields positive value in the form of persons, things, and relations, although it may be undone by sorcery and other malign forces. But *tiro* appears never to have been regarded as an abstract quality or a commodity to be exchanged. It cannot exist as alienable labor power. In the 1970's we were told that, *bogologolo* ("long ago"), even the toil of a serf was only available to his master as part of a total bond of interdependence. It could not be given over to another person unless the relationship itself was transferred. In short, "work" was, and is, the creative process inherent in all human activity; it is expressed in the "building up" of self and others in the course of daily life. In doing it, Alverson (1978:132) notes of the modern Tswana, "an individual not only produces for himself, but actually produces his entitlement to be a social person."

As this suggests, work has always involved the construction of a person in relation to others. The point is well captured in the various inflections of *go dira*. Its simple reflexive form, *go itira*, means "to make oneself" or "to pose as," a notion with ambiguous moral implications. It speaks of a form of self-enhancement both egocentric and antisocial; hence the common phrase *go itira motho* (lit. "to make oneself a distinct person") connotes "to be proud" or "haughty." By contrast, *go itirela*, the reflexive extension of *direla* ("work for"), translates as "to make (work, do) for oneself" in a positive sense. Alverson (1978:134) found, as did we, that this term continues to embody a critical set of values for Tswana: the building of wealth in family and social connections, clients and cattle, position and political influence. Such undertakings are dubbed "great works," a usage which indicates that the process of their production is inseparable from the value produced. The process itself depends on an active subject extending himself, in time and space, by cultivating a network of relations. To wit, the significance of objects, most notably cattle, is that they may be used to weave a chain of rights and claims over others (cf. Evans-Pritchard 1940:89); similarly, power is held to flow from the capacity to spread one's control across the social field.

While the early linguistic evidence lacks detail,[23] there is none to suggest that the meaning of terms like *tiro*, *itira*, and *itirela* changed much before the 1890's, when the first major Setswana dictionary was published.[24] It is true that, as the colonial era unfolded, they were to take on new poetic and ideological referents, especially in contrast to the European concept of labor (Comaroff and Comaroff 1987). But at the time with which we are concerned, it seems clear that *tiro/itirela* connoted the effort to fashion an identity and do "great works" by husbanding material assets and wealth in people. Cast in the active voice, it evoked an image of social life as a continuous, creative flow of events through which persons worked to construct themselves in relation to others. And it accorded with a particular notion of time (*lobaka*), which, far from being an abstract resource to be spent or wasted, was itself to be created as an integral part of the social world made by human action and interaction.

This imagery is also tied to another familiar fact: that, here as elsewhere in Africa, the building of identities, relations, and statuses was an active, ongoing process. For example, a Tswana marriage was forged by a gradual, cumulative series of incidents and exchanges, the last of which might occur after the death of one or both spouses (J.L. Comaroff 1980). And, as the union was nurtured and grew, so too did the identities, the "greatness," of the parties to it. In fact marriages, like most relationships, are best described as having been processes of becoming, not states of being. They existed (or, more accurately, matured) in the continuous present as long as men and women worked on them. Even in the 1970's Southern Tswana were reluctant to define social ties or personal identities as fixed states—and so to close them off from the possibility of growth or transformation. Such enquiries as "Are you married?" or "Do you have children?" were often answered with a curt "Not yet!" (*ga e se*)—even by very old men and women. John Campbell (1822:1,309) heard much the same thing in 1820, when he encountered an ancient Tlhaping rainmaker who sought material wealth and ritual knowledge and was prepared to travel far in pursuit of them. When the incredulous missionary asked how one so aged could still expect to become affluent, the man replied in all seriousness that "he was but a youth, [and] at any rate there was no harm in his getting rich, he could leave it to his children. . . ." Relations and identities were potentialities to be realized in the unremitting work of daily existence, *tiro* that continued until life itself gave out.

The work of "building oneself up" and of creating social value was not easy, however. For it was always threatened by negative forces, driven by conflicts within the social order itself. Above all else, there were always agnatic rivals seeking to "eat" one. A man who had been eaten—the metaphor suggested feminization—became not only a junior in rank but also a client, and could eventually lose all self-determination (Burchell 1824: 2,272, 346ff.; Lichtenstein 1973:66ff.; Campbell 1822:2,210f.). He became, as Willoughby (1932:227) was to note, "absorbed by another personality." Such a man and his family might be called on to supply labor to his patron during the agricultural season. Like a woman, he had relatively little control over his own movement in space and time—let alone over the movement of others. Sorcery also played a large part in these processes of destruction, its malevolent influence undermining all positive social activity. Not surprisingly, "great work" included the protection of one's efforts, and those of one's dependents, from the ever present danger of being undone (*dirologa*); men took pains to fortify their homesteads and other holdings against attack (Willoughby 1932:96; Lichtenstein 1973:73).

In stark contrast to the images of work soon to be nurtured by the mission, then, *tiro* and *itirela* invoked a world in which the making of the person, the accumulation of wealth and rank, and the protection of an autonomous identity were indivisible aspects of social practice. The converse of self-construction, as we said earlier, was the eclipse of personal viability, an over-shadowing caused by the invasion of malign human or spiritual forces. In extreme form it led to the death of the self. Brown (1926:137–38), who observed cases later in the century, describes the symptoms with chilling detachment:

> When a man's relatives notice that his whole nature is changed, that the light of the mind is darkened and character has deteriorated so that it may be said that the real manhood is dead, though the body still lives; when they realize that to all intents and purposes the human is alienated from fellowship with his kith and kin, then they apply to him a name (*sebibi* or *sehihi*), which signifies that though the body lives and moves it is only a grave, a place where something has died or been killed. The essential manhood is dead. It is no uncommon thing to hear a person spoken of as being dead when he stands before you visibly alive. When this takes place it always means that there has been an overshadowing of the true relationships of life. . . .

The object of *tiro* was to avoid social death: to continue producing oneself by producing people, relations, and things. But not everyone was equally capable of such activity. Chiefs and rainmakers, for instance, had unusually creative powers. Women, feminized clients, and serfs, on the other hand, lacked the capacities of the most ordinary of free men. And they were a lot less equal.

The stress upon self-contrivance and the active making of the social world led Western observers from the very first to describe the Tswana as rampant individualists (Burchell 1824:2,554; Campbell 1822:1,243). Even those missionaries who most rued their lack of private property seemed to detect a deep individualistic streak in them (Mackenzie 1871: 402, 501f.; Livingstone 1857:21). We have seen how the contemporary structure of their society served to individuate identities and ambiguate relations, making it necessary for men to construct their social ties and subjectivities—an activity visible both in the politics of everyday life and in the management of crises through litigation or healing. But such practices also revealed something else: an ontology according to which persons, spirit forces, and material objects participated in and could affect each other. Witness the case of an elder who was terrified lest the "spirit" of a powerful chief, living many miles away, might hear words uttered in criticism of his royal personage and inflict awesome mystical punishment (Campbell 1822:1,146). Or another, of a young man who was killed by the malign will of his affines, born in a bodily ornament given to him as a gift (Campbell

1822:1,192). This was a far cry from the ontology at the base of modern Western individualism, in which spirit and matter, people and objects, were definitively set apart, and in which every man and woman was responsible, on their own account and in their own right, for their spiritual, social, and material situation in a radically disenchanted universe. In short, while both cultures placed a great deal of weight on the active subject—the human being acting upon the world—the two forms of individualism had fundamentally different ontological roots. The Tswana might have recognized something familiar in the Protestant notion of the self and its construction. But as we shall see, their own conceptions of personhood and the production of value were to remain quite distinct, even under the prolonged assault of the civilizing mission. Apart from all else, these conceptions were difficult to disentangle from the social essence of material life; that is, from relations of production.

Relations of Production, Structures of Authority

In contemporary Tswana society, as we would expect, relations of production were centered on the household and the uterine houses within it.[25] Domestic units regularly cooperated with one another and exchanged labor and goods, but they worked hard to retain their own autonomy. Within them activities were sharply differentiated by gender and generation, and were part of a more pervasive division of tasks in an economy based on agriculture and pastoralism, supplemented by hunting and gathering (see e.g., Barrow 1806:394; Campbell 1822:2,60; Burchell 1824:2,425, 564). While cultivation yielded the bulk of daily subsistence, the cattle herded by preadolescent boys, impoverished clients, and non-Tswana serfs[26] provided for the ritual diet and for social exchange. Women also gathered the fruits of the wild, just as in the male sphere pastoralism was augmented by hunting. As noted before, however, these were not merely complementary spheres of production and use. The labor of women, youths, and retainers laid down the material base on which rested the transactions of agnatic politics; moreover, by freeing adult males from the need to contribute to the physical reproduction of the household, it allowed them to engage in the public domain (Burchell 1824:2,347; Lichtenstein 1973:76f.).

The contrast between the genders was reiterated in the way in which each was held to relate to, and produce from, the natural world. Women, corn, and bushfoods represented a fragile, unstable culling of the wild; men, stock, and game evoked the potent, stable domination of its forces. Cattle were the very embodiment of reliability and control over nature (Moffat 1842:451). Mobile in the face of drought and disaster, they were largely self-reproducing. Grain, on the other hand, was vulnerable to the climate, and crop failure often promised to wipe out seed altogether. Cows predictably yielded milk as a finished victual; the agricultural counterpart, corn beer, had to be made by women in a delicate operation that was easily disrupted, not least by their own bodily pollution. Indeed, the entire arable cycle was metaphorically linked to procreation, both being associated with instability and the risk of miscarriage.

The notion that pastoralism was an activity far more controlled than cultivation was reinforced by the perception that livestock gave security against crop failure. As Grove (1989:164) reminds us, severe droughts in the early, middle, and late years of the century devastated the indigenous economies of southern Africa and were to play into other forces of change on the subcontinent. In the short run, however, the relative capacity of herds to withstand such catastrophes, and to recover from them, seems to have confirmed the Tswana view of their enduring value in the struggle against the forces of nature. But the worth of domesticated beasts within the overall economy of signs and means stretched well beyond considerations of dietary utility or disaster insurance. If agriculture allowed men to subsist by the toil of others, cattle were the media for expanding their social identities.[27] Their herds enabled them to establish enduring bonds within and between communities; to communicate with the ancestral realm; to arrange marriages and so acquire reproductive rights and labor; and, especially through the loan of stock (*mahisa*), to forge relations of inequality and clientship. Burchell (1824:2,272, 347) was quick to observe that, for Tlhaping, "wealth" and "power" were synonymous—and that cattle were the key to both. These animals had not only the capacity to create and embody value but also the wherewithal to permit its transformation. In the context of exchange, sacrifice, and ritual commensality they could construct or disentangle human identities and relations, and in rites of passage their slaughter marked the alteration of social status (Willoughby 1928:187, 196, 330). The close iconic connections between beasts and humans did not escape the notice of the more acute among the early European visitors. Wrote Campbell (1822:2,206):

> When a woman has twins, one of the children is put to death. Should a cow have two calves, one of them is either killed or driven away. . . .
> When cattle die by disease, the proprietors must stick up a reed on the fence at the door. If any of the family are sick, a similar signal is placed on the outside, intimating that none must enter, unless invited.

Cattle, in sum, were the pliable symbolic vehicles through which men formed and reformed their world of social and spiritual relations. Deep into the twentieth century, long after a rinderpest pandemic and global political and economic forces had undermined the material bases of pastoralism among the Tswana, livestock would remain signs of enduring social wealth—albeit in a radically transformed environment (Comaroff and Comaroff 1987, 1990; Alverson 1978; cf. Ferguson 1985 on Lesotho).

Apart from their capacity to stand for particular identities and bonds, cattle also validated the authority of a specific worldview and the social order of which it was part. Thus they could only be owned by adult male citizens, whose identity they bore, and they had to be kept apart from females, to whom they had an innate antipathy (Mackenzie 1871:499; Campbell 1822:2,254; see above). As fully domesticated creatures, they were unfit possessions for beings themselves not fully socialized—women, children, and subject peoples—who were unable to control the value contained in them. Such persons were said to lack the distinctively male quality of endurance in time, a quality enshrined in agnatic genealogies, ancestorhood, and memorable public events. Of course, livestock also indexed the fact that, while all free men were equal, some were always more equal than others. Not only were they a medium of agnatic politics—wherein inequality was socially produced—but the essence of the chiefship lay in the fact that its holder owned the largest herd in the *morafe* (Lichtenstein 1930:2,413; Burchell 1824:2,347).

If Tswana economy was founded on the contrast between pastoralism and agriculture, male and female, it was also caught up in a tension between the centralized controls vested in the chiefship and the demands of domestic production. While all households were domiciled in towns, from which women took off for the arable season and youths were sent out to tend cattle, the regulation of residence and movement was a royal prerogative. A recurrent theme in both the practical management and the ritual symbolism of state power, the chief's control of space and time underpinned his dominion over the domestic periphery and its surpluses. Before he "gave out the seed time" (Willoughby 1928:226f.) each year, the ruler had the women of the community plant a field for him. Restricting their dispersal, therefore, was an aspect of his mobilization of tributary labor; anyone who left for their fields before the appointed moment courted severe punishment (cf. Schapera 1943:184, 1971:74). But the matter went yet deeper. The entire fabric of the polity, its administrative hierarchy and authority structure, was located in the town. Without the latter the chiefship became an empty shell. According to received convention, the temporal power of its holder rested heavily on his right to appoint men to offices (Lichtenstein 1930:2,414); to distribute land (Campbell 1822:2,193; Burchell 1824:2,348); to receive a portion of the spoils of raiding and hunting (Lichtenstein 1930:2,414; Burchell 1824:2,545; Livingstone 1857:48); to call up regiments for war and public works (Mackenzie 1871:375ff.); and to regulate external trade (Burchell 1824:2,539; Campbell 1822:2,194). All of these rights were seen to depend on the continued centralization of the *morafe*. As Lichtenstein (1930,2:413) put it, "The power of the chief . . . [was] a natural consequence of [the Tswana] having permanent habitations."

This pattern of centralization was in the material *dis*interest of household producers, however. In an arid region where rains were unpredictable and fell unevenly over the land, the timing of agricultural tasks was crucial. The evidence seems to favor Livingstone's (1857:22) view that Tswana had profound knowledge of their environment, notwithstanding the loudly asserted opinions of some of his brethren who held them responsible for the ecological ills they suffered (see Grove 1989). They appear to have been aware, for instance, that each day passing between the first rains and the sowing of their gardens would diminish their harvest. Yet in deciding on the "time for beginning to sow," rulers seem to have waited for rainfall at either the capital or their own holdings. The delay, along with the days spent on the royal field, prevented most women from planting at the best moment. This material factor, though, was only one piece of a larger picture. By its nature, cultivation involved dispersal and, therefore, was the very antithesis of centralization. In a world where the unit of production was socially individuated—and its independence culturally valued—the tension between chiefly control and household autonomy hovered close to the surface.

Many Tswana showed their antipathy to centralized control by leaving the town to set up permanent rural homes whenever they could. For those who could not depend on the labor of serfs and clients, dispersal was often preferable to participation at the center in poverty. Not only might their material fortunes improve, but they would avoid the risk of being "eaten"; as Moffat (1842:8) observed early on, even a life of relative hardship and isolation "in the country"[28] was "vastly preferred to . . . vassalage in the towns." As a result, the social ecology of production created a dilemma for the chief. Patently, the close supervision of time and movement was vital to his exaction of tributary labor—indeed, to his material and symbolic command of the polity *tout court*. Yet that supervision threatened the very means by which men might engage in the public domain, and so introduced a centrifugal force at the heart of the *morafe*. Thus it is that early visitors came across communities of scattered households with no center at all (above, p. 127).

As this suggests, the struggle between chiefly dominance and domestic self-assertion, centralization and decentralization, was endemic. Rulers had not merely to ward off repeated attempts by rivals to dislodge them. They had also to face a perpetual challenge to the authority of the office itself and to the social and cultural forms on which it rested. On the other hand, because the town was the site of the administrative hierarchy and the arena of all social management, any activity in pursuit of property and position contributed to the nucleation of the polity. The antinomy between centralization and decentralization, in other words, might have presented itself as an opposition between politics and production, the demands of the chiefship and the exigencies of agriculture. But it was not reducible to a simple antagonism between ruler and populace. This antinomy inhered rather in the very structure of Tswana economy and society. At the same time it was most openly expressed—and was worked out—in the political context, in which chiefly performance, power, and legitimacy were constant objects of negotiation and public debate.

Recall how images of the chiefship, *bokgosi*, reflected the dualistic character of the Tswana social world. The office, we repeat, was the symbolic core of the polity (*morafe*) at large; its holder, the personification of his people (*Morolong*, "[the] Rolong person"; or *Motlhaping*, "[the] Tlhaping person"). Within any chiefdom, *bokgosi* was the hub of everyday life, the axis around which rotated the cycles of production and ritual performance that yielded human, material, and spiritual value (J. Comaroff 1985:75f.). Its suzerainty in turn was mandated by the royal dead, whose potency emanated from their communal grave in the cattle-byre alongside the royal court. As we shall see, the chiefship was also invested with command over a system of age regiments, put into place by periodic initiation rites; these rites and regiments, each in their own way, underwrote the ruler's control over space and time. And yet in spite of all this, chiefs were taken to be fallible human beings whose authority could be questioned and in certain circumstances spurned. Even their succession, although phrased in terms of immutable genealogical status, was open to negotiation—and was on many occasions contested (J.L. Comaroff 1978:passim). In no sense was a Tswana sovereign divine, notwithstanding the spiritual resources he enjoyed by virtue of his access to the ancestors and, perhaps, to rainmakers and medicines (Schapera 1971). Witness a speech made by a Tlhaping headman in criticism of Chief Mothibi, of whom he had formerly been an active supporter (Campbell 1822:2,156):

> He began by asking how Mateebe dared to speak [to his followers] as he did; and declared that the young people loved independence, and would not bend for any one; that it was not good for people to be afraid of their King, who was but a man, and when he did anything wrong his people ought to . . . tell him publicly of it. . . .

Added Campbell (1822:2,157), now speaking in his own voice:

> Such is the freedom of speech at those public meetings, that some of the captains [headmen] have said of the King, that he . . . is not fit to rule over them.

In describing a *pitso*—an "imposing" gathering of adult male townsmen in the chiefly court—John Philip (1828:2,133) also remarked admiringly on the "perfect freedom of [the] debate" that took place. Noting how Mothibi had been chided for being "completely under the government of his queen, Mahoota [Mmahutu]," he observed that the outspoken criticism directed at the ruler and his personal circumstances had been received without animosity. The contrast between things said of the office and things said of its holder—the one honorific, the other brutally honest—could not have been more sharply drawn.

A thoroughgoing distinction was made, then, between the chief and the chiefship, *kgosi* and *bokgosi* (Schapera 1938; J.L. Comaroff 1978). The latter defined a context and a conventional stock of resources that enabled the former to construct himself as a ruler. While in office, "kings" had constantly to prove themselves and to account for their actions. Otherwise they could not expect their people to accept their authority; Moffat (1842:389), for example, tells us of one Rolong sovereign, ironically named Kgosi ("Chief"), who was deposed because of a "want of energy." It was in the *pitso*, the assembly, that the performance of such men was discussed and evaluated; and it was there that a ruler (and his close allies) had to convince the *morafe* of the quality of his administration.

The actual mechanisms involved in this process of public negotiation are beyond our present scope.[29] Suffice it to say, however, that, far from being decided purely by argument and oratory, the legitimacy of any office-holder was greatly influenced by the complex kaleidoscope of power relations surrounding him. Still, his right to regulate the affairs of the *morafe* was held, tautologically, to depend on his ability to demonstrate his effectiveness before his people. Forceful men, whose performance had been publicly sanctioned, could exercise almost dictatorial power. Weak ones, by contrast, had difficulty in imposing their wills, and their executive decisions, on anyone. As this implies, chiefly authority varied a great deal within and between reigns.

Not surprisingly, nineteenth-century accounts differ in characterizing the ability of Tswana chiefs to command their peoples, to extract surpluses, to regulate external trade, and to control the terms of engagement with such outsiders as missionaries, traders, and settlers. Lichtenstein (1930:2,414) described their power as "nearly uncircumscribed," their authority as unassailable; similarly, Burchell (1824:2,376), while noting the moderating effect of "inferior chieftains or principal men of property," stressed that when a "king" asserted his will, he was obeyed without question. Others (Barrow 1806:399; Mackenzie 1871:371) held that rulers were always required to consider "the sentiments of the people" in decision-making, and could never reign just as they pleased. And a few, like Moffat (1842:389), tell of virtually powerless sovereigns. Philip (1828:2,132) gives a somewhat more nuanced view:

> The form of government among this tribe [the Tlhaping] is monarchical, the office of the king is hereditary, and the theory of government is that of an absolute despotism; but the king is checked in the exercise of his power by . . . the circumstances of his chiefs [headmen]. The king is assisted by a council, composed of his chiefs, but this assembly is deliberative only, and the executive department of the government rests in the hands of the king. Several cases were related to me, in which the king exercised a despotic authority; but each of those cases was followed by a diminution of the number of his subjects. . . . [I]f a [headman] is dissatisfied, he may withdraw with his followers from under the king's authority, and join another tribe; and, in a thinly-peopled country . . . this must be a circumstance of frequent occurrence.

The contrasts among these European characterizations—as Philip seems to imply, and will by now be clear to us—reflect observable variations in chiefly authority at different places and times. Each represents one face of an office constantly in flux in response to the dynamics of the political and social context in which it was situated.

This brings us back, full circle, to economy and society, to the antinomy between centralization and decentralization in nineteenth-century Tswana life. It was when a ruler lost a large measure of his legitimacy, or failed to consolidate it in the first place, that he would gradually forfeit control over domicile and movement. Typically, households would then seize the opportunity to scatter, returning only when centralized authority was reestablished. The chiefs themselves appear to have been acutely aware of the danger. Thus, says Rev. Williams,[30] Sechele foresaw that his heir, an unpromising politician, would have great difficulty in preventing the Kwena from dispersing. He was correct. Not long after he had taken office, the new sovereign, Sebele, began to act high-handedly and quickly alienated his popular support. And so, "as the spirit of revolt grew in the town men remained away at their cattleposts or gardens" in defiance of his wishes "until he seems to have lost all control. . . ." Not coincidentally, he was challenged soon after by his younger brother. But centralization/decentralization was not always an all-or-none matter: the degree to which domestic units could and did disperse—or conversely were held at the center—was an index of the subtle fluctuations of chiefly command.

There is, however, one further twist to all this. Earlier (p. 140), we showed how the social order subsumed countervailing tendencies toward inequality and egalitarianism. The existence of those two tendencies was

closely connected to the tension, in political economy, between centralization and decentralization. Thus, for example,[31] when the social world was at
its most egalitarian and individuated, officeholders found it difficult to control space and time. For the exercise of real authority required a cadre of
personnel who commanded lower order constituencies—which, in a fragmented, egalitarian universe, was lacking. But where a field of unequal
relations existed, a ruler might build a power base by making alliances with
other influential persons, subordinating agnates and isolating rivals in the
process. He then could place supporters and clients in important offices, and
thereby consolidate a faction of "chief's men" for whom there was common
cause in centralization, the extraction of surpluses, and the regulation of
politico-ritual activities. These men might further exploit their own positions to extend networks of clientage around them, and so reinforce emerging
structures of dominance. Of course, social management of this kind had a
direct expression in economy: the process of eating agnatic rivals and others,
in the culturally-given manner, involved the social production of a workforce. In this respect, as in all others, cultural order and political economy,
symbolic forms and material life, composed an indivisible totality.

On the other hand, the growth of strong opposition to a ruler and his
regime could lead to the fragmentation of the *morafe* and, with the scattering
of households, to the breakdown of relations of inequality and servitude. As
it happens, however, most Southern Tswana lived in nucleated chiefdoms
during the early nineteenth century. The tendency toward centralization appears to have been clearly dominant, and was more consistently reproduced—
albeit with some internal variation—than it was to be in later periods
(Comaroff and Comaroff n.d.; see also Legassick 1969b). In part, this was
due to relations among contemporary Southern Tswana polities (see below,
p. 161f.). Above all else, chiefs were in a position to accumulate a fund of
power by virtue of their alliances, marital and military, with other sovereigns
of broadly equal status.[32] These men often united in defence and attack, and
sometimes helped one another to stop subjects from dispersing. Rulers also
consolidated their dominance by appropriating the spoils of war and raiding,
especially serfs and cattle,[33] and they regulated cross-regional and long-
distance trade (Smith 1939:1,278; Burchell 1824:2,537ff.; Campbell 1822:
1,249; 2,194; Lichtenstein 1930:2,409f.).

These relations and resources, then, buttressed a centralized polity, one
in which distinctly unequal classes enjoyed very different access to the
means of production and redistribution (e.g., Burchell 1824:2,347, 516–24;
Lichtenstein 1930:2,414; Moffat 1842:390). The control by ruling cadres
over serf labor and trade goods in particular facilitated the subordination of
the rest of the populace. For it enabled the production of surpluses and the
regular exaction of tax and tribute. And it was on these—as a contemporary

ruler told Campbell (1822:2,194; 1,249, 268, 316)—that the material trappings of government and politics depended. In sum, the emergence of a
centralized polity was favored by the engagement of the local community
with an external context that gave a dominant class the means to control
the flow of value. But in this dynamic world, where human action was never
a simple reflection or a mechanical enactment of "social structure," everyday practice could and did produce a subtle, shifting mosaic of social and
political forms.

Worldview, Ritual, and the Life of the Spirit

The social and productive arrangements of the period also entailed a classification of beings and forces, things and actions, space and time; in short,
a worldview. The signs and relations that made up this scheme, however,
were not neutral or arbitrary. In the early nineteenth century the perpetuation of a centralized, hierarchical society involved the symbolic assertion of the chiefship over the domestic periphery, agnatic politics over
matrilateral kinship, cattle over agriculture, men over women, and so on.
Indeed, this pattern of symbolic dominance was an essential component
of the prevailing hegemony; that is, of the representation of the universe
as a natural order of categories and conventions. While the latter was
given tangible expression in certain mythico-ritual texts and social contexts,
for the most part it remained unremarked in the flow of daily life. Even in
conversations with outsiders it was never voiced openly, a tendency which
John Mackenzie (1871:396) was to ascribe, perhaps more colorfully than
accurately, to the "misleading [native] custom of feigning extreme ignorance," of seeming so stupid "as to be seized with a violent headache whenever they tried to think." Some years later, Willougby (1923:46) came closer
to the mark. Like ourselves, he said, these people never "express the ideas
that matter most. . . . Such ideas appear so fundamental to a speaker that he
credits the listener with taking them for granted." Neither of the missionaries could quite put their finger on a yet more basic fact: that the Tswana
worldview could not be distilled into a "belief system," or into a rationalized
metaphysics, without reifying and distorting it. The term that was to be used
for a Christian (*modumedi*; "one who professes agreement") captures the
point well: it set apart those who identified with an explicit, systematic faith.
In the precolonial world, by contrast, "cosmology" diffused itself throughout
the fabric of social existence.

It will be remembered, for example, that Tswana social architecture distinguished the town (*motse*; above, p. 129f.) from the bush (*naga*). The wild
was the threatening realm of spirits, plants, and animals of unruly potential.
It provided the vital ingredients for both healing and sorcery, and, most

important, was the habitat of Sarwa ("bush" people) and other (less than social) clients and serfs. The town, on the other hand, was the apex of civil society and its achievements. It was the domain of free citizens, especially persons of wealth and worth. This opposition between *motse* and *naga*, the Tswana analogue of that between civilization and savagery, also laid down the coordinates of a chain of being. Like its European counterpart (chapter 3), it placed men of wealth and refinement at the pinnacle, beasts of the wild at the bottom, and people of the bush somewhere between. And it, too, grounded human inequalities in natural differences. Members of the Tswana "lower class," to use Mackenzie's (1871:131) term for *balala*, were treated as part of the animal kingdom. Adds Moffat (1842:8–9), these "poor ones"—literally, "those who had been laid low"—lived "a hungry life, being dependent on the chase, wild roots, berries, locusts"; to him, their language was a babble of "mongrel words," their "wild look" a result of their "constant intercourse with beasts of prey" (1842:11). Such semihuman creatures could not own cattle, though the most trusted of them might tend the herds of others (Mackenzie 1871:129). Nor could they enter the capital at their own initiative, even to bring the fruits of the wild to their masters. They had to do so, with permission, under the cover of night (Mackenzie 1871:368). In this manner the social and material inequalities between classes of men were imposed upon the face of nature.

Much the same point, as we have seen, may be made of the connection between sexual inequalities and the anatomy of the town. Or between relations of power and production and the gendered body. That much follows from the way in which the worldview of the Tswana saturated every aspect of their quotidian world. The latter, however, was also inhabited by non-human forces and beings.

1. Human and Superhuman Capacity

The indigenous cosmos was populated by a panoply of beings who interacted with living persons, beings with the capacity to affect the material and social circumstances of others for good or ill. These spirit forces ranged from the familial ancestors of the household, through the royal dead buried in the chiefly cattle-byre, to the residual supreme being, *modimo*, located in the "far distance" (*modimo wa go dimelela*; Brown 1926:113). As this implies, the superhuman realm traced out the major lineaments of the contemporary cultural universe, underscoring in particular the division between the domesticated and the wild.

The ancestors were the domesticated dead of the settlement. Their world was a projection, on a spiritual plane, of the dominant model of social relations among the living (e.g., Holub 1881:1,383; J. Comaroff 1974:

119). Death converted the animating essence (*moya*, "breath") of a person into -*dimo*, a penetrating superhuman power (from *dima*, "to penetrate" or "pervade with power"; Brown 1926:101f.; Smith 1950a:17). As life ended, *moya* left the body, rising like smoke to form a distillate that remained dangerously unstable if not contained through ritual (Willoughby 1928:10). Once the proper rites had been performed, however, the deceased became one of the *badimo* (the "beings of -*dimo*"). These ancestors had only a communal presence, there being no singular term of address or reference for any one of them.[34] Not only did they always act together, but individuals could not be singled out for veneration (Willoughby 1928:330; Mackenzie 1871:394), their subjective identities having been merged into a collective spiritual dominion. Predictably, given existing kinship arrangements, cults were largely domestic in focus. While matters of public concern might require intercession with the forebears of the chief (see below, p. 158), the *badimo* of major account for any household were its close agnates and mothers; its "living dead" (Mbiti 1969) were those who had helped to propagate it and who continued to be an active source of both power and punishment.

The subtle yet vital force of the ancestors was to be overlooked or misunderstood by most Nonconformist missionaries.[35] The Europeans, who sometimes likened *badimo* to demons (below, chapter 6), also failed to see that they intervened in the affairs of the living to defend the established moral order (Schapera 1953:59). In fact, spiritual potency began to grow *before* death, taking root in senior men, who could curse (*go hutsa*) junior agnates if they defied their authority (Schapera 1938:181; Willoughby 1928:194); the wrath of elders and ancestral sanction together served to protect social convention and political hierarchy. In this respect, more generally, the *badimo* were a significant presence in the male sphere of agnatic politics, and legitimized the activities of the public domain. Their strength, which Tswana took to be a real factor in the economy of everyday means, was tapped through sacrifice, a rite that could only be performed by senior agnates or household heads on behalf of their dependents. As Schapera (1953:60) has noted, estrangement from these men removed access to the greatest font of power in everyday life. Further, while veneration occurred at the grave sites of both males and females, there was no acknowledgement of matrilateral ties. The female dead too spoke in agnatic idiom. Thus the containment of matrilaterality by agnation was reiterated at the spiritual level. The ancestral cult also extended to the level of the state. Important communal rituals (rainmaking, firstfruits, initiation) centered on the royal burial place at the chief's court, where the ruler propitiated his dead kin on behalf of the body politic. The preeminence of past sovereigns in the superhuman realm was unambiguous; access to their spiritual vigor was, as we said earlier, a crucial timber in the symbolic scaffolding of the chiefship.

The cult of the dead, then, made agnatic rank and royal control the elements of an inscrutable cosmic order. The *badimo* were guarantors of civil society and centralized political authority, standing in contrast to those un-domesticated beings, probably known as *medimo*, left unburied in the wild. Such persons—bush dwellers and those who died "unnaturally" through violence—never joined the ancestral collectivity. They were not tied by moral or ritual links to the social world, and they acted toward the living with capricious nastiness (Willoughby 1932:110f.). These undomesticated spirits came to embody *naga*: nature, unpredictable and unknown, rank and menacing. Just as *badimo* were the guardians of *motse*—of the town, civil society, and the administrative hierarchy—so their wild counterparts repre-sented the unsocialized, entropic forces that endangered it. The opposition between these spirit forces, like the contrast between *motse* and *naga*, was critical: the very existence of the community depended on the triumph of the one over other (see p. 129).

At the very edge of that cosmos—beyond both *motse* and *naga*, beyond the expanse of bush known or imagined, beyond space and time itself—was the realm of *modimo*, the supreme being. *Modimo* was said to be "above where the clouds float and the lightning flashes" and "in the west where the sun sets and whence the streams flow" (Willoughby 1928:67). This, we stress, was not "heaven," a notion that only came later, but merely the in-conceivable fringes of the world. There seems to have been no explicitly developed connection between the "creation" of the universe and *modimo* (Moffat 1842:263; but cf. Schapera 1953:59), who did not intrude upon everyday events and relations. We are told, in fact, that prior to the advent of the mission this remote being was referred to as a "thing" (*selo*), a noun that did not take personal concords (Moffat 1842:261; Smith 1950a:118–20) and that was seldom even mentioned in ordinary conversation.

Although *modimo* was held accountable for such major catastrophes as drought and pestilence, its actions were utterly inexplicable; being indifferent to human intervention through ritual, it was a residual force at the margins of experience and control (Broadbent 1865:82; Burchell 1824:2,388). Perhaps this is why many early monotheistic visitors, including the observant Burchell (1824:2,550) and the knowledgeable Moffat (1842:244), thought that the Tswana had no religion to speak of (see also Philip 1828:2,88). The initial failure on the part of the first missionaries to elicit from them any response whatsoever to "Our Father in Heaven" was commented on with shock. It reinforced the impression that their dark minds were devoid of all spirituality (Broadbent 1865:81). These people did not even have the raw, exotic rites of heathen savages. Just "superstition" of the "weakest and most absurd kind" (Burchell 1824:2,550; below, p.208). Nonetheless, once the evangelists discovered the vestigial *modimo*—which connoted, among other things, "to pervade" or "to evaporate" (Willougby 1923:77; Smith 1950a:117)[36]— they seized upon it as a basis for instilling their concept of an omnipotent, paternalistic deity. For the incorporation of black South Africans into the purview of modern Europe was to be accompanied everywhere by the dissemination of an anthropomorphic image of God, the fountainhead and guardian of a highly rationalized, universalist cosmology (cf. Horton 1967). Most Tswana, however, were to regard Him—now gendered, of course— rather differently from the omnipresent Almighty of the Judeo-Christian tradition. Apart from all else, he was to be approached through the *badimo*, who were themselves to become increasingly individuated (Schapera 1953:59; J. Comaroff 1974; cf. Pauw 1960).

2. Ritual: *go thaya* and *go alafa*

For precolonial Tswana, ritual was an especially forceful mode of action. It was "work," *tirelo*, par excellence: the accomplishment of skilled human effort (see p. 140f.). This work involved the controlled and stylized manipulation of words, gestures, and substances—techniques, that is, that concentrated their properties and powers. While some *materia medica* were widely known, their potency depended on both the acquired knowledge and the innate creative faculties of those who administered them (Schapera 1953:62). The *ngaka*, or ritual expert, combined these qualities, having an enhanced ability to transform things and relations. It was he who maintained the fragile margins of civil society, mediating between the domesticated and the wild, the living and the dead. And only he could restore the integrity of the disrupted body, both personal and social (Campbell n.d.; Livingstone 1857:ch.1; Molema 1920:165).

The integrity of the body personal and social, it seems, flowed from the proper alignment of the categories of the cosmos, which shaped images of well-being and affliction, etiology and healing (Willoughby 1928). Thus, for example, the cooperation of men in government under the chiefship, the principles of agnatic rank, the gender-based division of productive and reproductive labor, and the separation of the social from the wild were all necessary for the regeneration of the human world. Their violation—indeed, any disorderly mingling of these conventional categories and activities—was held to bring illness and destruction. Excessive agnatic rivalry took the form of sorcery (*boloi*) and was an offence to the ancestors (see n. 12); disruption of physical relations between men and women gave rise to pollution (*bothitho*; Willoughby 1932:122f.); and confusions of the social and the wild unleashed the powers of the undomesticated spirits. These various modes of affliction came together in an etiological order: sorcery, ancestral punishment, pollution, and the vengeance of wild spirits composed a system of explanation of ever increasing scope. In an environment in which, despite surface appearances, people were always "suspicious and jealous of each other" (Mackenzie 1871:402), the most common and specific cause of misfortune was the *boloi* of personal rivals. But illness that persisted despite treatment might be the work of the *badimo*, the product of *bothitho*, or the caprice of *medimo*. And cases of affliction that did not fit into this scheme of things, or were utterly unyielding, were attributed finally to the residual supreme being, *modimo* (J. Comaroff 1974).

Misfortune, by its very nature, then, demanded both explanation and treatment, a process that involved the ritual expert and hinged upon his divination of cause and circumstance (Brown 1926:134ff.). As elsewhere in Africa, this process drew on a shared worldview to account for particular incidents of affliction. Its open-ended oracular conversations allowed healers and clients to exchange interpretations of events and relations and thus to subsume chaotic, usually painful, experience into available symbolic categories. Among nineteenth-century Tswana, as among their descendants, the divination of personal ills seems often to have occasioned searching analyses of social ambiguities and contradictions. While it may not have been self-conscious, these analyses seem to have led to the gradual reformulation of collective meanings, especially in response to discrepancies between individual perception and communal ideology. Such discrepancies were the result of continuous shifts not only within the social system but also in its relationship to the external environment. Healing was, and remains, a context in which cultural forms may be realigned, symbols given renewed value, established practices extended or transformed (J. Comaroff 1985:passim). The dice used by Tswana diviners provide graphic illustration of just this process. The basic set of four bones (representing senior male, junior male, senior female, and junior female) used a century-and-a-half ago permitted sixteen primary configurations or "lies" (*mawa*) based on sex and age. As the universe of meaning and causality changed under the impact of the colonial encounter, the set was greatly enlarged. In time it came to include bones for, among others, "non-Tswana blacks" (*batosa*), whites (*makgoa*), and God (*modimo*); as a result, it made possible an increasing array of diagnoses and explanations for affliction (cf. Reyneke 1972; J. Comaroff 1974).

Ritual action, uniform in its principles of operation, was categorized in terms of its intent. A clear distinction was made between *bongaka*, the beneficent work of the doctor, and *boloi*, destructive sorcery—although doctors were said to engage sometimes in the latter while pretending the former (Brown 1926:132f.). *Bongaka* in turn comprised two classes of rite: *go alafa*, to heal or reconstitute; and *go thaya*, to strengthen, affirm, or reproduce. *Go alafa* was occasioned by a dislocation in the life of persons and groups and corresponded to the "movable" or piacular rituals of other African societies. Occurring at the level both of the domestic group and of the chiefdom as a whole, it entailed divination (*go laola*) and treatment (*go hodisa*), the first to define the malady and its source, the second to reverse the condition. Because affliction—whether wrought by sorcerers, vengeful ancestors, or careless polluters—was associated with breaches of the conventional order, its repair usually involved an authoritative restatement of that order. This was most visible in rainmaking, a form of *go alafa* closely tied to the legitimacy of the chief (Schapera 1971).

Rain rites were orchestrated by the ruler himself, although he was often aided by *baroka*, a special class of "doctors of the nation" (*dingaka tsa morafe*), whose skills were particularly necessary when something had caused the clouds "to miscarry." This was typically put down to "remissness in administering the affairs of the town," or to the pollution let loose either by death or by uncontained female bodily processes; at times it was blamed on such disruptive agents of change as white traders and missionaries (Mackenzie 1871:386f.; Willoughby 1928:203f.; below, p. 211). Treatment began with an appeal by the headmen, in the name of the people, to the chief: "We seek rain from you, *Kgosi*. Where do you look (*bona*; also "focus" or "gaze"), that you do not give us rain?" (Willoughby 1928:205). Only the sovereign himself could intercede with the royal ancestors, without whose sanction no amount of medicine could be effective. And they would respond only if they were sure that *mekgwa* were being properly followed—above all, in respect of the governance of the (centralized) polity and the received division of labor. As we shall see in the later chapters of this volume, rainmaking was especially abhorrent to the missionaries. They were to view it both as the epitome of satanically-inspired, sinful imposture and as the essence of savage superstition.

Go thaya, for its part, affirmed or renewed the structure of the social world. It was the equivalent of what elsewhere have been called "fixed" or "commemorative" rites. Such rites accompanied the establishment of settlements (*go thaya motse*), the redrawing of boundaries around homesteads, fields, and villages (*go bapola lefatse*), and the redefinition of status at moments of passage. Where *go alafa* focused on personal affliction but also regenerated the social order at large, *go thaya* concentrated on communal reconstruction but also remade the individual participants. Both, however, applied the same underlying cosmological scheme to the contingencies of social existence.

Go thaya punctuated the agricultural cycle, too, marking out the rhythm of seasonal activities. Most notable, perhaps, were the "giving out of the seed time" and the "tasting of the gourd" (firstfruits), the rites which asserted chiefly control over space and time, over the productive labor of females and the autonomy of households. Violations of this aspect of sovereign authority were not lightly regarded; Campbell (1822:2,154) reports that in 1820 Chief Mothibi fined a woman heavily, and berated her angrily in public, for sowing a field before he had given the word. But *go thaya* rituals did more than just reflect the dominion of the ruler. They were, as we saw above, one of the means by which it was forged. As such, they were directly involved in the hierarchical construction of the polity. Thus, for instance, the firstfruits ceremony, conducted according to strict order of seniority, imposed an annual public reckoning on the negotiation of rank and position; in so doing, it restated the primacy of agnation in shaping the world, its dominant relations, and its values.[37]

In much the same vein, the initiation of adolescents, the most important event in the ritual calendar (Mackenzie 1871:375), recreated the basic principles on which Tswana society was founded. To be sure, it engraved them on the bodies of the novitiates.[38] Separate but coordinated sequences were performed: *bogwêra*, for immediately prepubescent boys, took place every few years (Lichtenstein 1973:72), when a royal son was old enough to lead the age regiment established in the process; *bojale*, timed to coincide with the conclusion of the male circumcision, drew in girls after the onset of menstruation. Everyone had to undergo this passage: an uninitiated adult was a contradiction in terms, a thoroughly unsocialized being who was unable to marry or participate in collective activities (Campbell 1822:2,172; Brown 1921:421). Held once the ingathering of the firstfruits had revitalized the *morafe* and ushered in the ceremonial season, *bogwêra* and *bojale* brought together youths of the appropriate age from all over the polity. They were set in motion by the chief, who alone had the capacity to will, and thus to effect, the reproduction of the social world. He also presided over their completion, when the initiates were welcomed back as full members of the community under his jurisdiction. But it was not only rulers or royals who stressed the significance of the rites. Commoners too appear to have viewed them as vital for the continued viability of the chiefdom. Indeed, their enduring salience—albeit under different conditions and with radically transformed meaning—is proven by the fact that some modern Tswana have tried to revive *bogwêra*, long moribund in many places, in order to regain control over their collective destiny.[39]

The rites themselves were intricately choreographed to remake persons and forge new groupings. Harnessing physical growth to social ends, they fashioned from the fruits of the domestic domain (children) the substance of an agnatically ordered community (citizens). Elsewhere (see n. 38) we have shown that the initiation cycle spelled out, in a subtle counterpoint of symbolic registers, the major contradictions underlying contemporary Tswana social life—the contradictions that made themselves felt in the tension between centralization and decentralization, agnation and matrilaterality, male control and female fertility, chiefly command and household production. It also played out their authoritative resolution, asserting and enacting the subordination of the individual to the collectivity, the domestic periphery to the political center, women to men, and so on. Thus were males made over into fully *social* beings, a state that highlighted the inherently less stable, less refined character of females. For above all, the rites set out to eclipse the threatening generativity and fecundity of the latter, bringing them within the purview of the masculine power to make society—of which male age regiments, the essential guarantors of the polity, were the supreme embodiment. As this implies, *bogwêra* and *bojale* ultimately grounded the complex contrasts of the Tswana world in the essential and distinct capacities of men and women. Of course, the rites could not banish all contradictions from that world. But along with other symbolic action that addressed and redressed social tensions, they could, and often did, hold them at bay.

For early nineteenth-century Tswana, in sum, ritual was a vital force in constructing and transforming the social and natural universe. As their supreme cultural product, it played a major part in sustaining structures of inequality and in managing the tensions and ambiguities inherent in their political communities. But ritual is never merely conservative. It is not simply an adhesive that holds together authoritative social arrangements and institutions. Under certain conditions, its power may be called upon to illuminate, interpret, and counter dissonance in the lived environment. This was to become especially evident later, once the colonial process began to act upon precolonial economy and society, to engender a discrepancy between received ideologies and practical experience, and to crystallize strains formerly implicit in everyday life. Also, as new contradictions and unfamiliar cultural forms were implanted into their social context, Tswana increasingly invoked "traditional" ritual itself as a symbol of a lost world of order and control.

THE UNIVERSE AND BEYOND

Earlier in this chapter we noted Legassick's (1969b:98f.) thesis that, during the sixteenth century, two large Tswana chiefdoms in the present-day Transvaal began to segment, scattering "lineage clusters" over central southern Africa. Given the composition of these chiefdoms, he argues, their division would not have disrupted material and social life very much. Each segment, being like the *morafe* in microcosm, would have emerged as a smaller version of the parent unit—as in fact happened often in later Tswana history, typically in the wake of succession struggles within royal descent groups. It follows too that the internal structure of the chiefdoms made it equally easy, under the appropriate conditions, for two or more communities to merge, or for a centralized polity to absorb immigrants and captives (see Schapera 1952).[40] This, Legassick goes on to claim (1969b:106–07), is exactly what occurred in the eighteenth century, when the period of fragmentation ended and small groupings began to amalgamate into large "confederations." Two factors are held to account for the process: (1) the assertion of a chiefly monopoly over the ivory trade, and (2) a pattern of population growth that made it "easier for a dissident group leaving one chiefdom to join another rather than establishing themselves autonomously."

Whether or not the details of Legassick's reconstruction of Tswana political history are correct,[41] he makes a number of important points. Among them is the insistence that, far from each being an island unto itself, by 1800 the various political communities already had a long history of interaction with one another; that the composition of those communities underwent considerable fluctuation, over time and space, due both to their internal workings and to external processes; and that trade played a critical role in such processes. These points echo our own earlier statements about the historical dynamics of Southern Tswana economy and society. They also anticipate our suggestion that the centralization of local polities—and, with it, the concentration of chiefly power—depended in large part on their external relations (above, p. 151). In addition to the regulation of trade, we said, those relations gave ruling cadres the opportunity to control the movement of people and cattle across their territories; to recruit the services of famed ritual experts from far afield; to reap the human and bovine spoils of attacks on weaker communities; and to forge military and marital relations with each other. These various forms of exchange, extraction, and alliance were all of a piece. Through them, the chiefdoms and their rulers were enmeshed in a complex network of links within and beyond the region.

1. Trade, Tariffs, and Tribute

The first missionaries, like early travelers, were quick to remark upon the external relations among the chiefdoms they visited. In due course they would become deeply embroiled in those relations. Nor is it surprising, in this regard, that they paid great attention to exchange and barter. Not only did they believe that their own dealings with African rulers depended on the proper bestowal of gifts (below, p. 181f.); any evidence of local trade gave them hope that there existed fertile ground for commerce and hence for civilization. They were not disappointed. The Tswana showed a keen interest in the exchange of objects, especially beads (see Beck 1989: passim). Lichtenstein (1930:2,387f.), for example, describes graphically the "formal market" set up by his party among the Tlhaping, who did not tire of the "tumultuary transactions" until the whites had "nothing left to sell." He also reports (1930:2,409) that these southern communities traded with others to the northeast, exchanging their cattle for "hassegais [spears], needles, earrings, and armrings," as well as for other iron and copper goods (see chapter 5).[42] What is more, this traffic sometimes passed through many hands along the way. The chiefs, who had "extensive knowledge of the country" (and a host of ambassadors, informers, and messengers), took care to monitor and direct all such trade, including that with the Europeans. In his very first encounter with the Tlhaping ruler, Campbell (1822:1,249–50) was upbraided because

> . . . some of our attendants had already exchanged beads with his people, which was contrary to their law; that all strangers ought first to lay their beads before him as ruler of the people, and if he could not please them with articles in return, then they were at liberty to go to other persons.

The Ngwaketse chief to the north, he notes later (1822:1,316), was even more strict. He disallowed *any* transactions between his subjects and "people from a distance," taking all their goods for himself. In some places, trade monopolies were accompanied by a form of protective tariff, imposed by the ruler as part of the control over movement across his realm. Mothibi, the Tlhaping chief in the 1820's, is a case in point (Campbell 1822:2,194):

> The mountain from whence the Bootchuana nations obtain the blue sparkling ore, which they pulverise to adorn their heads, is claimed by Mateebe and his people as their property, and they demand a tax from all strangers who travel to it for this commodity. Mateebe only permits his own people to visit the place once a year, perhaps to prevent its becoming too plentiful, and thereby reducing the price paid for it by more distant nations.

The missionary had not merely found "native commerce"; he had, he was convinced, discovered the elementary principles of European political economy in the African desert.

The articles most actively traded among the Tswana and their neighbors were ivory (Livingstone 1857:45), wild animal skins (Smith 1939:1,278), ostrich feathers (Mackenzie 1871:130), and the blue hematite (*sebilo*, a cosmetic with ritual importance) whose extraction was so carefully controlled by Mothibi. Furthermore, this trade covered considerable distances.[43] For instance, skins and ivory, especially when scarce, were brought from beyond the Kalahari (Livingstone 1857:45). But it was not only material objects that flowed across the chiefdoms of the region. Ritual expertise was also a

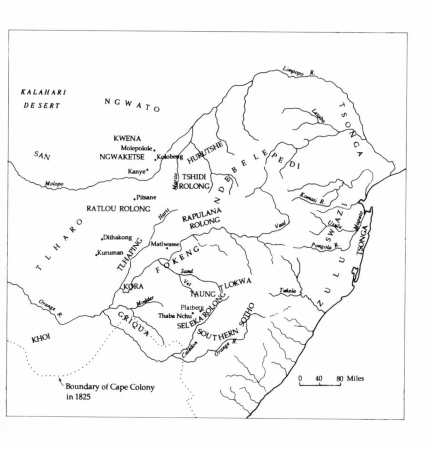

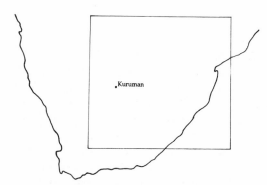

MAP 3 *Peoples of the Interior, circa 1830–40*

prime value sought out, and regulated, by Tswana rulers, many of whom continued to recruit rain specialists "from abroad" until well into this century (Schapera 1971:44). Even when the chiefs themselves were thought to have the requisite skills, they welcomed the support of foreign practitioners and went to great lengths to keep them at their capitals. More remarkably, however, there seems to have been a fairly lively long-distance exchange of medical knowledge itself. Campbell (1822:1,307f.) tells how Ngwaketse traveled for almost a year, to the north of the Tswana world, to learn techniques and obtain preparations that might bring them rain and cause their enemies drought. Nor was this an isolated odyssey: albeit perhaps not on quite such a grand scale, journeys in search of expertise and medicines were quite frequent.

2. Warfare, Raiding, and Alliance

The medical knowledge acquired in this way was also deployed in another sphere of external relations, raiding and warfare, which appear to have increased palpably during the eighteenth century (Legassick 1969b:109). Experts were called in, as a matter of course, to doctor the warriors who were about to fight, and to oversee "the consecration of the cattle . . . the possession of which [was] often the subject of the contest" (Lichtenstein 1930: 2,416). Under some conditions contemporary warfare led to the destruction of polities and their absorption into more powerful chiefdoms. More typically, however, it was a limited affair, with little loss of life, involving nocturnal ambush rather than open, all-out confrontation (Burchell 1824:2,534). In these circumstances it shaded into raiding—the covert removal of stock, if possible without even a skirmish—although more emphasis was placed on the taking of prisoners as *balala*, serfs.

The cattle and captives seized in these hostilities often found their way into the regional and long-distance trade nexus, where they were exchanged for other goods and valuables (see e.g., Lichtenstein 1930:2,397): combat and commerce were closely interconnected. So too were warfare and the hunt, between which there was a strong metaphorical and material identity. Both were forays beyond the safe confines of the polity; both yielded significant tributary proceeds to the chief; both were dangerous male activities, had to be prepared for in forceful ways, and were governed by the same taboos (Willoughby 1932:170f.). In each case, the participants met beyond the boundaries of the village, dressed and armed for the fray, and were subjected to careful ritual washing (*go fôka marumô*). A collective hunt (*letsholô*) sometimes actually preceded an attack on another community, the success of the former promising the same for the latter. The major difference between them, self-evidently, was that war might lead to armed reprisal, which was most threatening if an enemy succeeded in persuading others to join the counter-attack. This consideration lay behind the energetic efforts of most chiefs to sustain a network of external alliances and military pacts (Lichtenstein 1973:79). Burchell (1824:2,536) suggests that:

> In their political alliances and friendships, the Bachapins [Tlhaping], it would seem, are an inconstant people, guided only by selfish views and the prospect of booty. There is scarcely a nation around them, ... with which they have not at different times been both on friendly terms, and in a state of hostility: one year joining strength with some neighbouring tribe, to plunder another; and the next, perhaps, assisting that which they had robbed, to plunder their late ally.

Things were not quite as inconstant as Burchell thought. As he noted himself (1824,2:536), the Tlhaping and Ngwaketse chiefs had been antagonistic toward each other, and had fought bitterly, for as long as anyone could remember. On the other hand, some alliances, especially those cemented by the regular exchange of royal women in marriage, lasted for decades or even generations.[44]

These alliances, moreover, did not end at the boundaries of the Tswana universe, but extended beyond it in most directions. In the mid-eighteenth century, for example, the Rolong, under their heroic king, Tau, began to enlarge their dominion by conquering adjoining communities. Eventually their campaigns brought them up against the Tlhaping. The latter, being at a distinct military disadvantage, called upon the Kora, a (non-Tswana) Khoi people to the south with whom their senior chiefs had intermarried for three generations (Lye and Murray 1980:30). Together, the Tlhaping and the Kora vanquished Tau, forcing him to withdraw to his former territory. The defeat had major consequences, leading eventually to the fragmentation of the Rolong *morafe* into the four smaller chiefdoms (Ratlou-Rolong, Tshidi-Rolong, Seleka-Rolong, and Rapulana-Rolong) of modern Tswana history. As this suggests, patterns of alliance and conflict sometimes took on large enough proportions to affect relations across the region, abetting the rise and fall, the mobility or stability, of its polities and populations.

3. The Colonial Presence and External Relations

As the existence of the Cape Colony began to impinge on the Tswana, it became an ever more significant factor in their external relations. One white observer in fact blamed the increase in indigenous warfare and raiding on some of the Dutch settlers, pointing to the disturbances caused by their interference in the material life of the blacks.[45] But the first major area in which the colonial presence made itself felt was predictably that of trade: specifically, that of chiefly control over the movement of persons and the exchange of products. Burchell (1824:2,536–37), who complained about the "mercantile jealousy" of the Tlhaping, the southernmost Tswana people, tells how their rulers tried to gain a monopoly over the traffic of goods from the Cape. Having obtained beads for themselves, they took pains to deter Europeans from visiting, or even communicating with, the chiefdoms beyond. There was a good deal of unwitting irony in the way they did this: they portrayed their neighbors as "men of ferocious habits," making them out to be just the kind of stereotypic savages conjured up by genteel Englishmen in their parlors and benevolent societies. At times Tswana sovereigns went to great lengths in their duplicity. Thus, to prevent trade between Burchell and the Ngwaketse, Mothibi assured the traveler that he, like others before him, would be slaughtered by the devious tribesmen—and then promptly let it be known to the latter that mysterious, murderous white men were coming to kill their chief.

In the end, of course, the Tswana rulers were to lose their control over trade—first to the armed and mounted Griqua and Kora, and then to the interlopers from the Colony. But they had no intention of doing so without a struggle. Mackenzie (1871:130–31), speaking of chiefdoms somewhat further to the north in the 1860's, recalls the

> well-known reluctance of Bechuana chiefs to allow traders and travellers to pass through their country. The attempt on the part of a certain trader some years ago to enter the Kalahari country . . . from which the Barolongs are in the habit of procuring their ostrich-feathers, cost the life of the trader and that of his son. . . . [T]he Bamangwato . . . have lost property to the value of many hundreds of pounds through the opening up of the waggon roads. . . .

The opening up of those roads in turn weakened the mastery of Tswana royals over their serfs who, living in the countryside, could now trade with passers-by on their own account. Adds Mackenzie (1871:130–31):

> I was frequently offered beautiful ostrich-feathers for a bit of tobacco or a few strings of beads. . . . It has been found impossible by the Bamangwato to stop this "contraband" trade. . . . [T]he masters now are in point of fact competitors with the European hunters and traders for the purchase of ivory and feathers from their own vassals.

The colonial frontier, although still many miles from the edges of the Tswana world, was coming nearer all the time. So too were the complex relations among, and the conflicts between, the various segments of the white population of southern Africa—relations that were to play a part in the early encounter between the mission and the Tswana. Even before they did so, however, the colonial presence had begun to hook into the web of connections that bound the chiefdoms and their rulers in an expansive, dynamic regional system.

But the most tumultuous process of the period had its epicenter else-where—at least in the retrospective imagination of many South Africans, historians among them (Cobbing 1988:487f.). *Difaqane* (or *mfecane*),[46] the great subcontinental upheaval of the early nineteenth century, is generally attributed to the explosive rise of Shaka and the Zulu state. Its impact reached into the Tswana world in 1822–23.

4. *Difaqane*: Upheavals and Migrations

Accounts of *difaqane* differ widely in their details. Nonetheless, as told from the perspective of the peoples of the interior, a common narrative thread is discernible. Whatever its causes,[47] goes the story, the emergence of the con-quering Zulu state on the east coast led to a chain reaction, a "shockwave" of violent conflict throughout much of the southern African hinterland. As Lye (in Lye and Murray 1980:31) puts it, those who resisted Shaka's regiments, with their devastating and largely original military techniques, "either suc-cumbed or fled away. The refugees who escaped, thoroughly conversant with the new fighting strategies, burst upon their neighbors to precipitate a holo-caust in every direction." In retracing the topography of devastation and displacement among the Tswana, historians usually blame much of the "holocaust" on the Tlokwa (see e.g., Thompson 1969a; Lye 1969); other-wise known as "Mantatees," this Southern Sotho group had been put to flight by the Hlubi, a Nguni chiefdom itself ravaged by the Zulu. The Tlokwa were supposedly led by their female regent, MmaNthatisi—a shadowy fig-ure sometimes cast in the fantastic mould of a Rider Haggard heroine—and are said to have cut a swathe of destruction across the settled polities of the region. They were followed, in intermittent waves, by the Taung of Moletsane, the Fokeng of Sebetwane, and, most fearsome of all, the Ndebele of Mzilikazi. Where these warriors fell upon local communities, the desicca-tion of the countryside and the dislocation of social life appear to have been immense: "The land was strewn with human bones," observed Broadbent (1865:74–75) at the time, his description colored, it seems, by the evan-gelical sense that these were the battlefields of Satan. "Beautiful and fertile regions became depopulated, . . . towns and cattle-folds destitute of man or beast." Many, he added, died from starvation as they wandered across the wasted terrain in a pathetic effort to flee the roving soldiers of "savage and cruel Chiefs." By a century later, the tone of such missionary testimonies had insinuated themselves into scholarly reconstructions: so desperate were the victims of *difaqane*, writes Lye (1969:195), that some took shelter in "crevices of rocks," and subsisted "on the dregs of hunting and thieving."

Recently, Cobbing (1988) has cast a skeptical eye on *difaqane*, demonstrating that the evidence for the conventional scenario is extremely flimsy. His own view, offered in a controversial reanalysis, is that the period of turmoil had little to do with Shaka or his voracious army; that this myth, propagated both by white settler history and by the apartheid state, has long obscured even the most basic facts of the situation. The real cause of the upheaval, he argues, lay in European penetration and black defensive reaction: specifically, in (1) the efforts of the Portuguese at Delagoa Bay to push south in search of slaves (1988:504f.); and (2) the demand for bonded labor emanating from the Cape Colony, which the Griquas and Bergenaars were encouraged to procure by seizure from Sotho-Tswana communities (1988: 492f.). Many of the *difaqane* "battles," then, are reinterpreted as having been slave (as well as cattle) raids, rather than a chain reaction of black-on-black violence set off by Zulu expansionism. Whatever the merits of this radical revision—and it certainly warrants careful evaluation—Cobbing does show that we have only a vague idea of who actually took part in even the most celebrated *difaqane* "wars" (1988:490f.). Still, he does not deny that the period was dominated by "bewildering sequences" of attack and counter-attack, of alliances and aggression (1988:497), in which the missionaries also were caught up.[48] Nor does he doubt the fact that the loss of life and labor, cattle and crops, seriously depleted the communities of the interior.

Even this recast picture of destruction represents one extreme, however. For, while some Tswana, like the Seleka-Rolong, were severely battered during the 1820's, many fared better. And even those who suffered badly usually managed, often after a period of flight, to regroup and recover (Thompson 1969a:392f.). Chiefs, the Rev. Hamilton tells us,[49] took great pains to gather together their scattered peoples and quickly went about trying to recreate earlier social arrangements. In rare cases local polities actually defeated the invading warriors. The Ngwaketse, for instance, inflicted heavy losses on the Tlokwa, although the latter then proceeded to strike at other Tswana with added vengeance (Molema 1966:11f.). A few chiefdoms escaped the hostilities entirely, the most notable being the Tlhaping; the intervention of mounted Griqua commandos, at the behest of the recently-arrived Robert Moffat (see below, p. 266), succeeded in turning away an attack on Dithakong.[50] The military, material, and social effects of *difaqane*, in other words, were distinctly variable. And yet, even for those who were not directly assailed, this was an uncommonly troubled time. All Tswana seem to have lived in fear, and many felt it necessary to avoid conquering armies and marauding bands either by moving around or by withdrawing to inaccessible retreats. With few exceptions, local ethnohistories recall an epoch of danger and defensive migration. They tell stories of horror rather than heroism, sad tales of popular rulers killed, families violated, communities torn apart.

It was in this unsettled world, then, that the pioneer generation of missionaries was to try to establish itself. As we shall see in the next chapter, the encounter between the evangelists and the Tswana was deeply affected by the historical context in which it occurred. For the Europeans, *difaqane* confirmed the savagery of Africa. More immediately, it persuaded them that, in order to gain a foothold, they would have to abet the chiefdoms in the practical effort to survive. This complemented the Tswana perspective. In their affliction, local rulers were not slow to see the advantages in the political agency and military assistance of the whites. Not only did the latter have guns and horses—resources that made a difference in this theater of war— they also controlled other forms of power and knowledge. It did not go unremarked, for example, that the Tlhaping, who had a LMS station, survived *difaqane* largely untouched; some drew the confident conclusion that a *morafe* with a mission would never suffer military reverses (see e.g., Broadbent 1865:117; below, chapter 7). And so the frame through which the Tswana and the Europeans regarded each other was set, laying out the terms for their historical engagement. Let us go back to the opening scenes of this process, to the epic journeys, the ritual exchanges, and the material gambits that set it in motion.

FIVE

THROUGH THE
LOOKING GLASS

Heroic Journeys, First Encounters

About sunset the king, attended by his brothers and a few more per-
sons, came to our tent, and sitting down, remained silent to hear what
we should say. . . . I said that I had brought a small present for him,
as a token of friendship—while opening it he remained silent, not
moving even his head, only his eyes towards the parcel. I then took
from it a gilded copper comb and put it into his hair, and tied a silver
spangled band and tassel round his head, and a chain about his neck,
and last of all presented him with a looking glass. . . .

The Rev. John Campbell (1813)[1]

THE AFRICAN INTERIOR presented itself to missionary consciousness as virgin ground to be broken, landscape to be invested with history (Ranger 1987:158). In the Nonconformist imagination, this was not merely a matter of "taking hold of the land." It required seizing the hearts and minds of its wild inhabitants, rousing them from a state of nature by cultivating their self-consciousness. Only then might they recognize their true reflection in the mirror, see themselves as wayward children of God, and will their own transformation. The conceit that Africans would cooperate willingly in this bourgeois morality play masked the coerciveness of colonialism and the part of evangelism in it. It belied, too, the more complex dialectic at work in the process: while "the savage" was to see through the looking glass as a missionary ploy, he was also to find in it a new objectification of himself and his changing, endangered world—if not quite in the manner intended by the churchmen. Reciprocally, despite their metaphors of mastery, their sense of themselves as bearers of eternal truths, the Christians were to be deeply affected by the encounter as well. Bent on realizing a pious fantasy in the African wilderness, these Europeans had eventually to come to terms with the disconcerting image of themselves that the "wilderness" gave back—especially as the Tswana reacted to the dangers that seemed to lurk behind the mirror itself.

In this chapter we explore the initial meeting of two worlds, one imperial and expansive, the other local and defensive. The encounter presents itself most accessibly in the letters, reports, and published works of the missionaries, whose stories invariably begin with self-conscious accounts of their "outward" journeys to the "field" and their first dealings with "the natives." But there is also a discernible Tswana commentary on these events, spoken less in narrative form than in the symbolism of gesture, action, and reaction, and in the expressive play of language itself (see e.g., Burchell 1824:2,407, 432). The confrontation, patently, was between two parties of incommensurate power; their inequality being reflected in, among other things, the awareness of the evangelists that they had the capacity to "make" history—and in so doing to speak of, and for, the uncultivated native. As this suggests, their impact lay as much in their representation of Africa—in both senses of the term—as it did in any of their actions as participants.

To those who cared to listen, the Nonconformists would tell a tale of an inert continent slowly awaking to white initiative. Yet the blacks were no less historical actors, even though their assertiveness might have lain in the shadow of European self-representation. To be sure, they were soon casting the churchmen in a script of their own making. This first interaction between the Tswana and the whites was thus a dialogue at once poetic and pragmatic. Based on the exchange of words and things—and on profound misconceptions all round—it laid the ground for the long conversation, the drawn out process of colonization, that was to follow.

The signs and practices which the evangelists brought with them from Britain might have set the terms of the conversation from the outset; indeed, this had much to do with their success in seeding the state of colonialism in which the colonial state was to take root. And, as we shall see, those signs and practices might have been conveyed through rituals with great persuasive force—rituals at times theatrical, at times mundane. But do not be misled: despite the fact that the colonization of the Tswana began with polite ceremony rather than with a crashing military onslaught or a crippling economic invasion, there was, hidden in the politesse, oblique forewarning of later struggles. Both the assertion of the ruler and the riposte of the ruled were given expression in these initial moments. We shall examine the latter first from the perspective of the Europeans, seeking to illuminate the looking-glass world they implanted into Africa as a mirror for both self and other. Thereafter we move through the looking glass, so to speak, to recover, as counter-discourse, the Tswana point of view. It is an analytic journey that takes us, perforce, back to the elementary forms of social life.

THE EUROPEAN PERSPECTIVE
Narrative Journeys: Passages to the Field

Accounts of missionary "labors and scenes" had by the late nineteenth century become an established European literary genre, taking its place beside popular travel and exploration writings, with which it shared features of intent and style (cf. Pratt 1985).[2] This was a literature of the imperial frontier, a colonizing discourse that titillated the Western imagination with glimpses of radical otherness—over which it simultaneously extended intellectual control. What distinguished the reports of the evangelists from most travel narratives was their assertively personalized, epic form. Being soldiers of a spiritual empire, the churchmen described their deeds and achievements—and especially their battles with the forces of darkness—as conquests of civilization; here was history told, in the true spirit of Carlyle (above, pp.52,61), as the autobiography of heroism.[3] For its part, the African landscape was presented as virgin, devoid of society and history, waiting passively to be watered and tilled by evangelical effort. The texts, in other words, both personalized nature and naturalized humanity, portraying the "dark continent" as a vacant stage on which to enact a Promethean myth (see chapter 3).

Missionary narratives most often opened with the passage from civilization to the "regions beyond"; the crossing of "the great water," as one good reverend put it in his first meeting with a Tswana chief.[4] John Edwards (1886:38) captures the emotive tone of the moment of separation:

> As we gradually lost sight of England's favoured isle, in my heart I said: 'Farewell, honoured and beloved England, with all thy churches, Gospel ministers, Christian privileges and means of grace! Thou who art the "Queen of Nations, and the bulwark of eternal truth;" mayest thou be ever faithful to thy high calling in sending forth to the "regions beyond" the pure Gospel of Christ!'

On the great maritime highways of British imperialism, mission vessels plied a mythic course. Victorian children were to save pennies for the maintenance of the *John Williams*[5] and other ships engaged in the work of the LMS, their efforts rewarded with an annual booklet depicting the "sharp-witted young savages" who were their swarthy "school mates" in the distant mission field.[6]

As Beidelman (1982:63) notes, however, the essential rite of passage into the African reality was the overland trek from the coast to the interior. As they edged away from the comforting civilities of the Cape Colony toward territory unknown, these latter-day crusaders sought a reference point for their grand visions on the "empty" landscape. But what appeared to them as a featureless desert was, as we have seen, a country colored by a history of social conflict, one in which they were already cast in an equivocal role. Far from a slumbering wasteland awaiting their benign attentions, it was an arena fraught with struggle between colonial factions for control over indigenous resources, especially human capital. Almost from the start, the part played by the churchmen in local power relations was mapped out for them both by whites and by blacks. And, as they took up their position between the two, they quickly learned the costs and returns of active mediation.

The only secure path over the uncertain terrain was the so-called Missionary Road, a chain of established stations that proclaimed a new moral topography on African soil. This route struck out into the wilderness, linking it to the noble empire of the spirit: "You will look in vain on the various maps of Africa to find the place where I write," Broadbent declared from the capital of a small Tswana chiefdom, "for till now it has been unknown to Christendom."[7]

The stylized narratives of these overland travels reveal an important dimension of the evangelical enterprise: a pervasive belief in the author's passage itself as emblematic and hence as worthy of record. For his was an odyssey of sacred and imaginative incorporation, bringing the "regions beyond" under European gaze. It reenacted, at least in spirit, the greatest of all Puritan journeys—a *Pilgrim's Progress* across the worldly wilderness to the Celestial City.[8] Through it, the ideal of Christian transcendence became a model for imperial conquest. From the vantage of their oxwagons, the missionaries constructed a pristine vista, extending the horizons of their European audience—and, with them, the conceptual frontiers of empire. At times they traveled with colleagues, at times with traders either black or white, but they were always accompanied by African laborers familiar with the terrain: drivers, guides, and where possible, interpreters. These companions give lie to the evangelists' act of discovery, but they remained behind the scenes painted by the narrator, brought forward only to serve specific rhetorical purposes in his account (Pratt 1985:128).

The narratives, then, were highly self-conscious texts that positioned European and native on the moral and colonial margins. The journey, retold in the indicative mood, framed the encounter, stressing the unreconstructed savagery of the land and its inhabitants. The Christians looked upon the

wild to find in it affirmation of eternal truths. Burridge's (1973:17) claim—
that, since the Renaissance, missionaries have prepared the European mind
for an appreciation of otherness—must be challenged. Their writings gave
insight into the great beyond, but through a moralizing lens, focused on the
lamentable distance between savagery and civilization. In South Africa these
writings assimilated the countryside to the categories of a specific vision,
laying the basis for a more aggressive colonialism. Whatever had not been
surveyed by the European eye had not been invested with light:[9]

> . . . I went on a journey of six weeks from Klaar Water to the City of
> Latakkoo [Dithakong], in the Bootchuana country, and to the Coran-
> nas and the Bushymen in the vicinity of the Heart River, a river never
> before seen by a white man's eye, so you may easily conjecture the
> dreadful state of dark heathenism in which they must be involved.

The inhabitants of the wilderness shared its qualities, moreover, merging
with it like feral children unaware of their own humanity. The most apt
examples were those who "prowled about"[10] in the bush, incapable even of
cultivation. According to Edwards (1886:65–66):

> Wolves and wild Bushmen were very destructive on the Station. . . .
> The sheep, when they went out in the day-time to feed, were shot
> down by the poisoned arrows of the Bushman, often three or four in a
> day. . . . The Bushmen would not touch the carcases; these would lie
> for the vultures to eat. It was therefore obvious that these acts of law-
> lessness were prompted by a spirit of wanton cruelty, and were not the
> result of hunger. The country, too, being bushy, favoured their wicked
> doings, as it afforded a secure cover for their diminutive bodies.

Joined in an uncouth alliance with its inhabitants, the landscape itself was
frequently described as "desolate" and "lonely," bereft of the human marks
that the Nonconformists associated with productivity and culture. Its occupants, incapable of imposing themselves effectively upon it, left mere
"scratches on the face of the country" (Pratt 1985:124).

The vastness of this unconquered terrain overwhelmed the small-scale
tidiness, the nice demarcations of the British ideal of spatial order. Notwithstanding its dryness in comparison to England, the country through which
the missionaries passed was hardly a desert; a century later, in fact, the new
Resident Commissioner of the Bechuanaland Protectorate, Charles Rey, was
to remark that even its thirstiest parts, the Kalahari, were "misnamed Desert" (1988:6). Its extreme lack of fertility to the eyes of the evangelists was
a metaphor made matter-of-fact. In part this was a function of the contemporary European invention of Africa as "wasteland" (cf. Mason 1987 for

American parallels). But it also evoked the long-standing symbolic contrast between church-as-garden and world-as-wilderness, of Eden and the banishment after the Fall.[11] Once innocent Africans, having suffered Satanic reverses (above, pp. 109f.), were clearly still consigned to the dark nether regions; only the implanting of the church in their midst might remedy their miserable state. These tropes of subtropical deserts and desiccation, of wasteland and wilderness, were to provide natural reinforcement to those already predisposed, like Moffat (1842:17), to see themselves as irrigators:

> The Karroo country, which is the back ground of the colony, is . . . a parched and arid plain, stretching out to such an extent that the vast hills by which it is terminated, or rather which divide it from other plains, are lost in the distance. The beds of numberless little rivers (in which water is rarely to be found) cross like veins in a thousand directions this enormous space. . . . Excepting these, . . . [n]owhere appear any signs of life, nor a point on which the eye can dwell with pleasure. The compass of human sight is too small to take in the circumference of the whole—the soul must rest on the horrors of the wide spread desert.

This was a desert, in short, because it lacked definition, disconcerting because it defied surveillance. The eye searched in vain for recognizable margins and limits. In this void it was the very act of narration that imposed an order of space and time, making the metaphorical leap from these formless wastes to known cultural referents. Thus the Rev. Broadbent (1865:2):

> We travelled through a barren and desolate land, in which we saw no living creature beside our own party, except when the quagga or zebra passed; reminding us, in their lonely course, of some impressive imagery of the Hebrew prophets [Jer.ii.24, and Hos.viii.9].

And again (1865:5):

> . . . The earnestness with which we dug, the manner in which the water sprang, and the gratification we enjoyed at our success, forcibly reminded me of the Israelites in the wilderness. . . . [Num.xxi.17].

Here a coherent chain of images closes the gap between the evangelical journey and the sojourn in Sinai, the distressing African wastes and the dynamic formlessness of the biblical desert. Poetic trope locates the progress in a well-established vision of history, validating the right of the wandering prophet to take possession of the Promised Land. This mythic theme had long been susceptible to Judeo-Christian manipulation (cf. Walzer 1985; also Hill 1989:207 on the connections between Exodus and *The Pilgrim's*

Progress). It was later to be put to work yet again by dissenting black Christians in an effort to escape the bondage of colonialism.

The African desert might have evoked long-standing European images, but its people were adjudged in terms of a particular nineteenth-century notion of civilization (above, chapter 3). They represented the natural obverse of enlightenment, of developed human potential. We have already noted how the bestial "Bushmen" were seen as one with their wild surrounds. Note what Edwards (1886:61–62) says of the blacks who conveyed him the four hundred miles from the coast to the Methodist station of Platberg:

> We made a start with a train of three waggons, in one of which was the printing-press for the Mission. The mode of travelling involved great loss of time, and . . . nearly cost me the surrender of my patience and temper too. . . . It was provoking, when we were about to inspan the oxen, to see one man sit down composedly to mend his *veldtschoen* (shoe); another rectifying a reim [rein]; while a third would be tying up something, and a fourth rolling up his scanty bedding. . . . Hours were often wasted in this manner. It was very trying for one just from England, where everything was orderly. One day I said to Mr. A[rchbell]—: 'You say these men are members of the Society . . . ? It has not made them active, industrious, or time-saving.' Just such were the natives of that country then, and just such were the impressions of a man who had lately opened his eyes upon Africa.

Once more caught in the candid English gaze, the disorderly savage shows himself incapable of rational foresight, unable to see time as a scarce resource to be put to work in the cause of improvement. The European observer finds his urgency and self-control foundering in the timeless sloth of Africa, and his narrative establishes at the outset the fundamental tension that his mission must transcend. A visual depiction of "The Waggon in a Hole" from this section of Edwards' text unwittingly conveys the predicament: as the black drivers struggle to extricate the wagon, two missionaries in hats and jackets watch them resignedly, one recording the scene in his journal (plate 6).

This illustration also gives an uncensored glimpse of the labor relations that underlay the mission journey. While the text decries the lack of native industry, the picture shows the black drivers wrestling with the oxen, the whites contemplating them from postures of evident repose. Similarly, Edwards' (1886:73f.) description of an encounter with beasts of prey might evoke the dragon Apollyon barring Christian's progress. But it also reveals the extent to which the success of these travels depended on the

PLATE 6   *The Waggon in a Hole. Reproduced from Edwards,* Reminiscences *(1886:57).*

African laborers. As a lion and lioness appear close to the road, the missionary party draws to a halt. The Europeans confer, and one instructs the driver (1886:74):

> 'Take my gun and go as near to them as you can, and shoot, not to wound them, but . . . to frighten them. If they run towards you, you retreat to the waggon.'

The animal chases the driver, who swiftly withdraws. A second man is sent toward the lions as decoy, while the marksman fires again, the evangelists watching from the wagon. In a pinch, African practical skill obviously suffices. The lions retreat, and both the journey and the narrative resume. The blacks become invisible again, their knowledge of the physical and social geography being the absent presence that guides the party to its destination. Edwards, though, concludes: "the Lord was our Protector in the hour of need."

As they moved northwards beyond the boundaries of the Colony, the Christians scanned the horizon for something "pleasurable to look upon," an oasis where they could plant the seeds of civilization. What they sought were minimal signs of physical and social hospitality. Campbell describes his first view of Dithakong (Lattakoo), site of the future LMS station, in these terms: [12]

... in 10 days, travelling almost due north, we reached the top of a hill
where we all at once [had] a full view of Latakkoo, lying in a beautiful
valley. The town being divided into a great many districts, standing a
little distance from each other, makes it cover a great deal of ground,
perhaps five miles in circumference. . . . [W]e were much pleased to
see fields enclosed with hedges, a rare sight beyond the limits of the
colony.

The eye, weary of unbounded, uncharted landscapes, could at last come to
rest on the rudiments of cultivation: a large settlement, with visibly bounded
subdivisions and, most portentous of all, enclosed fields.

The Rise of the Tswana Mission

In our opening chapters we sketched the general historical background to
the Nonconformist thrust into South Africa. Let us pause here, before the
encounter between the churchmen and their would-be subjects, to consider
the specific conditions and processes that opened the Tswana world to evangelism. Recall a few of the details outlined earlier. John Campbell, a director
of the LMS, had been sent to the Cape in 1812 to survey the progress and
prospects of mission work in the interior.[13] An astute observer—his account
has furnished much material for our discussion here—he set out by way of
the Society's posts in the Colony, making for Klaarwater in what was to
become Griqualand, north of the Orange River (du Plessis 1911:138). This
station, which had been founded in the early nineteenth century, was just
over one hundred miles south of Dithakong, then the capital of Chief Mothibi of the Tlhaping. Efforts had already been made to establish a foothold
among the latter, but in 1802 the LMS had abandoned the project (du Plessis 1911:111; see below, p. 190). Thus, by 1813 Campbell was aware that the
Tlhaping were the southernmost of a large cluster of "Bechuana" peoples
who shared a language and a centralized residential pattern conducive to
evangelization. Learning at Klaarwater that Mothibi had, via intermediaries,
expressed interest in receiving missionaries, he proceeded to the chief's
court "to ask his permission" to send one or more.[14] But the ruler replied[15]

> that his people had no time for their instructions, having to attend to
> the cattle, to dig, sow and reap the fields. . . . Besides, the things which
> these people teach are contrary to all our customs. . . . It would not do
> for [the missionaries] to live at Latakkoo, but were they to live at a
> distance, I should . . . send some of our children to them to learn the
> Dutch language.

Campbell insisted that his colleagues were themselves industrious people;
just how industrious the Southern Tswana would soon find out. Whites, he
continued, had made all the fine goods he brought, and would reveal the

secrets of their manufacture—and of the greatest act of creation, that of man himself. The evangelists would only instruct those "willing to be taught" and would not interfere with chiefly government. To this the ruler is said to have replied: "Send instructors, and I will be a father to them!" [16] The sentence was destined to reverberate loudly through mission circles back home.

It is significant that this exchange turned on issues of production and time, for these were to mark out the central arena of debate and struggle between colonizer and colonized. The key misrecognitions in the relationship between them are already visible. Campbell's notions of time, work, and self-discipline were drawn from the natural lineaments of the industrial capitalist world. The Tswana, however, soon indicated that his understanding of personhood, property, and production was by no means self-evident or shared by them. Campbell simply failed to see that the attraction of whites to the Tlhaping flowed from the mystical qualities attributed to them and their things in a hinterland where raids were endemic and where guns, beads, and tobacco had become prime valuables. Pursuing a "rational discussion" with Mothibi, he took the ruler's agreement to signal his considered acceptance of the mission. The early evangelists felt the need to reason with the Africans, to convince them of superior truths, and to gain their voluntary compliance, even through the medium of inadequate interpreters. Yet on this and many other occasions, it was the nonverbal signs of the Europeans that spoke most cogently to the Tlhaping. The chief's response suggests that he conceived of a missionary presence in the usual terms of black-white exchange on the frontier: those of trade. The Christians would supply desired goods and techniques for the conventional return: cattle, the spoils of the hunt, and general protection. But it was to be a symmetrical exchange, one that would not alter the existing order. As Campbell noted ruefully, Mothibi ended the interview by remarking: "When the missionaries have got enough they shall be at liberty to depart."

Nonetheless, Campbell returned to the Colony well pleased with his mandate, and, despite some government obstruction, we find Rev. Read writing from Dithakong in 1817 that the chief had "fulfilled [his] promise." Yet neither he nor his senior advisers would permit any preaching: [17]

> They believe that the very day they give their consent to receive the gospel they that moment must give up their political authority, their manner of dress, marriage, circumcision, etc. and although we affirm to them the contrary they say they have eyes to see how it has gone at Griqua town (formerly Klaarwater).

This was both a bold observation and a bald prevarication: the Tlhaping *were* convinced of the potentially subversive impact of Christianity; and, in spite of disingenuous affirmations to the contrary, the condemnation of African culture *was* an axiom of the civilizing mission. So sure were they of the dangers of the church that some Tlhaping royals urged the ruler to expel the LMS, arguing that its continued presence would end in their subjection (Moffat 1842:229f.). While Read managed, after a long struggle, to persuade Mothibi to move his seat to the better-watered banks of the Kuruman River, he was unable to sustain a station there. It was to fall to Robert Moffat to revive the mission in 1821 and to make it the cornerstone of Tswana evangelism.

It will be remembered that the Wesleyan Methodist Missionary Society (WMMS) was founded in 1813 and that its first evangelist arrived at the Cape in 1814, only to be denied permission to preach (above, p. 48); that in 1816 the Society was allowed to set up a station in Namaqualand, beyond the frontier, where they heard of a hinterland of "Bechuana" peoples who seemed amenable to evangelization; and that in 1821 two missionaries were posted to these peoples. At the end of chapter 1, we left the Rev. Kay just as he was setting off, traveling with a large party of Griqua and Tswana who were returning from a trade expedition to the borders of the Colony (Mears 1970:1). The very existence of such a party, and its movement along the frontier, confirms that these populations were already caught up in complex flows of knowledge and commodities well before the missionary advance into the interior (see chapter 4). In fact, Broadbent and Hodgson, who were to follow Kay later that year, were dismayed to find that the "so-called Christians" at the LMS station at Campbell would offer their labor only in exchange for money.[18]

Kay was met en route by Moffat and his wife, and was taken to Kuruman, where he spent several months surveying the surrounding countryside for a suitable site. Denominational cooperation was common in those early years, although rivalry was always close to the surface; Moffat was to refer to the "cabinet of Methodists" who had passed through Kuruman by 1825 as "a heterogeneous mess of inconsistencies."[19] Once in the interior, Kay came face to face with the effects of *difaqane* (above, p. 167ff.). Rumors, raids, and flight were the order of the day, and by the end of 1821 he concluded that such turmoil was not conducive to the mission.

But Samuel Broadbent, sent to join him early in 1822, was less easily dissuaded. Taking advantage of the knowledge of his LMS colleagues in Griqualand, he decided to make contact with "a large population of Bechuanas" northeast of the Vaal River. And when the Hodgson family met him later, they set off to "a region where no missionary had been, where Christ had not been named" (Broadbent 1865:16). Making their way without the benefit of an adequate guide or interpreter, and mindful of the fact that they were crossing a land of "darkness and war," they continued eastward,

Broadbent's narrative becoming ever more rhapsodic as they seemed to approach their goal. After two weeks they reached a Korana town, whose chief made strenuous efforts, through a Dutch-speaking subject, to persuade them to remain with him. While still seeking to extricate themselves from these ardent attentions, Broadbent (1865:28) and Hodgson

> saw clouds of dust ascend into the air, then heard the lowing of hundreds of cattle, bleating of flocks of sheep and goats, driven by a mixed multitude of men, women, and children, accompanied by a host of armed warriors. These were a part of the tribe of Bechuanas, the Barolongs, to whom we were journeying.

This section of the Barolong boo Seleka (or Seleka-Rolong) was fleeing from the pursuing MmaNthatisi, who had sacked Thabeng, their village to the north. The evangelists determined to join the main body of the same chiefdom, now settled at Matlwasse under their ruler, Sefunelo. Significantly, once the marauding MmaNthatisi warriors heard that there were white men with the Seleka-Rolong, they gave them a wide berth;[20] we are told that when the Wesleyans, en route to Matlwasse, actually came upon a party of these warriors, the latter fled at the very sight of them. The Europeans had not entered history on a blank page. They had been assigned a role in an African saga of long standing, a saga whose parameters they dimly understood.

The Methodists were to be uprooted several times before they managed, in 1833, to build a settlement securely under their control at Thaba 'Nchu. But their accounts of the countryside around Matlwasse were positively Edenic, especially by contrast to their descriptions of the "wilderness" through which they had passed. A "cluster of mountains and gently rising hills," it was, for the usually severe Mr. Broadbent, "most delightfully romantic—very fruitful and salubrious."[21] Here, it seemed, was a place in which the seed might fall on fertile earth, where the community imagined for Africa might take root.

"Glass and the Ego": Initial Exchanges[22]

The initial meetings between the evangelists and the African rulers were the subject of careful forethought on the part of the whites. In some respects like courtly rituals, they bespoke the intentions of each side as it tried to construct the other in its own image. At the center of the ceremonies was a set of material and verbal exchanges whose terms soon became a matter of convention, laying the bases for future interaction between the Tswana and the Christians. But the very first exchanges were visual, aural, and tactile, a trade of perceptions. Take Campbell's description of the entry into Dithakong:[23]

We were led to what may be called their Royal Exchange, in which our
waggons were unyoked. The place was constantly crowded . . . and
there was no small uproar. . . . Now we were completely in their power,
and we who had been so long unaccustomed to hear any other human
voices but our own, felt strange at this confusion of tongues. Some
were squeezing through the crowd to see us, others to examine our
waggons, our tent, our various things just as it struck their fancy. . . .
[W]ithout ceremony they touched us as if we had been so many statues
fallen down from the fixed stars. I must confess I felt rather anxious in
the midst of this bustle. . . . Our poor women kept very close within
our waggons, which formed a square with our tent in the centre . . .
hither a crowd followed us, feasting their eyes by earnestly looking to
the plates and other articles on our table.

In fact, it was the whites who feasted, sitting down then and there to a
meal—a sacrament?—served by their black servants before the assembled
crowd.[24] Especially notable in their recollections of the occasion was their
feeling of impotence in the face of the heathen babble; a barely hidden discomfort at being "completely in [the] power" of those whom they would
make into subjects of God and Empire. The colonial encounter, it seems,
began in an awkward moment of ritual irony. Great must have been the
impact of the dramatic entry of Campbell and his entourage into the chiefly
court. It is not clear how many Tlhaping had seen whites before, but virtually
everyone must have heard of them and of their association with goods of
strange power. There could have been no better affirmation of these preconceptions than the procession of wagons that encamped in the midst of
the town. The Tlhaping seem to have related to the Europeans as objects,
touching and bearing in on them, enjoying a closeness never again permitted
by the etiquette of the mission, with its deference to racial separation and
the spatial discreteness of person and property.[25] In this regard the square
enclosure and all that "took place" at the center of the most public of
Tswana spaces was ominous, foreshadowing a methodical reconstruction of
their symbolic map. At the same time Campbell was discomforted by the
intimacy of the encounter and by his lack of control over it. His party was
surrounded by people who showed no awe or respect whatsoever. Even their
speech was a disorderly "confusion of tongues."

Campbell's style here expresses his intent. In the narratives of these
early exchanges, the role of the confessing self is very evident. Lévi-Strauss
(1976:35) has said, of ethnography, that the "observer apprehends himself
as his own instrument of observation." In an utterly foreign landscape, the
European self, already divided as a matter of cultural principle (see chapter

2), becomes the only yardstick of experience, making itself "other" to the "I" who uses it. In the process it provides a "self-centered" reading of a strange world. Thus the ethnographic career "finds its principle in 'confessions', written or untold." But as Campbell's testimony reminds us, this was even more so in the case of the evangelical enterprise. Foucault (1978:60) argues that the modern church, both Catholic and Protestant, long ago established confession as a mode of self-discipline, making the bourgeois subject and his conscience into the undisputed measure of all surveillance and evaluation. The mission societies, cast in just this mould, monitored their agents in the field through their detailed and introspective reports. In Campbell's despatch from Dithakong we see the confessing self in full operation. Self-disclosure textures his construction of the Tlhaping, as he projects himself now as subject, now as object.

This self bears with it an entire worldview, of course, and it is palpable in the early exchanges between evangelists and local leaders. If we accept, with Mauss (1966), that the gift constructs a social relationship by acting as a vehicle for the self, the goods handed by the Christians to the chiefs were the bearers of a particular kind of selfhood. Campbell, it will be recalled, gave the Tlhaping ruler a copper comb, a silver headband, and a chain, all of which he placed on the royal person, so that the culminating gift, the looking glass, might reveal to him his transformed visage. Later the missionary also presented some tobacco, a gift, he said, from those who hoped to come and work among his people. The chief reciprocated by bestowing on Campbell and his colleague, James Read, a "fine ox" each.

The "tokens of friendship" that the Christians gave as their opening gambit anticipated the more complex transactions that would incorporate the Tswana into the culture of empire. We have noted that European commodities circulated quite widely in the South African hinterland at this time; beads, tobacco, and knives had become prized trade goods, and by 1820 Tswana parties were traveling to the borders of the Colony to obtain them (Moffat 1842:239; chapter 4). Evangelists seeking entry into the Tlhaping chiefdom after Campbell's visit had been advised to say that well-wishers across the Great Waters had sent with them "a plentiful supply of articles to make [the chief] and the people happy." This information, it appears, "produced the desired effect on Mothibi's mind" (Moffat 1842:235). The opening gift of the missionaries soon became standardized, as did the response of the Tswana. The chiefs had no intention of remaining long in the Christians' debt, however. Almost immediately, they made the return prestation of two oxen and sundry small stock,[26] a gift rated highly in both the local bovine currency and the white oxwagon economy.

Let us look more closely at this exchange, for it was a significant moment in the engagement of the two worlds. Objects passed in each direction, bearing with them a set of values and intentions largely misread by the recipients. Some of the goods given by the evangelists to the Tswana had already become the conventional currency of black-white relations in southern Africa; others were to be associated exclusively with their own presence. Broadbent's (1865:47) account of his first meeting with the chief of the Seleka-Rolong treats the matter as routine:

> A fire being made on the ground, and a circle formed around it, I had an opportunity of presenting the Chief with the presents I had brought consisting of beads, rings, snuff-box, mirror, knife, etc. etc., all of which appeared to give him great pleasure. . . . Tobacco was in great demand. . . .

It is often said by historians that traders in search of skins, ivory, and cattle "taught the natives" of South Africa to want such commodities as beads, buttons, tobacco, and knives (de Kiewiet 1936:818). That wants were fostered in this manner seems clear, but there was also indigenous precedent for most of these tastes. The Tswana, as we saw in the last chapter, had long traded among themselves, southern peoples such as the Tlhaping exchanging lead hematite, a glittering hair cosmetic (*sebilo*) mined in their territory, for iron implements, copper rings, tobacco, and beads from the Ngwaketse to the north (Shillington 1985:11). Of tobacco, Lichtenstein (1973[1807]: 67) remarked very early on that "it is one of their needs and there is nothing they like to barter more" (see also Campbell 1822:1,276; Burchell 1824:2, passim).[27] And of beads, Philip (1828:2,131) wrote that they were the quintessential "representatives of value." With unusual insight he added that, because "utility is, perhaps, more connected with beauty [here] than it is with us," such aesthetic objects may condense signs of wealth into marks of social distinction; that is why those beads adjudged desirable were so avidly sought.[28] Sheffield steel was to displace African iron, and glass baubles were to take the place of the bodily adornments of a prior fashion. Yet none of these objects was introduced into a void, and while they brought novel values into the Tswana world, they also acquired meanings different from those intended by their donors.

Besides the inevitable beads, knives, and tobacco, the missionaries chose the sorts of shiny trinkets that contrasted sharply with their own sober sense of modesty and true inner value, the latter often being set against base, outward things in their writings.[29] The allure of such "splendid trifles" had ironically been established by former generations of slave traders, who had calculated them to be instantly appealing to the Africans, with their "childlike" lack of refinement and their dependence upon physical gratification.

In his epic poem denouncing the evils of the slave trade a generation before, Roscoe (1787:8–9) was unequivocal about the motives of such gifts:

> Thou to their dazzled sight disclosest wide
> Thy magazine of wonders, cull'd with care,
> From all the splendid trifles, that adorn
> Thine own luxurious region; ...
>   ... pointing out
> Wants which before they knew not; mirrors bright,
> Reflecting to their quick and curious eye
> Their sable features; shells, and beads, and rings,
> And all fantastic folly's gingling bells,
> That catch'd th' unpractis'd ear, and thence convey
> Their unsuspected poison to the mind.

While they saw their enterprise as the moral inverse, the Nonconformists were to be condemned to a similar historical judgment. They directed most of their goods to the chiefs for their personal consumption, goods calculated to flatter and adorn, to quicken desire. The European vision of monarchic power assumed that African polities rested on the exclusive sovereignty of the ruler and his close kin, and it was to them that they wished to underscore the material advantages of cooperation. "Most of the captains, having tasted bread, long for wheat to be served," wrote Read from Dithakong. "By this means the Gospel may get a footing." [30] As we shall see, the chiefs had a less self-centered, more strategic purpose in mind for the evangelists, a purpose soon to be brought home to the latter in no uncertain terms. In the meantime, while the churchmen might have winced at the need to pander to primitive vanity and greed, doing so was justified as a means to a greater end; namely, the exorcism of superficial conceits through inner revelation. But are *we* justified in taking for granted—as the missionaries did—the practical and symbolic meaning of these seductive objects? What, for instance, was the role of the looking glass, a ubiquitous presence in these opening exchanges?

The looking glass astonished those seeing it for the first time. It was a fairly cheap gift of maximum effect. "To break the ground," Read tells, "I gave them a looking glass, some beads, some tobacco etc. for their king with which they were very proud." [31] Clocks and telescopes were to follow closely upon mirrors as devices capable of working transformations, although, being more costly, they were seldom given at the start. Clearly, glass was taken to be the window into a new way of seeing and being. Mumford (1934:124) and others have claimed that the development of its large-scale production was the most significant factor in the evolution of the modern, techno-empiricist worldview. While we do not ourselves regard this technical advance as a sufficient cause—or for that matter a necessary consequence—of cultural reformation, its impact on enlightenment self-conceptions was certainly palpable. If the first axiom of the new empiricism was "seeing is believing," then glass—in the form of spectacles, telescope, and microscope—became its prime medium.[32] As Mumford says, it seemed to make many of the mysteries of nature "transparent" (1934:131).

Glass had been used as a mirror by the Romans, but the modern looking glass was developed in sixteenth-century Germany and Venice, when improved surfaces were coated with silver amalgam. It was not until the mid-seventeenth century, however, that the "domestic-and-fancy" glass trade made hand-mirrors an inexpensive, common possession throughout England (Thorpe 1935:117, 151). Although glass beads were also being manufactured in Britain by this time, they became an item of mass trade to the colonies only when they began to be imported in quantity from Venice in the late eighteenth century (Nesbitt n.d.:93).

Our missionary texts have already given plenty evidence of the role of optics in the early nineteenth-century imagination. These images, of course, were drawn from a well-used cultural stock. Mitchell (1986:166), for one, has noted the centrality of optical metaphors—metaphors of rational "transparence"—in the writings of both enlightenment political theory and its critics, most notably Burke and Marx. The repeated reference in evangelical narratives to vision, reflection, mirrors, and glass shows how these figures also lent themselves to Nonconformist thought. Once the divine light entered the world, it created the conditions for human beings to distinguish truth from falsity, and to recognize their own likeness in all its imperfection. In the "nocturnal regions" of heathenism, however, no such differences could be recognized, for "man in his natural state was blind."[33] As bearers of the light, therefore, the Christians had to persuade those long accustomed to darkness to "open their eyes" and let "brightness illumine their hearts." To the children of an evolutionary age, such images of enlightenment made cultural imperialism seem like a moral duty.

While they decried Godless modernity, the missionaries were advocates of technological advance, seeking to harness it to the progress of Christ's Kingdom (see chapter 2). Campbell, writing of the pathbreaking visit to Dithakong, mentions Read's wish that their brethren in London had a "glass" in which they could witness the historic event.[34] Telescopes and pocket compasses were indispensable tools in navigating the uncharted landscape, and the evangelists made sure they had the instruments to impose their civilizing plan upon it. After all, surveying and mapping were a crucial part of the European incorporation of others. Hence, before he left for the interior, Moffat apprenticed himself to the government surveyor in Cape Town and wrote to the LMS requesting a sextant, an 'Artificial Horizon' with two spare glasses, and two compasses.[35] The vacant countryside would be charted, measured, and entered onto the colonial map.

It is against this cultural background, then, that the missionary held up the looking glass to the Tswana. As we have noted, the gesture itself was not unprecedented. Burchell (1822:1,461) put it to "scientific" effect when he explored the peoples of the interior in 1811–12, gauging their relative intelligence by their response to seeing themselves in his shaving-mirror. The "Bushmen," he says,

> laughed, and stared with vacant surprize and wonder, to see their own faces; but expressed not the least curiosity about it; nor do I believe it excited in their minds one single idea; and I may not, perhaps, be doing them an injustice by asserting that, whether capable of reflection or not, these individuals never exerted it.

The extension of the mirror-image to the notion of reflective thought is unquestioned here. But the missionary seems to have held up the looking glass with a yet more specific intention, one that embodied evangelical values and purposes. Evidence of this is discernible in their rhetoric. For instance, Moffat, in a fit of despondency, was to write:[36]

> Once or twice during every week day I illustrate and apply a portion of scripture. I cannot complain for want of attention: but alas! How many see their face as in a glass and straightaway forget!

And Broadbent (1865:88), musing on how the Scriptures show man his wickedness and "bring to light the things of darkness," concludes: "Yes, they describe human nature, and, as in a mirror, man sees himself in this the word of God."

Is it surprising that Adam Smith (1976:204–05), political economist of preference in evangelical circles, should have envisaged the self-awareness of economic man as taking shape like an image in the mirror? The symbolic association of the looking glass and the contained, reflective individual in European thought has received much comment (see e.g., Cooley 1964:183f.; Abrams 1953; Babcock 1975; Hannerz 1983; also Frazer 1964:203–04). Thus, for example, Mumford (1934:129) notes that the evolution of the hand-mirror as a common possession among the bourgeoisie coincided with the rise in art and literature of a concern with introspection and the self as object:

> The self in the mirror . . . was the self *in abstracto*, only part of the real self, the part that one can divorce from the background of nature and the influential presence of other men.

This was the self that the missionaries were to try to liberate from the "socialistic" mesh of "tribal" life, which snared people in an unholy tangle of superstition and social dependence. Being a self divided, it was capable of a searching inner dialogue; a self able both to recognize the truth of its own finitude and to exercise reflexive discipline. It was the self, in sum, of bourgeois individualism nurtured by the Enlightenment and the Industrial Revolution (see chapter 2). The image in the mirror blocked out the encompassing world, turning that self back on itself, dissociating the ego from its context, and fragmenting a formerly continuous perceptual universe. The "native," though he might not have known it, had come face to face with the Christian subject.[37]

THE AFRICAN PERSPECTIVE

We have no way of knowing, of course, what the Africans actually saw in the mirror. But there are strong grounds to believe that they were bothered by its arresting gaze.[38] Hodgson, for example, writes:[39]

> We offered [a chief] a gift of beads, tinderbox and looking glass. He refused to take the looking glass, because if it remained with him, he and his people could not remove from their present residence.

The missionary says nothing more, but it seems that the chief understood the reflection in the glass to be turning the viewer back on himself, rooting him—like Narcissus?—to the spot and preventing his growth or movement. In contrast, late nineteenth-century photographers were to find Tswana reluctant subjects precisely because the snapshot seemed to separate a human being from his or her own image; it threatened to capture the self, draw it from its center, shatter its integrity, and negate its ability to act on its own account (cf. Alloula 1986:92). Common to both the transfixing mirror and the captivating lens, however, was the power that glass might give to others to grasp a person's very essence. It was, in short, both wondrous and dangerous, potent and potentially eviscerating.

There is evidence from another place and another time in the Bantu-speaking world that also points to the capacity of the looking glass to frame, individuate, and seize personal identity. In her classic discussion of "A Modern Movement of Witch-Finders" in Central Africa, Audrey Richards (1935: 448) described the activities of bands of wandering wonder-workers who dressed conspicuously in European clothing:

> Arrived at a village, they summoned the headman, who was bidden to gather his people together and to kill and cook a chicken for the ritual meal of which all were to partake. Once assembled the men and

women were lined up in separate files, and passed one by one behind the back of the witch-finder, who caught their reflections in a small round mirror by a turn of his wrist. By his image in the glass it was claimed that a sorcerer could be immediately detected. . . .

The witch-finders held that, once captured in the "magic mirror" (1935: 449), witches could no longer conceal their evil activities or abilities by blending into the surrounding community. Divination by looking glass seems to have been especially appropriate for identifying and capturing a hidden malevolent, whose offence was the assertion of unbridled self-interest in violation of the common good. This form of divination, we stress, was a quite explicit deployment of European tools and techniques (1935:451). For here, as among the Tswana, what appeared to lurk behind the mirror were the still mysterious powers and practices of the whites.

Through the Looking Glass

Although there are no Tswana texts that recount their early perceptions of whites, it is possible to recover something from the record of their actions and reactions. Sometimes those reactions were highly visible—and very voluble. Take Campbell's (1822:1,222) entry into the Hurutse capital which, being far north of Kuruman, had not been formally visited by Europeans before:

> The street through which we went was crowded with people, and many hastened to their doors to see us pass. The sight of white men threw them into fits of convulsive laughter; but the young were more seriously affected, they screamed, and in the utmost horror fled to the first place of concealment they could find. The noise was tumultuous. . . .

Being the only language open to the missionaries themselves, such sounds and gestures—and the less boisterous exchanges that followed—were subject to careful scrutiny on the part of the Europeans. As Rev. Broadbent wrote regretfully of his first meeting with a Rolong royal, "We could only communicate . . . by signs."[40] Consequently, he took pains to describe the nonverbal features of the encounter in exquisite detail. Nor were his efforts unusual; despite the fact that the Tswana speak through the texts of others, they are not rendered voiceless. In this regard too it is to be stressed that, in the earliest dialogues between the whites and the blacks, the former were less than fully in control. And so, in their accounts, a counter-discourse is to be heard: a discourse which may be illuminated by playing it off other cultural materials—among them, linguistic usages and poetic expressions— that give insight into contemporary symbols and meanings, relations and categories.

Burchell (1824:2,559), the perspicacious naturalist, observed that the Tlhaping used the term *lekgoa* (pl. *makgoa*) to refer to whites. The full term in fact was *makgoa ma shweu*, literally "white bush lice," *kgoa* referring to a tick or a louse commonly found on the hindquarters of domestic animals. Evoking, perhaps, the notion that Europeans were first sighted clinging to the backs of horses (J. Comaroff 1985:137), it is a noun of the class (sing. prefix, *le-*; pl., *ma-*) that usually denotes plants, animals, and persons of debased status (*leshahé*, "albino"; *legodu*, "thief"; *lethwalwane*, "foundling"). For all their extraordinary powers, whites were regarded early on as less than completely human, as were "mixed-race" peoples like the Griqua (*lesetedi*). Note that it was such "mixed-race" peoples, themselves associated with horses and armed soldiery, who first brought Tswana into contact with European culture. Burchell (1824:2,559) writes:

> The first men whom the Bachapins [Tlhaping] ever saw wearing the European dress, were some Colonial Hottentots, who about twenty years before the date of my visit, began to find their way into this country. . . .

By 1802 direct contact with the whites had been well established, and Kok and Edwards, who had set up the first mission station near the Tlhaping and Tlharo, were heavily involved in commerce with these peoples. Wagons bearing ivory were being driven to the Cape by local recruits, returning with a variety of goods for barter; and, in a dispute over remuneration, two Tlhaping employees shot and killed Kok (du Plessis 1911:112). This incident, and the subsequent execution of the culprits by their chief, was a graphic illustration of the life-determining power being vested in European goods, power that was increasingly symbolized by the gun (see chapter 7). When Burchell (1824:2,376f.) reached Dithakong, Chief Mothibi wasted no time in pressing on him a "matter of national consultation": while Khoisan traders had armed some of the inhabitants of the region, Tlhaping efforts to obtain muskets from the mission at Klaarwater had been fruitless. The chief demanded that Burchell part with one of his firearms, doing all he could to force his reluctant visitor's hand. Like other travelers, Burchell reflected uncomfortably on the fact that the Tswana believed *makgoa* to be inexhaustibly rich (1824:2,451). Yet he himself fed this assumption in order to promote the "mercantile enterprises" that he saw as the key to civilizing the interior (1824:2,440):

> I invited him [a senior Tlhaping royal] to make a journey to *Cape Town*, where he would, I assured him, not only get beads in abundance, but would behold so many extraordinary and handsome things, that he

would never afterwards find time enough for relating [them] to the people of Litakun [Dithakong].

What the Englishman failed to realize was the extent to which the valuables he bore were viewed as an extension of himself. Earlier we saw how the predatory hordes in the interior fled at the sight of the white churchmen, and how the vanquished tried by all means to attract them as protectors. This suggests that the evangelists, as repositories of powerful goods and techniques, had themselves become supreme values. Soon after Read arrived to set up the station at Dithakong, a group of Tswana, who had journeyed from afar to trade, congratulated Mothibi for "residing with God in one city," an idea the missionary hastily tried to dispel.[41] More sustained observation of European technology revealed ever greater powers. As Hamilton wrote, in 1818, from Dithakong:[42]

> The clock which was sent by the Directors for the church . . . is to the Bootchuannas a great wonder. Some of them were asking us whether the three little wooden men that strike the hours eat meat and milk. They have much disputing among themselves whether the three men were made by men or God.

Such elementary manufacture as the hewing of wood and dressing of stone were performed by the missionaries for all to see. Here the principle of production was plain. But machines and technological tools from Britain were introduced ready-made into the Tswana world. The seeming vitality of the machine, more than anything else perhaps, confounded indigenous distinctions between the animate and the inanimate; this being dramatized by the little mechanical men of the LMS clock, whose wooden humanity was designed to draw attention to the genius of their own impersonal workings. Here was irony indeed, for it was the evangelists who were to portray time as an abstract, objective measure. The Africans, by contrast, took it to be man made, an implicit dimension of all human activity.

There was yet further irony in the Tswana concern about the origin and nature of the mechanical men. By virtue of their apparent ability to breathe life into the inanimate, the whites had taken on superhuman power. But that power was soon to be perceived as part and parcel of an ominous order of domination. What the Rev. Hamilton does not tell us is that these little men were in fact "strutting" European soldiers (Moffat 1842:339); before long, they became miniature embodiments of colonial coercion. Moffat, who inherited the clock in 1820, recalls:

> [A Kora chief], and others, had poisoned the minds of some of the leading men with the idea, that the missionaries were only the precur-

sors of the Government, who would soon follow in their train, and make soldiers of every one of them. The little images in the clock were soon magnified into Goliaths, and the place of worship looked upon as an *eintlu ea kholego*, a house of bondage. It was necessary to take down the fairy-looking strangers, and cut a piece off their painted bodies, to convince the affrighted natives that the objects of their alarm were only bits of colored wood. Many, however, thought themselves too wise to be thus easily deceived. Though perfectly convinced of the egregious folly of believing that the little *liséto*, "carved ones," would one day seize them by the throat in the sanctuary, they nevertheless continued to suspect, that the motives of the missionary were anything but disinterested.

Already the would-be subjects of the church were turning its own rhetoric against it, calling on the fertile potential of the Bible to ally themselves with righteous sufferers elsewhere. Although the mission tried to exorcise the menace in its emblems, it clearly failed to dissociate itself from the colonial state at its back.

Another element in the portentous power of the missionaries was literacy. As we shall see in chapter 6, it was to be an essential tool in the colonization of Tswana consciousness. The evangelist had his Bible with him at the very first encounter, for while tinsel might catch the African's attention, his real gift was to be the word. Unlike trivial outward things, the ability to read opened a window to the truth by cultivating the inner being of the person (above, p. 63). The ways in which the value of literacy—and the power of the book—were conveyed to the Tswana could only have magnified their sense of the potency of the whites themselves. Campbell writes: [43]

> We explained to [Mahutu, the chief's wife] the nature of a letter. Mr. Anderson shewd her one he had got from his wife since he had left home, by which he knew all that was going on at Klaar Water. This highly entertained her, especially when she was told that Adam Kok brought it, yet did not know anything that was in it, which we made her understand by explaining the use of the wax [seal]. The Bible was lying on our table, which gave rise . . . to our explaining the nature and use of a book, and particularly that book.

Like the ability to transform the world through ritual, literacy seems initially to have been understood less as a learned skill than as an innate mystical capacity. Even after the Tswana no longer thought this, the written word retained a good deal of its potency for them. Thus, for example, the treatment of the body with script and newsprint later became a regular part of healing rites, particularly among the illiterate poor in apartheid South Africa, for whom the appropriation of the word presented itself as one of the few possible ways of gaining some control over a hostile, changing world (J. Comaroff 1985:203).

As with the magical word, so with the tangible body. Recall how African physiognomy intrigued Europe in the age of revolution, how it was seen as all of a piece with African mentality. Albeit from a quite different perspective, the Tswana were similarly intrigued, and took the fantastic capacities of the whites—literacy being just one among them—to be an integral part of their physical being. Not surprisingly, then, in the unusual, liminal space opened up by first encounters, each party contemplated the corporeal exoticism of the other with frank fascination, even desire. One of Robert Moffat's biographers tells how the fearsome Ndebele chief, Mzilikazi, insisted on "riding in Moffat's wagon, lying on Moffat's bed, sleeping near him, handling his possessions, getting Moffat to rub his feet, stroking Moffat's beard"; all these being "naive expressions of happiness" at the presence of the evangelist, who responded with "reserve" (Northcott 1969:xvi). Here we gain insight into the intimacy, even eroticism, of these early meetings (cf. Pratt 1985:132), a physical playfulness across the lines of race and gender that the bodily politics of colonial hierarchy soon forbade. In similar vein Burchell (1824: 2,453–54) describes a meeting with royal women who had never before seen a white man: "I felt now and then some person behind me cautiously feeling my hair." When he removed his hat, they gazed "with surprise at the extraordinary sight." The European's hair was regarded as a tangible embodiment of his essence and was sought after by Southern Tswana in their efforts to grasp his vitality (Burchell 1824:2,504). For their part the English visitors wrote lovingly detailed descriptions of the physiognomies and physical attractions of the Africans, caressing them, almost, with strokes of the pen.

The Christians, of course, did differentiate the physical from the mental and spiritual capacities of persons. And they took every opportunity to persuade the Tswana of the importance of doing so. But they encountered great difficulty in teaching them to "have no confidence in the flesh,"[44] precisely because the Africans saw the powers of whites to be part of their substance, suffused through their entire being. What is more, despite their dualistic ideology—the insistence not only on a distinction between mind and body, but also on the primacy of the former over the latter—the churchmen were committed to a corporeal semantics of their own. They intended to transform the heathen person by transforming his or her physical state.

The Tswana enchantment with the substantial force of the Europeans would, over the long run, turn to distaste as they experienced its coercive effects. Still, their perception of the foreigners remained rooted in bodily form for many years, as these lines from a late nineteenth-century praise poem illustrates:[45]

> *Oêtsa Makôpyê mosenya-lefatshe,*
> *ona atlhwa aredira nyampêtla;*
> *aregolêga aresema diôsê,*
> *aregôgisa dikôta tsamanyêla,*
> *arebinisa lenya rele banna.*
> *Mekgakwana borrankô-êmoriti. . . .*

> He is like Makopye ["protruding forehead"; a local Boer],
>   a spoiler of the country;
> he used to make life hard for us,
> he inspanned us and used us as oxen,
> he made us pull the shafts of refuse-carts,
> he made us play 'scratch' [a children's game], though we
>   were men.
> Red-faced people with jutting noses ["that cast
>   shadows"].

The particular characteristics of *makgoa*, physical and cultural alike, were attributed to their distinct origin: they came not merely from the south but from over the Great Water. The Rev. Hamilton recounts a detail that explicitly makes the connection between the foreign origins of the Europeans and their exotic qualities: "The Queen one day asked if we got our clothes from the sea water, as she had never seen any beasts with such skins."[46] The irony, it seems, was lost on the missionary. Not so, however, when Moffat, Hamilton's successor, sought to persuade Mothibi's rainmaker of the futility of his ritual procedures. The man listened in a "friendly" manner, and then replied with typical Tswana diplomacy: the God of the whites, he suggested, "dwells in the south, . . . the Bootshuana God dwells in the north."[47] This neat image of theological relativism anticipated what was quickly to occur: a process in which *Setswana* (Tswana ways) and *Sekgoa* (European ways)—each with its own cosmology, "customs," and conventions—came to be constructed, in opposition to one another, as distinct, objectified cultures. And, in turn, to be locked in a dialectic from which neither could escape. It is to this process that we return in the next chapter.

The whites did not present themselves as a single category for long, however; almost from the start, the English set themselves visibly apart from other Europeans. Like earlier visitors to the interior, Burchell flew his national flag on his wagon. To his surprise, the chief's brother noticed that it resembled that borne by one previous party but contrasted with that of another (1824:2,429–30):

> In this he was quite correct; for the former was sent by the *English* government, and the latter, by the *Dutch*. This naturally led to an explanation that these were two different nations, and that they came . . . from different countries and spoke different languages: facts of which he was totally ignorant. . . .

If this was an early lesson in the trappings of European nationalism, it was quickly learned: awareness of a differentiated white "other" did not take long to impinge itself upon Tswana consciousness. Burchell (1823:2,429ff.) found one resident of Dithakong, respected as a man of information, who had lived at Klaarwater and had learned some Dutch. Like other multilinguals in such situations, he was a cultural broker who was able to set the local world in more global perspective; he knew well that there were important distinctions among Europeans, at least with respect to their relations with blacks. These distinctions were to become complex and contradictory realities in the experience of the Tswana as the impact of competing colonizing forces worked itself out (J. L. Comaroff 1989:passim). Indeed, their historians would muse for decades on the perverse commonalities and differences among whites (e.g., Molema 1966:136).

The brief moment that allowed European and African to confront each other in frank fascination soon passed. Although their relationship continued to have an erotic dimension, this was to remain the dark underside of public segregation and inequality. For all its physical closeness and its stress on Christian love, the mission was to reinforce the taboo against intimacy across racial lines and hence to give support to the basic premise of colonial hierarchy. This was brought home to the Tswana very early on when the Rev. Read became a "recluse in the desert" to escape the wrath of the LMS for having fathered a child by a black woman.[48] He had fallen from the "dignity of the ministerial character," as his brethren put it, having succumbed to the seductions of Africa. But Read's sin was not merely that he had defiled his body, the "temple of the Holy Ghost," by committing adultery. He had also committed a primal offence against the emerging caste-like structures of South African society. For such intercourse, and its halfcaste product, breached the physical separation of white and black and mocked the sense of European distinction that was the *sine qua non* of colonialism. As Pratt (1985:121) has remarked, "nowhere are . . . systems of difference in greater jeopardy than on the imperial frontier."

Some Tswana leaders were quick to observe that, in pressing the distinction between black and white, the object of the Europeans was to unite the two in a single structure of inequality. By the second decade of the nineteenth century, as we have noted, Tlhaping royals were voicing the opinion that the Klaarwater mission was subverting local authority and values. What is striking about the perception is the consciousness that the church threatened to unravel the Tswana social fabric in its entirety. Thus Mothibi told Read[49] how his headmen "understood that as soon as his full sanction was given [and] due *submission* . . . paid to all what the missionary proposes [there would be] a change in *their whole system*" (our emphasis). The continued resistance of a few of these men seriously impeded early attempts to evangelize among the Tlhaping, and when in 1820 Mothibi seemed to become more amenable to the whites, several of his close advisors fled to the neighboring Rolong, declaring: "the missionaries will make [the chief] their servant" (Campbell 1822:1,77).

Rolong royals were to raise similar objections to the activities of the Methodists. As this suggests, local rulers were finding themselves caught up in the contradictory implications of the missionary presence. On the one hand, these *makgoa* embodied power, gave access to goods, and afforded protection against enemies. As Broadbent perceptively put it:[50]

> I say not that the good will they have hitherto displayed towards us is because we are the ambassadors of Christ, for they know not that. Their motives probably are very different. I believe, in some of the principal men, it is ambition and covetousness. They are proud to have it known to other tribes that "Makoas" . . . reside with them. They consider our name a defence, they have the means of obtaining many things of which they are proud through us. . . .

The potency of the whites, however, was highly ambiguous. On the one hand, their presence, like their powers, became ever more attractive as the century unfolded and the Tswana found the situation on the troubled subcontinent growing worse. On the other, the incipient dangers posed by the imperial intentions of the mission were plain to see. The evangelist was an intrusive, forceful figure within the chiefdom, a figure not subject, finally, to indigenous control. Not only did his knowledge and technology challenge their categories, conventions, and forms of creativity, but his commanding bearing also contested existing lines of authority. The Rolong nickname for Samuel Broadbent mimicked this. They called him "Kom hierso," Dutch for the imperative "Come here!"[51] He and his colleagues had come to work transformations, and, as we shall see, they were soon disputing the sovereignty of basic tenets of Tswana life.

Yet this African world was already beset by destabilizing forces, *difaqane* being followed by a colonial expansion on the part of settlers, who were casting their political and economic net over the interior. What is more, while the chiefs sought to enlist missionaries in an effort to protect their communities, the churchmen had already begun their own colonizing project on the planes of everyday life. Without knowing it, the Tswana were being groomed for an image of themselves to be seen, not merely in the evangelist's mirror, but in the prism of the modern nation-state. They were being drawn into a long conversation from which there could be no turning away.

S I X

CONVERSION AND CONVERSATION

Narrative, Form, and Consciousness

> *In our relations with this people we were simply strangers exercising no*
> *authority or control whatever. Our influence depended entirely on per-*
> *suasion; and having taught them by kind conversation as well as by*
> *public instruction . . . we saw that our teaching did good to the general*
> *mind of the people by bringing new and better motives into play.*

David Livingstone (1857:21)

A S THE INITIAL meetings between the "Bechuana" and the
evangelists gave way to the conversation of which Livingstone
speaks, both tried to make good the intentions signaled in their
first halting transactions: the Tswana, to draw on the power of
the mission to protect an endangered world; the missionary, to cast the native as a savage "other," whose difference was to be "converted" into the
currency of the Christian commonwealth. To each, the other was indispensable in making real his own fantasy—although the European was to prove
more capable of imposing his imperial designs on the reality they would
come to share. For the conditions of struggle between colonizer and colonized were as unequal as their visions of history were distinct. Even so, the
Britons and the blacks were to remain locked, for the rest of the century, in
a mutually constraining embrace.

In this chapter we attend to the opening up of the long conversation, to the actions and interactions that laid the bases of an intelligible colonial discourse. This conversation had two faces. Its overt content, what the parties most often talked *about*, was dominated by the substantive message of the mission and was conveyed in sermons and services, in lessons and didactic dialogues. As we shall see, the gospel, delivered thus, made little sense along the South African frontier in the first half of the nineteenth century. More often than not, it was ignominiously ignored or rudely rejected. But, within and alongside these exchanges, there occurred another kind of exchange: an often quiet, occasionally strident struggle between the Europeans and the Africans to gain mastery over the *terms* of the encounter. The earliest objects of this struggle were the forms that the churchmen sought to impose on the conversation itself: among others, linguistic forms, spatial forms, the forms of rational argument and positive knowledge.

The early colonization of Tswana consciousness, in other words, advanced at two levels. At its most tangible it involved what the evangelists termed "direct influence"—the effort, that is, to convert the heathen by exposure to the divine truth, to a persuasive account of the sacred narrative. But at a deeper level only partially distinguished from the first, the Nonconformists set their sights on a "revolution in the habits of [the] people" (Philip 1828:2,355): on re-forming the African by engaging him in an argument whose terms they regulated, and whose structure bore the hegemonic forms, the taken-for-granted tropes, of the colonizing culture. The churchmen were often explicit about working on both planes at once (see e.g., Philip 1828: 2,355). They were aware that the kind of being and consciousness they wished to instill did not arise from dogma and revelation alone. Yet, despite their hopes and intentions, the two levels of transformation—conversion and conversation—did not complement each other in a neat, orderly counterpoint. Quite the opposite: the discontinuities between them were to feature centrally in the making of modern Southern Tswana consciousness.

In the first part of the chapter, then, we examine the struggle to dictate the terms of conversation, its "deeper" dialogue of forms. We do so in three crucial domains: the politics of space, in which both parties tried to appropriate the physical context in which their interactions (literally) "took place"; the battle to control dominant material and symbolic values, best exemplified here by a war over water; and the contest over the media through which the conversation itself was proceeding, over the very nature of language and representation. Thereafter, in the second part, we go on to scrutinize the explicit content of the evangelical message—the gospel as presented to the Tswana—and the responses to which it gave rise. This, finally, will bring us back full circle to a reexamination of conversion and conversation themselves—both as modes of historical practice and as analytic categories.

THE LONG CONVERSATION:
ESTABLISHING A COLONIAL DISCOURSE
The Politics of Space: Or, "Taking Place"

We have dwelt at length on the spatial semantics of the missionary vision—on the way in which the churchmen went forth to chart the terra incognita of the interior onto the glorious map of Christendom. The "regions beyond" might already have been a playground of the early nineteenth-century European imagination. But the drama of conquest had yet to be played out along the imperial frontier. At this time, as we have seen, the British administration showed little interest in extending the borders of the Cape of Good Hope and in the end left the Nonconformists to their own devices.[1] For their part the newly-founded Societies put the task into the hands of their evangelists in the field, trusting to their inventiveness and good sense. There was little else in which they could put their faith. The first generation of LMS and WMMS emissaries to the Tswana had limited vocational training and often scant theological education (see chapter 2): recall that Moffat, for one, left England with virtually no formal religious instruction, being content, in his spiritual endeavors, "to acknowledge the sovereignty and dominion of God in all . . . events" (Northcott 1969:vi). He served his apprenticeship as a missionary by touring the few stations that had gained a tentative foothold in the Colony. Yet like all initiatives and inventions, those of the early evangelists were conditioned by the world from which they sprang. Campbell's priorities in the initial encounter with Chief Mothibi made this plain. The mission was to establish itself at the heart of the indigenous social order, beside the ruler—just as church and state stood side-by-side in Britain. From there, it would spread the "kernel" of knowledge and truth, and work profound, civilizing transformations. The savage would "willingly [become] subject to His Government" (Northcott 1969:vi) and to the cultural empire of European Protestantism. Over the long run, these gentle soldiers of God's Kingdom were to prove themselves every bit as effective, in making subjects, as were the stormtroops of colonialism.

The politics of space were integral to this process. In setting up their first encampment among the Tlhaping, Campbell and Read appear to have been acutely aware of the symbolic impact of seizing the center. So, it seems, was Chief Mothibi. In response to their offer to "send instructors," he had suggested that "it would not do for [evangelists] to live at Lattakoo [Dithakong]," his capital. Rather, they might reside at a distance and have some children sent to them for teaching (above, p. 178). It will be remembered, too, that when Read returned in early 1817 to settle at the Tlhaping town, he met with considerable resistance. Senior royals urged Mothibi to expel him, arguing that the churchmen had already reduced other rulers to servitude. In order to resolve the contradiction posed by the Europeans—whose power to protect from external threat was also the power to undermine the polity from within—the chief tried to hold them at arm's length. He insisted that a station could be established only at the Kuruman River, in uninhabited country some thirty miles to the southwest, the site of the earlier, ill-fated trading post and mission of Kok and Edwards (above, p. 190; Moffat 1842:231).

The letters of the persevering Rev. Read confirm that the struggle between him and Mothibi was framed almost entirely in terms of location. Each sought to place the other in a map of his own making. The chief wished to keep the evangelist on the borders of his realm, close enough to be a source of valued goods and skills but too far away to have direct access to his subjects. Read, on the other hand, wanted to situate his station where it might insinuate itself into the moral landscape of the Tlhaping, visible both as an inspirational example and as an epicenter of the godly rural nation he hoped to cultivate. But the ruler obstructed him in this, even thwarting his attempts to hold prayer meetings or to conduct rudimentary instruction from his wagon. In the end the dejected churchman was compelled to "convince [Mothibi] of his sincerity" by giving him what he most wanted—his own gun. Only when the Tswana sovereign could command (what he took to be) the most condensed source of European power would he permit a more lasting missionary presence.[2] Mothibi also took the opportunity to turn the triumphant moment to political advantage. Speaking of those royals who had criticized him for allowing the LMS to gain a foothold, he is alleged to have declared:

> . . . let them now come and let them now talk. I have now got what my forefathers never had; the news will be through the city immediately and all will come to see this great present.

Read may have been extremely reluctant to give away his firearm, but he made full use of the room for maneuver it gained him. By his own account his efforts soon had a noticeable effect:[3]

> Today finished thatching my house. . . . Had great numbers of people flocking to see [it] which was as a wonder to all. Mahootoo the Queen in particular was greatly pleased and signified her wish to have one made like it which I promised to make for her.

We are not told the exact location of the new mission house, but it was well within the confines of the capital. Standing before it, Read preached the gospel each day, albeit through the medium of "very imperfect interpreters" (Moffat 1842:238). While people showed no more than bemused interest in this performance, they seem to have been quite captivated by the industrious acts of fabrication through which the evangelist laid claim to the space he had been allotted. Alongside his house, he built a smith's forge and, to the "astonishment" of many Tlhaping, began fashioning the tools of peasant production.

When Hamilton joined Read some weeks later, he soon took to hewing millstones, and was also watched in amazement. His account of the incident shows a keen awareness of its impact: "The people were struck with wonder when I made a hole in the middle of [the stone]. One of them said 'these men must be from God that can do such things'."[4] Here, then, was the matter-of-fact theater of Protestant industry, setting forth bit by bit the mode of rural production through which the evangelists hoped to shape the servants of Christ. Spanish Catholicism in seventeenth-century Mexico used ritual drama to impress pious submission upon the Indians (Trexler 1984), and colonizing Anglicanism in Rhodesia took hold of the Shona by making their landscape its own icon (Ranger 1987). But the Nonconformists in South Africa sought to reconstruct the inner being of the Tswana chiefly on the more humble ground of everyday life. Not only were they predisposed to such methods by their puritan creed; their ritual parsimony also struck a chord with Setswana practice, which lacked obvious symbolic or ceremonial elaboration. Moffat (1842:243–44) gives insight into the implications of this spiritual economy for the mission:

> The situation of the missionary among the Bechuanas is peculiar, differ-
> ing . . . from any other among any nation on the face of the earth. . . .
> He seeks in vain to find a temple, an altar, or a single emblem of heathen
> worship. . . . Thus the missionary could make no appeals to legends,
> or to altars, or to an unknown God, or to ideas kindred to those he
> wished to impart. His was not the work of turning the stream back-
> ward to its ancient course.

Moffat was correct. Rather than flow between clearly visible banks or pro-claim itself to the European as overtly "religious," Tswana symbolic practice operated on another plane entirely. It saturated everyday activity, breathing life into the habitual forms of social existence. It was on this terrain that the missions had to battle for control over the salient signs of the world they wished to conquer (cf. Voloshinov 1973)—a battle not for sacred sites but for mastery of the mundane map of lived space.

It was on this terrain too that Chief Mothibi sought to bring the evan-gelists to heel, converting them into subjects of his own. His allocation to Read of residential and arable plots—the royal gift that conferred citizen-ship on immigrants into a Tswana polity—clearly expressed the intention to make the European his dependent. The missionaries might have planted English seeds in African soil in the hope of cultural harvests to come. But

for the Tlhaping their cultivation of the chief's land signaled their acceptance of his sovereignty—even though the "natives" were so scandalized at
the sight of men tilling the fields that the ruler's wife offered to relieve them
of such "women's work."[5] Their outrage was reciprocated: the evangelists
were convinced that female agriculture was unnatural and immoral, and
vowed to bring it to an end (see volume 2, chapter 2).

Since Read's arrival, good rains had fallen. But this auspicious sign appears to have been attributed largely to a Shona rainmaker who had reached
Dithakong at the same time.[6] The obvious awe in which the Tlhaping held
this visiting ritual expert alerted the Christians to what they were up against.
Not only did it emphasize the ecological salience of *pula* ("rain," "well-
being") in the African "desert," but it also "proved" that the savage lacked
all technological reason—two factors, they concluded, that combined to
make the Tswana easy prey to the trickery of "magicians." Although the
missionaries were not fully aware of the complex values invested in water,
they nevertheless perceived it to be a critical arena in the struggle for the
hearts and minds of the Tlhaping. We shall return to this struggle below.
For now, it is enough to note that it had a direct expression in the politics of
space and place. Almost immediately the Nonconformists began to press
Mothibi to move his seat to the banks of the Kuruman River, to which he
had previously wanted to banish them. This site, they suggested, was easier
to irrigate and to defend; it was also more amenable to their own techniques
of control.[7]

The matter of defence was not trivial. As we know, the shockwaves of
difaqane were palpable among the Southern Tswana at the time. These
threatened communities often turned on one other, and lived in constant
fear of attack. Read had repeatedly refused to lead raiding parties against
neighboring peoples, who were said to have stolen Tlhaping cattle. But he
did take responsibility for defending the capital during the chief's absence
on such excursions. One of these forays served the cause of the mission well.
When Mothibi attacked the Kwena, some two hundred miles to the northeast, his regiments were so soundly routed that he reconsidered the evangelists' plea to move from his vulnerable town. As soon as he intimated the
possibility of settling on the banks of the Kuruman, the Christians took it
upon themselves to select a suitable site—and began, there and then, to
build a water mill. They were determined to wrest control over water and
well-being from the rainmaker, thereby to invade the spiritual politics of the
chiefship. Only by meeting the challenge head on, they believed, could they
ensure that a civilized division between church and state would be established from the start in "New Lithako (Kuruman)."[8]

The integrity of the Tswana social order was not so easily disrupted,
however. Nor was the architecture in which it resided. Nineteenth-century

Europeans, in fact, were to remark on its resilience and portability: each "new settlement," Mackenzie (1871:370) wrote later, "is as much as possible a counter-part of the old." In it was to be found "the whole scheme of their social life." It is not surprising, therefore, that in their efforts to recast Tlhaping society, the missionaries were drawn into a lengthy contest with the chief and his advisors over the establishment and ground plan of the new capital. Mothibi kept the evangelists in prolonged suspense as to whether his people would join them at the Kuruman River. Refusing to call a general meeting to declare his intentions, he complained that the opponents of the LMS accused him of "running after" the white men, of "giving the place over" to them.[9]

Read and Hamilton had chosen a site alongside an abundant spring and had begun the arduous task of digging irrigation ditches. They recounted the eventual arrival of the chief at the river bank with some annoyance:[10]

> He was followed by a vast convoy of men and women, each with an ax in the hand. The rule is that no-one may cut a bow till [the chief] has cut the first. No attention was paid to the goodness of the soil, nearness to water etc. but only to where most Camel Thorns grew for shadows, and ordinary thorns for making kraals. We all walked about for an hour before a fit tree was found for Mothibi.

There was no doubt who had seized the initiative in creating the settlement, or upon whom it was centered. Although close to the Kuruman mission station, it was definitively set apart and given its own name, Maruping. The churchmen found themselves once again at the periphery, having to go on Sundays to "Mothibi's tree" in search of an audience. The chief prevaricated in response to their plea for a new site *within* the mushrooming town. If they were to move nearer, he insisted, they would have to build in a place of his choosing, "under his eye."[11]

In the politics of space that surrounded the establishment of the LMS among the Southern Tswana, then, each party tried to draw the other into its own scheme of things. Just as Mothibi sought to make the evangelists' actions "take place"[12] on a terrain he controlled, Read set out to encompass the chief's court in the rationalized ground plan of European civilization; in due course, his brethren would also attempt to reconstruct Tswana settlements after the model of the idealized English village, a rectangular grid of square cottages and enclosed gardens owned by yeoman families. But the Tlhaping showed no desire to relinquish the social, spatial, and symbolic forms of the *motse*, the town at the core of their universe (see chapter 4). Mothibi prevailed in the early rounds of this contest, as did his counterparts in other South African communities; Chief Kreli of the Galeka on the eastern frontier, for example, frustrated the spatial designs of the Anglican mission in a similar manner (Merriman 1957:218f.). The churchmen had to settle down to the laborious task of working within the given constraints of the Tswana order, devoting themselves to colonizing the microcosm, the everyday realm of domestic arrangements and activities. This, as we shall see, was to become the primary focus of the civilizing mission, especially in its earlier phases.

Wherever it was situated, however, the mission station would strive to dominate its surroundings:[13]

> The foundations of the church were laid this day. It is made of Camel-thorn poles and reed, 40 feet long, 15 feet wide, with a rung in the middle 20 foot long and 15 foot wide which gives it the form of a cross. Adjoining that is a room 15 foot square for a stone house to put the society's goods in. All hands are now hard at work. . . . It appears a huge building compared to any one here at present.

Here was a portent of the long run. Over time, the social and material presence of the LMS would come to loom every bit as large.

The history of the Methodist mission among the Rolong was marked by a similar politics of space, if in even more dramatic form. For these peoples were closer to the path of the storm of *difaqane*, and their agrarian base was more radically destabilized by it. When the evangelists first encountered the Seleka-Rolong in January 1823, their ruler was in flight from pursuing marauders (above, p. 181). And while the presence of the Europeans gave them some periods of respite, they were caught up in a cycle of raids and counter-raids, removals and migrations, for many years. As a result the Wesleyans were forced to follow them on their peripatetic course. Nonetheless, they persisted in the belief that, because the Tswana "reside together . . . in large and populous towns" (Mears 1970:15–16), a station among them was both possible and desirable. But the disadvantage of such conveniently centralized communities was their cultural density and the concentrated power of their chiefs—both of which increased the difficulties under which the churchmen had to toil. Missions among more scattered populations, whatever their denomination, were to have greater success in founding discrete Christian communities in nineteenth-century South Africa (Hutchinson 1957).

The Methodists spent nine restless years wandering with the Seleka and two other groups of refugee Rolong who subsequently joined them. In 1832 they secured a large tract of land at Thaba 'Nchu from the Southern Sotho sovereign, Moshweshwe, working through his own resident evangelist (Broadbent 1865:180; Molema 1951:12–40; above, p. 181). There they finally settled down with the three Rolong groups and built a permanent station. In the course of the decade of migration and upheaval, the Wesleyans had taken an ever greater part in the public affairs of "their" people. Although their actions did not grant them entry into the Tswana religious imagination, they did drive a deep wedge into the indigenous sociopolitical order—despite the stated intention of the mission societies to keep out of local politics (see chapter 7).

The growing presence of the WMMS among the Rolong was reflected in its changing place on the social landscape. At first, of course, there was no Methodist station at all; just two mission families tagging along in the wake of the harried Seleka as they shifted from place to place. When the latter came to rest temporarily at Matlwasse, the earliest mission building was erected. It was constructed "in the manner of the natives, though of a different [rectangular] form," and was "separate . . . yet accessible" to the royal capital (Broadbent 1865:61). With each successive move thereafter, the evangelists became more central. It was they who eventually led the migration—they likened it to the biblical Exodus—to the relative security of Thaba 'Nchu, which they believed themselves to have "bought" on behalf of the Rolong peoples. The new station here was situated on a mound in the very midst of the town, roughly where the discrete territories of the three Rolong chiefs met. In it, the so-called Documents of Purchase for the new Jerusalem were carefully preserved.

The WMMS had at last penetrated to the heart of local economy and society. What is more, to the European eye at least, there was a world of difference between its austere, neatly fenced buildings and the surrounding "heap of Bechuana huts jostled together without any apparent order" (Broadbent 1865:189; Mears 1970:19). This difference foreshadowed some of the oppositions that were to pervade the long conversation between the Africans and the whites. For it described two distinct maps, two spatial embodiments of social order, social being, and social power. Most fundamentally, the landscape itself began to give expression to a dawning confrontation between two *cultures*—each becoming ever more visible, ever more objectified by contrast to the other, as they struggled for dominance. The churchmen might not have persuaded the Rolong, by "public instruction," to forsake their social architecture for that of a phantasmic English country village. But as they led their lives on this terrain, the Southern Tswana would slowly internalize the distinctions and relations inscribed in it—including the built forms of the mission and all they stood for. Let us bear this in mind as we move to a second register of the conversation, the politics and poetics of water.

The Politics of Water: Irrigation and Iconicity

The British evangelists were predisposed by both climes and times to conceive of themselves, in horticultural idiom, as irrigators of the African desert. "Her vast moral wastes," wrote Moffat (1842:614), "must be watered by the streams of life." It was a productive metaphor, for it captured the dual meaning of Christian cultivation, referring both to the pragmatic and to the persuasive dimensions of tilling a mission field. Grove (1989) has argued that European conservationist writings also had an effect on the thinking of these churchmen: the contemporary idea that drought was caused by human desiccation of the environment seemed to account for the ecological state of Africa, and it resonated well with the moral image of the dark continent as a "wasted garden." It is true that, soon after the early Nonconformists arrived, there were repeated periods of drought in the interior of southern Africa. And Moffat (1842:168ff., 326ff.) does give evidence of having appreciated the material and rhetorical uses of the "desiccationist" thesis in blaming the Tswana for despoiling their own land (Grove 1989:166–72). Nonetheless, the influence of conservationist writings on the missionaries should not be exaggerated. At the time, their preoccupation with irrigation as trope and technique was part of a more general vision. "Fructifying the desert" linked technical reason and virtue not only to the naturalized forms of European cultivation and land use; it evoked the implantation of European culture *tout court*. For the evangelists, the African wasteland had more complex metaphysical origins than the mere mismanagement of the environment.

A regular water supply was vital, obviously, if the Nonconformists were to create a Christian peasantry in the "desolate vineyard" (Moffat 1842: 330). And so, once they had taken their place on the landscape, the evangelists began to dig irrigation trenches and wells. Their actions soon set them at odds with local values and interests. The Rev. Hamilton writes from the Kuruman River in 1823:[14]

> Our channel from the spring ran through the land of the Great Lady [chief wife, Mahutu], who refused last year to let our water pass. We appealed in the matter to Mathebe, who upheld the women's right to do with the land and water as they please. At present we are supplied from a fountain about two miles east of us and the water of this fountain is a bone of contention betwixt us and the women. They will have it for the town and we will have it to our gardens. . . . It gives us a great deal of trouble every evening to walk four miles to turn it in that we might have it for the night.

The ecological uncertainties of the Southern Tswana world had already called forth a torrent of indigenous tropes and techniques to conserve its most precious and capricious resource.[15] The control over water, as we have noted, was a crucial aspect of sovereign power: the annual rains were the inseminating force bestowed by a virile ruler on his land and people, setting in motion the entire productive cycle (above, p. 158). Here, then, water and land were given not by nature, but by the chief; and, as primary producers, it was women who had practical, everyday use of them. In this dryland region, water was a particularly scarce domestic resource, and its appropriation for the evangelists' gardens was seen as an imposition. These "gardens," a term seldom used by the churchmen to refer to Tswana horticulture, gave great pride to the Europeans. Laid out almost at once within neat fences, they became icons of the civilizing mission at large and were described in dispatches home as "examples to the natives of industry." [16] It was in their cultivated shade that the few would-be converts who died in the early years were laid to rest.[17] The Tlhaping, for their part, reacted to the presence of the gardens by repeatedly stealing their fruits.

When Moffat took over the station on the Kuruman, the battle with the women over water continued unabated. This battle affords perhaps the earliest evidence of a protracted popular protest on the part of the Tswana against Christian incursion. "It was in vain that we pleaded, and remonstrated with the chiefs," wrote the missionary (1842:285). "The women were masters in this matter." Mounting complaints by the evangelists finally brought matters to a head. The women were so roused as to take their tools and destroy the dam that Read had built, permitting the stream to return to its original course (Moffat 1842:286). Mrs. Moffat, always a model of Godly cleanliness, had to send her linen a hundred miles away to be washed. And her husband, irritated by the intransigence of the Tswana, resolved even more firmly to reform their division of labor and "lead the minds of the Bechuana men to agricultural pursuits." [18]

While the war with the women was waged over the practical deployment of water, a more elevated argument raged over its ontology. In the absence of elaborate ritual or iconography, the rites of rainmaking presented the Europeans with Tswana "superstition" in its most tangible form. In these revered rites, performed at the direction of the chief, the missionaries read the essence of savage unreason. "Rainmakers," said Moffat (1842:305), echoing many similar statements made by his brethren, "are our inveterate enemies, and uniformly oppose the introduction of Christianity amongst their countrymen to the utmost of their power." The evangelists in fact became fairly obsessed with the problem—so much so that they regarded the eradication of the rites as a major measure of their success (J. Comaroff 1985:139).

Yet the Tswana were to misunderstand this preoccupation with rainmaking and irrigation, for there was an ironic contradiction in the stance of the missionaries. On the one hand, as we shall see, they introduced innovative techniques and quasi-scientific meteorological explanations, seeking to demystify the magic of water. Yet, on the other, they attempted to restore ultimate authority over the elements to God alone: only He could bring the rain, they claimed, and only by prayer could He be approached. The contradiction was widely visible in evangelical practice in southern and central Africa at the time. A corollary of the attempt to harness rational knowledge for the divine cause, it turned on sensitive European distinctions between ritual and technology that had no indigenous counterpart. A frustrated Rev. Elmslie (1970 [1899]:169), for instance, describes how the drought-plagued Ngoni attributed evil effects to his consultation of the meteorological instruments erected in his garden. Was *this* the white man's divination? Here, as elsewhere (cf. Reyburn 1933), the actions of the churchmen seemed to confirm that they were really rainmakers of competing power.

It was the wells sunk by the WMMS that first challenged the font of indigenous ritual authority among the Rolong. In the absence of a flowing river, Broadbent dug a simple waterhole to irrigate his garden. Seeing this, the Seleka chief insisted that "water comes from the clouds" (Broadbent 1865:99)—whereupon the evangelist and a growing band of excited helpers set about proving him wrong. People thronged to witness the spectacle of water issuing from beneath the earth. Soon, however, the Methodists were confronted by the ruler and his key advisors in full battle dress, as was required when the polity as a whole was threatened (1865:100). The churchmen had recently refused to participate in rain ceremonies held to alleviate a prolonged drought, and the chief now responded by demanding that they dig him a well. But Broadbent declined on the ground that the Africans appeared to think that "the result depended on some peculiar influence" of his own (1865:101).

This sequence of events had complex implications for the encounter between the Tswana and the missionaries. The latter wrote home joyfully that they had earned the "respect and gratitude" of the Seleka rank and file, having proved once and for all that rainmaking was a "vile imposture," a "transparent deception." They were less quick to note the resentment of the ruler, although fully aware of it (Broadbent 1865:102). His reaction was to be expected. The displacement of water from the domain of chiefly ritual to that of "technical management" directly challenged his control, since any wealthy man—that is, anyone who could muster the labor—might now sink his own wells. In the upshot, the Seleka sovereign, with consummate political skill, deflated the Methodists' triumph by taking ritual credit for the enhanced water supply. At least for the time being, rain ceremonies continued undiminished.[19]

Reasons for the misunderstanding and conflict over rain are not hard to find, the ethnohistorical record on the matter being especially rich.[20] Not only did the Nonconformists fail to see the contradictions in their own actions, but they also lacked all grasp of the complexities of Tswana ontology. The ancestral rainpots of the chief might have stored the essence of his ritual potency, and rainmakers might have known how to release that essence in order to activate the clouds. But their power was said to work only when the community was in a state of moral rectitude, a state of "coolness" (*tsididi*). Any breach of proper relations among humans, or between them and the nonhuman realm, might pollute this order, generating heat and drying up the rain. The ritual expert was the mediator between the living and the potent dead. He "made" the rain only insofar as he ensured that the condition of the social world met the requirements of ancestral beneficence—in particular, by removing the pollution that closed up the heavens. In this sense, he no more manufactured rainfall than did a clergyman praying to God, a point lost on the missionaries at the time. As a result, most of them made some attempt to convince rainmakers, in "reasoned" argument, of the fallacious dishonesty of their activity (Reyburn 1933). While a surprising number of them recorded their efforts, Livingstone (1857:25f.; also 1960:239f.) alone described his debate with a Kwena practitioner in such a way as to suggest that there was little to choose between their positions:

MEDICAL DOCTOR: So you really believe that you can command the clouds? I think that can be done by God alone.

RAIN DOCTOR: We both believe the very same thing. It is God that makes the rain, but I pray to him by means of these medicines, and, the rain coming, of course it is then mine. It was I who made it for the Bakwains for many years . . . ; through my wisdom, too, their women became fat and shining. Ask them; they will tell you the same as I do.

M.D.:   But we are distinctly told in the parting words of our Saviour that we can pray to God acceptably in his name alone, and not by means of medicines.

R.D.:   Truly! but God told us differently. . . . God has given us one little thing, which you know nothing of. He has given us the knowledge of certain medicines by which we can make rain. *We* do not despise those things which you possess, though we are ignorant of them. We don't understand your book, yet we don't despise it. *You* ought not despise our little knowledge, though you are ignorant of it. [Original italics.]

M.D.:   I don't despise what I am ignorant of; I only think you are mistaken in saying that you have medicines which can influence the rain at all.

R.D.:   That's just the way people speak when they talk on a subject of which they have no knowledge. When first we opened our eyes, we found our forefathers making rain, and we follow in their footsteps.

You, who send to Kuruman for corn, and irrigate your garden, may do without rain; *we* can not manage in that way. . . .

M.D.:   I quite agree with you as to the value of the rain; but you can not charm the clouds by medicines. You wait till you see the clouds come, then you use your medicines, and take the credit which belongs to God only.

R.D.:   I use my medicines and you employ yours; we are both doctors, and doctors are not deceivers. You give a patient medicine. Sometimes God is pleased to heal him by means of your medicine; sometimes not—he dies. When he is cured, you take the credit of what God does. I do the same. Sometimes God grants us rain, sometimes not. When he does, we take the credit of the charm. When a patient dies, you don't give up trust in your medicine, neither do I when rain fails. If you wish me to leave off my medicines, why continue your own?

Livingstone presents himself as an uneasy advocate of God and Science in this carefully crafted dialogue, permitting his opponent to confront him with the logical impasse of the mission. The parallel use of the title "doctor," as much as the symmetry of the actual debate, implies an ironic conviction that the contest is being waged on equal ontological ground. Thus he allows his interlocutor to suggest a functional correspondence between Tswana material icons and European verbal signs, and to call into question the Christian distinction between sacred and secular activity. In so doing Livingstone anticipated by eighty years Evans-Pritchard's (1937) spirited defence of the rationality of African "magical" thought.

In light of this kind of confrontation, it is predictable that rainmakers would begin to blame their failures on the defiling presence of the mission— and that evangelists would hold rain services, claiming any success as proof of divine intervention in the works of Satan (cf. Elmslie 1970 [1899]:169; Reyburn 1933). Each became grist for the other's mill, athough each was constrained by the other in their escalating ritual contest. This struggle captured in microcosm the whole encounter between the Southern Tswana and the Europeans. Consider the following report sent by Archbell from the WMMS station at Platberg in 1832:[21]

In the sermon, the preacher observed to them that some of the Rainmakers had resumed their employment, and had been making rains all the last week, but had produced none, he therefore recommended them to put no confidence in their ability, but themselves pray to God that he might graciously look upon our land, and send down the dew of heaven. The people prayed to God . . . and shortly after the heavens gathered blackness and the rain commenced which continued through the night. The people were greatly rejoiced at so reasonable a supply, while the Rainmakers were ashamed and confounded.

If anyone had harbored doubts that the evangelists were really rainmakers from abroad, this, surely, would have removed them. But the matter runs deeper than merely an impression confirmed. Evans-Pritchard (1937) made another well-known observation long ago: that criteria of technical efficacy are culturally specified, and that established knowledge is not easily falsified by arguments or evidence external to its (tauto)logical structure. What the churchmen took to be definitive disproofs of the "[native's] vain pretentions" in no way undermined Tswana ontological assumptions. Instead, such things merely confirmed the notion that the whites had introduced a distinct and competing power into their world (cf. Hodgson 1977:23). It seems no coincidence that some key signifiers of the European presence were quickly seized upon to explain the failure of indigenous rites: in one case, for example, the missionary's "long black beard"; in another, the church bell (Moffat 1842:323; Reyburn 1933:148). The fact that the color black and rhythmic sound were important in rainmaking, and that bodily parts were used in potent medicinal concoctions, seems to have suggested to the Tswana that the foreigners intended to use their own capacities to usurp local ritual forces.

Clearly, the struggle to control water, as both sign and substance, took place in terms that were at once prefigured yet fortuitous. Perhaps this paradox is in the nature of all cultural encounters. Here the flow of exchanges between the mission and the Tswana was shaped by determinate, historically prior social and symbolic forms. But its precise content was decided by a serendipitous and superficial overlap of two very different orders of meaning and value. As the participants communicated through a clutch of terms they seemed to share, each side began to recognize the differences between them: differences that became visible, simultaneously, in other domains— not least, on the surfaces of the landscape. And each came gradually to objectify their world in relation to a novel other, thereby inventing for themselves a self-conscious coherence and distinctness, even while they accommodated (often unwittingly) to the new relationship enclosing them. For the Tswana, the encounter slowly brought forth an explicit sense of opposition between *sekgoa* (European ways) and *setswana* (Tswana ways), the latter being perceived for the first time as a *system* of practices (see Moffat 1842: 246f.). The coherence of that system seemed to be located especially in certain contained areas of thought and action. *Mekgwa le melao*, "law and custom," was one such area; a body of conventions long in existence, it was now rising to consciousness, in increasingly reified form, under the impact of the colonizing culture. As we shall soon see, Tswana language was another.

Increasingly, then, the argument over such issues as rainmaking became a confrontation between two cultures, two social orders, in which each had a palpable impact upon the other. The Nonconformists' battle with rain magic might have convinced them that the "[natives] . . . looked at the sun with the eyes of an ox," and were incapable of the argument or reflection required of a true Christian subject (Broadbent 1865:177; Moffat 1842: 245, 309). But the impact of Tswana ritual pragmatism, and of their non-dualistic worldview, also had tangible effects on the mission. We shall see, for instance, that the evangelists would try to invent rites that would extend their ritual calendar and make their worship more compelling to the Africans. Some even went so far, eventually, as to introduce special rain services into the regular cycle of church activities, albeit with great reluctance; over a century later, in fact, we ourselves would attend such services. Similarly, while Rolong and Tlhaping royals might have resisted the polluting power of the white interlopers, they also sought to bend that power to their own will. And in so doing, they joined the conversation that was so profoundly to alter their sense of themselves and their world.

Here, once more, lies the point. In being drawn into that conversation, the Southern Tswana had no alternative but to be inducted, unwittingly and often unwillingly, into the *forms* of European discourse. To argue over who was the legitimate rainmaker or where the water came from, for instance, was to be seduced into the modes of rational debate, positivist knowledge, and empirical reason at the core of bourgeois culture. The Tswana might not have been persuaded by the substance of the claims made by the churchmen, and their world was not simply taken over by European discursive styles. Yet they could not avoid internalizing the terms through which they were being challenged. Even to respond to the arguments of *sekgoa*, after all, meant using some of its signs and adopting some of its practices—in short, assimilating its forms and conventions. A critical feature of this colonizing conversation was that it presupposed the sanctity of the written word. Behind the talk of the missionary lay his texts, the ultimate repositories of eternal, global truth. We turn now to the effects on Tswana consciousness of exposure to this imperious ideology, an exposure embedded in the politics of language itself.

The Politics of Language: Fountains of Civilization, Life-giving Words

For the Nonconformists of the period, it was the Word more than anything else that bore the divine light into the dark recesses of human hearts and minds. Its dynamic force had the capacity to transform the blindness of man in his "natural" state. A sermon given by Read through an interpreter at "New Lattakoo" (Kuruman) captures this well: [22]

> ... I told the Bechuanas that when God's word began to work in their hearts their tears would wash away all the red paint from their bodies.

We shall return to this vivid image of conversion, in which the material signs of heathenism are dissolved by the power of the Word. Note how water and words are rhetorically braided together here, so that each chain of metaphors comes to imply the other: words convey reason to the mind as tears bear tangible witness to affected emotions—water distilling the force of God's moving message, be it as rain from the heavens or the weeping of the human heart. Evidence of this pattern of association is everywhere to hand. The verbal truth, evangelists were wont to say, would irrigate the desert of the African's mind just as moisture would fructify his blighted habitat. The blessing of Christian cultivation was to provide such life-giving potency, fertilizing at once the soul and the soil. No wonder that, in the early years, the Tlhaping referred to the letters of the alphabet, which the Nonconformists strove to teach them, as "seeds" (Moffat 1842:600).

Moffat's initial struggle to control the Kuruman stream soon gave way to a battle to gain command of the indigenous word, which had to be made into a worthy instrument of divine truth. To this end, he devoted himself unsparingly to the task of mastering Setswana. In 1849 a LMS observer tells that: [23]

> Mr. Moffat's time seems mainly occupied in the translation of the scriptures. . . . It is a sight worth travelling some distance to see—the printing and binding operation at Kuruman. The Fountains of Civilization so far up in the interior of South Africa! And scores of men, women and children having renounced heathenism, intelligently reading the Word of Life. . . .

The Tswana mind was being watered by the Word of life, whose truth was to be discovered independently by each self-willed citizen of God's Kingdom. The Nonconformist "Word," of course, was the written word; its faith, the faith of the book (cf. Beidelman 1982:14). The spoken word might have called the world into being in Judeo-Christian tradition, but it was the Word carved in stone by the very finger of the Lord that conveyed the divine law to all living creatures. Sinners, those tempted by heathen images and idols, fetishes and falsehoods, were to be "blotted out of the Godly book" (Exodus 32:32).

While the relation of words and pictures has fluctuated through the centuries and sectarian pathways of Judeo-Christian symbolism, the graven likeness has tended to remain secondary, an often mistrusted medium for bearing the "truth" (Mitchell 1986). An enduring stress on the sanctity of the original inscription made a textualized faith out of early Christianity, laying the basis for its unity and control. It also set medieval scribes to their painstakingly imitative task of preserving the holy writ in its pristine form. But the faith of the book was to be gloriously democratized in the age of the Reformation, when the ideal of literacy put a Bible in the hands of every child of God. As we have noted, this process was founded on an ethos of universalism, the same ideology that spawned the imperialism of the Non-conformist mission, with its assumption that all peoples had some capacity to reason, to love, and to receive the written word. Yet it remained the sacred text itself that held the ultimate power of transformation. Thus wrote the Rev. Hughes, in a personal letter to Moffat (1842:618):

> ... the simple reading and study of the Bible alone will convert the world. The missionary's work is to gain for it admission and attention, and then let it speak for itself.

Added Moffat (1842:618), now speaking for himself:

> The vast importance of having the Scriptures in the language of the natives, will be seen when we look on the scattered towns and hamlets which stud the interior, over which one language, with slight varia-tions, is spoken as far as the Equator. When taught to read they have in their hands the means not only of recovering them from their natu-ral darkness, but of keeping the lamp of life burning even amidst com-paratively desert gloom.

Moffat was not alone among the Nonconformists in seeing the mastery of Setswana as a primary objective, *the* key to the civilizing mission. "The lan-guage was still the principal subject of my waking thoughts, day and night," wrote Broadbent (1865:111), "for my mind was so much taken up with it, that it often kept me awake in bed."

The men who brought the light unto the nations of Africa were prod-ucts of a Europe whose various spoken tongues had shown that they could bear the holy word as faithfully as did Latin, Greek, or Hebrew. It may be argued, with hindsight, that the very act of biblical translation had trans-formed those modern vernaculars in important respects. But the "fever for translation" often held to have overtaken Europe in the sixteenth century (Simon 1966:123–24) flowed from a growing conviction that language, a human creation, could be made into a global medium of communication. Behind this conviction lay a fundamental epistemological principle: that

naming and knowing the truth was a matter of managing signs and corre-
spondences in a world of verifiable realities (Cohn 1985). As the philologist
Max Müller (1891:1,30) reminded his contemporaries, the Bible itself supported the view that language was the invention of man; he did not add,
though he might have done, that the good book also seemed to affirm the
notion that to name was to know: "We read," he said, "[that] 'The hand of
God formed every beast of the field, and every fowl of the air; and brought
them unto Adam to see what he would call them'." This act of original
nomination was to be emulated by evangelists in South Africa and elsewhere
every time they bestowed biblical names on persons and places incorporated
into Christendom (see below, p. 219). Indeed, it was precisely because all
human beings shared the potential to know things by their correct name that
they could become heirs to God's Kingdom, a universal civilization with no
cultural barriers. This in turn mandated a "benevolent" ideological imperialism: those who already had the knowledge were morally bound to teach
those without it, so that they too might realize their potential. It was a mandate that made bold assumptions about the ("indexical") properties of language and the possibility of knowledge that transcended human differences.

Three things followed directly from these assumptions. The first was
the naive faith of the earliest missionaries, like many imperialists before
and since, in the capacity of interpreters to facilitate communications free
of intervening cultural "noise." There was a great dependence on these
mediators in the speech field established along the colonial frontier (cf.
Samarin 1984). Initially, most of them were Griqua with an imperfect command of Setswana and Dutch, their role as brokers between the African and
the Europeans being a function of their political, spatial, and racial marginality.[24] In the social world brought into being by the evangelists, these
vital middlemen held unusual power—they were the best paid of the work
force that undergirded the mission—and there is evidence that they took full
advantage of it, much to the despair of their employers.[25]

At the same time, secondly, the missionaries were convinced of the need
to learn the vernacular themselves as quickly as possible. Colonial administrators, whose authority was backed ultimately by force, might have had
control over the "language of command"; their "command of language,"
that is, lay in a mastery over the structures and terms of communication
(Samarin 1984; cf. Cohn 1985). But evangelists faced the task of winning
over the savage "inner man" in a context of equivocal power relations. Since
their mode of persuasion was heavily discursive—a "kind conversation"
centered, in their own view, on the message of the gospel—fluency in Setswana was obviously vital. Without it they would remain, for all practical and
spiritual purposes, woefully dependent on their would-be subjects. Moffat's

(1842:293–94) energetic and authoritarian spirit railed against this contradiction, ever more so as he lost his faith in interpreters:

> A missionary who commences giving direct instruction to the natives, though far from being competent in the language, is proceeding on safer ground than if he were employing an interpreter, who is not proficient in both languages, and who has not a tolerable understanding of the doctrines of the Gospel. Trusting to an ignorant and unqualified interpreter, is attended with consequences . . . dangerous to the very objects which lie nearest the missionary's heart.

Once more, the divine message was to be preserved at all costs from corruption through ignorance and error.

It is worthy of note, thirdly, that while Moffat often scorned the competence of African speakers, he did not question the potential of their language to bear the meanings that civilization might demand of it. Similarly Livingstone (1857:128), who wrote:

> The capabilities of [*Setswana*] may be inferred from the fact that the Pentateuch is fully expressed in Mr. Moffat's translation in fewer words than in the Greek Septuagint, and in a very considerably smaller number than in our own English version. . . . *Language seems to be an attribute of the human mind and thought*; and the inflections, various as they are in the most barbarous tongues, as that of the Bushman, are probably only *proofs of the race being human* . . . ; the fuller development of language taking place as the improvement of our other faculties goes on [our italics].

Africans might have appeared to lack a reflective mentality and hence a capacity for abstraction. And they might have seemed so stupid as to confuse homonyms; although when Moffat (1842:292, 294) tells us that Tswana were liable to "introduce an ox-tail into some passage of simple sublimity of Holy Writ," it is he who fails to grasp both the salience of cattle analogies and the expressive character of the language. But the churchmen never doubted that Setswana would yield to the painstaking effort to translate literally and precisely the English message they wished to convey.

For Moffat (1842:302), "a mass of rubbish . . . paralyze[d] the mental powers of the natives." Such detritus was easily removed, however, whereupon the vacant savage mind would be receptive to the biblical text. Equipped with this optimistic belief, he followed in the footsteps of the Protestant evangelists in India, who had already translated the Bible into Bengali and were busy rendering it into other Indo-European and Dravidian languages (Wonderly and Nida 1963:122). Both Testaments were later published in the vernacular and had an unparalleled impact on the orthographic standardization of Setswana. So salient was the Setswana Scripture to become in the missionaries' perception that some of them were actually buried with it on their caskets.[26] But Moffat's action had consequences far beyond his own intentions, for he had not merely held up a Setswana mirror to the English text. He had created a counterpart of the scriptures, at least as he read them, in the tongue of the natives—as he had come to understand it. In short, he had transposed the Bible into a cultural register true to neither, a hybrid creation born of the colonial encounter itself.

Thus, for example, Moffat's use of *badimo* ("ancestors") to denote "demons" (Mathaio [Matthew] 7:22; 8:28, 32)[27] did violence to both biblical and conventional Tswana usage. Nonetheless, it reflected the missionary ideology of the time, and was to become standard church usage (Brown 1926:103; above, p. 154). The longer-term consequences of such mistranslations for indigenous consciousness were complex. Clearly, as we know from twentieth-century ethnosemantics, the Tlhaping and Rolong did not simply accept the revision of their key constructs. Few Setswana-speakers would ever have attributed to *badimo* the (English) connotation of "demons"; after all, there intervened an entire cultural order in which the dead had, and still have, a hallowed place. And while the substance of that order was to change under the impact of colonialism, it was not to do so as a direct result of the mistranslation of words. The latter, however, did have an indirect effect: it helped to develop in the Tswana a sense of the relativity of meaning, of the politics of cultural distinction. All Tswana, whether or not they entered the church, were soon to learn that "ancestors" held different valence in *setswana* and *sekgoa*. Within the realm of colonial semantics, they were signs of the "primitive."

As this suggests, the effort to subvert indigenous terms was part of a broader struggle that took place within the speech field of the mission. The Nonconformists spoke of their linguistic efforts as preparatory to the work of conversion proper; they were to provide a medium capable of bearing the powerful, transforming truths of the gospel. But, as Fabian (1983b, 1986) says of Catholic evangelists in the Belgian Congo,[28] the colonization of language became an increasingly important feature of the process of symbolic domination at large. Indeed, Setswana was to carry the lasting imprint of Christian Europe in its lexicon. This was evident in the commandeering of everyday terms like *moruti* ("teacher"), which took on the connotation of "minister of the church," and *modumedi* ("one who agrees"), which came to imply "Christian believer" (above, p. 152); unlike *badimo*, these were subtle acts of appropriation rather than bald mistranslations and hence were potentially all the more invasive. The process was also marked by the use of Dutch and especially English loan-words for features of the emerging colonial universe: for example, *kereke* ("church") and *mmèrèkò* ("wage labor") from Dutch, *sekolo* ("school") and *madi* ("money") from English.[29] Such linguistic innovations traced the hardening outlines of a symbolic order that was already beginning to cast a shadow over Tswana cultural identity.

The invasive yet ambiguous impact of the linguistic colonialism of the mission on Tswana identity is neatly exemplified by changing conventions of personal naming. As we noted above, those who entered the church were given new names. An act enshrined in the Pauline model of conversion and widely practiced in Africa and elsewhere (Ajayi 1965:269; Genovese 1974: 443), this was an evangelical refraction of the general tendency of imperialisms of all stripes to impose themselves by redesignating people and places; such is the illocutionary force of nomination in the (re)construction of reality—and personal status. In fact, the early Nonconformists among the Southern Tswana were not as immediately assertive in this respect as were some of their brethren elsewhere (cf. Beidelman 1982:139). Initially, only their personal servants and non-Tswana assistants were christened with Old Testament names (see, e.g., Read 1850:446). The first generation of Tswana converts continued to be called by their Setswana designations (Read 1850: 446), these being single words, often comprised of verbs with pronominal prefixes and suffixes, describing the distinctive circumstances of birth or early childhood. (For instance, *Lotlamoreng*, "What will you [pl.] do with him?"; or *Kebalepile*, "I have observed them.")[30] Mission records and genealogies show, however, that second generation Christians, particularly those who entered church schools, were referred to at least formally by two first names, one English and the other Setswana. What is more, the bureaucratic conventions of the religious (and, later, the colonial) authorities soon required that "Christian names," given at baptism, be complemented with "family names," which were derived from the eponymous heads of local agnatic descent groups. In this manner Christian subjects were defined and set apart, although vernacular alternatives remained. It seems that code-switching in address and reference between the two (first) names became a highly personalized means by which individuals might signify their relative attachment to *setswana* and *sekgoa*—and the contexts in which one or the other was of primary salience. In colonizing the Tswana world with its nominal forms, then, missionary linguistics played out, in yet another register, the contrast between the two cultures and their everyday practices. But it also introduced a vehicle by means of which persons could make, and remake, their subjective identities on a changing social stage.

There was another way in which naming underscored the contrast between *setswana* and *sekgoa*. The Southern Tswana understood the notion of a "family name" in a manner quite different from that intended by the Europeans. The vernacular term that came to be used for "surname," *sereto*, implied "a totem," a sign of collective identity with particular connotations in this cultural context (J.L. Comaroff 1987b; Schapera 1952); in due course it would also acquire the modern meaning of an "added name" (Brown 1931:283). But *setswana* did share one thing with *sekgoa*: the assumption that naming had unusual illocutionary force and was implicated in changes of status. Consequently, the Southern Tswana responded to the colonial linguistics of the mission by, among other things, reciprocally naming some of the Europeans in their midst. Perhaps the most pointed, poignant case comes from further north and later in the century. In 1894, Rev. Willougby wrote to the LMS from Phalapye, telling the Society that his wife had just given birth to a son:[31]

> The rain has fallen at last. It came with the baby. And since then the weather has been delightfully cool and fresh. . . . The arrival of the two together made the natives urge that the boy should be called "Monna-pula" (master of rain) or else "Rramasimo" (father of the gardens); but we begged to decline the honour.

We do not know whether Willougby's polite refusal put an end to the matter; the long-standing Tswana tendency to nickname does not always respect the desires of those so named. But it does seem significant that the heir of the missionary, the white boy born amongst them, should personify rain and cultivation, the domain of the most bitter struggle between *setswana* and *sekgoa*. If the latter was to invade the everyday world of the former, it was not going to do so without a reaction.

The colonization of language had another, less obvious dimension. It arose from the axiom, shared by all the Nonconformists, that African tongues were all of a piece with African civilization and mentality. Being very simple, they would present little challenge to the industrious European scholar (Samarin 1984:437). As Campbell wrote in 1813:[32]

> The language appears to me so easy . . . that a missionary [with] a turn of mind for learning a language I think in six months would understand it so well, that [he] could be able to begin a translation of the Scripture. . . .

Livingstone (1857:128; above, p. 217) might have thought that the simplicity of the language, given its copious vocabulary, was a mark of its sophistication. Most of his colleagues drew the opposite conclusion, however, and casual analogies were often made with the peripheralized "folk" tongues of Europe. Rev. Hughes, for one, claimed that his knowledge of Welsh was helping him to learn Setswana;[33] similarly, Samarin (1984:436) writes of a Belgian colonial doctor who thought that the Breton he had picked up from a servant at home made it easy for him to communicate with

Central Africans in the vernacular. There is evidence that the confident but incomprehensible babble of some evangelists caused great amusement to the Tswana. Livingstone (1857:128) talks disparagingly of colleagues who, "after a few months' or years' study of a native tongue, [cackle] forth a torrent of vocables," ostensibly to convey instruction; in so doing he gives us a glimpse of the play of disruptive forces, born here in laughter and mockery, that threatened the sedate assertions of civilization and order on the part of the mission.

Such nineteenth-century notions about "folk" languages were innocent of the impact of structural linguistics, of course. But the missionaries generally had some education in normative grammar and in a few cases had studied Greek, Latin, or Hebrew.[34] Once they set about trying to master Setswana, they drew upon this knowledge. For "bringing the language under some organization"—reducing it, that is, to "simple grammatical form"[35]— was a prerequisite of the symbolic incorporation involved in colonialism (cf. Cohn 1985). In this respect, linguistic classification and translation were metonyms of an embracing process of "conversion": the process of making difference into similarity, of reducing the lower order diversities of the non-European world to the universalistic categories of the West. Nor did the methodical Nonconformists see any difficulties standing in their way; while Tswana culture in both its material and immaterial form struck them as elusive and illogical, the vernacular presented itself as more tangible, more amenable to management. It displayed some recognizable order and thus could be used to render the holy word. Most of all, it might be made to submit to the refinement and control of writing. This is why its mastery became emblematic, for the Christians, of the progress of the civilizing mission as a whole. Broadbent wrote indignantly to the WMMS in 1824:[36]

> In a letter presented in Missionary Notices in for January 7, 1823, I found the following account of [the Setswana] language: "The language as yet professes no regular form but is filled with all the unsoftened barbarity of savage sound." I think it necessary to correct the impression such a statement calculates to make. . . . Any person acquainted with different languages, whether ancient or modern, will be astonished at the regularity Sichuana contains, considering it was never written that I know of, though I suspect we shall ultimately discover that it is a dialect of the Arabic. . . . As to the 'unsoftened barbarity of savage sound' . . . I am bold to assert that [no language is] more free from such sounds as this.

This statement assumed a global standard of linguistic comparison as well as a genealogical model of relations among languages and dialects (cf. Moffat 1842:226). Broadbent went on to write the names of thirty-nine "different tribes" on the "blank area of the map" between his station and the Indian Ocean, and to define his evangelical sphere of interest as the greater speech field of Setswana, albeit erroneously specified; he concluded his report by begging the Society to send a party of missionaries to learn the vernacular so that they might bring its speakers under Christian dominion. As Harries (1988:39) notes, churchmen in Africa acted on the contemporary western view that people who spoke the same tongue shared a common mode of thought—almost a "soul"—that bound them together as tribe or nation. It was language, in short, that provided the fixed categories through which an amorphous cultural landscape became subject to European control. As Sinclair (1977:18) put it: "words [were] the devices by which priests and administrators net[ted] men from the wilderness for their service."

There was some early debate among the Nonconformists over the exact degree to which Setswana was rule bound,[37] but exposure to the language seems to have persuaded them of the applicability of Indo-European forms in grasping it. In any event their efforts to learn it were founded on the models of normative grammar and vocabulary they had acquired in school. Moffat (1842:292), however, was quick to point out that the unreflective native was utterly ignorant of "the grammatical structure either of his own or the Dutch language." This structure was to be excavated and presented back to him by his white mentors. Working mainly with the categories of Latin, English, and French (nouns, verbs, cases, declensions, and the like), the evangelists proudly offered to their overseers samples of the most "unembarassed and simple" Setswana grammar.[38] But these European categories did not always correspond nicely to their apparent Bantu equivalents. Thus the lack of conjunctive writing in English led to the early rendering of vernacular words as meaningless strings of discrete grammatical particles (see Wonderly and Nida 1963:127 for a comparative discussion). And missionary linguists, predisposed by Indo-European influences to look for gender-based noun classes, had difficulty making sense of Southern Bantu classifications, which drew on more diverse and subtle semantic distinctions; by modern consensus, Setswana has fifteen noun classes.[39] In addition to grammar, the churchmen paid a great deal of attention to vocabulary in the attempt to achieve linguistic competence. For language was seen by them to consist, at root, of words whose referents were self-evident properties of the world. They took it as axiomatic, therefore, that Setswana terms should be synonymous with their English counterparts (see Moffat 1842:xiv). Not coincidentally, the first secular mission publications in the vernacular, alongside hymnals and biblical texts, were wordlists in the form of spelling books.[40]

In order to produce their texts, the Nonconformists had to develop an orthography; Lepsius's *Standard Alphabet for Reducing Unwritten Languages*, later recommended by the Church Missionary Society, did not appear until 1855, long after the work on Setswana had begun. The latter, it should be added, was regarded as "mellifluous" by comparison to the barbaric speech of the "Cora and Bushmen," whose "claps with the tongue, . . . snorting, . . . clucking [and] croaking" were thought to fall outside the familiar human phonic range.[41] Relying in this prephonemic era on modern European alphabets, the early conventions of the mission were unstandardized and idiosyncratic, Welsh and Spanish sometimes being used to augment the English sound system (Moffat 1842:226n). Furthermore, the Methodists devised their own orthography independently of the LMS, although they soon began to exchange transcriptions and cooperate in translation and printing.[42] Once Moffat commenced publishing the Setswana Bible in 1830, however, his system became the dominant one. And the written language became a *sine qua non* of Christianity and civilization.

The impact of missionary linguistics on the professional study of Bantu phonetics was to be significant, epitomized by the seminal studies of C. M. Doke, an evangelist, Bible translator, and professor of Bantu at the University of the Witwatersrand in Johannesburg (Wonderly and Nida 1963:127). More far-reaching, though, were the sociopolitical consequences of the evangelical onslaught on Southern Bantu languages. The classification of these languages, which originated in the nineteenth-century work done at mission stations across the region, was to justify the division of African peoples into putatively closed ethnic groups (Harries 1988:29); in the age of apartheid, in fact, "Bantu" would become a racial label and an epithet of inferiority. The potentially serious implications of the linguistic labors of the churchmen were not to be lost on African intellectuals. The first protest by literati against the colonization of Tswana culture was to seize upon the appropriation of Setswana—and especially on mission orthography—as the object of its wrath. But all this was still decades into the future.

More immediately, by rendering the Southern Bantu speech field into a series of standardized, written languages—and by expanding its modes of communication and representation—the churchmen interpolated themselves into the local politics of knowledge. In the process they reduced the uniqueness of Setswana, making it into one of several similar "native tongues" brought under foreign linguistic control. And, eventually, they re-presented it back to its speakers, in its now orthodox form, as the gift of civilization. Like Junod (1927:2,618), who held that teaching the Thonga their own grammar would train them in the ways of analytic thought, the Nonconformists regarded the newly-disciplined vernacular as a tool of reason. Taught in schools and spoken in church, it was intended to be a "simple, unvarnished tongue," ostensibly free from the confusions that the evangelists read into indigenous poetics. Most pedagogic texts were written, as we shall see, in a "thin" narrative genre. They told spare, childlike stories in which language itself was portrayed, true to the spirit of rational empiricism, as an instrument of naming and knowing, speaking and specifying. Livingstone (1857: 128), ever sensitive to the ironies of the evangelical enterprise, remarked;

> It is fortunate that the translation of the Bible has been effected before the language became adulterated with half-uttered foreign words, and while those who have heard the eloquence of the native assemblies are still living; for the young, who are brought up in our schools, know less of the language than the missionaries. . . .

Of course, the poetic can never be flayed from any language. Even the most simple of utterances have symbolic potential. And while we cannot know exactly how Tswana understood the lessons they were taught in church and school, available records of late nineteenth-century oratory and praise poetry suggest that their creativity was sparked by biblical idiom and the cadences of English preaching (J. L. Comaroff 1973:ch.5).

The representation of Setswana as a "native dialect," whose reduction to literate order had rescued it from primitive disorder, was an integral aspect of the colonization of consciousness; all the more so, since the indigenous ideology of language, in which words shared in the reality of their referents, was dismissed by the Europeans as "animist," part of the heathen baggage of "spells and superstitions" (see below, p. 228). Even praise poetry, an enormously rich literary tradition, was devalued. It was not, according to the churchmen, an aesthetic form for civilized people. Later, as we shall see, when mission-educated black intellectuals were to build a new literary canon, they began by writing life-stories, chronicles of events, lyric poems, novels, even translations of Shakespeare (see Willan 1984). They had internalized the lessons of linguistic colonialism and the bourgeois ideology that lay silently behind it, concealed in such genres as narrative history and individual biography, such precepts as moral universalism and semantic transparency. It was this process of cultural imperialism that the iconoclastic work of radical black poets in late twentieth-century South Africa was to protest (McClintock 1987). Although the Nonconformists might not have realized it, the media of the long conversation were to have more profound effects than was their evangelical message. For it was those media that bore the essential forms of colonial culture. They were, in short, one of the modes of induction—and an especially powerful one—by which the vital signs and practices of a new hegemony were instilled into Tswana consciousness.

But what part did the Tswana, their ideology and actions, play in the process of linguistic colonization? To the extent that such things can be recovered, they seem not to have regarded language as an object in itself; interestingly, the word that denoted it, *loleme* ("tongue"), falls outside the noun class usually associated with abstract concepts. Rather, it was embodied, literally, in the power of speech, a taken-for-granted capacity of persons and an integral feature of social being. In fact, "Setswana," the term the Nonconformists translated as "the Tswana language," would have been more accurately rendered as "Tswana culture"; it included all the signs and conventions, the symbolic forms and everyday practices, that flowed from, and through, life in a particular community. The spoken vernacular was merely one of its aspects.[43]

Just as there was little sense of a collective Tswana identity prior to this period, so Setswana embraced many distinct dialects. Even a century later, an expert missionary linguist was to express "despair of any homogeneous and comprehensive language ever forging itself out of the multitude of divergent forms" (Sandilands 1953:vii). In the absence of either a single, overarching body politic or of a paramount sovereignty, there was no central authority to impose standardized cultural forms, no hegemony secured by an expansive elite over popular orders of knowledge. Perhaps this is why, in their ways of seeing and being, the Tswana were highly relativistic (below, p. 244f.)—in sharp contrast to the universalism of postenlightenment Europe. The Christians might have believed that they had brought the exclusive truths of civilization to the natives, truths that could not but displace existing heathen customs. But for the Africans it was quite possible for such bodies of knowledge to coexist without threatening each other. This tolerant relativism encouraged them to try to adopt piecemeal into *setswana* those elements of *sekgoa* that might enhance their lives. It was an attitude that the missionaries condemned as "syncretistic"; although, as it turned out, the interplay between the two cultures was to be more complex and pervasive than either imagined.

If the Southern Tswana took language and culture to be part and parcel of particular local identities, they also saw them as growing out of physical being. We have seen how the technical skills of the first white visitors were regarded as an extension of their bodily powers. So it was with speech. In Setswana, "to interrupt someone's conversation" is to "enter into his/her mouth" (*go tsena mo leganong;* Sandilands 1953:358). Given the connotation of *loleme* ("language"/"tongue"; cf. the comparable English folk usage), this suggests that language was perceived to arise, in practice, from the act of speaking itself. It follows, then, that the power of speech was all of a piece with the ability of persons to impose themselves positively on the world—

most effectively through curses, spells, praise poetry, and oratory, the "great words" (*mahoko a makgolo*) that men might use as weapons and resources (Alverson 1978:140; J. L. Comaroff 1975). Livingstone (1857:129) once remarked that "both rich and poor" spoke Setswana correctly; that, apart from "the *patois* of children, there was no vulgar style."[44] But not all speech was equal. That is why women, as beings of limited social competence, were excluded from such *mahoko* ("words") as public debate, poetic recital, or ritual incantation (Kinsman 1983:49; above, chapter 4). Among word-smiths, moreover, utterances were given their relative weight by personal status: the rhetoric of the ruler bore his full sovereign authority; the curse of the elder, his enhanced spiritual potency. Reciprocally, it was through speech that those personal forces and powers were called up.

Men might also increase their prestige and standing by public displays of oratorical skill. As Alverson (1978:192) has observed, Tswana males em-powered themselves through a reflexive verbal process:

> To appreciate the full meaning and significance of the heroic, we must first understand the power of naming and self-naming to create what one is. . . . Among the Tswana a traditional part of growing to man-hood entailed learning to compose skillful and artistic praises for the heroic in poetic form, especially praises *of one's own putative heroism* [original emphasis].

To orate in this manner was to "create experience" (Alverson 1978:192), to construct a reality. And to orate well was to establish potent and plausible connections between men and the world. No wonder that Tswana Christians retained a rather distinctive attitude to prayer, seeking, as one evangelist put it to us in 1969, "to sway God with many words." *Mahoko* were not merely effective manipulations of learned formulae. They were the audible media of the creative impulse.

While utterances bore the imprint of their speakers, they also estab-lished tangible links with their referents, a property that was taken by Victorian scholars as evidence of "primitive mentality." It was this property that Tambiah (1968) was later to dub the "magical power of words." Brown (1926:114), for example, explains why the missionaries encountered "a great silence" in respect of Tswana notions of the supreme being. It was because "the word *modimo* . . . is a great taboo, the mere mention of which in the ears of the people would cause death to the profane one." The Old Testament contains a similar taboo, of course, a fact of which the evangelists were surely aware but which they chose to ignore: their own eagerness to "speak God's name" was born of a very different notion of the relationship of signifier to signified. Consequently, they noted with surprise that the Tswana seldom mentioned life-threatening beings or forces by name. They had "as many euphemisms for death as China has," Willoughby (1932:241) was later to say; rather than evoke its specter, they felt more comfortable in speaking of it as "the thief."

In this, and in their scrupulous use of kin terms instead of names to address and refer to each other, Southern Tswana echoed an assumption widely noted by early writers on non-Western religions: to know the names of persons or beings was to have some control over them, to be able to summon them for good or ill. And just as these names were not neutral signs but an integral part of their "owners," so all terms participated in whatever they denoted. "The power of words, uttered under appropriate circumstances," adds Horton (1967:157) of African thought, can "bring into being the events or states they stand for." Such "magical power" goes well beyond the scope of Western ideas of the capacities of speech, further even than the missionaries' belief in the potency of the Word. For it implies verbal connections among forces unwilled and inanimate. Words are enmeshed in dense fans of association that might unwittingly be activated by their mere utterance. Tswana have long explained their reluctance to use the term *shupa* ("seven") by observing that it also means "to point out" (i.e., with the right index finger, the digit that stands for the number "seven"), a gesture which connotes "to curse" (Willoughby 1932:143).

In the conception of cause and effect, of relations and events, then, words were not set apart from actions. The taboo on taking a firebrand (*serumola*) into a domestic courtyard, to give another example, was explained by the fact that *go rumolana* meant "to quarrel"; the action would, as a result, itself lead to family discord (Willoughby 1932:43). This is an instance of a widespread metonymic principle; it is most evident, in central and southern Africa, in healing concoctions, the names of whose ingredients are frequently homonyms for a desired quality or state (cf. Turner 1967:299f.). In such cases objects actually serve as words, just as words act on the world as invisible things. Each medium enhances the power of the other, this often being the explicit intent behind the juxtaposition of spells and actions in ritual processes (cf. Tambiah 1968). Not coincidentally, as we shall see, the Tswana were to respond to the missionary's creed by talking *simultaneously* with words and things.

As has become plain, the potency of words lay not only in "great works," in oratory or poetry, rhetoric or ritual. Their unintended effects were constantly felt in a universe in which the concrete and the abstract, the human and the nonhuman, were not definitively severed—a universe, that is, in which they could, and did, impinge on one another without the intervention of living persons. The grammatical forms of Setswana, in fact, suggested as much to missionary linguists. Commenting on the transitive verb *go kgopa*, the action of an inanimate object which "trips a person up," Sandilands

(1953:342) noted that it "shows how different from ours is the Bantu way of regarding many facts of existence." As a description of social practice, this is naive. The western world, past and present, offers ample examples of the presumed capacity of reified categories and abstractions—among them, statistical "artifacts" and ideological constructs—to motivate behavior. Nor was the English language or the culture of which it was part ever free of the magical power of words.

Nonetheless, there certainly were differences in the nineteenth century between the ontological bases of English and Setswana. Perhaps the most consequential was that western culture had come to define matter as neutral and to see man as prime mover in his interaction with his surroundings; *setswana*, by contrast, continued to speak openly of the ability of the inert to affect the living. Indeed, this was the core of the "superstition" identified by the evangelists as "animism": as the state of delusion, visible in the false connections made between people and things, which bound Africans to their world of tradition and limited their sense of personal independence. If it was from this world of connections and continuities that the Nonconformists hoped to liberate the Tswana, it was from this world too that the Tswana were to speak back, giving voice to their side of the long conversation.

One early riposte came in response to the repeated claims made by the churchmen for the "power of the Word," a power that was made to sound very concrete. The Good News of the gospel might not have conveyed much to African ears (see below, p. 236f.). But the manner in which it was spoken left the impression that the Word itself was the dynamic core of the mission: that it was, truly, potent and physically dangerous. Moffat writes (1842:576):

> Many, alarmed at the progress made by the "medicine of God's word," as they termed it, were loud in their complaints of the new order of things which was introduced, and some were so determinately opposed to this new word or doctrine, that they removed to a distance beyond the reach of the Christian atmosphere. Some were concerned, lest the water in the river which passed our houses might receive an infusion, and being drank [*sic*] transform them too.

Recall how substantive was the power attributed, in *setswana*, to "great words"; how spells and concoctions often enhanced one another in rituals designed to transform persons and conditions. Given the rhetoric of the evangelists and the awe with which they spoke of the divine truth, it is not surprising that the latter was perceived as a strong medicine, an infusion that bewitched all who imbibed it. Like other Africans who made no distinction between symbols and instruments (see Beidelman 1982:103 for a similar case), the Southern Tswana took the mission at its word, so to speak, treating literally the implications of its tropes. Eager to domesticate the new force in their midst, they identified the Bible as a major repository of the word of the whites. Moffat (1842:503), again, tells approvingly of a heathen chief who, "tracing civilization to its proper source," asked him:

> "What, is it the precepts of that book," pointing to the Gospel of Luke which I held in my hand, "which has made you what you are, and taught the white people such wisdom; and is it that mahuku a molemo (good news,) which has made your nation new [vital], and clothed you, compared with whom we are like the game of the desert?"

Similar exchanges and struggles over the Word occurred throughout much of Bantu-speaking southern Africa during the nineteenth century. Thus Elmslie (1899:169) writes of the Ngoni that "a book was in their eyes nothing but an instrument of divination." He adds that these people, imitating the churchmen, spoke about "The Book," assuming that there was only one (see Harries 1988:45 for the comparable Tsonga case). Later on, as we have noted, illiterate separatist Christians in South Africa would take hold of the Bible in ritual efforts to distil the power of literacy (J. Comaroff 1985:250), just as they would try to harness other media that seemed to bear the essence of white might.

What we see here, then, is a systematic misrecognition of European signs and meanings on the part of people whose own cultures did not segregate the word from the world or the concept from the concrete. This misrecognition led in turn to a misreading of the metaphors of *sekgoa* and to disruptions of the silent complicities on which its hegemony would rest. In the early stages of colonialism everywhere, indigenous peoples seek by their actions to fashion an awareness of, and to assert conceptual mastery over, a changing world. These are early pragmatic efforts to plumb the depths of the colonizing process, to capture the mysterious bases of the European production of value. They are also ways of creating historical consciousness. Out of the insights they yield come forms of experimental practice that attempt, by testing out relations between new means and ends, to forge both techniques of empowerment and modes of collective representation. For the recently colonized generally assume that there *is* something invisible, something profound happening to them. And that their future may well depend on gaining control over it.

With time and experience, colonized peoples invariably develop an ever more acute sense of the logic of the colonizing culture. Usually, too, their attempts to come to terms with it grow increasingly diverse. In the Tswana case the historical dialectic of challenge and riposte, of cultures in contest, became ever more closely tied to local processes of class formation; as we shall see in volume 2, distinctions of ideology and cultural style wrought by the colonial encounter tended to follow the deepening lines of social differentiation. In embryonic form, however, these distinctions and diversities were visible in the other side of the mission project, namely, its explicit techniques of conversion.

THE POLITICS OF CONVERSION: IN SEARCH OF THE SOUL

The elevation of a people from a state of barbarism to a high pitch of civilization supposes a revolution in the habits of that people, which it requires much time, and the operation of many causes to effect. By the preaching of the gospel, individuals . . . may be suddenly elevated to a surprising height in the scale of improvement, and the influence of such a person, on a savage tribe, must be great; but those on whom the power of divine truth operates in a direct manner, bear but a small proportion to the numbers who are only the subjects of an indirect or reflected influence. . . . [The] mass of people . . . are but slightly affected with divine truth. . . .

Rev. John Philip (1828:2,355)

The primary objective of the churchmen, of course, was to awaken the dormant intellect of the savage through the "direct" power of the Word. Dr. Philip might have realized that it would be necessary to take a more circuitous route via the laborious reform of habit. Yet he and his brethren believed that, if only the Africans would permit it, the gospel would, like a "sword . . . penetrate . . . the heart and mind," tearing away the veil of heathen superstition (Broadbent 1865:88); hence Read's limpid description of the capacity of God's word to bring forth the purifying tears of a penitent heart (above, p. 214). Here we explore the work of conversion in the terms that the missionaries themselves used to speak about it; that is, as an exercise in the persuasive telling of a truth which the Southern Tswana were free to accept or reject. In contrast to the earlier parts of the chapter, we consider not the media of the long conversation but its message, a new ideology to be impressed on black consciousness. This, then, is the more familiar terrain of narrative history, the realm of actors with explicit intentions, whose pursuits were clearly visible above the murky symbolic struggles we have discussed thus far. We shall allow the Nonconformists to tell their story, aware all the while that their verbal exchanges were never really independent of the other, less audible transactions of the colonial encounter. This, as we said earlier, will lead us to examine the limitations of theories of conversion in explaining radical processes of social, cultural and, by extension, religious change.

Sacred Schooling: Awakening the Intellect

The pioneer generation of Nonconformists in South Africa had to evolve their own techniques of conversion; their weak training in theology and evangelical practice gave them very few guidelines with which to begin. However, they were equipped with the revivalist ethos of mission work in contemporary Britain and with creeds that stressed self-reliance and divine inspiration. Following the command to "preach the gospel to every living creature," they took the sacred text as their manual, liturgical orthodoxy as their yardstick of piety. The holy narrative, for these purposes, was the New Testament. Moffat (1842:301) had called the Acts of the Apostles a "missionary book," and had noted that "he who takes the first propagators of Christianity as his models, cannot err." While the Lord's Prayer, the Apostles' Creed, the Ten Commandments, and various catechisms were among the earliest texts to be rendered into Setswana by both the LMS and WMMS, Moffat began his illustrious career as translator of the scriptures with the Gospels of St. Luke and St. Matthew, his versions soon becoming standard throughout the Tswana field (Broadbent 1865:111; Bradlow 1987:26ff.; above, p. 223). He went on to prepare translations of Proverbs and Isaiah, and subsequently the whole of both Testaments. But it was the story of Christ that was most widely told, first by the European churchmen and then by mimetic local preachers.

The Nonconformists arrived in the field impatient to tell the "Good News" to the heathen. Hardly had they parked their wagons when they began to preach from them in a gesture that became emblematic of the early mission at large (plate 7); their faith in the persuasive power of the Word was so literal that they paid no attention, at first, to the manner in which their orations were being translated and understood. Although they were eventually discouraged by the lack of response to these initial outpourings, the churchmen nonetheless worked hard to rouse what they took to be the sleeping African intellect. Moffat (1842:302), for one, noted that among the Tswana it was crucial to make every subject as striking, as dramatic as possible. Drawing on comparative evidence of evangelism among Jews, Greeks, and Greenlanders, he concluded that it was essential from the start to introduce the savage to Christ crucified. Merely to recount the attributes of God would not be effective. The stress on the spiritual millennium was to stand in sharp contrast to the theology of the independent churches which later seceded from the mission congregations; to their members, the Old Testament provided a more congenial model for *this*-worldly redemption, its

MISSIONARY
LABOURS AND SCENES
IN
SOUTHERN AFRICA;

BY

ROBERT MOFFAT,

TWENTY-THREE YEARS AN AGENT OF THE LONDON MISSIONARY SOCIETY IN THAT
CONTINENT.

FIFTH THOUSAND.

Preaching at Mosheu's Village.—(See page 596.)

With Engravings, by G. Baxter.

LONDON:
JOHN SNOW, PATERNOSTER-ROW.

1842.

PLATE 7 *Preaching from a Wagon at Moshweu's Village. Reproduced from Moffat, Missionary Labours (1842, title page).*

idioms of pastoralism, lineage relations, and food taboos resonating with the signs and values of their own culture.

The "lessons" delivered to Southern Tswana seem usually to have been succinct and direct (Campbell 1822:2,1):

> Many attended our worship. . . . [T]hey were told what great things the Son of God had done for the salvation of men, and in order to gain their love.

Or (Broadbent 1865:178):

> Mr. Archbell had preached on the words, "Prepare to meet thy God, O Israel;" and though the congregation was unusually crowded, they were exceedingly attentive.

In their early reports from the field, the missionaries gave meticulous account of how precisely they bore witness to the sacred truth, recording the details of verses selected, sermons preached, and services conducted.

The legacy of didactic philanthropism in postenlightenment Britain meant that, to the Nonconformists, evangelism was inseparable from education. It was not merely that the school was the "door to the church" (Etherington 1978:54). Schooling actually provided the model for conversion; conversion, the model for schooling. Each aimed at the systematic, moral reconstruction of the person in a world in which individuals were increasingly viewed as capable of being formed and reformed by social institutions (cf. Foucault 1979). Campbell had founded the mission among the Tlhaping in 1813 by offering to "send instructors" to those "willing to be taught" (see chapter 5). And it was on these terms—most explicitly, the desire for literacy—that Chief Mothibi initially accepted the LMS. Nor was it an accident that Moffat built his chapel like a holy schoolroom; in his native land, the state had not yet wrested control over education from the religious institutions. As we have noted, moreover, the Tswana term for missionary was to be *moruti* ("teacher"). "Inquirers," prospective converts, were known as *barutwi* ("students"). Spiritual and secular tuition ran parallel, organized in "classes" in which "diligent scholars" of all ages took "lessons," and became "candidates" for "examinations" (Broadbent 1865:197–99; Moffat 1842:570). If the lexicon of secular education in the West still speaks of its ecclesiastical roots, this influence was to be all the more marked in black South Africa, an issue to which we return in detail in the next volume.

Literacy, among the first capacities of whites to be identified by Tswana as potent and desirable, soon became much sought after, even by people "with no intention of converting."[45] Reading was taught by means of the interrogation of sacred texts, the catechism being seen to provide an ideal mode of instruction, of the process of inscribing categorical truths on blank minds. And so, between 1826 and 1860, Moffat supervised the printing of two editions of Dr. Brown's *Catechism* and three of the *Assembly Catechism* (Bradlow 1987:27–28). While not all those who came for instruction were children, young and old alike were treated as infants in the "nurseries of education" built by the Nonconformists (Moffat 1842:570). Enrollment in both day and night classes grew steadily, and the schoolroom became a major conduit through which potential converts were drawn to the church.

This form of teaching was the key to the Christians' "higher" objective of reconstruction. The curricula of church and school together set out to reorganize the flow of seasons and events that configured space and time for the Tswana. They separated the sacred from the secular, work from leisure, the public from the private, the inner from the outer, the biography of the scholar from the master narratives of Christian history. Sunday service, weekday classes, quarterly communion, and annual feasts introduced a new schedule of activities that encompassed local routines within a global time-table, a universal geography. We shall analyze the implicit imperatives of the schoolroom itself when we explore the practical reforms of the civilizing mission. For now, the point is that the religious calendar of the church marked out a moral order that would subsume all others, embracing the everyday lives of its participants in a continuous regime of instruction, veneration, and surveillance.

In an effort to make the church schedule yet more encompassing, and so to compete more effectively with the ubiquitous practices of *setswana*, the missionaries constantly elaborated their own ritual cycle. Sometimes they invented new ceremonies with a view to seizing the high moments of the indigenous calendar. Willoughby,[46] for example, describes his attempts to arrange an annual, three-day festival once the harvest was in. This was to be held in July, during the period of most intense Tswana ritual activity (J. Comaroff 1985:67). All Christians were to attend, even those from out-lying districts, and the proceedings were to include a public debate about the moral viability of potential new members, an "impressive" baptism service, several prayer meetings, and a "Magic Lantern lecture" on "Bible narratives." These rites of renewal were intended to replace *go loma thotse*, and all other forms of harvest thanksgiving (above, chapter 4). Although there is little evidence to suggest that Willoughby succeeded, it is clear by his own admission that he wished to inculcate a structure of regular vigilance and accountability:[47]

> At the New Year Service I mention the names of those who have been irregular at the Communion during the year. If I know of a valid excuse, I give it; and if not, I say so. . . . This not only serves to keep the

members up to the mark, but it serves also to show each member that notice is taken of his presence and absence. . . .

Thus was the progress of the humble pilgrim monitored and marked. All for his own good, of course: it cultivated in him a sense of Christ's path as a cumulative moral career.

But the Nonconformists regarded the regular round of Sabbath observances as their most significant evangelical activity. Hear what Mackenzie (1871:72–73) was to tell a late nineteenth-century audience:

> If you wish to see Kuruman to advantage, . . . come to church on Sunday morning. I do not mean to the prayer-meeting at sunrise, but during the hour before service, when the people assemble in groups outside the church, in the grateful shade of the syringa trees. Some read the Scriptures; others are going over the spelling-book; acquaintances are greeting each other; while occasional strangers from the interior stand in the background in their karosses, and gaze with mute wonder at the scene. Inside the church and school-room the children are singing hymns and listening to the instructions of their teachers. You see many people who are respectably dressed. Most of the men belonging to the station wear European clothing; the trousers, however, are frequently of skin, tanned and made by themselves. . . . Most of the women wear a handkerchief (or two) tied tightly round the head. . . . You observe that a good many have brought with them a pretty large bag . . . [that] contains the Sechuana Bible . . . and the hymnbook, which, here as elsewhere, is a great favourite. . . . The bell rings for service, and the people hasten into the church. The mothers who have little children remain on forms near the doors, so that in case of a squall they can readily make their exit.

This is a carefully composed portrait of a decent, self-disciplined community going through the motions of Godliness. The description continues with the minister's ascent of the pulpit, his only concession to clerical dress being a black coat; the LMS, we are assured, is a very "broad" institution, its clerics often preaching in a "smoking cap and wrought slippers" (1871:74–75):

> The service now proceeds with the reading and exposition of Scripture, succeeded by solemn prayer. A sermon or lecture follows, in which the preacher strives to reproduce some incident in the sacred narrative,—some parable or doctrine, so as to impress its lesson on the minds of his audience. . . . The church was lighted with tallow candles, one of which was on each side of the reading-desk. . . . An hour-glass is beside the snuffers in the pulpit—articles not usually found in pulpits now-a-days.

The anachronistic timepiece reminds us yet again how thoroughgoing were the disciplinary and didactic techniques of the evangelists; how intent they were upon colonizing both the temporal and the spatial axes of this African world. But Mackenzie's description tells of later days, by which period the missions were well established. At what stage did some Southern Tswana at least begin to listen to the gospel?

Singing a New Song: Internalizing the Word

In light of what we now know of the methods of the missionaries, it should not surprise us that their message was less than enthusiastically received. The first reaction of Southern Tswana to the Christian word, it seems, was one of utter bemusement. Moroka, the Seleka-Rolong chief, for example, said to Broadbent (1865:178) that "the things [the churchmen] told him were great things"; but that he, and many others, "could not comprehend them all." Likewise, Edwards (1886:91), who concluded that his preaching was "incomprehensible to the . . . unsophisticated minds" of the heathen, noted that they described it, dismissively, as "talking."

It is indeed difficult to assess just what the Nonconformist message might have meant to early Tswana listeners. Most seem to have interpreted the admonitions and promises of the mission in highly literal, immediate terms—this being characteristic of the response of many nonwestern peoples to millennial Christianity (Mbiti 1969; Worsley 1968). The evangelists were graphic in their accounts of the wages of sin and the fruits of redemption,[48] eliciting reactions which suggest that the Tlhaping and Rolong took the Protestant deity to be a pragmatic being, different from their own otiose *modimo*. "Where is God?" they asked. "Has He hair?" "What food shall we eat in heaven?" (Broadbent 1865:81, 177). As later observers were to note (e.g., Horton 1967), these were questions that Africans seem never to have asked about their own disembodied divinities.

It was not, as the churchmen thought, an inability to transcend the carnal that shaped early Southern Tswana perceptions of the white man's God. These perceptions grew, rather, out of a misreading of mission metaphors. The Africans, according to available testimonies, understood the Christians to be claiming that their deity was able to deliver human beings from dangers inconceivable yet fearsome, dangers especially acute as life on earth came to an end.[49] This emerges with particular clarity in deathbed conversions; minutely described by many evangelists, such scenes typified the drama of snatching savage souls from the abyss (see plate 8). But more sustained exposure to the exhortations of the Nonconformists deflated the initial awe and fascination of the Tswana. Livingstone (1857:25) recalled a "sensible" Kwena man telling him that "we like you as well as if you had been born among us. . . . [B]ut we wish you to give up that everlasting preaching and

PLATE 8   *The Dying Hottentot Boy. Reproduced from* The Missionary Magazine and
Chronicle *14 (September 1836): 419.*

praying." And Moffat (1842:285) wrote that the Tlhaping seemed to treat
the Word like an "old and ragged garment." This, as it was to turn out, was
a highly loaded simile.

It was not merely that Southern Tswana found the evangelist's message
less and less appealing. They soon became aware that it was fundamentally
antagonistic to their mode of existence. Very early on, as we saw in chapter 5,
Chief Mothibi is alleged to have complained to Read that "submission"—

the pun could not have been intended—would change "their whole system" (above, p. 196). Many years later, Wookey,[50] who worked among the Tlhaping in the second half of the century, confirmed that once local people began "to know something of his work, they oppose[d the missionary] ... tooth and nail." This was hardly remarkable. The doctrine borne by the Word was explicit in its attack on the entire edifice of customary practice. Once the divine light of truth had fallen on it, savage innocence became original sin, its ways to be loudly condemned as the path to death and damnation (Broadbent 1865:193). Royals were most directly threatened by such moral tirades, seeing the onslaught on rainmaking, initiation, and polygyny as a serious challenge to their sovereignty. Nonetheless, while Southern Tswana elites—"the heathen Party," Willoughby was to call them[51]—flatly refused to hear the gospel, they continued to converse with the church, not least for strategic purposes. As Molema (1951:58) was to note, the chiefs responded to the contradictory implications of nineteenth-century evangelism by "listen[ing] to the missionary with one ear and tradition with the other. . . ."

The strategic benefits of the church were not inconsiderable. Nor were they underestimated. The physical security offered by LMS and WMMS stations in the unsettled interior ensured that by the early 1830's they were usually surrounded by sizeable populations, even when peripatetic chiefs moved their seats elsewhere (as had Mothibi from Kuruman in 1828; Shillington 1987:13). Predictably, those who opted for the protective arc of the mission rather than that of the royal court were typically marginal people: sometimes they were Tswana or even Sotho from other communities. Edwards (1886:91) writes of a station he established with a small number of Rolong at Lishuani, near Thaba 'Nchu, in 1833:

> The natives of that country who . . . were through fear living in the mountains, gained courage from seeing we were settling down quietly and living in peace, and they came down and began to settle at and near the Station.

For a long time, however, the vast majority of Southern Tswana remained reluctant to enter more closely into the society of the church. They refused to give the anxious evangelists what they hoped for most, some sign of the intention to convert; although, as we have already said, a more diffuse process of conversion to the signs and practices of European Protestantism was already well under way. As the civilizing mission gradually began to make its inroads, increasing numbers came to services, and appeared to show a growing respect for their decorum. Yet virtually all of the earliest candidates for baptism were non-Tswana outsiders: first were the employees of the churchmen, then people who had either been left destitute by the ravages of *difaqane*, or were *batlhanka* (serfs) in local chiefdoms (Moffat 1842:473, 480, 501; Broadbent 1865: 80, 98, 186; see Peires 1981:72 for the comparable Xhosa case).[52]

The Christians ensured that the baptism of these first converts made an impact on the surrounding community (Moffat 1842:497; cf. Broadbent 1865:178–79):

> The scene . . . was deeply impressive and exciting. Notwithstanding all our endeavours to preserve decorum in the crowded place of worship, strong feeling gave rise to much weeping and considerable confusion; but, although it was impossible to keep either order or silence, a deep impression of the Divine presence was felt. The work which had commenced in the minds of the natives received an additional impulse from the above circumstance. . . .

The fact that uncharacteristic emotionalism now replaced apathy in many Tswana onlookers seems to have been taken as evidence, by the evangelists, of the "work of the Divine Spirit" (Broadbent 1865:178). The Gospel, declared Moffat (1842:496), was "melting their flinty hearts." The tears that the mission had so long tried to evoke now became a veritable flood:

> The moral wilderness was now about to blossom. Sable cheeks bedewed with tears attracted our attention. . . . Our temporary little chapel became a Bochim—a place of weeping; and the sympathy of feeling spread from heart to heart, so that even infants wept. Some, after gazing with extreme intensity . . . on the preacher, would fall down in hysterics, and others were carried out in a state of great exhaustion.

This evokes, once more, the emotive image of conversion as "tears washing away the paint of heathenism" (above, p. 214).

Such rhetoric was far removed from indigenous expressive forms, however. *Setswana* did not include a tradition of possession or ecstasy. It was only after years of exposure to evangelical expectations that a few Southern Tswana, under the leadership of mixed-race mission employees from the Colony, began to talk about matters religious in the terms demanded by the churchmen—and to exhibit signs of spiritual arousal. While delighted by these outbursts of enthusiasm, the Christians had some qualms about their vehemence and lack of control. Emotionalism, already regarded ambivalently in British Nonconformism (Thompson 1963:368f.), was particularly troubling in those but one step away from nature. For their part the Africans seem yet again to have read ambiguous mission metaphors quite literally; perhaps misrecognition of this kind is inherent in signs that cross social frontiers bereft of their cultural nuances. It resulted in the Tswana and the Englishmen finding each other banal, incapable of richly textured understanding or poetic subtlety.

The first converts would appear to have been made sensitive to the Protestant message by their very marginality; the promise of equality before the Lord, of an unfettered moral economy, must have appealed to those who had long been treated as less than human. However, a second category of people, peripheral in a quite different sense, soon showed itself susceptible to evangelism. Both among the Tlhaping and the Rolong there were junior royals who drew close to the mission and availed themselves of its knowledge and resources; in the celebrated Tshidi case, Molema, a half-brother of the heir to the chiefship, became leader of a small Methodist congregation in the 1840's (Molema 1966:27f.; see chapter 7). These men were more securely rooted in their communities than were the first catechumens. But their exclusion from positions of authority by virtue of rank, age, and prevailing power relations seems to have attracted them to Christianity. Apart from all else, the church presented itself as an alternative, and an altogether new, source of meaning, control, and influence.

In addition to junior royals, women of all ranks began to show an interest in the church. This was widely the case throughout southern Africa: wherever the egalitarian rhetoric of the gospel was heard in communities based on gender inequality, it seems to have had a much greater and quicker impact on females than on males (Mackenzie 1871:230; Holub 1881:1,296; cf. Peires 1981:72; Murphree 1969:160; Wilson 1952:136; Kuper 1946: 183f.). Our discussion of Tswana economy and society in the early nineteenth century made it clear that even women of high status were excluded both from positions of authority and from formal control over material and symbolic resources. Some early converts said explicitly that Christianity would reverse these disabilities, that it "raised them to an equality with their husbands" (Holub 1881:1,296). This is not to suggest that conversion was, or is, reducible to the terms of a simple social cost-benefit analysis (J. Comaroff 1985:29). It implies, rather, a subtle relationship between social predicament and the degree to which novel signs and ideologies are perceived as potent—and received as a recipe for changing the world.

Much to the gratification of the Nonconformists, then, there slowly arose a small, heterogeneous population who sought the skills of *sekgoa* and were happy to listen to the Word. The chiefs would later try to use these converts— especially their junior kin—to tap the resources of the church from a distance (Molema 1966:35; Broadbent 1865:178). But, as we shall see, the ploy tended to backfire, contributing to the consolidation of Christian elites with competing bases of authority. The baptized sported badges of their new identity in the form of European dress and filled the air with their preaching and singing (Moffat 1842:497; also Edwards 1886:91). Sensing the Tswana fondness for song, and its centrality in both ritual and everyday life, the missionaries made hymns a priority in their early translations. The sounds of Sankey soon reverberated in local communities, being intoned even by those otherwise unmoved by Christianity.[53] Here again the evangelists showed themselves willing to use "indirect" means of reaching their target: "Being constantly sung," Moffat (1842:478) noted, "the great truths of salvation would become imperceptibly written on the minds of the people." Added Mackenzie (1871:74) some years later:

> [A]t Kuruman a great improvement took place in the singing in a very short time. Lessons in church psalmody were given by the Misses Moffat, assisted by an excellent harmonium kindly sent . . . by some Christian ladies in London. The singing is now as good as in an English or Scotch village church. Many of the Bechuanas showed themselves possessed of a fine musical ear. . . . Instead of thumping the dusty earth the whole weary night long, to a monotonous recitative, as in the olden time, the villagers of South Bechuanaland now collect in little parties round a neighbour's fire, and sing hymn after hymn till a late hour. At present all music is sacred among the Bechuanas. . . . Thus "Jock o' Hazeldean," usually sung at a marriage service . . . . [is] connected with a match approved by the parents and ratified by the church.

To sing and to dance, in *setswana*, was *go bina*, which also meant "to venerate." The "sacredness" of song was nothing new here. But in the evangelists' view, such performances were a "monotonous thumping" to "barbarous airs" (Edwards 1886:91)—just as Tswana agriculture was no more than "scratching the earth's surface," and Tswana dress no better than brute "nakedness." The choreography of rustic Christian life in Africa would be set to a different tune, the very sounds of which—it was hoped—would signify conformity with church orthodoxy. But there is also evidence that some resisted the seductive power of the songs of praise. As late as 1888, when Price visited a group of recalcitrant Tlhaping near the Harts River, he and his drivers tried to "sing some of Sankey's hymns." They were prevented by the men of the place, however, who drowned them out by setting up a cacophonous din.[54] In fact, mission music was to be widely domesticated in southern Africa, most notably in the secessionist churches. Its cadences would be made to take on the pulse of indigenous self-assertion, to harmonize the aspirations of an independent, black salvation.

By the second half of the nineteenth century, Mackenzie (1871:75–76) was able to describe the "religious attainments of the Christian Bechuanas" with measured optimism:

It is not to be expected that a loquacious news-telling people, unaccustomed to solitude and to consecutive thought or study, should on
their conversion to Christianity become at once remarkable for their
elevated spirituality, and for delighting in protracted seasons of prayer,
meditation, and communion with God. . . . [But] the minds of many
are deeply impressed with the truths of religion. If not Godly in the
highest sense, they are sincerely religious. They believe in God, and
their faces and hearts are turned towards Him. . . . Even the most ignorant of the members of the church, those who have become Christians in advanced years, have got fast hold of a few leading truths. God
loves them. Christ died for them. God will help them if they cry to
Him. They are like lean scraggy oxen that have grown up unaccustomed to the yoke. But at all events they will put that yoke on their
necks, and if they cannot pull much, they will at least walk with the rest
in the team.

Given the richness of their cattle symbolism, their own poetics of pastoralism, Southern Tswana might not have appreciated the missionary's
metaphor. Or the intention which lay silently behind it: that savagery
was to be tamed, and a docile Christian yeomanry trained, by the re-
straining efforts of God's ploughmen and by the civilizing effects of agrarian toil.

To what extent was Mackenzie's cautious optimism justified? How do
we read his effort to put an acceptable face on half-a-century of hard work
devoted to converting the heathen? Others, from the same mission field,
offered more doleful diagnoses. Thus Brown, with unfeigned pessimism,
concluded in 1909 that "Insincerity might be written in large capitals over
the lives of the bulk of the people," a statement meant to apply to Tswana
both inside and outside the church.[55] Optimists and pessimists alike seem to
have agreed on one thing, though: that conversion meant little in isolation
from more thoroughgoing changes in disposition and habit. As Livingstone
(1857:129) had mused many years before:

When converts are made from heathenism by modern missionaries,
it becomes an interesting question whether their faith possesses the
elements of permanence, or is only an exotic too tender for self-
propagation when the fostering care of the foreign cultivators is
withdrawn. If neither habits of self-reliance are cultivated, nor op-
portunities given for the exercise of that virtue, the most promising
converts are apt to become like spoiled children.

Plucked from the wild, African converts appeared to lack the capacity to
reproduce themselves in the missionary's carefully cultivated field. Their

ability to mature seemed still in doubt, still utterly dependent on the sustaining hands of God's gardeners. With the growth of a second generation in the church, taming the heathen became less of a concern. Now the problem was to perpetuate the fragile communities of Christians tilled and nurtured by the evangelists. Given mounting evidence of the "shallow-rootedness" of the new faith, the meaning of conversion itself became debatable. And, as an analytic category in the historical anthropology of religion, it remains debatable. We conclude this chapter by exploring some of the ethnographic and conceptual problems raised by it. We do so by attending to two sets of issues: first, the consciousness of difference wrought by the evangelical encounter; and, second, the relationship, in that encounter, between conversation and conversion.

CONVERSION, CONVERSATION, AND CONSCIOUSNESS
Recognizing Difference

In the long conversation between the Tswana and the churchmen, we discerned a growing objectification of the difference between *setswana* and *sekgoa*, Tswana and European values or ways. As we know, the first generation of evangelists were heirs to a European self-awareness that had long been sharpened on the contrast with the non-European; and they continued this reflexive process on the moral frontiers of empire, where civilization and savagery met. For the Southern Tswana, the encounter with a people so preoccupied with techniques of self-representation and rationalization encouraged them to perceive their own world with a new distinctness and coherence—and to oppose their "customs" to the "belief system" of the whites. Revealingly, they referred to the latter as *tumelo*, which took on the connotations of "faith" or "dogma," but which denoted "agreement" or a notion of conviction as consensus (Brown 1931:66, 333, 343).

Evidence of the emerging sense of difference abounds in the early mission records. And it raises a question long asked by students of African systems of thought (see Horton 1967): Why did the confrontation with Europe have this effect on peoples like the Tswana when their frequent contact with others on the continent did not? Of course, the question itself presumes a lot, since we know relatively little of the cultural dynamics of contact and conquest in precolonial Africa; in part, as we are now all aware, this is because functionalist anthropology, with its emphasis on synchrony and integration, ignored such things as long-distance trade, regional ritual and social movements, and the like. It hardly needs saying, any longer, that local communities *were* caught up in complex processes of internal change; that they *were* engaged in continuous relations with others, exchanging goods and meanings, practical and ritual knowledge. Recall, from chapter 4, how complex were the external connections among the Tswana polities at the turn of the nineteenth century, how their conceptual horizons included distant peoples endowed with their own unique resources and rites.

These external relations were predominantly of two kinds. The first were among discrete political communities whose members spoke mutually intelligible languages; such communities were part of a cultural commonwealth in which collective identities were marked by totemic affiliation. The second were with those who appear, then as now, to have been referred to as *banna ba ditshaba*, usually translated, literally, as "men of the tribes." These peoples, with their generically distinct social, cultural, and physical forms, were taken to be truly different. They were the "others" in a fragmentary world that seemed to know no absolute assertions, no universal meanings. Interestingly, African polities that embarked on processes of expansion and state-building usually followed their military predations with campaigns of cultural imperialism in the effort to consolidate their authority. We are told, for example, that the rulers of the nineteenth-century Pedi federation sought to regulate the chiefly ceremonies of those whom they subordinated (Sansom 1974: 268f.); that the consolidation of the Swazi tributary state rested on an aristocracy seizing control over local rites of social reproduction (Bonner 1983: 88); that Ngoni conquerors tried to abolish autochthonous cults and shrines (Rau 1979); and that Shaka suppressed lineage shades and local diviners, setting up ritual and military structures focused on himself as the embodiment of the Zulu polity (Kelly 1982; Walter 1969). And yet in none of these cases was there any attempt to forge a new universalism, a global hegemony, like that envisaged by bourgeois Europe in the name of its civilization. Nowhere was the assumption made that there could only be one "true" way of knowing and classifying the world, one absolute standard of value. These remained efforts of manifest conquest, campaigns to assert Pedi or Swazi or Ngoni or Zulu predominance in a universe recognized to be populated by others with their own ways and means, their own refractory knowledge and values, their own spirits and specialists.

The churchmen, speaking the language of European ethical and cultural universalism, pressed upon the Tswana a hitherto unfamiliar notion of difference. According to their rhetoric of contrast, it was precisely the things that marked the Africans as distinct that made them and their world inferior—that had, therefore, to be erased if these heathens were to be incorporated into the socio-moral order of global Christendom. "Conversion," the ultimate objective of the Nonconformists, was a process involving the removal of difference and distinction—a process whereby the Tswana were to be assimilated into the moral economy of civilized man, in which human worth was evaluated against the single currency of absolute truth. Over the long run, the process would not efface human differences but would extend the European system of distinction over Africa, drawing its peoples into a single scale of social, spiritual, and material inequality. In the short run, however, the Tswana did not concede to the universalistic ethos of the mission, or to its discriminatory logic. Neither did they simply admit their inferiority.

Instead, they set about recasting the message of the evangelists into their own language of cultural relativism, mindful of the hardening opposition between *setswana* and *sekgoa* as distinct ways of knowing and being, each with its own powers and capacities. Thus it was that a Tlhaping rainmaker told Moffat, who was trying to convince him of the Lord's universal love, that the "God of the whites" lived in the south, the God of his people in the north (see chapter 5, n. 47)—the spatial metaphor clearly being intended to underscore both the *co*existence of the two divinities and the relativity of their realms. Compare another famous rainmaker, the man who debated Livingstone: the burden of his argument, it will be remembered, was that Kwena ritual and healing had its own integrity and value; that its logic ran parallel to that of European medicine, albeit on the basis of different knowledge and techniques. Many years later a northern chief challenged Rev. Lloyd, in much the same terms, on the issue of circumcision:[56] "You told us that we should not practise [ours]," said the ruler, but "we read [in the Bible] how God commanded Abraham" to do it for his people. To each, their own. As we shall see in the next chapter, a group of Tswana, contrasting *setswana* rites with those of the Christians, told Archbell as early as 1833 that initiation was essential to their very being as a people.

These are not just a few isolated examples. The documentary record is filled with reports of ordinary men and women trying patiently to explain to the churchmen the unique significance of conventions such as bridewealth, polygyny, or rites of passage. It is also replete with instances of Tswana comparing the ways of the whites with their "customs"; *mekgwa* being the term they used in the language *they* now began to label "*Sichuana*" (Burchell 1824: 2,295). Says Moffat (1842:246–48), the Tlhaping made it perfectly obvious that they "could not see . . . any thing in our customs more agreeable . . . than in their own."[57] Worse yet, "they would, with little ceremony, pronounce our customs clumsy, awkward, and troublesome"—even at times "laugh extravagantly" at them. Disturbed, perhaps, by the subversive force of savage mirth, Moffat was overstating matters somewhat. From the start, as we already know, there were European techniques and knowledge that the Africans were happy to absorb. But one thing does seem clear. The missionary was unwittingly being given a lesson in cultural relativism, a lesson that most modern anthropologists are also made to learn: whenever he challenged the Tlhaping to account for their ways, he was told "it was custom" (Moffat 1842:465).

One corollary of this form of relativism was the refusal to bow to the assimilating power of any dominant culture, any master narrative of a universal civilization. Another, we repeat, was the presumption that peoples of different worlds might learn, and might incorporate, one another's ways and means without repudiating their own; the demand of the Nonconformists that a choice be made between *setswana* and *sekgoa*, heathenism and Christianity, must have appeared utterly quixotic to the Africans. As we saw in chapter 4, their worldview fostered a highly acquisitive and eclectic disposition toward cultural exchange. That is why even those royals with a pronounced interest in checking the mission and protecting *setswana* were so quick to seek the power and knowledge of the whites, notwithstanding their effort to remain detached from the European embrace—and why, as a result, they became increasingly enmeshed in the forms of *sekgoa*, despite contesting the explicit message of the mission. To be sure, as Christianity played into the cracks of local polities and the expanding colonial arena—finding its access, ironically, in the cultural openness of the ostensibly close-minded savage—no Southern Tswana could avoid its implications.

We shall return in due course to discuss the objectification of *setswana*, and its hardening opposition to *sekgoa*, in the encounter between the evangelists and the Africans. For it was to have a profound impact on the colonization of Tswana consciousness. At this point, however, it is enough to note that, as the process unfolded, a new set of implicit *forms*—unremarked ways of seeing and being, of construing and representing the world—were beginning to insinuate themselves into the worldview of the Tlhaping and Rolong. And they were doing so, often unrecognized, amidst all the ideological arguments and contests of images. Not, we stress, in spite of those arguments, but because of them. It is our contention that the very structure of the long conversation itself was a crucial vehicle by means of which those forms took root, bearing with them the hegemonic signs and practices of European culture.

Of more immediate concern, however, is the implication of the contrast between *setswana* and *sekgoa*, of the dialectics of difference and its negation, for the Nonconformist effort to gain converts. Not only did the relativism of Tswana culture resist the universalism of Christianity—and consequently make the very notion of conversion difficult for the Africans to grasp. It also laid out the syntax of "religious" transformation here. Those royals who actively opposed the mission, notwithstanding their efforts to seize the powers of the missionaries, did so expressly in order to protect the integrity of *setswana*; recall the Tlhaping headmen who claimed that the presence of the evangelists put "their whole system" at risk (chapter 5, n. 49). By contrast, those marginal men and women drawn into the church soon realized that they had to accept, in no small measure, its methodical, rule-governed regime: to be seen to adopt, that is, the conventions of *sekgoa*. "Interested inquirers" who wished to drink at the fountains of the LMS and WMMS—to cultivate their irrigated fields, use their tools, learn to read their books, rely on them as a defensive shield—were expected also to acknowledge their beliefs and assent to their "laws." That much was implicated in being a *modumedi*, "one who agrees," the vernacular term for "convert" which derived from the same root as *tumelo* ("faith"). This was not an altogether unfamiliar notion for the Africans. In their own world too a set of taboos (*meila*) defined the boundaries of any social community and regulated the flow of superhuman forces within it, although moral breach was not seen in the same light as the Nonconformists regarded sin. Similarly, the Christian concern with "laws" resonated with the indigenous stress placed on *mekgwa le melao* ("law and custom") in ordering the flow of everyday communal life. More than a century later, anthropologists were to be struck by the extreme legalism of Tswana Christianity of all types (J. Comaroff 1974:262; Pauw 1960:218; cf. Murphree 1969:161f.; Peel 1968:298)—this legalism emerging from the articulation, under particular historical conditions, of two cultures that placed complementary weight on rules and conventions in establishing membership in, and shaping the life of, any community. But even for those who first chose the church in the face of chiefly opposition, "conversion" was always mediated to some extent by the forms of *setswana*; the new wine, as Sundkler (1961:238) put it for the comparable Zulu case, was poured into old wineskins. And this in spite of the fact that the neophyte Protestants, those who agreed, came progressively to be associated with the world and worldview of *sekgoa*. As in most situations of "religious" transformation, professions of new belief belied the fact that older modes of thought and action were never fully laid aside.

By far the majority of Southern Tswana, however, ranged between the two extremes in their response to the evangelical outreach: between the blanket refusal of those who championed *setswana* and the positive identification with *sekgoa* of those who became "believers." It was this large population in the middle that would attempt to engage with the mission, to domesticate and harness its resources, while rejecting its order and discipline. Inadvertently perhaps, Moffat (1842:288) gives us a telling glimpse of the manner in which the Tlhaping expressed themselves in this respect during the early days, attending the church yet maintaining their distance:

> Our attendance at public worship would vary from one to forty; and these very often manifesting the greatest indecorum. Some would be

snoring; others laughing; some working; and others . . . would be employed in removing from their ornaments certain nameless insects . . . while sitting by the missionary's wife. Never having been accustomed to chairs or stools, some . . . would sit with their feet on the benches, having their knees, according to their usual mode of sitting, drawn up to their chins. In this position one would fall asleep and tumble over, to the great merriment of his fellows.

Mission order might have been flouted, its seriousness of purpose subverted by hilarity. But the novel ritual forms and productive techniques brought by the churchmen were ever more widely adopted by the mass of Tlhaping and Rolong. And, modulated to meet local symbolic and material imperatives, they were put to work in various causes. Such modes of creative appropriation and defiance were common in the early phases of colonization. As we shall see, they were to be characteristic also of the longer-term reactions of the Southern Tswana rank and file to the culture of the colonizer.

The evangelists were less than delighted at this development. They took it to be an unmistakable sign of childish misunderstanding, of the sheer incapacity of the Tswana to grasp the refined knowledge and rational technology of western civilization. And they responded to it with a mixture of paternal tolerance and ill-disguised exasperation. But what they did find particularly wounding were instances of ritual syncretism, the reconstruction and representation of the liturgy of the Holy Service. One noteworthy case, to which we return in volume 2, was reported by an indignant Rev. Monro (1837: 396–97) in the *Missionary Magazine and Chronicle*, under the title "Pretences of a Bechuana Woman to Immediate Communion with the Divine Being."[58] Monro tells of a former candidate for baptism who had attracted a large following by concocting a synthetic rite, a brilliant bricolage of Christian and indigenous words and objects; she chanted fragments of the Lord's Prayer, hymns, and scriptures while laying out an orderly arrangement of patches torn from a Baptismal gown. In her claim to tap the condensed might of the mission God, this "technician of the sacred" (Eliade 1964) anticipated generations of secessionist clergy and ritual practitioners who would likewise seek access to the divine powers of *sekgoa*—and would, in the process, talk back to the colonizers in a register of their own choosing.

The Meaning of Conversion

In musing on conversion in Africa, David Livingstone (1857:123) cites an "intelligent chief's" characterization of the moral status of Tswana Christians:

> . . . "some feign belief to ingratiate themselves with the missionaries; some profess Christianity because they like the new system, which

gives so much more importance to the poor, and desire that the old system may pass away; and the rest—a pretty large number—profess because they are really true believers."

Whatever else we may make of this reported conversation, its unspoken frame of reference was the Nonconformist axiom that conversion involved two things: sincere personal belief and committed membership of a community in Christ. In the moral economy of Protestantism, it was up to every individual to arrive at a rational choice among alternative, mutually exclusive faiths—and then to act upon it. But, for the Tswana, the matter was not so straightforward. As Livingstone's interlocutor was trying to tell him, affiliation to the church meant quite different things to different people. It is the evangelist's perspective, however, that has survived to become part of the discourse of the social sciences. Conversion, defined as a transfer of "primary religious identification" (Peel 1977:108), continues to be isolated as a relevant analytic category—and a "problem"—by those concerned with religious and ideological transformation in Africa (Horton 1971; Fisher 1973).

The Pauline model of conversion has become deeply enshrined in modern western thought. Having been absorbed silently into the bourgeois ideal of spiritual individualism, it permeates both theological and popular conceptions of religious change. Within sociology and anthropology, efforts to explore the latter, and to deploy this image of conversion as an analytic construct, have been associated primarily with scholars in the Weberian tradition. Speaking of the spread of Christianity in the Third World, these scholars have suggested that a rapid explosion of social horizons, such as occurs under colonial and postcolonial conditions, often engenders a felt need for a more coherent doctrine, a more highly rationalized faith than is offered by "native" religions. However logical in their own right, goes the argument, those religions are ill-equipped to make sense of the forces unleashed by European modernity. Shifts in spiritual commitment, in short, are attributed to the responses of individuals in situations of intellectual and experiential crisis. This perspective assumes that any religion is a discrete *system* of belief—the corollary being that symbolic or ritual activity which draws from more than one is "syncretistic."

The most well-known example of this position is, perhaps, Horton's (1971, 1975) thesis that African conversion arises from the quest for meaning in the face of modernization: that shifts in spiritual identity occur as a result of the incapacity of "traditional" cosmologies to account for existence outside the local "microcosm" (1971:101f.). This thesis has been called into question for, among other things, its intellectualist and teleological assumptions. But even for those who criticize it, or who treat the phenomenon in more sociological terms (e.g., Peel 1977), the concept of conversion itself retains its commonsense European connotation. And so the problem remains: how well does it grasp the highly variable, usually gradual, often implicit, and demonstrably "syncretic" manner in which the social identities, cultural styles, and ritual practices of African peoples were transformed by the evangelical encounter? How well does it capture the complex dialectic of invasion and riposte, of challenge and resistance, set in motion among the likes of the Southern Tswana? Here, after all, was a politics of consciousness in which the very nature of consciousness was itself the object of struggle.

Among the Southern Tswana formal church affiliation was certainly salient in marking out members of an emerging Christian community and, especially, its elite. Yet far more definitive, in local terms, was the degree to which these people adopted the practices of *sekgoa*, of which attendance at religious services was merely a part. Indeed, the growing concern of the churchmen with "backsliding," and their frequent excommunication of individuals and congregations, indicates that the act of conversion was *not* a reliable index of the values or spiritual commitment of those concerned. Most Tlhaping and Rolong, in the nineteenth century, took part in Christian ritual as selectively as they took on other mission innovations. They were not constrained by a sense of systematic theology or universal truth, by any meaningful idea of personalized professions of faith or by the notion that adherence to one religion excluded involvement in all others. Like our technician of the sacred with her patchwork of cloth and catechism, they were bricoleurs of the spiritual, as well as of the material, domain—if less flamboyant ones. And so they remained, even when they followed their chiefs into the church to become what Schapera (1958) has dubbed "nominal Christians."

The missionaries might have written the history of Tswana civilization as a chronicle of conversions won or lost. But it will be clear now why *their* perspective cannot, and does not, yield a sufficient account of cultural change or spiritual bricolage. And why *we* hesitate to treat "conversion" as a significant analytic category in its own right. The case of the Southern Tswana simply underlines the truism that changing religious identity, itself a highly complex problem of meaning and action, is always an element of more embracing historical transformations. It is a matter of novel media as well as messages, of cultural form as much as content. What is more, the significance of conversion to Africans themselves cannot be assumed to conform to European preconceptions—a serious point, to be sure, since it is their experience that the concept is meant to illuminate.

Other, more general, analytic dangers also lurk behind the concept of conversion. We shall mention just two and let the matter rest. The first is that, in the African context at least, it tends to conflate changes in individual spiritual identity with cultural transformation, thereby muddying the historical relationship between subjective experience and collective existence. The two are obviously connected. But the nature of the connection can be neither assumed nor ignored. It demands explanation. Secondly, the very use of "conversion" as a noun leads, unwittingly, to the reification of religious "belief"; to its abstraction from the total order of symbols and meanings that compose the taken-for-granted world of any people. This abstraction makes spiritual commitment into a choice among competing faiths, and "belief systems" into doctrines torn free of all cultural embeddedness. As we have stressed, however, modern Protestant conversion is itself an ideologically saturated construct. Framed in the imagery of reason and the reflective self, it is a metonym for a moral economy, representing personal conviction as a form of resource allocation that echoes, on the spiritual plane, the material economies of the marketplace. To pretend, therefore, that it may be an analytic tool, an explanatory principle, is to dress up ideology as sociology—and to ignore the fact that, in the context of European colonialism, "conversion" has always been part of its apparatus of cultural coercion.

While Protestant ideas of personhood, belief, and conversion had little resonance with Tswana values, the long conversation between the missionaries and the Africans had an enormous cumulative impact on the latter. This protracted exchange reshaped the "heathen" world not by winning souls in spiritual or verbal battles but by inculcating the everyday forms of the colonizing culture. As we have noted, the Nonconformists—despite their own ideology of religious transformation and their stated goal of gaining converts—were aware that they had to work on both planes at once: that to become cultivated Christians, the Southern Tswana had to be converted *and* reformed. They also knew that the kind of subjectivity and selfhood they wished to instill did not arise from dogma and revelation alone. It inhered as much in the quotidian practices of the "civilizing mission." Conversion, whatever its status in the formal rhetoric of the church, was no less partial and problematic an objective to churchmen in the field than it is to modern anthropologists of colonialism, culture, and consciousness.

S E C U L A R   P O W E R ,
S A C R E D
A U T H O R I T Y

The Politics of the Mission

I N ENTHUSIASTIC ACCORD with the Spirit of the Age at home (above, chapter 2), the mission societies accepted—indeed, positively urged—the separation of church and state, the sacred and the secular.[1] These categories and contrasts may no longer serve us as sufficient *analytic* terms with which to dissect historical agency, but they were critical tropes in the worldview of the nineteenth-century Nonconformists. Nor was the line between the spiritual and the temporal merely a convenient boundary in the imperial division of labor. As a received convention, it ran to the core of contemporary European images of the universe; a universe divided "by nature" into discrete domains, each associated with an appropriate sphere of practice. Just as God and man, divine authority and worldly power, were palpably distinct, so were politics and religion.[2] Evangelists in the South African field took the difference between them to be self-evident: the former involved the control by sovereigns and parliaments, "modern" and "primitive" alike, over public policy and the affairs of men; the latter, which included the effort to gain converts, to spread moral enlightenment, and to teach the arts of civilization, was accountable to God alone. Any confusion between them was itself a profanation. Robert Moffat (1842:206–09), for example, spoke of the "unhallowed union" of religious duties and political functions. To prove the point, he recounted, in high moral dudgeon, the dramatic failure of two missionaries who had accepted "diplomatic engagements" and become Confidential Agents to the Colonial Government. What is more, he noted, the confounding of spiritual and temporal roles has "no warrant from Scripture." Just the opposite: when Christ said "My kingdom is not of this world," he meant it quite literally.

On the less ethereal plane of the practical mission, however, the distinction between church and state, the sacred and the secular, was to raise two closely interrelated problems. The first concerned the line of demarcation between them. For all its supposed clarity, this line often turned out to be anything but obvious, and it demanded active interpretation. Sometimes, in the single-minded effort to build up the empire of the spirit, it was ignored or not seen at all. Thus when in 1815 the LMS directors wrote to Lord Somerset, Governor of the Cape,[3] asking him to assist the mission to the Tswana (above, p. 46), they added, "We hope that the information which [this mission] may obtain respecting remote nations will be gratifying to your Excellency." Did not the supply of intelligence to the colonial government blur—or even violate—the distinction between "religious duties and political functions?" If the possibility occurred to the LMS directors they did not admit it. Nor did it seem to cross the mind of a visiting LMS notable, who, afraid that conflict on the frontier might threaten the Society's stations, took Moffat to see the highest colonial officials in the district: "Our Brother," he wrote to a colleague, "can supply them with valuable and practical information" and so abet British control over the hinterland.[4] In principle there may have been a sharp cleavage between the realms of Cross and Crown. In practice it was as protean, as hard to pin down, as any other boundary between imagined domains.

The second problem was yet more difficult. Given the ultimate moral precedence of the sacred over the temporal, when and how far was it justified to stray deliberately into the political realm to do God's work? This was a question that arose frequently and, whether the missionaries liked it or not, sometimes required a practical answer. For on occasion, as almost every evangelist found out, turning one's back was as patently political as any intentional action could have been (see e.g., Broadbent 1865:82f.). A few of the Nonconformists addressed the issue explicitly, among them Moffat (1842:207–08):

> No missionary, however, can with any show *of Scripture or reason*, refuse his pacific counsel and advice, when those among whom he labours require it, nor decline to become interpreter or translator to any foreign power, or to be the medium of hushing the din of war arising either from family interests or national claims; nor is it inconsistent with his character to become a mediator or intercessor where life is at stake, whether arising from ignorance, despotism, or revenge. . . . A missionary may do all this, and more than this, without endangering

his character, and what is of infinitely more importance, the character of the gospel he proclaims [our italics].

Coming from an evangelist of great note and seniority, this view carried considerable weight. For some LMS and WMMS clergymen, it could as well have been a statement of common policy. The union of God and government might have been "unhallowed." Yet in allowing that "a missionary may do all this, and more," Moffat gave himself and his colleagues tacit licence to intervene in worldly affairs, provided only that they did so in the name of religion. Of course, this very general principle did not specify when and how. That would always have to be decided, if at all, in the murky light of circumstance.

The ideological distinction between church and state did more than just raise awkward practical questions and challenges of conscience for individual evangelists. It gave rise to an uneasy relationship between secular power and sacred authority, a relationship that was to have major consequences for the Tswana—and in time for the colonial process at large. These consequences flowed from inherent, but as yet invisible, contradictions in the politics of the mission. As we shall see, far from remaining aloof, many of the Christians found their way into affairs of government and became embroiled in decidedly worldly relations of power and dominance. Some even emerged as active public figures and administrators. Nevertheless, because of the nature of mission ideology and the colonial division of labor, their role in this arena was *intrinsically* indeterminate and ambiguous. Taken together, in short, the Nonconformists were ineffectual players on the conventional political stage.

It is here that the thrust of our argument lies. As we said in the Introduction, we do not suggest that the political implications of mission activity were trivial. They were not. But the capacity of the evangelists to act on the indigenous world, to impose upon it new ways of seeing and being, lay primarily in the diffuse processes of the civilizing mission, in the inculcation, among Tswana, of the values and conventions of modern European culture.[5] Processes of this sort—which we began to trace in the last chapter—rarely entail the overt exercise of power or coercion. Seldom do they occur in the domain of institutional politics, although they may play into it. Often all but unseen, they infuse such media as aesthetics and religion, built form and bodily presentation, medical knowledge and mundane habit (Bourdieu 1977:184f.)—the media through which human subjects are incorporated into a "natural" order. Indeed, there was to be a yawning gap between the power of the missionaries to transform Tswana cultural life and their powerlessness to deliver the new society promised in their evangelical message: a contradiction, that is, between their worldview and the world created by colonialism. Where the former at its most idealistic portrayed a liberal democracy of self-determining individuals, the latter yielded a racially-coded, class-ridden system of domination. It was in this contradiction, in which the mission churches were themselves to be implicated, that the first florescence of organized black resistance was to take root.

In order to analyze the politics of the mission, we do not offer a chronicle of events. Instead, we shall explore the three planes, each of them dynamic and fluid, that came to compose the political field for the evangelists and the Tswana alike: the internal government of the local chiefdoms; the expanding regional frontier, with its growing population of black and white inhabitants; and the subcontinental theater of colonial and imperial relations.[6] We treat these planes both in chronological sequence and in order of increasing scale, the point being to grasp the unfolding, ever more intricate field of power relations wrought by the spread of a colonial dominion across the face of southern Africa.

THE POLITICS OF THE MISSION

Church and Chiefship: Paradoxes of Power, Moments of Misrecognition

In their early dealings with the Tswana, the LMS and WMMS missionaries spoke openly of their intention to claim the spiritual realm for God, leaving intact the secular powers of the chiefs.[7] Inasmuch as the latter were the local temporal authorities, the evangelists treated them with almost exaggerated respect—albeit, they sometimes confessed, for strategic reasons. For many years they referred to even minor local rulers as "Kings,"[8] and took pains to ask their permission for everything from establishing residential sites to holding religious meetings, from trading to tree-felling.[9] The Christians' insistence that they sought only to rebuild the lost Empire of God (above, chapter 2) reassured the Tswana royals, who had strong views on the propriety of their involvement in public affairs. As Rev. Hamilton reported to the directors of the LMS:[10]

> At a general meeting called by [the Tlhaping chief] Mateebe, senior "captains" said that we must by no means interfere with their government. . . . [W]e have liberty only to preach the Gospel among them, and indeed this is all that the Great Master Christ hath laid upon us, and those that will be rulers and judges as well as preachers, it is no wonder that they bear a heavy Cross.

The warning not to intervene in local affairs reflected the ambivalence of the Tlhaping toward the political designs of the Europeans. For his part, the chief—who still grasped his trophy, Read's weapon—argued that their respectful conduct and cooperation gave proof of their intention not to intervene; to wit, Mothibi took the incident of the gun as evidence that *he* controlled the evangelists, not vice versa (above, p. 201). But the suspicions of many of his royal kin and followers were never fully allayed, perhaps because they were fed by the other black inhabitants of the region who had closer experience of colonialism. It will be recalled that Moffat (1842:339), in telling the incident of the wooden Dutch clock (see chapter 5), noted how the Kora to the south had

> poisoned the minds of some of the leading men with the idea, that the missionaries were only the precursors of the Government, who would soon follow in their train, and make soldiers of every one of them.

If we substitute "workers" for "soldiers" (or, more imaginatively, think forward to the era of the "reserve army" of black labor in South Africa), the Kora had a remarkably prescient sense of history. It is no surprise, as Moffat went on ruefully to remark, that Southern Tswana "continued to suspect that the motives of the missionary were anything but disinterested."

We have already seen how quick the Southern Tswana were to appreciate the temporal, and especially the political, advantages of the missionary presence; how soon the Europeans were put to use—often unwillingly, now and then unwittingly—as diplomatic agents, military allies, and advisers. We have also been told repeatedly by the evangelists themselves that, while they were kept at bay, their preaching ignored or even thwarted,[11] they had to accede to the natives' requests in order to pursue their goals.[12] The story of the Rev. Read's gun was merely a climactic moment in the ongoing battle of wills, a struggle that centered on such things as place and space, words and water, but suffused through everyday existence. At the same time the demands made of the mission were not always antithetical to its objectives. On occasion, in fact, they gave the Christians a chance to introduce their goods and messages into the Tswana environment: thus, when Campbell (1822:2,9) was told that many chiefs wanted evangelists because they had seen how "Mateebe's missionaries" were "a shield to his back," he took this as both an optimistic sign and a great opportunity. And later, when others were asked to dig wells, build houses, and make implements—particularly for the royals they most hoped to convert—they readily complied, knowing that, in bestowing the gifts of civilization upon some and not others, their actions were playing into local power relations. Political pragmatism and Protestant ideology, far from countermanding each other, frequently made common cause.

And yet the Nonconformists continued to sustain their view that it was both possible and desirable not to "interfere with [the] government" of the chiefdoms. Coming from a world that had conjured up a hard-edged distinction between politics and religion, secular power and sacred authority, they failed to see that sovereignty in Tswana communities simply could not be apportioned in such terms (see chapter 4). That is why it seemed quite reasonable to Moffat or Livingstone to oppose the rainmaker as a bitter enemy and yet to act with uncomplaining respect toward the chief.[13] The mutual misunderstandings that pervaded many aspects of the encounter between the Christians and the blacks, in other words, were to surface here too. In the process, forces were unleashed that would pick away at the seams of the indigenous politico-ritual order. But these forces were also to escape the control of the evangelists and would subvert their endeavors in important respects.

The key to the misunderstanding is evident from the first. It is foreshadowed in Hamilton's notes on the meeting at which the Tlhaping told the churchmen not to interfere in "their government." Reading his statement in light of contemporary Tswana political ideology, it becomes clear that much was lost in the translation, lexical and cultural alike: "their government" (*bokgosi*) meant something quite different to speaker and listener. For the Tlhaping, it evoked the total, indivisible fabric of authority that regulated social and material life—embodied in the chief, spiritualized in the ministrations of the ancestral realm, signified in the conventions of *mekgwa*, and realized in the proper conduct of all communal activity. For the Europeans, on the other hand, it applied purely to formal proceedings in the public domain and to matters concerning the worldly authority of the ruler.

For example, Broadbent (1865:93) offers, as proof of the careful distance kept by the Methodist mission from the affairs of government, the fact that he and Hodgson had "attended a *pietcho*, or council, . . . not to take any part in the proceedings, but merely as spectators." Their visible presence at the head of the polity was clearly intended by the embattled Seleka-Rolong chief, Sefunelo, to make a point to his followers; for the Rolong had become convinced of the invulnerability of any sovereign to his enemies, internal and external, as long as he had an evangelist by his side (Broadbent 1865:117; see Cope 1979:4f.). To Broadbent and Hodgson, however, passivity and silence masqueraded as nonpresence, almost invisibility. It did not occur to them that being there was itself a blatantly political act. On the contrary, it was only on the rare occasions when they openly contested a chief's temporal authority that they understood themselves to be doing something that could be construed as "political." This happened, for instance, when the Methodists gave asylum to a youth who, having stolen from them, had been sentenced to death by Sefunelo at the hands of his adolescent sons (Broadbent 1865:83). Here the interference of the Christians, at least in their own eyes, fell squarely within the guidelines laid down by Moffat (above, p. 253): they were interceding pacifically when a life was at stake. Under these conditions, their actions were a matter of pure moral conscience, and they had to bear the consequences bravely. Thus Broadbent (1865:84) tells, melodramatically, how, having kindled the fury of the "despotic Chief" on whose mercy their lives now depended, they

> stood calmly before him, and as it appeared that the secret of all this ire was jealousy of our interference with his authority, I said, "Siffonello, *Kossi*, (Chief,) hear me. We are not Kings; you are King here; this land is yours, these cattle are yours, and these people are your subjects, not your property. There is a King of Kings, Modeema [*modimo*], to whom all Kings and people must hereafter give an account of their conduct; human life is at His disposal only."

Broadbent thought that he had appeased Sefunelo. His text recounts, in a self-satisfied voice, that the chief was struck with "awe" at his arguments, although he did come back later to ask the whites whether *they* were kings—and, if not, whom they recognized as such. The evangelist realized that his answers were regarded as somewhat vague and incoherent. But he seems not to have connected this with the fact that the situation of the mission changed palpably thereafter. Before, its property had been treated as inviolable by the Africans; from that day on the station suffered constant intrusion and petty theft. Perhaps this was because the churchmen had been seen to deal leniently with someone who had stolen from them; instead of taking their complaint to the *kgotla*, as a Motswana would have done, they had simply forgiven the offender. But there is another possibility. Whatever Sefunelo's reaction to Broadbent's views on the difference between kings and Gods, it may be that, by removing his well-publicized protection from the Methodist station, he hoped to teach the Nonconformists a lesson about the totality of his control. The lesson was only dimly understood, however. The process of misrecognition continued unabated as the Christians sought an explanation for this "new irritation" in a familiar axiom, the natural greed of the savage.[14] Far from impressing the Europeans with his sovereign power, the chief merely fed their stereotype of the primitive as a being driven by passion, not political foresight.

Perhaps the most palpable symptom of misrecognition—that is, the interpretation of practices from one culture in the taken-for-granted terms of another—lay in the paradox of chiefly power and its subversion. Later, in 1855, the Nonconformists were to be criticized by Archdeacon (later Archbishop) Merriman (1957:223) for the "avowed attempt" to weaken indigenous authority in order to facilitate their work; by contrast, the clergy of his own church, claimed the Anglican leader, taught obedience to the chief "as part of the doctrine of God's word." But the matter was not quite so straightforward. Apart from their ideological commitment to the separation of church and state, most of the first generation of LMS and WMMS evangelists saw practical advantage in a strong chiefship. It ensured a stable polity within which they could toil to build their Kingdom of God (cf. Ayandele 1966:31 on Nigeria).[15] However, their own intervention into regional relations, in the name of moral advancement, could not but erode Tswana sovereignty—whether they actually "interfered" in public affairs or not. Thus the encouragement of commerce, ostensibly to bring civilized goods to the heathen and so help him earn his own humanity, had the effect of undermining chiefly control over trade. Indirectly, too, it loosened the hold of royals on their serfs (above, p. 166). In addition, the gradual pacification of Bechuanaland removed from rulers a prime source of tributary wealth—cattle and captives[16]—just as the introduction of a new well of power and knowledge, *sekgoa* (European ways), put an end to their monopoly over the well-being of their subjects. In short, the evangelists might have wished for potent chiefs and secure polities, but their own actions subverted the very political capital on which Tswana government rested.

The process of misrecognition, and the paradox of power to which it led, were brought into its sharpest focus when the Christians intervened in what they took to be matters spiritual. It was here, of course, that they believed it permissible to make their entry onto the public stage; here that they might legitimately drive a wedge between secular power and sacred authority. For them the religious "darkness" of these Africans—spirituality degenerated into brute superstition—was the insidious work of Satanic forces. Even worse, in extinguishing all light from the heathen mind, these forces had cast a pall over the social and public life of the Tswana. Marking off the religious domain from the political, therefore, was a first step in isolating the battleground on which Satan was to be defeated. We have already seen how, to the Nonconformists, the contest with rain doctors was both a means and a measure of their heroic quest. Another theater of struggle was communal ritual, especially rites of initiation and circumcision, *bogwêra* (for males) and *bojale* (for females),[17] the most powerful of all indigenous ceremonial (above, p. 159). As Mackenzie (1871:378) explains:

> The early missionaries opposed circumcision as a religious rite; . . . [saying] in effect, to the people, "There are two ways and two rites: the way of God's Word and the way of heathenism; the rite of baptism and the rite of circumcision. Let all give up the one and adopt the other."

To the mission, in other words, circumcision and baptism had become metonyms for heathenism and Christianity, respectively. Both rituals of reproduction in the broadest sense of the term, their stark opposition symbolized the uncompromising choice between the past and the future, benighted damnation and enlightened salvation. But the triumph of the latter over the former, to be counted in the hard currency of conversion, was not going to

be easy. While the evangelists poured scorn on the "ridiculous and profane"[18] initiation ceremonies, they acknowledged that they were "prodigious
barriers to the Gospel" (Moffat 1842:251). Once more, this was put down
to the deep hold of custom ("*mekua*"; i.e., *mekgwa*), of "the sanctions of
immemorial usage" (Mackenzie 1871:378); to "gross superstition, and inveterate habits";[19] or more practically to the fact that these rites indoctri-
nated Tswana children "in all that is filthy, in all that is deceitful and
unrighteous, and in all that is blasphemous and soul-destroying."[20] For their
part the Tswana seem to have tried to explain to the whites that *bogwêra* was
essential to the existence of the polity—that without it people could not
marry or be fully social beings, let alone become persons "of eminence."[21]

But the missionaries would not, because they could not, see the existential roots or the political implications of the rites. As a result they saw no
reason why chiefs should not excuse "people of the word" from taking part
in them—especially if these people gave proof of their loyalty. Mackenzie
(1871:378) again, speaking now of Chief Sekgoma of the Ngwato:

> I once pleaded with Sekhome that he would institute some new token
> of obedience . . . and to dispense with the present ceremony [*bogwêra*]
> for all who did not wish to attend it. I admitted that I wished the
> people to leave him as priest, but declared that I desired his people to
> be subject to him as commander of the army of the tribe. I wished all
> to be Christians, and yet all to remain Bamangwato.

In claiming religious freedom for their converts, the missionaries might have
thought it possible to avoid challenging the secular authority of the chiefship.
But for Sekgoma and other Tswana rulers, withdrawal from communal ceremonies was tantamount to withdrawal from the political community itself;
there was no such thing as religious freedom that was not also a repudiation
of their dominion. Moreover, since the success of these ceremonies was held
to depend on a state of harmony among the living and the dead (above,
p. 158f.), such defections endangered the well-being of the polity at large.
As the Seleka-Rolong chief, Moroka, put it to Rev. Ludorf, it was this
"rite by which the subjects were knitted to their chiefs, and the whole
race to their ancestors."[22] The claim that Christians could abjure initiation
and yet remain loyal to the chiefship, therefore, rang hollow to the local
sovereigns.

In the upshot, the struggle over circumcision was to be both bitter and
drawn out. As they did when counting victories against rain doctors and
"native dances," the evangelists repeatedly announced the impending demise of the rites. Already in 1833, Archbell[23] wrote that "the universal reformation is fast approaching," the whole edifice of *bogwêra* and *bojale* having
"fallen to the ground." His optimism was premature, however. At a Meth-

odist conference more than seventy years later,[24] a Southern Tswana speaker owned that "we have no power to stop *bogwêra*." Another went on to say that its persistence "is in the power of the chief and people," who want to keep it going. And this in spite of the fact that some Christian rulers banned initiation in the late nineteenth and early twentieth centuries (Schapera 1970:126). As we recalled in chapter 4 (n. 39), we witnessed the rite ourselves in 1970.

Two things stand out in this contest over sacred authority and secular power. One has already been noted: that it was the marginal, disempowered members of Tswana polities who first chose baptism over circumcision and attached themselves to the mission (above, p. 238f.). There is evidence that such people saw in Christianity an opportunity to reverse the disabilities under which they labored; Holub (1881:1,296), recall, said that women defended the church because "it raised them to equality with their husbands." The evangelists tried to convert chiefs, but drew only their junior brothers and cousins, wives and daughters; they sought to recruit a free citizenry for the Kingdom of God, but filled their pews with serfs and clients (Mackenzie 1871:230; Holub 1881:1,296; also chapter 8).[25] Molema (1951:58), a grandson of the earliest Tshidi Methodist leader,[26] argues that it could not have been otherwise. For those central to the political process—chiefs, royals with ambitions, and powerful commoners—Christianity seemed to violate the very foundations of their social world. They were correct. The Nonconformist commitment to economic individualism and commodity production, to the nuclear family and private property, was flatly inimical to contemporary Tswana political economy. Molema (1951:58) goes on to say that, to the royals, it was soon clear that the church would implant a "state within a state." By "state," he means a condition of being, not just a political institution. Whether this observation is a post-hoc reconstruction or a faithful reflection of Tswana historical consciousness is not clear. But it does capture the fact that, in place of social marginality, the mission offered "people of the word" a positive social identity, a *society* of the saved based on the power and knowledge of *sekgoa*.

Here lies the second point of note about the struggle. As the mission made inroads into Tswana communities, it was the confrontation over ritual participation that drew the line between "people of the word" and the chiefs and their followers; the line that gave political definition to the two "states." The evangelists, in pleading the right of "the People to pray and sing—attend Church, and abandon many of their practices,"[27] asserted the reality of something they called *Bogosi yoa Kereste*, the "kingdom of Christ."[28] Note the use of the term *bogosi* [*bokgosi*]. Until the Nonconformists began the task of cultural translation, it denoted the chief*ship*. More broadly, it evoked the values that lay at the core of Tswana government and politics, economy and society. It makes sense, then, that rulers and royals would be offended by the claim that Christianity was also a *bokgosi*, a competing *state*; that they would resist the effort of its adherents to turn away from communal rites; and that they would try hard to contain its activities.

Take the reaction of the Tshidi-Rolong chief, Montshiwa, to the rise of a Methodist congregation under Molema, his half-brother.[29] As this congregation grew larger, Tshidi converts began to absent themselves from initiation and other rites (Holub 1881:1,296; Mackenzie 1871:228f.). Deeply disturbed by their "disloyalty," and angered that his daughter had secretly joined them, the ruler declared that he would only tolerate the church if its members first took part in *setswana* ceremonies. In so doing he tried to encompass *Bogosi yoa Kereste* within his own sovereignty, demonstrating that it existed on his terms and by his permission. The converts continued to resist, however, and the conflict between chief and chapel, personified in Montshiwa and Molema, festered for many years. And, throughout, as the ruler was forced to make concessions to the swelling congregation, he looked for ways to keep it within his dominion. But he never fully succeeded: Christianity came to provide an alternative focus of political mobilization and action.

Much same the story was repeated all over the Southern Tswana region—perhaps most passionately, certainly most vividly, among a branch of the Tlhaping situated at Taung. In an effort to subdue the church, their chief, Mahura, showed lively symbolic imagination. As Rev. William Ross recounts:[30]

> . . . in a great passion he [Mahura] broke one of the windows of the chapel, threatened to set fire to the whole building, took down the bell, and carried it to his own kchotla [*kgotla*, "court"] to call his own picho [general assembly]. The only reason for his outrage was, that believers would not obey him.

The outburst had been sparked by a report—mistaken, according to the missionary—that a group of Christians had caught, convicted, and sentenced a man for stealing. Mahura was outraged, believing that they had deliberately usurped his judicial function, the very essence of his office. In seizing the bell, and by using it to call the populace to *his* court, he seems to have intended two things: first, to put the Christians on trial for their contempt, subjecting their il*legal* activity to his legal jurisdiction; and, second, to underscore his right to summon the entire *morafe*, of which the "people of the word"—and their *kgotla*, the church—were just one part. Significantly, he would only return the bell to Ross himself, and then only in public, all of which the evangelist found "strange." But these actions are easy to understand from the chief's perspective. Knowing now that Christianity could not be eradicated, all he could do was try to contain it—and show that the changes had, literally, to be rung at his behest; that he alone had the authority to "give" the bell, the means to call people together, to the "believers"; and that the only worthy recipient was the European, who had brought it, and the power of the church, in the first place. After all, the capacity to control space and time, movement and public meetings, was the acid test of a ruler's potency. For all its assertiveness, however, Mahura's response recognized the reality of a fractured polity, a fragmented world.

Here in fact lay the denouement of the process of establishing a state-within-a-state. By implanting Christianity as they did, the Nonconformists[31] did not just impair chiefly command over people and property. Nor did they merely subvert the relations of inequality on which rested the extraction of labor and tribute (Mackenzie 1871:230; Livingstone 1857:123). More fundamentally, by seeking to unravel the fabric of sovereignty—indeed, of social life—into discrete domains of religion and government, the LMS and WMMS engendered a new form pluralism; one that clothed ideological distinction in transparently political dress. For, whatever the secular intentions of the mission, its converts remade the political sociology of the church in their own image. Around it they created another center, with its own leadership, power relations, and symbolic resources. Where before the chiefship had been the core of the social and symbolic universe, it now became one of two foci of authority (cf. Chirenje 1976:401). Nor was the church any less political, in the usual sense of the term, than the royal court. To return to the case of the Tshidi, Montshiwa made this very point in a dramatic meeting at Moshaneng on 11 June 1863. Held in the wake of one of his public confrontations with the Methodists, the gathering was attended by Rev. Ludorf, who recorded the proceedings.[32] By the ruler's own account, his action against the Christians

> "was brought about because [my] brother Molema would not submit to [my] orders. . . . Molema stood as teacher of the tribe in my place. . . . [Then] he left, [and] set up a chieftainship of his own. . . . These Christians are obeying the Book more than the King; ultimately the tribe will split and perish."

Molema later made a direct bid to unseat Montshiwa (J.L. Comaroff 1973:310), and for almost a century his descendants were to contest the legitimacy of the ruling line. With their resources on the wane, officeholders were to find it ever more difficult to ward off such challenges or to limit the growth of the church from whence they came; the Tshidi Methodist congregation appears to have increased from 279 in 1882 to at least 1,200 by the end of the decade (Mears 1955:11). Not surprisingly, there were times that the Molema faction gained *de facto* control of the polity.

But the final irony was that, once he had built a firm power base in the church, Molema rejected the evangelists, making it hard for them to work amongst Tshidi (Holub 1881,1:280; Mackenzie 1883:33; see below). It was Montshiwa, the heathen chief, who, making virtue of ever growing necessity, now encouraged their presence, and who, when Molema died in 1882, was to declare "spiritual freedom" (Molema 1966:204). In the early 1880's he was being continually and violently harassed by the Boers, his capital under virtual siege. More than ever, he felt in need of agents, advisers, and assistance.[33] Adds Shillington (1987:323):

> [The] very existence [of the Tshidi] as a state was under threat from Boer mercenaries. . . . Montshiwa needed the full cooperation, support and unity of all Barolong in Mafikeng. This was no time for religious semantics. Montshiwa's request for missionary assistance was . . . a cry for British diplomatic and military assistance rather than any real conversion to religious toleration.

Whatever Montshiwa's "real" views about religious toleration,[34] eventually, at his bidding, Methodism became the Tshidi-Rolong "state" church.[35] While it is not clear who first used the term here, or when, the double entendre could hardly have been more pointed. To add one last symbolic twist, it is said that, at the insistence of the old ruler, the Christians' bell was now rung at his court each morning (Mears 1955:11): if the presence of the mission could no longer be denied, perhaps its potency could still be appropriated. And so a pagan ruler ended up in alliance with the evangelists cast aside by his devout brother—to the extent that the District Chairman of the WMMS at Kimberley, Henry Barton, wrote to Montshiwa, noting:[36]

> . . . your continued attachment to our Church. We have carefully and prayerful [sic] considered the necessities of your Nation, and we are desirous to do whatever we can to help you, and your people, in all good things. . . .

But the Europeans had acquired an ally weakened by their own actions. They had also created a local Christianity that they could no longer fully reign in.

The overall pattern is clear. From the viewpoint of the Nonconformists, their involvement in local politics was always indirect, almost incidental; in opposing circumcision and other rites, they intended only to reclaim religion for God, leaving secular authority intact. But Tswana culture made this impossible, and their activities set in motion a process with very mixed, contradictory implications.[37] Most notably, in forcing a practical distinction between the "political" and the "religious," the mission produced a dualistic order with competing foci of power and knowledge. This in turn put the evangelists themselves in an equivocal position. Sometimes they were caught between a weakened ruler who courted them and a strong congregation that was less keen to do so. At other times the chiefs converted to Christianity and then took over the church, simultaneously leaving the "traditional" political domain to their opponents or juniors[38] and seeking to isolate the mission. For example, among the Ngwato to the north, Khama's domination of religious affairs eventually led to a break with "his" evangelist, Rev. Hepburn (Chirenje 1976:412).[39] Similarly, Sekgoma of the Tawana so antagonized the LMS that it pressed for his replacement, despite a policy of noninterference in the designation and removal of officeholders (Maylam 1980:145, 157). In many places, in fact, control over the church became deeply embroiled in succession disputes (Mackenzie 1871).[40] The most ironic denouement of all, however, occurred where it all began, at Kuruman. Here, toward the end of the century, "*heathen*" rulers were to try to found "chief's churches" under "native evangelists," men who were "subservient to the chief and consulted [him] in all things spiritual as well as secular."[41]

Given the similarities in Tswana social organization, the impact of Christianity on the fate of different chiefs and chiefdoms was inevitably mediated by particular, highly situational, conditions. Although the process tore at the political fabric everywhere, its precise character—as with all such historical processes—depended on the interplay of local forms and external forces. One thing is unmistakable, though. The missionaries rarely escaped being caught in the fissure that they had opened up between church and chiefship.[42]

Along the Frontier: United Natives, Divided Nations

As we noted in earlier chapters, the encounter between the Southern Tswana and the missions occurred within the context of an expanding, at times explosive, colonial frontier. Before the 1830's the Cape of Good Hope had little significance for the Tlhaping, Rolong, and other communities: being the place from which came white men—merchants and missionaries among them—it was primarily a remote source of valued goods (above, p. 40f.). However, in the wake of *difaqane* and the Great Trek, the epic Boer migration into the interior,[43] the frontier moved much closer. And as it crossed the Orange River, it divided into two axes: the older one, to the south, focused on Griqualand; the newer one, to the north, east, and southeast, took in the Transvaal and Orange River Territory, later to become Boer republics and, in 1910, provinces of the Union of South Africa. The first involved the Tswana in dealings with the Kora and Griqua (both non-Bantu speakers) and with agents of the Cape Colony over matters of commerce and sovereignty; the second drew them into relations with white settlers over land and labor, water and beasts. Each, furthermore, was a distinct theater in the politics of the mission—at least until the late nineteenth century. After the discovery of diamonds in 1867, these frontiers were to merge into a single vortex of conflict as the Boers and British, Tswana and Griqua, scrambled to establish rights to the new wealth.

1. The Old Frontier

For the Southern Tswana, Griqualand was an ambiguous feature on the historical and geopolitical landscape. On the one hand, they had long traded with its inhabitants, the Kora and Griqua, exchanging cattle, beads, and cosmetic ore, the goods acquired from this traffic being put to profitable use in transactions with communities to the north (Shillington 1985:11; Legassick 1969a). In addition, Griqualand was the conduit to the Cape Colony and its itinerant merchants, who supplied valued objects and paid well for the products of the hunt. On the other hand, the armed and mounted Griqua, the dominant group in the region,[44] had the capacity to threaten the independence and economic fortunes of the Tswana (Legassick 1989:395f.). This was underlined by the fact that they had by turns been heroic allies and dangerous enemies of the various chiefdoms. At Moffat's request, for example, they had saved the Tlhaping and Tlharo from destruction during *difaqane* in 1823—and yet, just a year later, had attacked them in strength. The ambivalence of the Tswana toward the Griqua and Kora was at once material and symbolic. People of marginal cultural identity, they were blacks who appeared to possess some of the powers of whites. And they stood, both physically and metaphorically, between the chiefdoms and the south, with all its wondrous wealth and lurking danger. The threatening aspect of their presence was to come into especially sharp focus over the issue of guns and commerce.

As the colonial market for the products of the wild began to expand and military conflict burgeoned, Southern Tswana felt a growing need for guns—notwithstanding their dubious efficacy as weapons of war at the time (see below, p. 275f.). The Griqua and Kora, however, did everything they could to monopolize the arms trade; since its sole source was to the south, they were well-placed to do so. As a result the Tlhaping, Rolong, Tlharo, and others were unable to obtain the weapons they desired for hunting, raiding, and defence. Some chiefs made strenuous efforts to extract the odd musket from a missionary or a traveler (Burchell 1824:2,376, 388). And later a handful of wealthy royals were successful in persuading individual Griqua to part with theirs. But there were relatively few guns in Tswana hands until the end of the 1850's, when the supply from across the Cape border grew rapidly (Shillington 1985:21). As we shall see, this was to draw the evangelists into bitter controversies, especially along the second frontier, over the provision of arms to the Tlhaping and Rolong. For now, though, the important point is that in the early nineteenth century the struggle over guns and commerce led to open tension between Griqua and Southern Tswana. It was in this context that the Nonconformists entered directly into the politics of the region for the first time.

Shillington (1985:12, 29n) has reconstructed a story that points to the general pattern. It is based on letters from Rev. Holloway Helmore to his mother (August 1841) and wife (June 1842). The LMS had a large station in Griqualand, where Helmore was posted, as well as its establishment in Southern Tswana territory. Relations between the missionaries at these two stations were to play out the politics of frontier relations among the peoples with whom they worked. In 1825, in response to local upheavals, the evangelists with the Tlhaping had retired to Griquatown, promising to return as soon as possible. This they did in due course, Moffat taking the lead in reestablishing their presence at Kuruman. Nonetheless, as Shillington (1985:12–13, following Legassick 1969a:364 here), tells it:

> ... the Tlhaping felt they had been betrayed. Their Bergenaar [Griqua/Kora] enemies were being supplied with arms from the Cape Colony, and the Tlhaping, assuming this was with the support of the Cape Government and the missionaries, believed that the latter were conniving to destroy them.

When, a few years later (1839), Helmore tried to found another mission among the Tlhaping, this one in a community under one of Mothibi's sons, both the young leader and his aged father were suspicious, "distrustful of the fact that the missionary had come to them from Griquatown." Neither wished to "acknowledge Griqua suzerainty" of which, it seems, the evangelist was taken as a representative.

This was not in the least farfetched, for behind the carefully managed front stage of united missionary endeavor, a backstage struggle had been going on. Its chief protagonists were none other than the contemporary giants of the evangelical scene, John Philip and Robert Moffat—the former being allied with the interests of the Griqua and "their" mission, the latter with the Southern Tswana and the Kuruman station. Since this struggle has been recounted several times,[45] there is no need to do so again in much detail. For our purposes it is enough to note that, aside from their deep personal and temperamental differences (see e.g., Lovett 1899:1,591), the argument between the two men hinged on Philip's plans for the future of Transoranjia, the borderland of the Cape Colony beyond the Orange River. Or, at least, that was the issue over which it surfaced. Its broader ideological context was the very question of the role of the church in colonial politics—of the proprieties and promiscuities in the link between frontier evangelism and secular imperialism.

Among the early generation of evangelists, Philip was the quintessential "political missionary"; the epithet has been used alike by his critics and admirers (Hattersley 1952:88). He was from the first the "subject of the most extravagant laudation and the most unmeasured vituperation" (Du Plessis 1911:148; cf. Findlay and Holdsworth 1922:272ff.; Theal 1891: 343–44), a man who drew extreme reactions not only among his contemporaries but also among the many historians who were to write of him.[46] His long and complex career as superintendent of the LMS at the Cape came to be dominated by his fight for the protection of the rights of "coloured peoples"; in particular, for their entitlement, as free persons, to bring "their labour to a fair market" (Macmillan 1927:216). Predictably, he was quick to anger the Boers, whom he held in moral contempt and blamed, in large part, for the continuing vassalage of the "aborigines" of South Africa. But he also took the fight into the inner reaches of the colonial state. As Philip himself explained in his *Researches in South Africa* (1828:1,346–47):

> The landed proprietors of South Africa . . . depend on the price of labour, and the number of hands they can command; and it is obvious, while things remain in this state, while the magistrates are under such strong temptations to oppress the people by enslaving them, and keeping down the price of labour, the latter have nothing to look for without the interference of the British government, but an increase of suffering.

The "interference" of the British government, in his stridently voiced opinion, was neither timely nor comprehensive enough. And when it came, it was usually ill-judged (Philip 1828:passim).

There were times and situations in which Philip enjoyed a good deal of influence in colonial circles. But he frequently antagonized the administration, quarrelled with its governors, and irritated its officialdom with his "meddling" in the affairs of state (Walker 1928:158; Macmillan 1936a, 1936b, 1936c). Indeed, his *Researches* were written for expressly political purposes: their publication propelled his campaign onto the British public stage where, with the backing of the abolitionist lobby, he railed equally against Boer aggression and British inaction.[47] The tone of his literary polemic could hardly have been endearing to the authorities at the Cape; the statement quoted above, for example, comes from a passage entitled "Interest of the Colonial Functionaries in the Oppression of the Aborigines" (1828:1,345).[48]

According to Macmillan (1936a:245; also 1927, 1929; see n. 46), Philip did not come to the Cape "thirsting for [political] battle." Neither was he "doctrinaire." On the contrary, "he was something of a Whig in politics, abhorrent of radicalism, a thorough believer in middle-class respectability . . . and deferential to constituted authority." Like other mission apologists (e.g., Clinton 1937:140f.), Macmillan (1936a:245) goes on to suggest that Philip, philanthropist extraordinary, was drawn into politics as a matter of pure conscience, his moral sensibilities offended by the abominable conditions prevailing in the Colony. Perhaps. It was a view that the man himself was careful to fuel in his letters and published works. More critical commentators (e.g., Theal 1891:343f.; Corey 1919), even liberal historians (e.g., Walker 1928:158f.) and missiologists (e.g., Findlay and Holdsworth 1922:272f.), have suggested otherwise. More to the immediate point, Moffat seems to have believed otherwise too, and expressed his belief most openly in his antagonism towards Philip's superintendency of the LMS in South Africa (Macmillan 1929:192n; also Moffat 1886; Legassick 1969a). It was not only Sir Lowry Cole, sometime Governor at the Cape, who thought the good doctor "more of a politician than a missionary" (Theal 1891:344).

For all his own ambiguous statements and equivocal actions in this respect (above, p. 257f.), Robert Moffat was much less ready to indulge his moral conscience in the political domain—or to find any reason whatsoever to become embroiled in the everyday workings of colonial government. Of course, while Philip spent most of his time at Cape Town, the hub of the small South African world, Moffat remained steadfastly at the evangelical workface. From his vantage along the distant frontier, any effort to assail the corridors of power at the colonial center was at best distasteful. Worse yet, it could be extremely dangerous (Legassick 1969a:ch.12).

Philip's designs for the political future of Transoranjia had their origins in ca. 1820 (Macmillan 1929:39) but gained momentum during the 1830's. Baldly stated, he feared that increasing Boer expansion into the interior, culminating in the Great Trek, threatened to reduce much of the black population to slavery. As small farmers, these settlers had no less need of labor now than they had had before at the Cape—where, had their views prevailed, the "aborigines" would still have lived in the most abject bondage. Once free of the British government and absolved from the laws abolishing slavery within the Colony, they would surely seize whatever labor they could on their own terms. Griqualand, he believed, was the place, literally, to draw the line. If the Boers were not stopped there, nothing would prevent their cynical domination and dispossession of the chiefdoms beyond the frontier; almost certainly, too, they would make it impossible for the missions to pursue their work. The scenario might have rung of melodrama—Philip's rhetoric was often highly theatrical—but its political implications were serious. Among them was the claim that Griqualand had to be absorbed immediately and fully into the Colony.[49] All that remained was to persuade the dramatis personae to play their parts.

Philip's strategy had two prongs. The first was blatantly material. "By increasing their artificial wants," he had written in the 1820's,[50] "you increase the dependence of the Griqua on the Colony." In this way they might be absorbed, as free laborers (and, not incidentally, as taxpayers), into the liberal economy of Empire (cf. Cochrane 1987:22, 37). Where the Boers wished to dominate the blacks through relations of production, the missionary set out to control them through relations of exchange—to make them subjects, as we have said, by means of objects. In the end, however, each had to rely on other techniques as well. In Philip's case the second string to his bow was overtly political. He championed the Griqua chief, Andries Waterboer, as supreme ruler over the region, arguing that he be incorporated formally into the Cape Colony (or, at minimum, be acknowledged by Treaty) and given military and material support. In return the chief would be expected to govern the territory at the behest of the British. In fact, Waterboer was not the only local leader of the period. The Griqua polity had recently broken into four divisions each with its own head, and his authority, buttressed by the LMS, centered primarily on Griquatown itself (Ross 1976: 20–21). What is more, colonial policy on the status of these Griqua leaders had been rather ambiguous. At times they were treated as if they were already part of the Colony and its administration (Macmillan 1929:40), at other times as unreliable brigands. Notwithstanding such problems and inconsistencies—or perhaps by exploiting them, it is not really clear—Philip succeeded in having a missionary, Rev. Peter Wright, appointed in 1834 as a confidential government agent to Waterboer. It was understood, by the two evangelists at least, that Wright would also further this Griqua ruler's claim to paramouncty over the region (Macmillan 1929:40).

When, sometime in 1836, Moffat and the evangelists at Kuruman found out about Wright's appointment, they were furious. So too were the Wesleyans in the area.[51] Indeed, this was one of the cases that Moffat had in mind when he published his attack against the entry of missionaries into government (above, p. 252); he and his colleagues also addressed a stream of angry correspondence to the LMS directorate. Philip for his part responded by writing equally acrimonious letters to the Society in London. Not only did he reiterate his defence of Waterboer and the importance of the Griqua to the moral and evangelical frontier. He also censured Moffat for his hypocrisy and unreason (Legassick 1969a:590, 586ff.). As Lovett (1899: 1,591) explains, the "serious difficulties . . . between the brethren at Kuruman and those at Griqua Town" conflated personal, ideological, and political differences:

> Local jealousies further embittered the position. Waterboer, the chief of Griqua Town, looked with an envious eye upon the growing pros-

perity of Kuruman, and developed towards that settlement a very un-
generous spirit. Wright and Hughes, the missionaries at Griqua Town
took the side of their own chief; and when scandalous charges were
circulated about Moffat [alleging that he had committed adultery with
a local woman], did not show the readiness to discredit them which
they might have done. The Bechwana refused to accept the chieftain-
ship of Waterboer, and the Kuruman missionaries steadily refused to
allow Griqua Town influence to gain any power over their people.

In the end Moffat triumphed over Philip, Kuruman over Griquatown
(Legassick 1969a:ch.12). Although Wright continued to act as government
agent until his death in 1843 (Ross 1976:53), the colonial administration
was not moved to incorporate or annex Griqualand; at least, not until the
discovery of diamonds in the territory, many years later, remapped the economic topography of southern Africa (below, p. 282f.). But the political history of Griqualand and the old frontier is not of immediate concern. For
our purposes three things are to be stressed.

The first is that the evangelists, already caught up in the secular affairs
of "their" chiefdoms, could not avoid being drawn into temporal relations
among those chiefdoms. But—and here is the point—in doing so they set in
motion political conflicts within the LMS that came to parallel those between indigenous communities. This is a point that even some missiologists
concede, although they ascribe it to the fact that the Nonconformists were
everywhere dependant on chiefly favor for their success (see e.g., Lovett
1899:1,592). The matter is more complex, however. It derives from the very
nature of a frontier.

Inasmuch as a frontier is a space of cultural and material engagement
as yet unmarked on the maps of sovereign politics, it is a context in which
strangers have necessarily to construct a common world—a world of apparently understandable practices, meaningful symbols, and power relations.
But since it has few agreed referents or fixed lines, this world looks different
to the various people who inhabit it. For the Christians at Kuruman, gazing
northward to the African interior in a spirit of congregational independence,
the landscape did not appear at all the same as it did to those at Griquatown,
for whom the Colony, with its battles over aboriginal rights and labor relations, was inescapably closer. To the Griqua, oriented southward, life in
Transoranjia was a question of exerting dominance over the region or being
subverted by Boer expansion; to the Tswana, the hope for the future seemed
to lie in protecting their political autonomy. Here lay the *fons et origo* of the
struggle between them. The dissension among the "brethren at Kuruman
and those at Griqua Town," of course, was the same struggle writ ecclesiastical. Like all other players who happened upon the frontier, to make and

be made by it, these churchmen could not avoid its politics. After all, what made it a frontier in the first place was the very fact that it *was* a political theater of cultural confrontation.

But, secondly, if the frontier drew the missionaries inexorably into its politics, it did not do so everywhere in just the same way. The quarrel between Moffat and Philip, Kuruman and Griquatown, as we have noted several times, appeared to be a dispute over the very nature of the relationship between church and state. But, once more, the issue is somewhat more complicated than it seems. It is not just that Philip was a "political missionary" while Moffat confined himself to matters spiritual. Both were profoundly political men. Both agreed that there were conditions under which engagement in worldly power relations was necessary; recall that Moffat (1842:207–08) made this every bit as explicit as did Philip. Further, both men were committed to a project of cultural colonialism, to overrule in a pervasive sense, and were locked in struggle with indigenous authorities. And both argued that their actions, even the most obviously "political" by their own ideological lights, were governed *entirely* by the moral imperatives of the mission: the ethical demands, that is, of the Empire of the Spirit. Even Philip claimed not to have strayed one bit from these imperatives.

The point is that, while the missions could not escape secular entanglements—their place on the colonial frontier assured that Moffat's conditions for political engagement were always present—their ideology failed to specify the terms of that engagement. Congregationalism, with its stress on the decentralization of authority and its moral individualism, its lack of doctrinal coherence and the diversity of its personnel, fostered a great deal of independence in just this respect. (Much the same applied to the WMMS in this particular historical context.)[52] Hence it was perfectly understandable that the LMS stations at Griquatown and Kuruman, once lured haplessly into the conflicts of the frontier, should take opposed sides. Again, as we have explained, it is not that the Griqua evangelists abetted Waterboer while their colleagues among the Tlhaping held out against all involvement. Noninvolvement here was an active political cause, an alibi for the support of Tswana autonomy.

The general principle is one that we shall encounter over and over again: that, while Nonconformism drove a wedge between church and state, it did not prevent the entry of the evangelists into the formal arena of colonial politics. Quite the contrary. But neither did it lay down *what* stands should be adopted, what courses of action ought to be followed. Philip and Moffat could differ—and their colleagues could quite reasonably divide in support of one or the other—since there was nothing in mission ideology or moral precept to determine the substantive position, the political role, of the mission itself. The latter, in a word, was indeterminate. Its intrinsic ambiguity was the corollary of a Christian culture which, albeit erected on an elaborate set of binary oppositions (church:state::religion:politics::cloth:crown . . .) remained audibly silent at just the point where those oppositions were called to action: namely, to decide when, where, and on what terms entry into the secular domain was warranted.

The third point, too, is one that will reappear many times. It is that, even where the missions, or individual missionaries, entered the political arena, their effectiveness was notably limited. Because of the indeterminacy of their role in both the temporal state of affairs and the affairs of state, the evangelists could not partake of the political process as a coherent force. Nor could they assume that the church might be counted on as a solid constituency. At the same time, being bound by the ideological discipline of the missionary societies, it was well-nigh impossible for churchmen to build power bases in the "outside" world. Consequently, they had to rely on relatively unstable alliances and informal networks for their strategic ends—alliances that might win a particular issue but rarely could be sustained over the long run. It is no surprise, then, that even the most "political" of missionaries tended to lose their secular influence long before their energies ran out. As Davies (1951:16) notes, John Philip's career ended in a long period of "political quietude." It was a pattern often to be repeated.

The impotence of the evangelists in the political arena was to have important implications over the long run. Apart from all else it contributed to the deepening fissure between the seductive promises of the church and the irreducible realities of colonialism. It was also to reveal contradictions between the message of the mission and the actions of the missionaries. In these furrows between promise and reality the first hybrid seeds of Christian resistance were to germinate. But that is a story—indeed, a very general theme in the history of colonial politics—which we shall pick up later. Let us return, first, to the South African frontier; this time, however, to the new frontier, the borderland between the expanding world of the Boer settlers and the contracting world of the Southern Tswana. In reality, the old and the new were not all that discrete, since the one was already in the process of absorbing the other.[53] The new frontier, rather, was simultaneously a state of mind, an unfolding set of power relations, and a formless landscape over which people with infinite ambitions strove to assert a very definite form of control.

2. The New Frontier

As we noted earlier, the dominant motif of the new frontier was the struggle over land and labor, cattle and water. It was a struggle into which many missionaries were to be drawn—including a few of those who had supported Moffat against the political involvement of the likes of Philip. In truth, they had little option: the Boers who settled the interior regarded the British Christians as unyielding advocates of the Tswana. Accustomed to painting the divisions of South African economy and society in terms black and white (see e.g., Muller 1969:129f.), these settlers were especially offended by the LMS and WMMS evangelists: being whites who preferred to ally themselves with blacks, the churchmen defied not only the political interests but also the ideological categories of a nascent Afrikanerdom. As such, they were treated, singly and collectively, as part of the enemy (see e.g., de Gruchy 1979:11f.). One community went so far as to make its members "take a solemn oath to have no connection with the London Missionary Society, . . . a political association, disseminating doctrines on social questions subversive of all order in society" (Theal 1902:228). As Rev. Freeman pointed out in 1849 to the foreign secretary of the LMS in London:[54]

> . . . there is no doubt that they feel the missionaries are in their way. The missionaries are the protectors of the Natives and the latter cannot be so easily outraged and driven out . . . under the direct observation and remonstrances of the missionary.

David Livingstone (1974:5), in a letter written before his own aversion to the Boers had reached its highest pique, was less self-righteous:

> They have in general a great aversion to missionaries. The cause of their dislike seems to be an idea that we wish to furnish the natives with fire-arms, and whether right or wrong always take [their] side.

The issue of firearms was to arise time and again, and as aversion deepened into conflict in the 1840's, a few of the evangelists were to be driven out of their stations by angry frontier farmers. Not that the latter were unprovoked. As we have seen, the churchmen did not hide the fact that they regarded the Boers as degenerate "rogues," utterly lacking in "taste and genius" (Ludorf 1863:203)—or that they blamed them for the predicament of the Griqua, the Tswana, and others. Some of the Christians, moreover, resuscitating the spirit of John Philip, had campaigned loudly to have the British administration protect the chiefdoms against settler predations. Matters first came to a head in the early 1850's, when, by the Sand River and Bloemfontein Conventions, the overextended colonial government gave up all effort to control the Boers and recognized the independence of their republics across the Orange and Vaal Rivers.[55] It was a capitulation which the Nonconformists and black leadership alike saw as wanton abandonment of the Africans to those who would enslave them (Molema 1951:85ff.). The mission correspondence of the period is filled with reports of the seizure of land by the whites (e.g., Ludorf 1854, 1863:203, 1864:163), their plunder of cattle (Livingstone 1974:13), and their indiscriminate reduction of the local communities to "abject vassalage."[56] Livingstone (1974:8; cf. 1857:36f.), in a piece written for the mass British public, told how "the Bechuana spirit was broken" when the whites laid claim to their land and people, compelling them "to erect houses, dig watercourses, make dams, prepare gardens,—indeed, [do] everything their Boerish masters required." The pun was obviously intended.[57] So was the point that those masters had made their way into the South African hinterland largely to "indulge in their propensity to slave-holding." The canvas he painted was deliberately and unremittingly bleak (1974:9):

> Whoever required a piece of work done, just rode over to the nearest
> Bechuana town, and ordered the chief to furnish twenty or thirty
> men or women, as the case required. In the majority of cases when
> the work was finished they were dismissed without even a morsel of
> food. . . . [This] is now grinding the natives to the earth.

There follows a graphic description of the conditions of labor, of whippings and unrequited toil under the blazing sun. Whatever its basis in fact, it was an account that resonated in Exeter Hall and in the abolitionist conscience of its British readership (see also Livingstone 1857:passim).

In much the same spirit the imminent fate of the chiefdoms and the future of the mission were sometimes openly elided, both subject to the dire threat posed by the Boers. Once more, the peripatetic Rev. Freeman:[58]

> . . . there is abundant ground to apprehend the danger to the mis-
> sions—an interference with their labours, and the ruin of the indepen-
> dence, if not the very existence of some of the Native Tribes among
> whom they are labouring.

The Nonconformists found it easier, in all conscience, to take up the cudgels on behalf of the blacks against the settlers than to take almost any other political action, although, as we might expect, this did not mean that a uniform missionary stance emerged. Those who chose to act did so for the most part by appealing to the British administration yet again.[59] Others interceded, at times successfully, with the settlers themselves: Ludorf, for example, persuaded one group to return some Rolong fountains and springs to their original owners.[60] Yet others are said to have taken much more direct action, providing intelligence and guns to the chiefdoms; in fact, some of the earliest shots in the conflict between the Boer Republics and the British missionaries were fired over the supply of weaponry. Along this frontier all the protagonists seem to have believed that a little ordnance went much further than even the most far-reaching ordinance. As it happens, firearms did *not* always assure their possessors a decisive military advantage; given contemporary technology, at least until the second half of the nineteenth century, they were sometimes even a liability. But as Shineberg (1971:61f.) has shown for Melanesia, this did not prevent them from becoming "among the earliest, most consistently and most eagerly sought of the borrowings from European material culture."[61] Southern Tswana similarly paid little attention to their technical shortcomings. It was enough that they appeared to have an almost magical power to maim and kill from afar.

It was perhaps David Livingstone who was accused most persistently by the white settlers of gunrunning. So serious did the allegation become that Freeman, prior to his tour of the LMS stations at the behest of the directorate in London, wrote to Philip in Cape Town, asking whether there was any truth in it. The reply, written on Philip's behalf,[62] was rather equivocal:

> In reply to your question as to whether the missionaries have traded in firearms, Dr. Philip wishes me to say that he thinks they have *not* done so, at least to any extent. But he thinks the point is one it will be well for you to inquire into among the Brethren, as you go along. The Doctor thinks that Mr. Livingston [*sic*] was of opinion, that the natives *ought* to have firearms and ammunition for their own defence; in that Mr. L. will readily admit the fact and explain the course he has taken in the matter. . . . Dr. Philip thinks that if it shall be found that Mr. Livingston obtained for the people any guns etc it was not as a matter of *trade* or *gain* that he has done so; but to help them to the attainment of what he thought necessary for them.

Livingstone (1974:14), in a dispatch to the *British Banner* (1849), poured scorn on the allegation. Quite the opposite, he claimed: it was Boer traders who, unable to resist the enormous profits, were selling weapons to the blacks—despite orders to the contrary from their leaders. The traffic was so large, he went on, that any Boer authority who thought he could stop it "might as well have bolted his castle with a boiled carrot."

Carrots and castles aside, there is plenty of evidence that Livingstone *did* supply guns and ammunition to the Kwena (Livingstone 1974:41f.). For all Ludorf's insistence that the missionaries were there "to furnish weapons not carnal, but spiritual,"[63] other churchmen were caught up in the trade too. In 1858, for example, William Ashton[64] told his LMS superiors that Moffat's son, Robert, Jr., an entrepreneur, had brought a large amount of powder and lead shot to Kuruman. Some had been sold to Tswana who were engaged in border hostilities with the settlers. The rest "was stored away in his father's garden," buried, it seems, amidst the carrots. "What will become of the Station," asked the nervous pastor, "if the Boers get to know that the powder magazine is in the missionary's garden?" To compound the irony, Ashton wrote again three weeks later,[65] lamenting that all this had occurred while Robert, Sr. was in Cape Town trying to secure government

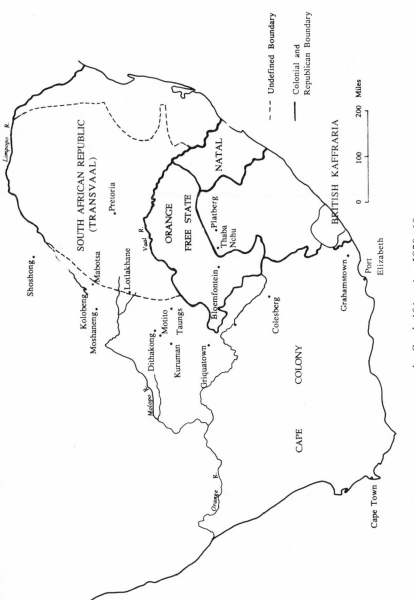

MAP 4 *South Africa, circa 1850–60*

permission for the supply of ammunition to two "trustworthy" Tlhaping chiefs. "Powder and lead," he commented acidly, should not enter the country "by the means of either missionaries or their sons." Far from being the business of Christians, they "should be left to the proper authorities and the traders." He did not add that the presence of those very traders had been encouraged by the LMS and WMMS in the first place. Despite his plea, several evangelists continued to help Tswana obtain weaponry and ammunition. But the scale of their efforts was much too limited to alter the balance of forces on the frontier (cf. Schapera, in Livingstone 1974:41f.).

As this suggests, the supply of firearms to the Tswana by the evangelists was more of a symbolic than a material issue along the frontier; access to the means of violence, whatever its real magnitude, lay elsewhere. But this does not mean that the matter itself was insignificant. Apart from all else, the war of words, of accusation and denial, made it clear to those concerned that they were caught in the middle of a new process of colonial domination. For the nascent Boer republics were extending their control over indigenous populations by asserting their sovereign capacity to impose taxation, to regulate land and movement, and to extract labor.[66] Alongside the state colonialism of Her Majesty's Government and the civilizing colonialism of the mission, settler colonialism was taking its intrusive place (J.L. Comaroff 1989). This process, and the resistance to which it gave rise, gained inexorable momentum in the three decades (1837–67) before the discovery of diamonds. Thereafter, with the opening up of the diamond and goldfields, previously parochial conflicts among and between colonizers and colonized alike were to fuse and explode into an all-embracing regional struggle for the future of South Africa. The "mineral revolution" was to mark the transition of the interior from a frontier, settler society into the core of a subcontinental political economy.

As the long-term process of domination and reaction unfolded, the Nonconformists were given many painful reminders of the difficulties of their own historical role. At times these lessons took an especially vivid turn. Just prior to the Sand River Convention, for example, when the Boers were most concerned about the political impact of missionary "interference," their warnings to the churchmen to keep their distance became extremely belligerent. So much so, that rumors began to circulate in the LMS: two respected evangelists, it was said, had actually been taken prisoner. The dispatch that bore the "news" to London[67] also announced gravely that "the Dutch Boers . . . [had] peremptorily ordered Livingstone to remove from his station and never to return to it." A letter written some months later,[68] by which time it was known that the report of the abduction was untrue, predicted that "as the result of the next general meeting or council of the Boers in January," all missionaries in the area would be commanded to withdraw.

This would place them in an impossible position, for—and here is the crunch—"to resist seem[ed] useless and to obey [was] to [give][69] up the natives to certain ruin." Appeal to the government, it went on ruefully, was also useless, since the British administration had "recognised the right of the Boers to this part of Africa, and promised that they would not interfere. . . ." The dilemma was brought home even more dramatically in 1852, when the settlers destroyed Livingstone's house and station among the Kwena at Kolobeng. The simultaneous sacking of the mission and the royal capital[70] asserted the common destiny of church and chiefdom as long as they were united in their resistance to the republics.

Not only did these events, and many others like them (see n. 63), underline the dilemma of the evangelists as they saw it—to resist the Boers or to sit by and allow the "ruin" of the blacks. They also elicited the usual range of responses, from (1) simply doing nothing other than to reassert that any political response whatsoever was beyond the moral charter of the mission; through (2) pleading with the British government either for a reversal of policy or for some intervention to protect the chiefdoms; to (3) interceding "pacifically" with the Boers themselves; and, in a few instances, to (4) taking direct political action on their own account. Perhaps most striking, since it exemplifies the entire span of possibilities, is the curious case of Joseph Ludorf.

A Methodist of German extraction, Rev. Ludorf was first posted to Thaba 'Nchu but spent two years (1850–52) at Lotlakane with the Tshidi-Rolong after Chief Montshiwa appealed to the WMMS for a missionary.[71] It was during this period that he interceded with a group of Boers, persuading them to return fountains and springs they had recently taken from the Tshidi (above, p. 275; Theal 1893:487–8). Recall, from chapter 4, the material and symbolic importance of water to the Tswana; the very dominion of a chiefdom was defined by the furthest ring of water sources that its ruler could hold (Comaroff and Comaroff 1990). In interceding with the whites, Ludorf, who spoke the language of each party fluently, must have known that the matter was of profound political significance to both: to the settlers, as much as to the Tswana, the possession of land and water sources beyond the colonial frontier was the *sine qua non* of their "freedom" as social beings. How the evangelist actually managed to gain acceptance as a mediator by the Boers is not clear from the documentary record.[72] But for us the significant fact is that he chose to act in this capacity at all.

It becomes yet more significant in light of his actions of just a few months later. In 1852 Ludorf left the Tshidi, stating that, given the troubled state of the country and the antagonism of the settlers, the mission among them was doomed.[73] The whites were about to fall upon the Kwena—Livingstone's station, the royal capital, and all—and they demanded that

Montshiwa join them as an "ally" or be attacked himself. By the Boers' account (Theal 1893:517f.), the Tshidi now lived on Transvaal territory, land claimed by right of conquest; having been released from labor tax at their ruler's request, they were "free" citizens of the republic and thus obliged to do military service. Ludorf was asked by Montshiwa to appeal again to the whites on his behalf and agreed reluctantly to do so. But this time they would not listen to him (Molema 1951:92; 1966:45f.; see n. 69). After a dramatic nocturnal meeting with the Tshidi, the evangelist spelled out the options open to them:

> I said there are three deaths, choose the which you will die. Ist, Take some cattle and go to the Boers, and pray to have peace; give up all your guns, pay taxes, become their slaves. Or 2nd, Look without delay for a hiding place, but look to the consequence: no water, and a burning sun. Or 3rd, Stand and fight like men for your lives, property, and freedom. As for me, I cannot say which will be best for you. God give you wisdom.

Montshiwa chose to the second option. He ignored the Boer order, eventually going into exile among the Ngwaketse. And Ludorf returned to Thaba 'Nchu. Where before he had been prepared to play an active role in frontier politics, now he appeared utterly disinclined to do so. Indeed, in his first sermon after he arrived,[74] he asked his Seleka congregation why they thought he had come amongst them. "Was it to extricate you from your political difficulties" caused by the Boers? If so, be advised that "those who sent me charged me expressly not to meddle in politics." It sounds rather as if the evangelist, faced by the contradictory implications of his own position, had suffered a failure of nerve. Or perhaps he was merely musing aloud on the conditions of his survival as a missionary. Either way, his volte face was striking.

Two years later, in 1854, we find Joseph Ludorf still laboring at Thaba 'Nchu. Once again a direct Boer threat loomed, this time endangering the autonomy of, among others, the Seleka-Rolong. Now, however, the Reverend was ready to act once again on behalf of the chiefdom. As he told his colleagues (1854:194), he had written to Sir George Clerk, Her Majesty's Special Commissioner, and had traveled to interview him several times "to secure to our people the rights to their lands [and] the liberty of their persons." The response was encouraging: Sir George had promised "to promote the welfare of the [Seleka-] Barolong." Appeased but not yet fully satisfied, Ludorf prompted the local ruler to write to Clerk as well. Chief Moroka's "letter," ostensibly translated verbatim by the missionary, accused the British queen and government of favoring the Boers over the Seleka

(1854:194–95). The chosen metaphor of this communication was a "House of God," which the colonial administration had built for the whites but not for the blacks:

> When our mother, the Queen of England, sent her Government into this country [in the early nineteenth century], she showed us her *power*. And after the thunder of the gun was silent, we saw her gathering her children, the shy ones, under her wings. . . . She [then] built for the rich ones houses, great, for prayer; but for us, the poor, will she not also build one? Our house is fallen down; we have tried to erect another one, but did not succeed for want of means. Now it is a long space (time)[75] that we stand in the sun, and are killed by perspiration. . . . Are, then, the Boers alone children of our mother's love? . . . has our mother only one breast?

And, if the queen would only intervene,

> Our enemies [would] be afraid to touch us, seeing we have such a powerful, glorious, and good provider.

Ludorf, taking seriously both the metaphor and its political point, appended his own plan for a church and an appeal for five hundred pounds to construct it. He seems to have believed that, once Her Majesty's Government had erected a House of God for the Rolong, it would also guarantee their physical welfare in the face of their enemies. In the event, Clerk agreed to give financial assistance for the project—although he never fully explained why he should take such an extraordinary step. Here, finally, was a perfect—indeed, perfectly ingenious—fusion of the spiritual and the temporal: a missionary persuading the administration to allocate funds to build a church as a symbol of political protection. No wonder an authoritative general history of the WMMS (Findlay and Holdsworth 1922:4,328) refers to Ludorf as "extraordinarily versatile."

But his story has two even more singular twists. The first is that, notwithstanding his deep commitment to the Rolong mission for over twenty years,[76] Ludorf left the WMMS rather abruptly in the late 1860's. It seems that, for all his active support of the blacks against the settlers, the Reverend, who had gained a reputation as a healer, was also tending to the spiritual and physical needs of Boers in the Transvaal. Somewhat out of the blue, another churchman, John Thorne (1867), wrote to the WMMS *Notices*, complaining that Ludorf was giving them "medicine and sermons for 250 pounds *per annum*"—without severing "his connexion to our Church." But, admitted Thorne, the senior evangelist of the circuit knew of the matter and had told him *not* to resign. For his part Ludorf did not think that his ministrations to the whites compromised his calling or affected his championing of the Rolong cause.

In the end, however, the complaint prevailed, and Ludorf was advised to resign from the Mission Society, at least formally (Findlay and Holdsworth 1922:4,330). But his day-to-day ties with the Tswana mission—and with the Rolong peoples—were so close that it made little difference. Nor were all his brethren put out by his behavior. Rather, his practical activities divided them along the fault lines of Nonconformist ideology that we have laid bare, revealing yet again the political indeterminacy of the mission. This became even more apparent in the final years of his life.

The last chapter of Joseph Ludorf's story begins with the discovery of diamonds, in 1867, near Hopetown on the Orange River.[77] Later, major finds were also made along the not-too-distant Vaal and Harts Rivers, bringing a rapid influx of diggers, dealers, and speculators into a region that cut awkwardly across Griqua, Southern Tswana, and settler territory.[78] Over the following three years, six parties laid claim to the diamond fields: the Boer republics of the Orange Free State and Transvaal, which fought the dispute in alliance with one another, and four indigenous peoples. Each had its protagonists and agents, some of them unscrupulous manipulators; all were caught up in byzantine political ploys and bitter fights over land and mineral rights. Among them, it was the Griqua who found the strongest ally: the colonial government at the Cape. Although the Governor had in 1870 refused to be drawn into the affairs of the region and had turned down a Tlhaping plea for protection, his successor, Sir Henry Barkly, was less reluctant to get involved (Shillington 1985:40). Hence, when Chief Nicholas Waterboer once more asked for help against Boer expansion, the matter was given serious attention. It was a request that could be interpreted as an invitation to annex Griqualand, including the contested frontier—a prospect that the Cape administration now regarded with unfeigned interest. In the meantime, the Seleka claimed half of the disputed area on the ground that it had been theirs prior to their enforced flight to Thaba 'Nchu during *difaqane*. The Tshidi asserted that the other half belonged to them by "ancestral inheritance." And the Tlhaping chief, Jantjie Mothibi, in whose realm many of the early diggings were actually situated, made his case on the most obvious basis of all: past and present possession of, and political jurisdiction over, much of the territory.

The minutiae of the dispute are not of concern here. It is enough to know that it went to arbitration, at least after several ill-tempered meetings among the parties (Walker 1928:340f.; Theal 1900:ch.13)—and some far-fetched strategies to establish prior ownership. Perhaps the most quixotic was a gambit by the Transvaal to claim the land by cession from the King of Portugal through his "local" representative, the Governor of Quelimane in northern Mocambique; the Portuguese, said the Boers, had acquired the whole region south of the Limpopo River "by virtue of an ancient treaty with the Mwenemutapa, semi-legendary ruler of east central Africa" (Sillery 1971:42; cf. Molema 1966:62f.; Theal 1900:239f., 355). But equally dubious was the behavior of one of the British arbitrators, who denied Chief Jantjie Mothibi permission even to bring his case to the court. The Tlhaping, he decided on no good grounds, were subject to Waterboer and therefore not a party to the dispute.

The Bloemhof hearing of 1871, under Lieutenant-Governor Keate of Natal, looms large in both white South African history and the collective consciousness of the Tswana.[79] It ended predictably. The Seleka and Tshidi were given a portion of the land they had claimed, some of it country that the Transvaal considered its own. But, alas, no gemstones. Waterboer was awarded the most valuable parts of the territory, which were duly ceded to the colonial government. Shillington (1985:53) has argued that "the Keate Award and British annexation of the diamond fields were not the *consequence* of arbitration . . . [but] an elaborate rubber stamp to lend authority to British interests and designs." Very likely. After years of unconcern, the Crown now urged the Boers of the Transvaal and the Orange Free State, who were infuriated with the outcome,[80] to respect the rights of "native tribes in friendly alliance with her Majesty's Government" (Molema 1966:57).

The Tswana case at Bloemhof was led by none other than Joseph Ludorf, although none of the available historical sources, primary or secondary, explain how he actually came to the task. But, it is said, he undertook it with "skill and devotion" (Matthews 1945:9; cf. Walker 1928:344). The evangelist, it seems, was profoundly upset by two things. One was that a large number of blacks, converts among them, were being drawn to the diggings,[81] where labor arrangements had produced unhappy, immoral social conditions. Some Nonconformists (see Findlay and Holdsworth 1922:4,313) were to see advantages in the growth of the diamond fields[82] for both the missions (a "congregation within easy reach") and the workers ("comparative wealth")—especially since in recent years poverty had forced many rural Christians to migrate to colonial towns in search of employment (Brigg 1867:30). Not Ludorf. He was appalled. But he was even more concerned that the chiefdoms might lose their ancestral lands and political autonomy. Goaded into action, he tried to mobilize public opinion, before the hearings, by writing a series of articles in the *Diamond News* (Lindley 1873:16). There is also some basis to believe that in preparing the Tswana suit he went well beyond the bounds of Christian ethics by counterfeiting an "early treaty" between the Tshidi and a Boer leader. This document was to be a crucial piece of evidence at Bloemhof (Theal 1900:363).

By all accounts Ludorf was elated at the result of the arbitration pro-

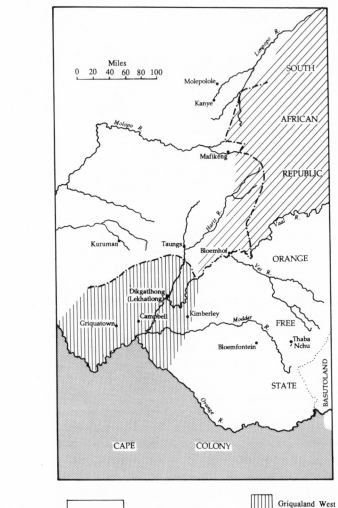

Miles
0 20 40 60 80 100

SOUTH

AFRICAN

REPUBLIC

ORANGE

FREE

STATE

BASUTOLAND

CAPE   COLONY

Limpopo R.

Molepolole

Kanye

Molopo R.

Mafikeng

Harts R.

Vaal R.

Kuruman

Taungs

Bloemhof

Vet R.

Dikgatlhong
(Lekhatlong)

Campbell

Kimberley

Modder R.

Griquatown

Bloemfontein

Thaba
Nchu

Orange R.

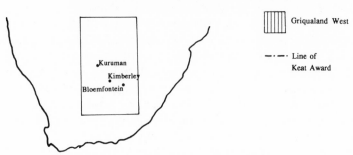

Kuruman

Kimberley

Bloemfontein

▮▮ Griqualand West

— · — Line of
Keat Award

MAP 5   *The Interior, circa 1870–80*

ceedings, despite having failed to have the Tlhaping case heard. And here is the nub of the story. Soon after the Keate Award, at the very moment when the Boer republics were angrily denouncing it, the missionary was drafting a manifesto and constitution for a "United Barolong, Batlhaping and Bangwaketse Nation" (Theal 1900:368–69). Its capital was to be at Klipdrift, in the awarded territory, and Ludorf was himself to be its commissioner and diplomatic representative. In this spirit, he wrote to the chiefs, evoking Isaiah (Molema 1966:66–67):

> And now chiefs: rulers of the land, I appeal to you. Awake: arise and unite soon before your trophy is torn asunder by wolves; come ye together, make protective laws; stop all breaches and gaps and close your ranks. Safeguard the heritage of Tau your ancestor. Hear ye chiefs: Come together and unite.

This must surely rank as one of the more remarkable documents of South African mission history. Ludorf was convinced, correctly as it turned out, that the republics would try to make it impossible for the chiefdoms to take possession of the land.[83] The only antidote, as he saw it, was a confederation of Southern Tswana polities with a representative government, an army, a judiciary, and an independent economy (Theal 1900:369; Molema 1951:136): in short, a sovereign state with full jurisdiction over all the citizens in its realm, black and white. Note that this "United Nation" was *not* to be absorbed into the Empire. Just as it was to be free of settler dominion, Ludorf wanted it merely protected, not colonized, by Britain.[84] The plan came to nought, though. Ignored by the Crown and derided by the Boers, the evangelist took ill and died a few weeks later.

Here, then, is the odd spectacle of a missionary defending Tswana from Boer subjugation by striving to found an autonomous state in the crevice between settler colonialism and British imperialism. Ludorf's strategy clearly violated the separation of church and state. Yet, significantly, his actions were *not* dismissed as frivolous or misguided by his colleagues. Apologists for the Boers might have ridiculed him (e.g., Theal 1900:368f.), but he was to be celebrated in Methodist histories among those whose "names shine like stars" (Whiteside 1906:339; Findlay and Holdsworth 1922:4,328). From the perspective of the Christians, after all, the protection of the Tswana from Boer "enslavement," from "tribal" wars, and from unscrupulous freebooters was vital to their work. In this situation it was difficult to avoid being drawn into politics not spiritual, but secular. And where it happened, it made as much sense, in principle, to promote an independent "native state" as it did to call for British overrule—which might later place constraints on the evangelists, who would themselves be subject to its authority. Both stances fell within the compass of mission ideology: it was an issue on which reasonable men could, and did, differ. Of course, even if Nonconformism had mandated a clear line of action, the churchmen had insufficient political capital to guarantee that any position they advocated would be adopted—whether or not it bore the visible imprimatur of imperialism.

But Joseph Ludorf's story does more than just affirm what we learned earlier about the role of the mission in colonial politics. What is noteworthy about it is the fact that, in the course of a single career, Ludorf took up every possible political stance—and acted in every possible way—open to an evangelist. Thus, at one extreme, he refused steadfastly to involve himself in the worldly affairs of the frontier; at the other, he wilfully set out to create a sovereign state, as "temporal" a gesture as one could imagine; and, in between, he engaged in a wide range of variously secular activities. Such inconsistent behavior, however, cannot be blamed on the rank perversity of an erratic mind. Nor was it simply the product of ambiguities in WMMS (or LMS) ideology. Remember how the churchmen, from their situation on a bitterly contested frontier, saw little choice other than to resist the Boers or give "up the natives to certain ruin" (p. 279). This perception, correct or not, flowed from their entrapment betwixt colonizer and colonized, between the dominant and the subordinated. And it led into a double bind: violate fundamental Nonconformist principles or surrender the objects of evangelism. One way or the other—or, as was more often the case, one way *and* the other—the conduct of the Christians could not appear anything but fickle and contradictory. We stress, though, that this grew out of their structural position in the historical topography of South Africa, not from individual caprice. Ludorf was not alone in his political behavior. The biographies of most evangelists in the region show similar inconsistencies, if not in quite as extravagant a form.

The situation of the mission between colonizer and colonized had another, related consequence. In mediating between the Boers and the indigenous peoples—and more generally in representing black and white to one another—the Nonconformists gave expression to emerging collective identities, identities at once political and cultural. These identities, on both sides of the growing racial abyss, were constructed as a nesting hierarchy. On one side, "Europeans," an inclusive category in opposition to "natives," were divided into Boer and British "nations," each of which in turn subsumed lower order differences of social background. On the other, the blacks were also divided into "nations." Thus "the Bechuana" were treated as a single entity, as if they shared common cause, a common culture, and a collective sense of themselves—although they were also encouraged to distinguish among what were to become known as "tribes," political communities with divergent interests and attachments, and even distinct dialects (see below, p. 288). Not that this imagery lacked a concrete foundation in the sociopolitical processes of the epoch. The content of contemporary Tswana identity was shaped in the colonial theater, as the power relations of the frontier played themselves out; and, over the long run, it was transformed by their incorporation, as peasants and workers, into a developing regional political economy. But, inasmuch as new modes of representation conjure up new realities—distilling from inchoate images the palpable signs of a historical consciousness—the evangelists, classical "intercalary" figures (Gluckman 1963:ix), were the vehicles of a nascent *Tswana* ethnicity.[85] Ethnicity, everywhere, associates cultural differences with social categories (J.L. Comaroff 1987b). Here it involved, first, citizenship in a local chiefdom; second, attachment to an aboriginal commonwealth;[86] and third, by implication, membership of a racial group.

Tswana ethnicity, then, far from being a primordial impulse, was a profoundly historical creation. Indeed, when the Nonconformists first engaged the peoples of the interior, they encountered a rather different mode of collective self-representation: a form of totemic consciousness that stressed the contrasts among *merafe*, similarly structured polities centered upon ruling dynasties (J.L. Comaroff 1987b). Beyond that, the social landscape was populated not by "Bechuana" at all, but by *batho hela*, just human beings—save, that is, for some semihuman bushpeople not worth speaking about or consorting with (above, chapter 4). Now, from that undifferentiated humanity (*botho*), under the appropriate conditions, arose ethnicity. Embodied in *setswana*, the social and symbolic substance of things Tswana, it had begun to grow—as we saw in chapter 6—into an ever more articulate consciousness in contrast to *sekgoa*, the ways of the whites (who, recall, were not perceived as unambiguously "human" either). For all their failure as politicians, missionaries like Ludorf were catalyzing the Africans into a distinct form of political self-awareness: into the perception, that is, that all who shared a common language and culture ("customs") also shared common (and exclusive) material interests. Such are the conjunctures of history. The Tswana, caught up in a process which called on them to objectify themselves as a social entity, had passed a critical point on the road to a generic black consciousness.

And so the Christians, by turning the visage of shared identity back on "their" people, became a medium for its construction and representation—the human equivalent, almost, of the mirrors they had given the Tswana fifty years before, except that now the reflected image was not individual but collective. Sometimes the fabrication of ethnic consciousness involved such flamboyant gestures as founding a state, a "United Nation." But most of all, it lay in the way in which the missionaries tried to remake the everyday world of these Africans and, as they insinuated themselves into it, to redefine its significant coordinates and constituencies.

For example, both the LMS and WMMS established a "Bechuana District"; and, within that District, each evangelist was posted to the "capital" of a chiefdom, likened here to the court of a European nation-state, as a diplomatic envoy of the Empire of the Spirit. The two levels of ethnic identity (local/"tribal" and regional/"national"), in other words, were represented in the very organization of the Nonconformist societies. So too was the contrast between European and native: the distinction between the mission church and the church proper, the spiritual home of black and white congregants respectively, inserted a racial wedge into the unity of each denomination. As we have seen, moreover, this hierarchy of oppositions underlay the involvement of the churchmen in the politics of the frontier.

It will become clear in volume 2 that every aspect of the civilizing mission was implicated in the formation of these nesting ethnic identities (see also chapter 6 above). Thus, for instance, in their work on language, and especially in writing their vernacular texts, the evangelists broke the Tswana world up into discrete (tribal) speech fields, asserting that distinct dialects were spoken in the different chiefdoms. Sometimes they went so far as to suggest that these dialects were mutually unintelligible. Yet as the century unfolded, the same evangelists were publishing newspapers and journals that envisaged a larger Tswana linguistic community. The precise degree to which this contributed to the emergence of an ethnic identity may be impossible to ascertain. But it is significant that, when the first locally-owned and managed weekly was established in 1901 at Mafeking, it was called *Koranta Ea Batswana*, "The Newspaper of the *Tswana*." Financed by a Tshidi Christian royal, a son of none other than Molema, it circulated among literate Tswana in both urban and rural areas. Interestingly, it was edited by Sol T. Plaatje, a mission-educated Motswana from another area who later became a major cultural figure in the development of Setswana language and literature; he was also to be the first corresponding secretary of the South African Native National Congress (forerunner to the African National Congress) and a strong advocate of black brotherhood and civil rights (Willan 1984). In the short run the evangelical reconstruction of "Bechuana" identity was intended to encourage converts to fit easily into the larger, unifying hierarchy of Empire and Christendom. In the longer run these efforts were to feed into the politics of consciousness in South Africa in complex ways.

The Regional Theater: Colonial Scenes, Imperialist Schemes

The hostilities that followed the diamond field dispute gave the evangelists cause to fear for the survival of the missions.[87] From their perspective the lines of political cleavage in the South African interior had previously seemed clear enough—indeed, as unambiguous as their own moral and material support for "their" native communities. In this respect most of them saw matters no less starkly in shades of black and white than did the citizenry of the settler republics. At the same time, however, they expected the Tswana to distinguish among Boers, English farmers and traders, the colonial government, and themselves. Thus they were horrified when, in 1878, in the wake of the Keate Award, the disturbances of the frontier blurred such distinctions—and when, in the course of the most serious armed resistance by Southern Tswana to date, two LMS stations came under attack. In comparison to the Griqua rebellion of the same year, the trouble was relatively minor and localized. But for the Nonconformists, it crystallized their political predicament on a volatile, violent landscape. Some time back, in 1851, Isaac Hughes had written: [88]

> We missionaries are blamed by the Natives as forerunners to them of oppression and destruction from the hands of our fellow white men. The Colonists, on the other hand, blame us as sacrificing their interests for the Natives.

This, plainly, was an early expression of the contradiction we encountered in the Ludorf story. Hughes' observation, ignored by those of his colleagues who continued to misrecognize the situation of the mission, seemed more acute with each passing year.

The origins of the crisis of 1878 may be traced back "as far as the time when the Diamond-fields were taken over," explained John Brown. [89] For most Tlhaping—now divided into three separate polities under Chiefs Jantjie, Mankurwane, and Botlhasitse—the annexation of Griqualand had been the start of another era of upheaval. Those who had been incorporated into the new Crown Colony by imperial fiat had much of their land taken, their ruler's authority subverted, and their chiefdom reduced to a scattered patchwork of "native locations" under foreign rule. They were also offended by the actions of local colonial administrators, who were quick to use force in policing the frontier zone, and by the depredations of traders and farmers—British no less than Boer—who violated their territory, seizing water sources, felling trees, and privatizing pasturage. As Brown (see n. 89) went on to point out:

> They saw the country in which they had been born and grown up, and over which their old chiefs had exercised undisputed authority for years past, out of their hands, without regard being had to their wishes and interests. They saw strangers come and take possession of fountains at which their own cattle had hitherto drunk unhindered. They were suddenly made subject to laws about which they knew but little;

and legal forms connected with execution of justice seemed in their eyes as if adapted to secure the interests of the white man and militate against those of the black. Under these circumstances it was no wonder that a spirit of restlessness and dissatisfaction became widely spread. . . .

Even the polities in southern Bechuanaland, although outside the annexed territory, were overtaken by the spreading discontent and antiwhite feeling. To many Tswana, moreover, nice distinctions among Europeans evaporated in the heat of conflict. The Rev. Wookey put it in no uncertain terms:[90]

Missionaries, traders, landjobbers, canteen keepers &c. have all been put down in the same catalogue as destroyers of the country. I have been told again and again that we are deceivers and only trying as Agents of the Government to get the country. The way in which Griqualand and much of Janke's country were taken over by the British Government has given rise to much of this sort of talk.

Rumors of impending trouble began to circulate among the whites in May and came to a head when a trader named Burness, his wife, and brother were killed along the Griqualand border (Mackenzie 1887:1,83ff.). Shillington (1985:76) has pointed out that Burness was master of the local cattle pound at a time when the government began to attach Tswana stock as "punishment" for various offenses (see e.g., Sillery 1971:43); he had also been involved in a land survey against which the Tlhaping felt deep resentment. As elsewhere in the colonial world at comparable moments of crisis (Stoler 1985), these "murders" of "respectable, fair-dealing"[91] people were read by the Europeans as dangerous political crimes that foreshadowed a general rebellion. One evangelist,[92] for example, wrote that according to his pupils Tswana families were being told "to rise upon the [whites] unawares and put them to death," missionaries included. Since there were also reports of stealing and killing along the Orange River, he added, all the Europeans of the district had taken refuge in the Moffat Institution, the new school at Kuruman. Barricading themselves in these buildings, they looked out at the world and saw themselves as besieged.[93]

We shall return to the significance of the Moffat Institution—and the Burness incident—in the colonial process. For now it is sufficient to note that a British volunteer column came from the south and, after two skirmishes en route, "liberated" the Kuruman station—though strictly speaking nobody was investing it at the time. The local chief had chosen not to fight; many of his people had recently been in government service as cattle herders and wagon drivers and were quick to accept the pieces of white cloth and badges that the evangelists offered to those who wished to remain "neutral."[94] Regular troops, who had been engaged elsewhere in bringing various "rebel" groupings to heel, then made for nearby Dithakong (Lattakoo), where, they had been told, a nearby mission church had been sacked (Shillington 1985:77). The "uprising" was put down without much further ado, and life on the Bechuanaland border returned to a state of restless quiet (Mackenzie 1887:1,102). But just as the military strength of most the Southern Tswana polities had been broken, so the missionaries had come up against another new reality: the implications of formal colonial overrule in the interior. The presence of the British administration, at least as it had shown itself thus far, was a distinctly mixed blessing for the civilizing mission.

Associated with the Moffat Institution at the time, albeit in contrasting ways, were two well-known churchmen—men who during the late nineteenth century were to figure prominently in the political discourse of the mission. Although both were formally to resign from the LMS, together they charted the alternative stances open to worldly Nonconformists. One was John Moffat, son of Robert, who had disagreed violently with his colleagues over the establishment of the Institution at Kuruman, had asked to be transferred to another station, and had been sent to Molepolole in central Bechuanaland (Moffat 1921:137).[95] The other was John Mackenzie, whom we have encountered before. He had already worked for some twenty years among the Tswana,[96] had devoted his energies to building up the school, and was commander of the "beleaguered . . . citadel" in 1878 (Sillery 1971:46).

As it happens, the two men detested each other. Of Moffat, Mackenzie wrote, "My time of connexion with [him] at Kuruman was the most trying and unhappy period which I have spent in South Africa."[97] Moffat reciprocated later by complaining loudly about the morality of Mackenzie's actions toward the Tswana (see below, p. 300). Nevertheless, their ideological convictions were very similar (Holmberg 1966:173). Both were unyielding protagonists of imperial rule; to be sure, the term "missionary imperialist," which each has been called (Dachs 1972; Moffat 1921; Sillery 1971; above, n. 15), would have struck either as a compliment. Both, moreover, were to become vocal critics of the colonial government at the Cape, to fight against local capitalist interests, and to protest the strong connections between the two. And this in spite of the fact that, during his career, Moffat was employed by the Cape administration, worked on behalf of the British South Africa Company, and abetted what he was subsequently to refer to, in disgust, as the "[Cecil John] Rhodes Gang" (Maylam 1980:66). The two evangelists, in short, stood at the intersection of the major political movements of the epoch, imperialism and colonialism; each, in his own way, was to be caught in the chasm between them. Black South Africans past and present may be forgiven for not seeing much to separate these movements or their historical impact (cf. Hall 1975). For the victim, such distinctions are at best ideological masquerades. However, to the Europeans, evangelists and others alike, the contrast was highly significant. For those drawn into the formal public arena, it mandated two quite different courses of action.

In order to capture the role of the mission in the dominant political process of the period, then, let us do as we have done before. Let us take John Mackenzie as our focal point, a prism for refracting the essence of the age. And where appropriate, let us cast him against John Moffat—as temporal circumstances were to do. Of course, this will not yield an "event history" of late nineteenth-century politics in southern Africa. But, we reiterate, such an account is not what we seek; there are many perfectly good social, political, and economic histories of the subcontinent, studies written from a number of perspectives. Our objective, rather, is to trace the contradictions and continuities among the various dimensions and discourses of the encounter between the mission and the Tswana—including those set apart by the Europeans as "*the* political."

John Mackenzie, who, like the other missionaries, hoped and believed that the Kuruman station would be spared in the 1878 uprising, took the events of the period as a major historical lesson—even if he read them in a rather idiosyncratic manner. As he saw it, the basic cause of the trouble lay in the nefarious intentions of the white settlers and the lack of a strong British presence to extend benign control over the region (1887:1,96ff.; Sillery 1971:ch.6, 7). In his haste to affix blame he did not look, for example, to the fact that the Moffat Institution had been built on Tlhaping ground, from which people had been "induced" to remove their houses (1887:1,75). Not, morally-speaking, an auspicious precedent in a land where the forced removal of blacks was to become both a means and a major symbol of political oppression. Nor did he note that much of the Tswana dissatisfaction was directed at the British presence itself.

Thus, when the Boers persisted in occupying land given to the Tswana by Keate, Mackenzie decided that only firm action on the part of the Imperial government would stop them. He had long entertained hopes of direct intervention. These were now encouraged not only by "the confused [state of the] Bechuana border, happy hunting-ground of Boers, deserters and adventurers" (Walker 1928:377). They were also sharpened by the general turbulence of the interior, fed by the rapid growth of the diamond and later the gold economy;[98] by continuing conflict over land claims along the frontiers;[99] by the escalation, throughout the country, of "native troubles"; and by schemes and struggles over the confederation of the subcontinent under British dominion. That such schemes had led recently to the annexation of the Transvaal by Britain fueled Mackenzie's enthusiasms still more.[100] As he had reminded the directorate of the Society in 1877,[101] "the LMS was long ago forbidden" in the republic. Now it, and the territories beyond, were thrown open. Exuberantly he added, "England is learning to annex justly and beneficently"; its strong dominion, "fair to all," should be extended over all of southern Africa.

Mackenzie, however, was not going to wait passively for this to happen. From the mid-1870's on, he fashioned his own imperial vision, a dream that was to evolve into a complex plan for the reconstruction of the subcontinent (Mackenzie 1887:vol.1; cf. Sillery 1971:ch.7; W. Mackenzie 1902). Like Ludorf, he assured his overseers that it was "no part of our duty as missionaries to meddle with [temporal] matters" (see n. 101); he insisted, and would continue to insist, that he was not party to "the political schemes and doctrines of the day" (1887:1,97). Nonetheless, like Ludorf, he believed that a political solution to the problems of the Tswana had become unavoidable. His plan entailed the full weight of the Crown and was detailed in a stream of books, pamphlets, and papers, culminating in his magnum opus, *Austral Africa: Losing It or Ruling It.* With this publication the heroic epics of discovery and revelation written by the earliest Nonconformists had finally given way to the mature political treatise. On its outer vellum binding was engraved a map of the region, from the Cape to the Zambesi, with the proposed boundaries of British South Africa embossed in relief. Quite deliberately, this was a book easily told by its cover. It brought to fruition, in textual form, the master narrative of missionary nationalism; a chart and a charter within which the ethnicities constructed for peoples like "the Bechuana" could take root. And, like all expansive nationalisms, it bore its own geography very visibly on its sleeve.

Although Mackenzie was no less paternalistic than his liberal contemporaries, his schemes were phrased in political language remarkable for the time.[102] Blacks should eventually enjoy equal rights in a federated, nonracial South Africa, he argued, so that "Class would not be arrayed against class; [and] the hatches would not be battened down over the heads of blacks, to be opened in bloodshed" (Sillery 1971:51; cf. Hall 1975:103). Although the term "class" was not intended in any conventional modern sense, it had an oddly prescient ring to it and was to appear often in his polemics. "One class of farmers," he would say, should never "legislate for another and unrepresented class": because both white settlers and black indigenes were largely pastoralists and agriculturalists, it was impossible for the former to rule the latter without conflict of interest (1887:1,52). It followed, then, that the Tswana ought not be governed by any colony, English or Dutch, but directly from London; that their territory and its borderlands should be annexed without delay. The founding of a Crown Colony in Bechuanaland would not only stop the Boers from preying further on local communities. It would also be a first step in creating the grand confederation of Austral Africa, a rich expanse of empire under secure British title.

As time went by and the vision became a manifesto, Mackenzie spelled it out—to, of all people, the LMS directors—in explicitly worldly, even materialistic terms: [103]

> I hope to see in the course of time—and to help to bring about, as God may give me opportunity—a *United or Confederated South Africa under the Queen, with a Territorial System of Government in outlying Native Territories under management of* [a] *Governor General and a South African Council*. Happy time for South Africa when this is *well* brought about—the Imperial vote and will of course predominating in Native Territories, but not excluding the assertion of local advice and opinion. Happy for Colonists: happy for Natives: happy for British Taxpayer [original italics].

Happy indeed. The "Territorial Government" envisaged for this Eden, and for Bechuanaland in particular, was simply a professional (expatriate) British administration empowered to regulate the affairs of blacks and whites as one population (Holmberg 1966:55f.; Lovell 1934:48f.). Such an administration would replace all "traditional" authorities, whose inability to control the influx of settlers had allegedly contributed to the disturbed state of the country. Unlike Rhodes and many other politicians of the period, Mackenzie opposed the establishment of reserves for the Tswana. The latter, he argued, should not be segregated and allowed to live under their old political, economic, and social arrangements (Hall 1975:102); they must, instead, be made to take their place as British subjects—albeit, presumably, ethnically distinct ones—alongside the Europeans, now an inescapable presence in the region. In fact, the evangelist hoped to encourage further immigration from England. If the right type of person were attracted, he believed, it would serve both the interests of the Tswana and the cause of civilization. Not leaving much to chance, or to bureaucratic inventiveness, he went on to formulate such things as a tax code and land tenure provisions. These codes and provisions, not surprisingly, bore all the hallmarks of the bourgeois worldview purveyed by the mission: private property and individual responsibility, the enclosure of the commons and "yeoman" farming, even the building of "good" houses (1887:1,ch.5; cf. Shillington 1985:153f.).

From the late 1870's, Mackenzie pressed his plan on British authorities whenever he could, and found a sympathetic ear in Sir Bartle Frere, High Commissioner and Governor of the Cape. Frere conceded that the regulation of the frontier was beyond the scope of his colonial administration; he was easily persuaded of the material and humanitarian advantages to be gained from an imperial presence. When this opinion was conveyed to London, the Colonial Office responded warily but slowly warmed to the idea of annexing Bechuanaland. Assuming that a protectorate was about to be proclaimed, the Governor went so far as to invite Mackenzie to become its Commissioner and asked the LMS for its approval. In his plea to the directors, he argued that the missions had effected great political change among the Tswana, but that by weakening their despotic chiefs—for the good of the natives, of course—they had opened the way for unscrupulous Europeans. In the circumstances, said Sir Bartle, it was only a man like Mackenzie, an evangelist with close knowledge of the blacks, who could now act successfully as Her Majesty's agent.[104] The Society, however, spurned "such a corporeal union of Church and State" (Mackenzie 1887:1,115), giving distinctly pragmatic grounds for its decision: native hostility toward the administration would further taint mission work "if one of [our] circle should become a government official."[105]

Mackenzie himself appears to have been in two minds about entering Her Majesty's service. Formulating constitutions and writing manifestos, it seems, was acceptable. It was the kind of "political work [which had] direct bearing on mission work, as well as the future prosperity of the country."[106] But actually becoming an *agent* of the administration crossed the invisible line between religion and politics. Clearly, that line had shifted a good deal since Robert Moffat's early injunctions on the subject (above, p. 253f.). But still it was acknowledged to exist. Writing just a few months before to a government official who had also requested his assistance, Mackenzie had explained, revealingly:[107]

> If there is one name more hateful than another to a native of this part of the country, it is that of "agent"—âh-gent—as they call it. For a missionary to leave his work and become an "agent" would be to descend to another level in native eyes. . . . [H]e would not be regarded by them any longer as their trusted friend.

But, at the same time,

> I am willing to place whatever influence I may have at the service of the Government. Indeed . . . carrying thro' a plan by which the Bechwanas can become accustomed to British rule . . . is perhaps the most urgent undertaking connected with the welfare of the natives. . . . I should be glad to be connected with such a work.

Mackenzie ended by saying that, as long as he was "not *called* an agent" and could continue to be *seen* as an evangelist, he would "give the Imperial Government [his] hearty and earnest service." Not only had the line between sacred and secular work moved. It had become exceedingly fine, even porous. For John Mackenzie it boiled down to little more than an artifice to be sustained by avoiding words unacceptable to the Africans. Few Southern Tswana were taken in by such semantic niceties, however. For the Tlhaping and other border peoples, the missionary and the maligned *â-gent* became increasingly indistinguishable. There were multiple ironies in this. The LMS and WMMS had long referred to their overseas emissaries as "agents," a usage which, not coincidentally, evoked the image of heroic men—men who, in the spirit of Carlyle, made history by imposing themselves upon the world through their "practic" action (see chapter 2). Indeed, it was in their self-appointed capacity to restructure the worlds of others, to draw non-Europeans into the spiritual and temporal purview of Europe, that their agency lay. However, face-to-face with the implications of that agency—of being *seen* to be *âh-gents*, itself a term with an uncomfortably political ring—Mackenzie and other churchmen took refuge behind the ideological oppositions that had played alibi to their actions and had rationalized their onslaught on Tswana society.

All of these exchanges and rhetorical exertions were premature, however. In 1880 Gladstone's liberal government came to power in England and soon vetoed the proposed annexation of Bechuanaland. In light of reverses elsewhere in the Empire, and with opinion at home turning against any further expansion, the acquisition of new Crown Colonies and protectorates lost its appeal in Whitehall. This was underscored by the first Anglo-Boer War (1880–81), when the burghers of the Transvaal, still smarting from the annexation of 1877 (above, p. 292), rose to inflict a humiliating defeat on an unprepared British administration (Headlam 1936:485). In the aftermath of the Convention of Pretoria, which laid down the terms for the retrocession of the Boer republic, the government of the day was especially wary in its dealings in southern Africa.

Mackenzie responded to this reverse by renewing his campaign with yet greater vigor. A complicated story,[108] its next stage included a furlough in England in 1882–84, during which he canvassed widely and, with other humanitarian and economic interest groups, formed the South African Committee (Dachs 1972:655). By means of newspaper campaigns, parliamentary lobbying, and appeals to public opinion, the Committee and its allies—the vocal Aborigines' Protection Society among them[109]—tried to sway foreign policy. Their efforts were probably helped by the fact that from 1881 to 1884 southern Bechuanaland was itself torn by war. Although the hostilities flared up as a result of differences among the chiefdoms, they soon became yet another confrontation between the larger Tswana polities and the Boers of the Transvaal borderland (Shillington 1985:130f.). Invoking a defensive alliance with the Ratlou, Rapulana, and others—but with their eyes firmly on land and cattle—white "volunteers" (*vrijwilligers*) from the republic mercilessly attacked the Tshidi and Tlhaping, leaving their victims all but destitute.[110] Mackenzie and his colleagues, not above offering lurid accounts of the situation, used pulpit and platform, the press and personal influence to make the very most of it (Northcott 1972:658; Mackenzie 1887:1,131ff.). They were quite successful. The politicians and public of the United Kingdom, stung by their own recent encounters with the Boers, were touched by the plight of the blacks.

Although it took an offer from the Cape Colony to shoulder part of the administrative cost, Gladstone's government finally agreed to establish a protectorate over Bechuanaland in 1884. When it did, Mackenzie was invited to become the resident Deputy Commissioner. He accepted the position and duly resigned from the LMS (Mackenzie 1975:164f.). Many of his brethren "rejoiced" at the "success of his [political] labours in England in behalf of the Becwanas"[111] and regarded his appointment in a highly positive light.[112] To be sure, his links with the Society and its activities in South Africa continued to be very close. Even in government service, he remained a *missionary* imperialist in all but name, both by his own lights and by those of his colleagues.

Several senior members of the Colonial Office, however, were unhappy with Mackenzie's appointment, expressly because it was not clear whether "the High Commissioner or H.M. Government would be able to control him" (Herbert, quoted in Sillery 1971:82); from the perspective of career politicians, missionaries—especially philanthropic, liberal ones—did not make reliable or compliant functionaries. But, they reassured themselves, they "could so easily get rid of him."[113] More seriously, though, their understanding of Mackenzie's mandate was the inverse of his own. For the Colonial Office, his usefulness lay in his "influence over the natives"—specifically, in his ability to dissuade them from acts of aggression.[114] For him, it was a chance to husband the interests of the chiefdoms, at least as he saw them, and so to protect the Tswana from the whites (Mackenzie 1887:1,168–78, 181–99).

In South Africa itself[115] the appointment was roundly condemned by the Boers, for obvious reasons, and by many English-speaking Cape politicians. Some of the latter enjoyed the support of the local branch of the Afrikaner Bond, an association that embraced Dutch-speaking settlers across the country. They were particularly anxious not to offend its members, who despised LMS missionaries, took it for granted that Bechuanaland should be absorbed into the Transvaal, and resented British interference in the affairs of the interior. Among these Cape politicians was Cecil John Rhodes, already a capitalist magnate and a cabinet minister, whose own expansionist agenda at the time required amicable relations with the Boer republics. For him, the "Imperial Factor" represented by Mackenzie was anathema: he envisaged an African dominion securely under the control of interests at the Cape. Bechuanaland, a vital link in its establishment, had thus to be absorbed by the Colony.[116] The High Commissioner and Governor, Sir Hercules Robinson, concurred. Unlike Sir Bartle Frere, whom he had replaced in 1881, he had little time for Mackenzie and his schemes. And so, politically isolated, the evangelist left to take up his office in Bechuanaland—not the large Protectorate that was later to become Botswana, but the much smaller, ill-defined territory of British Bechuanaland, consisting mainly of those parts of the Southern Tswana domain that had not yet been expropriated by whites.

Mackenzie's first task—an almost impossible one, according to some observers[117]—was to settle outstanding disputes among the chiefdoms, the Transvaal, and the white farmers and freebooters in Bechuanaland. In the course of the wars of 1881–84, the latter had formed themselves into two small republics, Stellaland and Goshen, and had continued to raid the Tlhaping and Tshidi, seizing their land and stock. As a Deputy Commissioner with few resources at his command, Mackenzie found it hard to put a stop to this or, indeed, to assert the authority of Her Majesty's Government at all. For years he had tried to persuade the Tswana to appeal for sovereign British protection. Now, when the chiefs had most need of it, he could give them very little (Shillington 1985:150ff.).

This is not to say that Mackenzie lapsed into inactivity. With his usual energy he went around asking the chiefs for their formal agreement to British overrule; pleaded with the whites for their cooperation in resolving the "native troubles"—and then castigated them for their recalcitrance; looked for ways to restore the property taken from the blacks; tried to raise a local police force to control cattle-raiding; and petitioned for armed help to quiet the region. But his actions, at times ill-judged and high-handed (see e.g., Holmberg 1966:6ff.), further alienated the Boers, the Cape government, and the High Commissioner. As the situation deteriorated, his requests for support met with increasingly irritable rejection from Robinson, who eventually recalled him for "consultation" and asked Rhodes to act in his stead. Mackenzie never returned to office. Opinion at the Cape was leaning toward the absorption of Bechuanaland into the Colony, Rhodes himself taking a lead in bringing the case before the public—and in painting the evangelist as an unreasonable champion of the blacks (Sillery 1971:105), and a danger to settler interests. With hostility toward him growing all round, Mackenzie resigned before he could be dismissed.

But he returned to Bechuanaland in 1885, this time with a British military force. The Colonial Office, reacting to subcontinental pressures, had finally decided to put an end to the frontier troubles, to protect the chiefdoms from further predation, and to forestall the annexation of more of their territory by the Transvaal.[118] The expedition was led by Sir Charles Warren, remembered by the Tswana as *Rra-Glas*, "Father Glass," for the monocle he wore. Much to the disgust of Robinson, but with the agreement of the Colonial Office, Warren sent for Mackenzie to join him as an advisor. The two men had come to know and respect each other during the frontier uprisings of 1878, and they shared an imperialist ideology.[119] The evangelist, having left government service, was acting as a propagandist and political critic in Cape Town at the time (Sillery 1971:117). Although he had not returned to mission work, the LMS had offered to pay him a salary—"to relieve your mind of care whilst you are carrying on your present agitation," Wardlaw Thompson told him.[120] The Society was knowingly funding a full-time political activist.

The Warren Expedition and the complex events it set in motion are, by any count, significant in the history of southern Africa. From our perspective, however, it is enough to note that, as a result of this foray, the uncertain protectorate over the Southern Tswana formally became the Crown Colony of British Bechuanaland;[121] and a second, much larger Protectorate (the Bechuanaland Protectorate, later Botswana) was extended over the northern Tswana. The latter, it should be pointed out, was *not* a product of Mackenzie's effort, even though he had strongly desired it. It was a preventative imperial response to rumors of German involvement in South West Africa; the struggle among expansive European states, yet another global process, had also insinuated itself into the politics of the region (Maylam 1980:26; Halpern 1965:86). Nonetheless, the evangelist lost no time in seizing the opportunity to which it gave rise.

When the establishment of the Bechuanaland Protectorate was explained to the northern Tswana chiefs, three of them offered tracts of land for European settlement, ostensibly in gratitude for British protection. Mackenzie, it turns out, was instrumental in prompting these (written) offers. They revived his old scheme for colonizing the interior with English settlers of the "right type," (above, p. 294)—thus to bring about his idyll of a country, ruled by Territorial Government, in which yeomen farmers, black and white, might toil away in an enlightened garden of liberal individualism, private property, and so on. It was a contradictory dream, of course. Intended to keep a free black peasantry on its own land—and safe from repressive, unfree labor conditions elsewhere—it envisaged giving away large tracts of that land. Nor was Mackenzie always open and scrupulous in his efforts to bring it about. For example, it is said on good evidence that he "deliberately concealed his own handwriting of the [Ngwato] offer" to cede territory to the whites (Dachs 1972:657; cf. Sillery 1971:130). Bluntly put, insofar as their full implications were only dimly understood and halfheartedly endorsed by the rulers concerned, these documents were at best the product of wishful imperial thinking. At worst, they were plain forgeries. In the event, the chiefly gesture was curtly declined by the High Commissioner, and Mackenzie's dream was not fulfilled. Still, the founding of the Colony and the Protectorate, under British rule, was a major step in the direction of his original design for Austral Africa.

It was thus only *after* he had left government service that Mackenzie saw his schemes partially realized—and then due to a totally extraneous, world-historical factor. It was also a short-term victory, as British Bechuanaland was absorbed into the Colony a decade later, eventually to become an integral part of South Africa; and the fate of the Bechuanaland Protectorate was to hang in the balance for many years, suspended amidst the machinations of Rhodes and his British South Africa Company (BSAC), the Transvaal, the "Imperial Factor," and other local actors and agents (see e.g., Maylam 1980). But most ironic of all, perhaps, is the fact that Mackenzie's own part in the process was criticized by some of his evangelical colleagues as a violation of Tswana interests. Already in 1884, just before the Warren Expedition took off, John Brown, minister at Kuruman, had written[122] that he could not imagine the Africans gladly handing over their land and fountains to white colonists. The whole plan, he added "must . . . be unwelcome to the large majority of the Becwanas; . . . the less the missionaries are identified with it the better." And then:

> I must say I have been a little disgusted with some of Mr. Mackenzie's recent utterances. . . . The spectacle of a missionary stumping the Cape Colony with a view to induce Cape Colonists to annex native territory[123] is certainly one new thing under the sun.

Note again that, for the Rev. Brown, Mackenzie remained, above all, an evangelist.

John Moffat, Mackenzie's old *bête noire*, was even more scathing. He described the "offers" elicited from the Tswana chiefs as "wholesale robbery of the Bechuana people under the guise of a philanthropic scheme for protecting them."[124] This statement was just one salvo in an intermittent exchange of insults between the two former colleagues. Being phrased in a moral key, however, it masks both similarities and differences in their political biographies and ideologies. More generally, it calls forth a comparison which, as we said earlier, is instructive for understanding the missionary politics of the period.

Moffat had himself resigned from the LMS in 1879 and had entered government employment the following year.[125] He took to the civil service much more easily than did Mackenzie and, after some time in it, wrote to his father that "political and magisterial duties can be gone about in a Godly fashion." As to "actual preaching," he added, "I have nearly as much of that as I ever had" (Moffat 1921:153). Like Mackenzie, he may

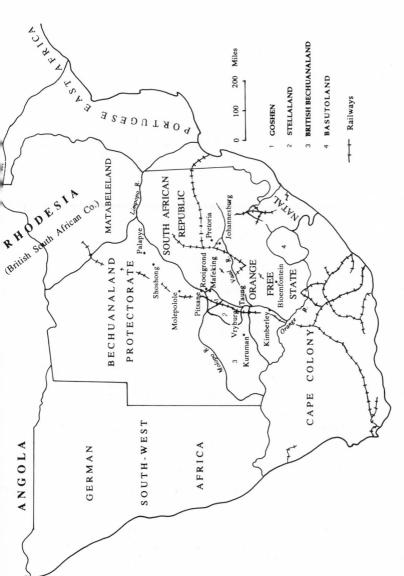

MAP 6 *Southern Africa, circa 1885–95*

formally have left the LMS, but he had certainly not left the church or the evangelical fold, even while working for the state. In 1880, in fact, he claimed never to having felt "more really like a missionary" (1921:153)—thereby rationalizing the apparent contradiction between his past and present roles—and was gratified to note that his entry into government was not viewed with disfavor by many of his erstwhile brethren.[126] In his early career as an administrator, John Moffat was a native commissioner in the Transvaal (1880–81),[127] a resident magistrate in Basutoland (1882–84) and British Bechuanaland (1885–87), and then Assistant Commissioner of the Bechuanaland Protectorate (1887). But he had barely taken up this last position when he was sent to Matabeleland—later a district of Rhodesia, now Zimbabwe—to act as British representative. The scramble for Central Africa had intensified: the Transvaal, Portugal, Germany, and the capitalists of the Cape Colony were all seeking a foothold in the deep interior. It is during this period that, ironically in light of his earlier attack on Mackenzie, Moffat made a treaty with the Matabele chief on behalf of Britain, and became an "imperial resident in the pay of the British South Africa Company" (Maylam 1980:28). The latter had been granted a charter over the territory, a major coup for Rhodes and the colonial capitalists.

For a while Moffat was happy to act on behalf of the Company and the colonists, fusing mercantile and political agency in his administrative role (Moffat 1921:247f.; Sillery 1971:160). Mackenzie, by contrast, never yielded for a moment in his fight against Rhodes and the capitalists. Not only did he contrast them, expressly and unfavorably, with imperialists and philanthropists (1975:259); he also took every opportunity to rail publicly against their mercenary objectives. And he was much quicker than Moffat to appreciate that the rise of the BSAC, and Rhodes's success in Matabeleland, was a serious reverse. Indeed, he must have been riled by the claim, made in his presence by a member of the Royal Colonial Institute, that the Company was "guided by Christian principles."[128] As Northcott (1972:663) notes, he was under no illusions that all his efforts

> had only paved the way for the coming of the British South Africa Company. That too was an imperial conception, but as Mackenzie knew it was essentially an invention of the colonial, land, and mining interests. Rhodes and his charter had triumphed both in Downing Street and on the veld.

In due course, as we said before, Moffat also was to turn against the "Rhodes gang" and to judge "the capitalists . . . worse than the Boers" in their treatment of blacks (Moffat 1921:46). But his objection, it seems, was not so much against the general principles of colonialism and industrial capitalism; it was directed towards the people who acted in their name (Moffat n.d.: 38–39). In fact, he seems to have remained no more sympathetic to rule from London than from Cape Town,[129] even when he fell out with local administrators.[130] And he was less approving of Her Majesty's ministers (Moffat 1921:183, 212) than Mackenzie, who stuck fast to his imperialist guns, never abandoning his scheme for Bechuanaland under the avuncular authority of the Colonial Office. Moffat, less trusting of British suzerainty, was always skeptical of this scheme, even when not accusing its author of "wholesale robbery." Of course, Mackenzie's capacity to bring it to fruition had, from the first, been limited by his lack of a power base. His influence diminished yet further after 1885; by 1892 a Colonial Office minute described him as an "extinct volcano."[131]

Moffat enjoyed a longer career in administration. After leaving Matabeleland in 1892, he went back to the Bechuanaland Protectorate as Assistant Commissioner. Here too he found himself pitted against Rhodes, who coveted northern Tswana territory as a road to the interior and was trying to persuade the Ngwato chief, Khama, to cooperate in his designs. Like Mackenzie, Moffat (n.d.: 36f.) was troubled by the seizure of Tswana land and, even more, by the new serfdom in which the Africans were being engrossed. Before, the churchmen had blamed the Boers for—in the official language of the time[132]—creating a "system of quasi-slavery" designed "to secure labourers in the interest of the industry of the whites." But now, they feared, such things were being done at the behest of Rhodes and his "gang" in the name of Britain.

Rhodes reacted to Moffat's opposition in Bechuanaland by undermining him in much the same way as he had done to Mackenzie. The Assistant Commissioner's standing soon began to ebb; in the end even Khama "turned against him" (Moffat 1921:281), demanding his removal when he criticized the chief's behavior in a local political struggle. Moffat was duly posted back to British Bechuanaland in 1895, where he ended his career in government, as extinct a volcano as Mackenzie had ever been. From there he saw British Bechuanaland annexed by the Cape Colony. And he watched the BSAC, over the complaint of the chiefs, almost gain control of the Protectorate. This denouement was prevented only by the abortive Jameson Raid (1895–96), in which the Company tried to sow insurrection in the Transvaal but succeeded merely in discrediting itself. Shortly after, Moffat followed Mackenzie to Cape Town to become a preacher, a propagandist for "pro-native" causes, and a pastor to political prisoners. In 1897–98 the LMS was to protest to Sir Gordon Sprigg, premier at the Cape, over a case of compulsory alienation of land and labor:[133] two thousand Tswana, who had "rebelled"[134] against the government, were being made to forfeit their property and serve as indentured workers on Cape farms.[135] Interestingly, when the Bechuanaland District Committee looked for someone to minister to these prisoners, they asked none other than John Moffat.[136] In his later years he was also to be an active voice in support of organized black protest against white domination.

Although this historical fragment deals with a pair of highly visible missionaries, it does much more than retail two unusual careers. Mackenzie and Moffat might have been more prominent than most of their brethren; in the corridors of power they certainly were taken to be the political voices of evangelical Christianity, and they were treated as anything from mild irritations to dangerous subversives.[137] Yet they were hardly alone in the manner and extent of their involvement in colonial politics. At times even the mission societies themselves trafficked in the affairs of state in ways most temporal and public.[138] It is, rather, the general implications of the narrative that are most salient here. For the story of Mackenzie and Moffat underscores and expands upon our earlier fragments in three important respects.

First, as we saw in those fragments, there was nothing in Nonconformist Christianity per se that prescribed one contemporary political doctrine above all others. Thus, for instance, both Mackenzie and Moffat saw themselves as champions of the natives. But one was an imperialist, while the other, for a time at least, advocated and served the cause of colonialism, Rhodes, and the BSAC. Nor was Moffat isolated in his early views. Long after he had changed his mind and become an active protagonist of black rights, there were many in the LMS and WMMS who supported the capitalists and who attributed their excesses to human, not ideological, failure. The more general point, once again, is this. The colonial history of southern Africa involved a long and sometimes bitter argument among the colonizers, an argument whose lines shifted over time. Not only did it divide Boer and Briton. It also cast metropolitan imperialist against settler colonialist, capitalist against philanthropist, and, on occasion, mercantilist against industrialist. For their part, the evangelists could not avoid being drawn in. And, often, they were forced to take sides. Yet, because of the silence of mission ideology on just such issues, they could not speak with a single voice. Far from it: as did their colleagues elsewhere in Africa, they adopted positions along all the axes of dissent, all the battle-lines of the secular discourses of the era (cf. Beidelman 1982:30). As a result, even though they were sometimes tarred with the same brush by outsiders, they had no *collective* identity on the institutional terrain of colonial politics. Having forced a distinction between church and state—a distinction regularly violated—Nonconformist dogma provided no chart of the ground between them, let alone of anything beyond. This, as we said before, is one reason for the inherently indeterminate role of the missions in the formal political processes of nineteenth-century southern Africa.

The second point involves the calculus of power. For a missionary who sought influence over worldly affairs, it seemed necessary to penetrate, somehow, into the inner sancta of government. This at least was taken to be the lesson of the many unsuccessful entreaties to Whitehall and Cape Town on the question of "native rights." Lobbying and propaganda campaigns, by either the evangelists or their societies, simply did not yield effective or enduring results. The Christians might have been significant agents of ideological persuasion in the colonizing process; but, being a "dominated fraction of the dominant class," they were well aware that they lacked the secular power to realize their vision. It is no coincidence, therefore, that most of the notable "political parsons" (Smith 1950b:66), like Moffat and Mackenzie, left the mission for the colonial service; or, like Ludorf, became legal representatives and agents of the chiefs. Those who took positions in government, however, soon found themselves in an impasse. Given the critical silences of its ideology and its lack of a coherent political voice, the Nonconformist church could hardly provide them with a base of support. Yet not being career politicians, they had no other constituency within the secular state, no independent social resources on which to call. Consequently, they were confined at best to purely *administrative* roles, usually in the lower reaches of the civil service. Having entered the public arena to shape a formal "native policy," they typically were charged with implementing one—one made largely by others, which they often found unacceptable but lacked the influence to change. It did not take long for these evangelists to run up against the contradictions of their situation. Faced with the stark reality of their political impotence, many of them resigned or were dismissed, and fell into bitter obscurity long before they reached old age.

Even the most politically active and imperialistically driven of missionaries, then, were quite ineffectual in the realpolitik of empire. Thus, for all Mackenzie's fervent campaigns, the creation of a Protectorate over Tswana territory came as a result of Anglo-German diplomacy, not through any actions of his own; for all his opposition to Rhodes, the capitalists, and the Boers, theirs were the decisive voices in the debate over Bechuanaland; for all his efforts to keep the chiefdoms out of the hands of the BSAC, it was largely the Jameson Raid that saved them this fate. What is more, even the most charismatic and canny of the evangelists sometimes saw their intentions disfigured by the force of circumstance or the will of others more potent. John Moffat's biography, to take one celebrated case, is a long litany of unintended consequences (Moffat 1921). But the same may be said of Philip, Ludorf, and many others.

As this suggests, the Nonconformists were often catalysts in the European domination of southern Africa—in ways they rarely would have chosen

305

(see e.g., Bundy 1979:36). In Griqualand, southern Bechuanaland, and Matabeleland, to be sure, their interventions paved the way for an especially violent form of overrule (see e.g., Shillington 1985). Always equivocal figures in the realm of institutional politics, the effects of their actions frequently escaped their own control and took on unexpected historical significance (cf. Crummey 1972:150). No wonder that the Tswana, particularly the non-Christians among them, were always suspicious of the motives of the mission and its connections with government and the military; that the churchmen were regarded, in their secular dealings, as little better than the maligned "âh-gent"; that, while they may have been used as diplomats and representatives, the chiefs often doubted their capacity to do much about the hostile actions of settlers in the region; that, even while they cooperated (usually passively) in the schemes of the "political parsons," the blacks increasingly asserted their will either by appealing directly to the administration or by mounting various forms of resistance. In this respect the evangelists suffered a fate that foreshadowed the destiny of white liberalism in twentieth-century South Africa at large: they were to find themselves ever more impotent in national politics and ever more mistrusted by those whose cause they set out to support.

But, third, however equivocal their role in colonial government, the evangelists were instrumental in recasting indigenous modes of political self-representation. It is here that the ideological imagery of the mission and the realpolitik of empire came together most forcefully. Quite deliberately, the likes of Mackenzie and Moffat, and others before them, inserted themselves as cultural brokers between the blacks and the whites. It was these men who introduced the Tswana to European techniques of diplomacy and taught them the terms by means of which they might engage with the strangers on their landscape. What is more, they wrote almost all the letters by means of which, increasingly, the chiefs engaged with the other players on the regional stage; indeed, by wielding the pen in the epistolary politics of the frontier, they exercised considerable influence over the language of negotiation and exchange.

This language spoke of sovereignty and hierarchy, of treaty and legality, of might and rights, of the state and the finality of imperial authority. And it confronted "the Bechuana" with an image of themselves as an ethnic group (above, p. 287) made up of "customary" political communities: simple precursors, that is, of the highly evolved European nation-state—but, in South Africa, a sad foreshadowing of the Bantustan. Whatever existed before (see chapter 4), Tswana were encouraged to represent their *merafe*—now translated as *both* "tribes" and "nations"[139]—as geographically and culturally defined units based on territorial jurisdiction, with formal courts and armies, administrative structures and responsible (secular) government. Thus in 1884, when Montshiwa concluded a treaty with the Crown, the document read: [140]

> I give the Queen to rule in my country over white men and black men. I give her to publish laws and to change them when necessary, and to make known the modes of procedure of the courts, and to appoint judges and magistrates, and police, and other officers of government as may be necessary, and to regulate their duties and authority. . . . [Also] to collect money (taxes) . . . which will go to defray the expenses of the work done in this country by the Queen; and to levy court-fees, to impose fines, and to employ the money thus obtained according to the laws of the Queen.

The words were drafted by Mackenzie, although, by the time they were written, Montshiwa was conversant with the style and probably knew perfectly well what they meant. His own letters, dictated to a "tribal secretary" when no missionary was available, were couched in a similar rhetoric and used many of the same phrases. [141] The Tshidi ruler was quick to learn the political language of colonialism, with its curious argot of bureaucratic and biblical terms. So too was his successor, who in 1903 would write unsolicited to Joseph Chamberlain, the Colonial Secretary, on behalf of the "Barolong *Nation*." [142] And he would ask Whitehall to recognize "our Native Laws," the jurisdiction of the chiefs, "our rights and privileges as loyal citizens," and the continued possession of "our Native Reserve Lands." Ironically, during the twentieth century, these remodelled polities, with their native laws and native reserves, were to be re-presented to "the Tswana ethnic unit" yet again—this time by a South African state seeking to construe them as "traditional." Apartheid may still have been a long way off when "the Bechuana" were first drawn into the struggle for their autonomy, for control over their land and labor. But from the start they were compelled to fight on the linguistic and conceptual terrain of the whites. Imperialism and colonialism alike implied the precedence of European signs and practices. Not only were the blacks being denuded of their self-determination. They had to suffer it being done to them in English and Dutch.

In teaching the culture of a new politics, the Nonconformists also had another lesson to convey: that, having themselves reached the apex of civilization, the British were more humane, more trustworthy, more committed to "native improvement," and, above all, better allies than the Boers. It was a short step from this lesson, repeated over and over again, to persuading the Tswana to appeal for imperial protection when threatened—and to do so by painting themselves as worthy subjects: responsible, law abiding, well-governed, and politically "advanced" according to the criteria laid down by the churchmen.[143] The chiefdoms were endangered often enough, as we well know, so there was plenty of opportunity to plead for British assistance. When protection (or, more precisely, a Protectorate) was granted, it appeared to come as a favor on the part of the Queen—and as a positive achievement on the part of Tswana, who had proven themselves sufficiently deserving of her patronage.

Here, then, is the ultimate imperial hegemony, the culmination of the moral offensive launched by the abolitionist movement and borne to Africa by the soldiers of the Lord: overrule as a kindness to the colonized. In the treaty quoted above between Montshiwa and Britain, the chief begins the second paragraph: "Rejoice today on account of the coming of the Representative of the Queen, according to my petition!" The "native" subject, under the careful tutelage of the evangelists, had become a willing citizen of Her Majesty's dominion. Or so it seemed. As this implies, the introduction of new modes of political self-representation was an integral part of the larger civilizing mission—of instilling the state of colonialism on which the colonial state was to be erected. The missionaries might not have been especially effective in the formal domain of "public policy." But by virtue of their practical intervention on the colonial stage, quotidian and institutional alike, they became agents of empire, conduits of its political culture; Gramsci (1971:12) might well have described them as the "dominant group's 'deputies' exercising the subaltern functions of social hegemony and political government."

There is another side to the story, however. The Tswana may have learned the political language of colonialism. And they may have conducted themselves according to its practical terms. But the more they were forced to comply with European forms of discourse, the more they came to rely upon, and invoke, the distinction between *sekgoa*, the ways of whites, and *setswana*, Tswana ways. We shall have much cause to return to this contrast. Present in embryo from the start of the long conversation, it was to emerge as a critical trope in Tswana historical consciousness. For now, its existence bore witness to the fact that the contradictions between the professed worldview of the mission and the world of material and social inequality in South Africa were becoming ever more acute. These contradictions were to reappear over and over in a variety of forms and phantasms. And in shaping black historical awareness, they were to fuel a long cycle of protest and resistance.

E I G H T

C O N C L U S I O N

THIS IS LESS a conclusion than it is a coda, a restatement of our original theme to mark the end of the first movement of a larger work. Thus far we have explored the early moments of a peculiarly modern drama: the colonizing thrust of European evangelists into the South African interior in the name of reason and righteousness, God and Great Britain. We began by tracing this drama to its roots in the new bourgeois world, a world whose tropes and tensions gave rise to the enterprise of "humane" imperialism, sending humble men on heroic missions. These men set out to save Africa: to make her peoples the subjects of a world-wide Christian commonwealth. In so doing they were self-consciously acting out a new vision of global history, setting up new frontiers of European consciousness, and naming new forms of humanity to be entered onto its map of civilized mankind.

The mission communities on the northern frontiers of early nineteenth-century South Africa grew out of the first stilted, stylized encounters between the evangelists and the Southern Tswana. In them, the whites sought to cast the "natives" as inverted images of themselves, while the Africans tried to grasp what lay behind the dazzling surfaces of this looking-glass world. The interaction that followed was characterized by contestation and compliance, fascination and repulsion; although the churchmen were to prove more capable of imposing their designs upon the colonial field, the Tswana were hardly passive recipients of European culture. Not only did they remain skeptical of some of its ways and means, but they also read their own significance into them, seeking to siphon off the evident powers of the

309

mission while rejecting its invasive discipline. From the start, their interest and inventiveness were stimulated by the goods and knowledge brought by the Nonconformists—the tools and techniques, rites and rhythms, songs and speech forms—and, wherever they could, they put these to work in ventures of their own. Some Tlhaping and Rolong, so disposed by their social marginality, were inclined to go further and developed a more thoroughgoing identity with the church. But most resisted the Christian campaign to reconstruct their everyday lives, to gain command over their means of producing social value and material wealth. Hence they struggled to retain control over space and place, words and water. And they argued over such things as the efficacy of rainmaking and the ontology of ritual—and, later, over mastery of Setswana itself.

At the same time the meeting of these two worlds was driven by a logic that transcended—indeed, shaped—the explicit intentions of the actors on either side. On the one hand, it was prefigured in the imperial thrust of Europe into the non-European world, itself a product of the postenlightenment imagination. The evangelists were not just the bearers of a vocal Protestant ideology, nor merely the media of modernity. They were also the human vehicles of a hegemonic worldview. In their long conversation with the Tswana, whether they knew it or not, they purveyed its axioms in everything they said and did. And yet despite this, they were themselves deeply affected by the encounter. Not only were they haunted by the image of the "native" they had conjured up; but in their effort to hold their converts, they soon began to imitate some of the very "heathen superstitions" they had so loudly condemned. Nonetheless, their assault was driven by a universalizing ethos whose prime object was to engage the Africans in a web of symbolic and material transactions that would bind them ever more securely to the colonizing culture. Only that way would the savage finally be drawn into the purview of a global, rationalized civilization.

For their part, however, the Tswana were motivated by quite different axioms. Their own taken-for-granted world was founded on the assumption of cultural relativity and political autonomy. It certainly did not equate exchange with incorporation, or the learning of new techniques with subordination. And it expressed itself in its own imagery of personhood and property, work and wealth, social relations and modes of rule. But even when they refused the overtures of the mission in favor of their own conventions, the Africans were subtly transformed by their participation in its discourse. For example, to argue over the efficacy of rainmaking in empirical terms—who actually had been better able to make the clouds yield their moisture?—was to concede a good deal to the epistemology of rationalism, the value of positive enquiry, and the cult of the fact. Similarly, to dig a well with the European tools was to not only to resituate the coordinates of material resources and ritual forces but also to enact a new notion of production and property. Or, to take a somewhat different example, chiefs who permitted the churchmen to act as their political agents in dealing with the advancing forces of settler colonialism soon found themselves speaking a new political language, one that presupposed a sharp, and for them unprecedented, division of church and state. It was also a language that presumed the reality of ethnicity and nationality, with all they implied for collective representation and the construction of interest. But perhaps the domain in which the encounter with the mission made its deepest inroads into Tswana consciousness was that of literacy and learning. Those who chose to peruse the Setswana Bible learned more than the sacred story, more even than how to read. They were subjected to a form of cultural translation in which vernacular poetics were re-presented to them as a thin *sekgoa* narrative—and their language itself reduced to an instrument of empirical knowledge, Christian prayer, and just-so stories. It is little wonder that the Tlhaping and Rolong became ever more self-conscious about their own culture as a distinct system of signs and practices; that *setswana* came to stand in opposition to *sekgoa* as, among other things, tradition to modernity.

The long conversation, as we have stressed, proceeded at two levels from the very beginning. Most overt was the tangible attempt to convert the Africans, to overwhelm them with arguments of images and messages, thereby to establish the truth of Christianity. Only partially distinguished from this in the evangelical enterprise was the effort to reform the indigenous world: to inculcate in it the hegemonic signs and practices—the spatial, linguistic, ritual, and political *forms*—of European culture. Notwithstanding their exertions, however, these two modes of transformation did not occur together as intended. They rarely do. Colonized peoples like the Southern Tswana frequently reject the message of the colonizers, and yet are powerfully and profoundly affected by its media. That is why new hegemonies may silently take root amidst the most acrimonious and agonistic of ideological battles.

In volume 2 we shall analyze the civilizing mission, a sustained campaign to remake the everyday world of the Tswana by refashioning such "external things" as modes of production and personhood, architecture and aesthetics, clothing and social calendars—in short, to replace one hegemony with another. While they did not succeed in converting many Tlhaping and Rolong into pious Protestants, the churchmen were to be ever more successful in implanting the cultural forms of bourgeois Europe on African soil. And yet even here they would come face-to-face with the tensions inherent in their enterprise. Eager to create a black yeomanry, the Nonconformists set out to instil appropriate structures of kinship, relations of gender and property, forms of commodity production and monetary exchange. Under prevailing subcontinental conditions, however, these innovations would engage with indigenous sociocultural arrangements to yield new social divisions and modes of consciousness. Above all, they would exacerbate processes of class formation and increase the vulnerability of the Southern Tswana to proletarianization. The evangelists were to watch in deep dismay as members of their rural flock—especially those who lost control over their land and livestock—acted upon lessons learned in church about the virtues of wage labor. Setting off to seek their fortunes in the burgeoning industrial centers, these early labor migrants were soon made aware of the harsh realities of life in a racially ordered colonial society.

This in turn underscored the fundamental contradictions of the missionary enterprise. As we showed in chapter 7, the churchmen simply lacked the power to deliver to black communities the world promised in their worldview. The brute inequities of the rising South African state seemed to mock the message of Christian liberal humanism, playing havoc with its assurances of British royal protection, its professions of universal civil rights. Given the structural predicament of the evangelists, their interventions in the making of modern South African were doomed from the start. Not only were their complex political maneuvers destined to be ineffective, but in retrospect it appears to have been inevitable that the Tswana should come to regard them as agents of colonialism like any other.

From such contradictions grew indigenous attempts to make sense of the European presence and to redress the tensions introduced by it. Many Tswana reacted against the Christian intrusion into their midst from the first, although they did so in very diverse terms. Some were outspoken in rejecting the churchmen and demanded their expulsion, others preferred the iconoclastic seizure of rites and practices sacred to the church; some argued openly with the missionary, others refused to talk back to him in his own terms, choosing rather to speak in a poetic voice of their own, a poetic of the concrete. Note once more, however, that expressions of resistance do not preclude the colonization of consciousness or the laying down of new hegemonies. The Nonconformists *did* succeed in seeding their culture on Tswana soil, especially in the fissures of local communities. And as they did, they provoked the Africans into making new conceptual and social distinctions—and into yet more diverse and urgent forms of defiance. These, too, will be a critical concern in volume 2, where we extend our discussion of hegemony and ideology to take in the distinct modes of perception, politics, and protest that emerged in a Tswana universe fractured increasingly along the fault lines of social class.

The issue of hegemony and ideology returns us to the concerns with which we began this account. In the Introduction we noted that there were lessons to be learned from critical postmodernism: among them, the need to address the indeterminacies of historical meaning and action, to regard culture as a set of polyvalent discourses and contestable practices in which power is always implicated. Thus we have taken pains to capture the interplay of structural constraint and situational contingency; our story recapitulates the global gesture of European expansionism that made the modern world, yet it also shows how such forces worked themselves out in particular local circumstances. Not only did non-European cultures limit what was meaningful and possible in the imperial project. Colonialism itself was less a monolithic movement than a complex response to a set of European arguments about the nature of humanity, civilization, and history; less a clash of abstract social forces or an epic battle of concrete interests than a drawn out struggle between ordinary people, human beings endowed with few resources and only partially coherent motives. What made the process distinctive was the fact that these human beings found their sense of themselves challenged by the radical confrontation with very different worlds, with others seeking to impose their own constructions on a shared reality. Here signs were cut free and contested in struggles over such mundane things as the nature of space and spirit, the control of water and words, the capacity to define the domain of the "political" or to determine the proper orthography of the vernacular. Because frontiers are uncharted spaces of confrontation—spaces in which people fashion new worlds by negotiating hitherto uncommunicated signs—they are a prime context for exploring the relations among culture and power, hegemony and ideology, social order and human agency.

The European colonization of Africa was often less a directly coercive conquest than a persuasive attempt to colonize consciousness, to remake people by redefining the taken-for-granted surfaces of their everyday worlds. In some places it was a combination of the two, effected by different agents at once; and even where it proceeded in an entirely noncoercive manner, the threat of violence was always immanent in it. As this suggests, overrule typically involved a complex interplay of power in both its *agentive* and its *nonagentive* modes—power exercised in purposive acts of the colonizer and power embedded silently in the diverse forms of the colonizing culture. This was especially evident in colonial evangelism among the Southern Tswana. On the one hand, the missionaries openly used all the resources and techniques at their disposal to make an impact on the Africans; that is, to convert people through reasoned argument, to bend chiefs to their wills, to affect the policies of the colonial administration. On the other hand, they were conduits of the power embedded in the practices of their culture, practices that were gradually inculcated into the Tlhaping and Rolong even as they refused to hear the gospel and struggled to limit the impact of *sekgoa* on their communities. These modes of power were complementary, as they always are, shifting in relation to each other as novel, purposive action slowly became social convention—or conversely, as the light of scrutiny fell, suddenly and searchingly, upon the force of habit.

Within any cultural field, we have suggested, the two forms of power are themselves associated respectively with ideology and hegemony—the first being a more or less coherent expression of values and meanings, of political and material concerns, that make up an articulate worldview; the second, an order of implicit signs that structure conventional ways of seeing and being. Neither is ever established or perpetuated as a mere reflex of administrative or economic control. Even at their most secure, ruling regimes strive to do more than just convince people of their ideological message. They seek to limit ambiguities of meaning and proliferations of power, to naturalize their worldviews in the commonplace. The colonial quest in this part of Africa was no exception, a fact underscored with particular clarity by the Nonconformist mission in its capacity as the ideological arm of empire. Although the product of self-conscious humanism, of a heroic history that constantly spoke of its intentions, its narrative was but a thin description of its own enterprise, its explicit message only one dimension of its total endeavor. Its most persuasive force lay in what it took for granted, in the hegemonic forms that would slowly make the Tswana into colonial subjects. We have just begun to examine the implanting of these forms here. In the next volume we continue to explore their pervasive power.

And yet as we have insisted, hegemony is invariably unstable and vulnerable. Never merely an assertion of order, it always involves an effort to redress contradictions, to limit the eruption of alternative meanings and critical awareness. From the mute experience of such tensions arise new kinds of experimental consciousness, new ideologies that point to the discrepancies between received worldviews and the worlds they claim to mirror. It is to this process that we shall turn as we trace the dialectic of domination and resistance among the Southern Tswana, following their passage down the road from revelation to revolution.

N O T E S

WE FOLLOW HISTORIOGRAPHIC convention and annotate all primary materials in the notes; at the same time, in accordance with usual anthropological practice, we include references to secondary writings (by author/year) in parentheses in the text itself and annotate them fully in bibliographies at the end of each volume. Wherever possible, archival documents are cited by author/source, place of writing, date, and storage classification (box-folder-jacket; or, if applicable, just box); in the case of Colonial Office documents, the fullest possible citation is given. Note that CWM is the Council of World Mission, whose papers (which include all the records of the London Missionary Society [LMS]) are housed at the School of Oriental and African Studies, University of London. So, too, are those of the (Wesleyan) Methodist Missionary Society (WMMS). The papers of Tswana communities, kept in their so-called "tribal offices," are listed by chiefdom, capital, file name, date and, if possible, document title.

O N E

1. Barolong boo Ratshidi, Mafikeng, Minutes of Council Meetings, 22 February 1960, "Minutes on the Discussions by Tribal Headmen on the Application for a Site by the Dutch Reformed Church."

2. See, for example, the *Chicago Tribune*, 1 March 1988, sec. 1, p. 3.

3. It is difficult to arrive at a coherent history of *Nkosi Sikelel'*. Walshe (1971: 35) attributes it to Enoch Sothonga, but Benson (1963:5) holds that it was written by "Enoch Sontonga and a missionary at Lovedale College for the African National Congress in 1912." Later (1966:8) she amended the date to 1897 and withdrew the statement that it was composed for the ANC; although Leach (1986:20) contends that it was sung at the initial meeting of the South African Native National Congress (forerunner of the ANC) in 1912 (but cf. Walshe 1971:35; also Gerhart and Karis 1977:103, who date its composition to 1927). Oosthuizen (1973:218) agrees that it was composed in 1897 by Sontonga, a mission school teacher, but asserts that it was originally performed "at the ordination of the first Bantu minister of the Methodist Church." Writing in a conservative South African encyclopedia, Oosthuizen does not so much as mention the link between the song and the ANC. He says only that it is a "devotional song or a song of national significance to the Bantu." One final note: it seems that only the first stanza was actually by Sontonga. The other verses were added later by Samuel Mqhayi (1875–1945), a nationalist poet of Xhosa extraction and also a sometime teacher at Lovedale (Gerhart and Karis 1977:103; February 1989:42).

315

4. Oosthuizen (1973:218) asserts that, apart from appearing in several anthologies of hymns, *Nkosi Sikelel'* was included in Clarence Gibbins' *An African Song Book* (1946). We have been unable to ascertain further publication details, however.

5. Mphahlele was not alone in this view. It was shared by, among others, the South African Students' Organization, a vocal representative of black consciousness in the 1970's. In 1971, SASO (1978a:309) took a resolution (No. 57) at a General Students' Council which noted that "Christianity as propagated by [all of] the white dominant churches has proven beyond doubt to be a support for the status quo, which to black people means oppression." Like Mphahlele and much of the Pan-Africanist movement, SASO was deeply concerned—also in terms reminiscent of Fanon (1967)—with the colonization of the black mind (SASO 1978b, 1978c).

6. Ranger (1975:166–67) makes a similar point with respect to colonial East Africa. As he puts it, "at the core of [the 'colonial relationship'] was the manipulation and control of symbols."

7. In South Africa, the term "native" has long had pejorative connotations. When we use it—with or without quotation marks—we do so not in our own voice but in that of the evangelists and other contemporary Europeans, who employed it often and unselfconsciously. (The same, of course, applies to "savage" and "heathen," whose pejorative connotations are hardly confined to South Africa.) Our prose is explicitly designed to capture the style as well as the substance of missionary discourse and to grasp the empowering rhetoric of the colonial encounter. To avoid its key terms, therefore, would violate the conceptual demands of our analysis.

8. We do not intend to review the literature on missions in Africa—or, for that matter, anywhere else—since it is simply not germane to our present task. Several references annotated in our bibliography do offer such reviews, and there seems little point in duplicating that rather specialized form of scholarly labor for its own sake.

9. See, for example, *Comparative Studies in Society and History* 23/1 (1981).

10. This is not to assume that "postmodernism" is a coherent "thing," even a concept, in and of itself (see e.g., Jameson 1984:53ff.; Hebdige 1988:181f.). However, there has arisen, in its name, a broadly identifiable genus of epistemological critique aimed at the kind of modernist discourses of which the social sciences are part. It is to this genus, and nothing more precise, that we refer in using the label here. For an especially useful introductory discussion of the topic, see Hebdige (1988).

11. Some of the earliest ethnographies and histories of Africa, as is well known, were written by evangelists with a "scientific" interest in their would-be subjects. Here colonial evangelism merged into a scholarly colonialism that foreshadowed and paved the way for modern anthropology. But this is quite another topic; we do not it address here.

12. Note, again, that we are speaking here of the *practice* of anthropology. As every anthropologist knows, there has recently been much programmatic and pre-

scriptive discussion about "writing culture"—discussion that has called, at times very suggestively, for new, experimental forms of ethnography. The intentions are undeniably worthy, as are the efforts to overcome the epistemological problems and limitations of older anthropological genres. However, it is always a far cry from program to production, prescription to practice; until we have a body of work to assess, the exercise remains little more than an interesting stimulant for the theoretical imagination. Thus far, there is, in our view, only one monograph that may claim to be postmodernist, *sensu strictu*: Taussig's *Shamanism, Colonialism, and the Wild Man* (1987). For a very thoughtful review of the theoretical, methodological, and ideological issues raised by the book, see Kapferer (1988). Kapferer also voices a number of general worries about postmodernist ethnography: (1) that, for all its radical stance—and accusations of fascism in others—it may conceal both political neoconservatism and methodological neopositivism; (2) that, despite its repudiation of order and totality, it is founded on a hidden systematicity of its own; (3) that its new rhetoric obscures unacknowledged continuities and similarities with older theoretical perspectives; and (4) that it is no less prone to appropriate the "other" than are its more orthodox predecessors. Inasmuch as these concerns are valid— and they appear to be—the problems raised by critical postmodernism seem not to be resolvable by postmodernist ethnography, at least as presently conceived.

13. The term "sociologies" is used here as a synonym for "social sciences." Hebdige's observations throughout the essay are clearly meant to include anthropology and history.

14. For reasons to which we shall return, this conventional understanding of hegemony owes less to Gramsci's own definition than it does to Raymond Williams (1977), whose commentary on the concept has insinuated itself into popular scholarly usage—and this in spite of the curious fact that it is written without a single page reference to, or quotation from, *The Prison Notebooks*.

15. See, for example, the passages on (1) the creation of a new culture (1971: 325); (2) the self-conception of a social group (1971:327); (3) contradictory consciousness (1971:333); (4) the "realisation of a [new] hegemonic apparatus" (1971: 365); (5) ideology as "a conception of the world that is implicitly manifest in art, in law, in economic activity and in all manifestations of individual and collective life" (1971:328); (6) the nature of philosophy (e.g., 1971:348, 370); and, in particular, of (7) "spontaneous philosophy" (1971:323), which is to be read in light of the association elsewhere in the text between (a) "spontaneity" and "social hegemony" (1971:12) and (b) philosophy, political action, and ideology (e.g., 1971:326). We shall return to (5), (6), and (7) in our discussion below.

16. The potential list of citations is huge. See, for just a small sample, Kraditor (1972); Femia (1975, 1981); Anderson (1976–77); Williams (1977); Adamson (1980); Laclau and Mouffe (1985); Lears (1985); and Hall (1986).

17. It follows that we find the term "cultural hegemony," which is used by some Gramscian commentators, a misguided conflation of two quite distinct (albeit theoretically related) concepts. The same, for reasons that will become clear, applies to "ideological hegemony."

18. Being less concerned with textual exposition than with the development of a conceptual framework, we have transposed the characterization of "contradictory consciousness" into our own conceptual terms; although, as it happens, we do not depart very far from the spirit of the original. For a brief summary of the precise terms in which Marx and Engels (1970:52ff.) and Gramsci (1971:326f., 333), respectively, characterized this contradiction, see Cheal (1979:110f.).

19. We work with a notion of the poetic most aptly captured by Friedrich (1979:491–92), who sees it as a pervasive aspect of all kinds of language and as characterized by "figures and tropes . . . intensification of forms . . . [and] association by analogy." It is the aspect that "most significantly interacts with the imagination."

20. The status of poetry is not the same here as it is among the Somali, whose oral tradition is described by Cassanelli (1982:270). In that case, poetic fragments "commemorate events," and their recitation serves as a mnemonic, calling forth the narrative exegeses of the episodes that comprise a group's history. The Tswana, we argue, actually *think* their history in poetic tropes; as social scientists often learn to their cost, they do not assume that exegesis is required to decode its truth into more "realistic" terms.

21. Others have also found this category useful for analytical purposes, although they do not always imply by it the same coverage as we do here (see Shillington 1985:xviii; also Schapera 1953:17 on differences of dialect among the Tswana).

22. This classificatory scheme continues to be applied to the languages and cultures of the peoples of southern Africa, in spite of criticism by linguists and social historians (Westphal 1963; Legassick 1969b).

23. Minutes of the second organizational meeting of the London Missionary Society (Lovett 1899:1,15).

24. The terms "Congregationalist" and "Independent" are frequently used interchangeably, as they are here. They do, however, have slightly different connotations which have been stressed more in some historical periods than in others. "Congregationalism" denotes a positive and specific doctrine of the powers and organization of the church, while "Independency" implies only the right of any society to meet together for worship, instruction, or exhortation without the interference of external authority (Dale 1907:375f.). Independency is thus a necessary but not sufficient basis for Congregationalism; in theory, there may be many Independent churches of differing creed.

25. LMS, London, 31 January 1815 [CWM, LMS Incoming letters (South Africa), 6-1-A].

26. The frequent and fairly complicated migrations of the Tlhaping rulers are summarized by Shillington (1985:15).

T W O

1. See Haldon (1912:246f.), himself a clergyman, for discussion of the way in which the spread of Christianity was treated by such writers as Milton (in the last book of *Paradise Lost*), Gibbon (especially in chapter 15 of *The Decline and Fall*), Herbert, Samuel Johnson, and Pope.

2. The "absorbingly complicated figure" of St. John Rivers (Eagleton 1975: 95–96) has been the subject of many literary analyses. Here we are concerned only with his characterization as a missionary.

3. All references to *Jane Eyre* are taken from the 1969 edition (ed. Jack and Smith).

4. For details on Patrick Brontë's political and religious convictions, see, for example, Winnifrith (1973:passim) and Eagleton (1975:9f.).

5. Interestingly, in *Shirley*, Brontë introduces a minor character by the name of Dr. Broadbent, who appears as a speaker at a Bible Society meeting (1981:111).

6. For a summary account of the Niger Expedition, see Curtin (1964:289f.). The government-funded Expedition was dedicated to the elimination of slavery and the spread of Christianity. It was mounted with wide political and humanitarian support, but its main protagonists were members of the abolitionist movement, led by T. Fowell Buxton. The Expedition ended in disaster as forty-one of its European members died of malaria.

7. It is to be noted, as Haldon (1912:254) points out, that Southey himself had as little sympathy with Nonconformist Christianity as did Smith.

8. Smith's response, in the April number of the *Edinburgh Review*, was also prompted by a pamphlet by John Styles attacking his earlier article. We have not been able to locate a copy of this pamphlet, which is entitled "Strictures on two Critiques in the Edinburgh Review, on the subject of Methodism and Missions."

9. Carlyle (1842:Lecture 4,153), quoted by Houghton (1957:305), but in another edition. The lecture, entitled "The Hero as Priest," was read on 15 May 1840.

10. Wordsworth (1954:3,353 [XXV]). The poem is from the Ecclesiastical Sonnets, Part I ("From the Introduction of Christianity into Britain, to the Consummation of the Papal Dominion").

11. As Hook and Hook (1974:9) suggest in their introduction to the Penguin edition of Brontë's *Shirley*, this is especially well captured by the "condition of England" novels published at the time or soon thereafter, "such books as Disraeli's *Sybil*, Mrs. Gaskell's *Mary Barton* and *North and South*, Dickens's *Hard Times*, and Kingsley's *Alton Locke*." They also go on to include *Shirley* amongst these novels.

12. Compare, say, Toynbee ([1884] 1969:85f.), Bowden (1925:1f.), Mantoux (1928:27), Dodd ([anon.] 1847), Hammond and Hammond (1928), Briggs (1959), Foster (1974), Thomis (1974), and Jones (1983); despite their very different ideo-

logical positions, these writers place similar emphasis on the significance of class formation in the Industrial Revolution.

13. See, for just a few examples, Hill (1969), Hobsbawm (e.g. 1962:18 et passim), Mantoux (1928:33f.), Briggs (1959:17ff.), Ashton (1948:2), and Cole (1932:1,32ff.).

14. This imagery was anticipated in the *Communist Manifesto*. See Marx and Engels (1968) and other writings of the left.

15. For an account of Luddism and machine-breaking as class consciousness, see Hobsbawm (1964:5–22); also Thompson (1963:pt.3). The Combination Acts (1799–1800), which fueled Luddite resistance, had banned confederations of workers, the forerunners of trade unions.

16. Briggs (1979:33f.) discusses the contrast, in literature and art, between "optimistic" and "pessimistic" representations of the Industrial Revolution. Elsewhere (1959:14f.), he deals with the same contrast in popular and intellectual debate. A reading of English historical texts, from Toynbee's celebrated *Lectures* ([1884] 1969) to Tawney's (1978) evaluation of the work of J.L. Hammond, makes it clear that the issue has run through a century of scholarly writing.

17. Of course, "class" did not mean then what it was to mean later, partly as result of the efforts of Marx and Engels—and the history of British labor politics. It referred more simply to "rank" or "estate." Nonetheless, much of what Dodd and Hall had to say about it had a decidedly modern ring. For a useful discussion of the language of class in the early nineteenth century, see Briggs (1960).

18. For an extended discussion of the influence of Benthamite utilitarianism ca. 1815, see Halévy (1924:462f., 502f.). In a more recent analysis of its impact on contemporary British opinion, Hobsbawm (1962:277f.) examines its internal contradictions and the kinds of debates to which it gave rise among the ruling classes. That Benthamism, especially in its extreme form, came in for criticism does not alter the fact that it resonated strongly with the dominant ideological conceptions of the age. To be sure, it tried to embody those conceptions, with limited success, into a systematic philosophy.

19. As Troeltsch (1949 [1950]:1,57; cited by Genovese 1974:166) put it in a somewhat different context, "absolute individualism and universalism . . . require each other." Their synthesis in the imperial project, then, is hardly surprising; if anything, it was ideologically overdetermined.

20. It is interesting that as early as 1865 Matthew Arnold (1903:ix) made ironic use of the metaphor of the "atom" to describe the individual "in the life of the world." As Halévy (1924:505) points out, Benthamite utilitarianism, to which Arnold had taken exception (see above), owed its image of the individual to Daltonian atomism.

21. Perhaps the best token of the type is Jabez Clegg, the hero of Mrs. G. Linnaeus Banks' naive novel, *The Manchester Man*. A rather more complex example is Robert Moore in *Shirley*. Although an ambiguous character in many

respects, this manufacturer is nonetheless regarded as a heroic figure (Brontë 1981:202).

22. The modern "divided self," as both metaphor and analytic construct, has appeared in many other places in the human sciences. Like the distinction between individual and society, it arises, a pervasive ideological trope, from the epistemological core of western social thought. This, however, raises issues that fall well outside the scope of our present study.

23. Thompson (1967:85) also observes that the revaluation of time, and the regulation of routine by the clock and the bell, were resisted by workers for a long while before being internalized.

24. It was not only French intellectuals like Halévy who regretted the aesthetic poverty of the age. With equal distaste, Hazlitt (1815:586) wrote, in his weekly column in *The Examiner*, of the "hardness and setness" of the Puritan tradition. In particular, he deplored its "aversion to [the] finer and more delicate operations of the intellect, of taste and genius . . . and the fine arts in general."

25. "Religious individualism" is the term actually used by Halévy (1924:511), who is well known for his view that Methodism was the factor that averted a revolution in Britain during the period.

26. Note, again, that we do *not* lay out in systematic terms the theology of Nonconformism. Not only does there exist a large literature on the topic, but, as we note throughout this study, the evangelists to South Africa were themselves not unduly concerned with abstract theological issues. To the contrary: they saw themselves as men of practical religion. (Indeed, this was itself a corollary of the weight placed by contemporary Protestantism on Good Works, method, and practical rationality.) What is more, as we have stressed, their mission to Africa was shaped by the Spirit of the Age at large—not simply by its spiritual aspect. Inasmuch as we discuss Nonconformist doctrine, then, we do so not by isolating an abstract ontology or a formal theology, but by situating it in its broader ideological and cultural context.

27. Sahlins (n.d.) notes that this reversal of signs had a number of significant corollaries—among them, the fact that human suffering and misery were no longer taken to be inevitable and universal. The sacralized pursuit of self-interest, after all, put the pleasure-pain principle into an altogether new light.

28. The phrase is from Ferguson (1989:31), quoting (but not annotating) Christopher Hill (1989).

29. There has been much debate over the precise periodization of the agrarian revolution (see e.g., Mantoux 1928:142f.)—and, more fundamentally, whether it was truly a "revolution" in the strict sense of the term (cf. e.g., Toynbee 1969:191 with Briggs 1959:41).

30. Prince (1841) is quoted, but not annotated, by Briggs (1979:15). There were others, it should be noted, who denied that the cities were as bad as they were often said to be. Some even spoke approvingly of their transformation, pointing

(1) to great civic buildings and capacious parks made with the profits of industrial expansion, or (2) to the rise of salubrious bourgeois neighborhoods. Such contrasts in perspective were, as we would expect, affected by class differences, political convictions, and geographical factors.

31. For a less positive view of the yeomanry, see Thompson (1963:219).

32. Earlier (Wordsworth 1948:45–46) we are told too that "every family spun from its own flock the wool with which it was clothed . . . and the rest of their wants was supplied by the produce of the yarn, which they carded and spun in their own houses, and carried to market."

33. There is something of a contradiction here. The image of England-as-garden, its expanses divided into neatly-walled or hedged fields, is based largely on the effect of enclosure on the landscape; but it was precisely this process that heralded the end of the old regime and, in particular, of the yeomanry. In sum, the picture of a tidy, geometric countryside, tilled mainly by yeoman households, merges two quite different historical periods.

34. Following Keith Thomas (1984:243), this may have been exacerbated by growing doubts, in eighteenth-century western thought, about man's place in nature. We return to the topic in the next chapter.

35. Note here the comparison with the earliest Protestant missionaries to the New World. As Bellah (1988:x) observes in his Foreword to Hughes and Allen's *Illusions of Innocence*, their "errand into the Wilderness" may be understood as an effort to recover the original, uncontaminated institutions of the church.

36. See Hill (1969:277).

37. Anderson (1983:ch.2) has analyzed the demise of religious authority—or, more embracingly, what he calls the "religious community"—in similar terms, although he links it to the rise of modern nationalism. Both, he says, flow from fundamental changes in "modes of apprehending the world" (1983:28), changes triggered by economic forces and, most notably, the rise of "print capitalism."

38. For a summary of this debate, see Knorr (1944:pt.2).

39. Similarly, where British interests were vested in commercial agencies, the latter often resented and sought to prevent the intrusion of missionaries; witness, for example, the well-known activities of the East India Company in this respect.

40. See J.G. Greenhough, "The Missionary Obligation" (Bloomsbury Chapel, London, April 1896); reprinted in Briggs and Sellers (1973:160–63).

41. Quoted by Warren (1965:53).

42. We refer to Marx's (1955:42) well-known statement that religion is "the heart of a heartless world, . . . the spirit of a spiritless situation."

43. On this general point, see Clinton (1937).

44. J. Campbell, Klaarwater, 26 July 1813 [CWM, LMS Incoming Letters (South Africa), 5-2-D].

45. Brantlinger was speaking mainly of explorers but, since Livingstone was

his prime target, the statement should apply to missionaries as well; the latter certainly fit into the thrust of his argument. (Sinclair 1977:24 makes a similar observation about Spanish "adventurers" in the New World.)

46. The exception was John Philip, superintendent of the LMS missions in South Africa for thirty years, whom we shall encounter several times in this account (see especially chapter 7). Well known in evangelical and colonial circles "as an uncompromising supporter of the rights of the black man" (Neill 1964:312), his reputation first grew out of his abolitionist activities (de Kock 1968:612–21). For a recent biography, see Ross (1986).

47. The celebration of Livingstone in LMS memorabilia ignores the fact that his relations with the Society were extremely tenuous for much of his life (see Jeal 1973).

48. Our sketch of Robert Moffat's background is compiled mainly from J.S. Moffat (1886), Smith (1925), and Northcott (1961), the three fullest sources.

49. For the purposes of this summary, we draw heavily on Blaikie (n.d.), Johnston (n.d.), Ward (1885), Campbell (1930), Seaver (1957), Jeal (1973), and Ransford (1978), although many other biographies cover the same details. Their only major disagreement is over Livingstone's birthdate: some give it as 1813, others as 1817.

T H R E E

1. Notwithstanding our particular concerns here, it goes without saying that stereotypic images of "others," in Africa and elsewhere, predate the age of revolution. So does their metaphysical significance in European thought and representation. For a valuable history of medieval conceptions of the "monstrous races," see Friedman (1981).

2. On Rousseau's views in this respect, see Cook (1936); also Curtin (1964:42).

3. We are grateful to our colleague Raymond T. Smith for making this point to us. The contrast between the Caribbean and South Africa underlines, once more, the danger of imputing homogeneity to contemporary British popular culture—or even to the Christian imagination. We stress again, therefore, the necessity of seeing these as *contested* discourses which became engaged, in varying ways, in the interplay between Europe and the non-European world.

4. *A New General Collection of Voyages and Travels* was published by Thomas Astley of London in four volumes. *Universal History* appeared in sixty-five octavo volumes (with a special luxury edition of twenty-three folio volumes); it is attributed, by the Library of Congress, to Sale, Psalmanzar, Bower, Shelvocke, Campbell, and Swinton (annotated in Curtin 1964:12–13).

5. This phrase was used by the anonymous editor of the 1816 edition of Mungo Park's *Travels* to describe the intellectual climate in which the African Association was founded.

6. Note the charming and often quoted couplet from a poem by Swift: ". . . Geographers in Afric-Maps/With Savage-Pictures fill their Gaps" (see Curtin 1964: 198). Of the latter, it seems, there were very many. Note also the stress on mapping as an index of knowledge; we shall return to it again later.

7. See the Prefatory Note to the 1816 edition of Mungo Park's *Travels*, which acknowledges the difficulty of reconciling the "distances computed according to journeys" with the latitudes and longitudes on the map (1816:xi).

8. Park (1816:iiif.), the son of a "respectable yeoman" who farmed near Selkirk in Scotland, went from grammar school to an apprenticeship with a local surgeon, and then to study medicine at the University of Edinburgh. Thereafter, he moved to London, where his brother-in-law, a gardener and self-taught botanist—later to become a leading European scholar—introduced him to Sir Joseph Banks, founder of the African Association. Witness the similarity in background between these men and those other footsoldiers of Empire, the Nonconformist missionaries (above, chapter 2).

9. The lyrics of this song by the Duchess of Devonshire extend Park's representation by placing us all in Africa's moral debt, all ostensibly summoned directly to secure her liberation (Fairchild 1928:489–50):

> The loud wind roar'd, the rain fell fast;
> The White Man yielded to the blast:
> He sat him down, beneath our tree;
> For weary, sad, and faint was he;
> And ah, no wife, or mother's care,
> For him, the milk or corn prepare.

Chorus:

> The White Man, shall our pity share;
> Alas, no wife or mother's care,
> For him, the milk or corn prepare.

> The storm is o'er; the tempest past;
> And Mercy's voice has hush'd the blast.
> The wind is heard in whispers low,
> The White Man, far away must go;—
> But ever in his heart will bear
> Remembrance of the Negro's care.

Chorus:

> Go, White Man, go;—but with thee bear
> The Negro's wish, the Negro's prayer;
> Remembrance of the Negro's care.

The words and music were included at the end of the second edition of Park's *Travels* (1799), and he introduced them by noting that they preserved the "plaintive simplicity of the original."

10. Park's family and biographers were to contest this opinion, but not with much plausibility (see Park 1816:xxxiv).

11. This scene ostensibly illustrates an attack on Park during his first journey. But, published well after his dramatic death, it strongly evokes the latter event.

12. Three seventeenth-century accounts were published in Dutch and Latin (see Schapera 1933); two in German followed during the eighteenth century (Kolben 1731; Mentzel 1785–87).

13. Barrow's biography was notably similar to that of Park. Both were self-made sons of northern British smallholders (Lloyd 1970); see also n. 8 above.

14. It will be recalled (see chapter 1) that the Cape was restored to the new Batavian Republic in 1803 under the Treaty of Amiens but was seized again by the British in 1806, after the resumption of the Napoleonic Wars (see e.g. Davenport 1969:273f.).

15. It is clear that Barrow meant "kaffir" here to include all "aborigines." In the nineteenth century the term (also "Caffre") was often used more specifically to describe the Nguni-speaking peoples of South Africa—although it was later to become a general term of abuse for blacks, much like "nigger" in the United States of America.

16. For an account of British images of and attitudes toward the Dutch settlers, see Streak (1974), who also discusses the writings of Barrow and Lichtenstein. We are grateful to Robert Gordon for drawing our attention to this reference.

17. Lichtenstein seems to have been the first writer in this genre to make use of missionary observations of black South Africans (see the Prefatory Note to volume 1 of his *Travels* [p.vi], republished by the Van Riebeeck Society in 1928). His work in turn became an important source of European constructions of Africa.

18. See Curtin (1964:58f.) on the role of the "tropics" in this discourse.

19. We are indebted to Nahum Chandler for this reference, included in his unpublished paper, "Writing Absence: On Some Assumptions of Africanist Discourse in the West."

20. Although, as Keith Thomas (1984:42) points out, talk of Hottentots as "beasts in the skin of man" also had earlier precursors.

21. As Williams (1976:77) has noted, "culture as an independent noun, an abstract process or the product of such a process, is not important before lC18 [the late eighteenth century] not common before mC19 [the mid-nineteenth century]." Prior to this, "culture" was a noun of process, implying the "tending *of* something," usually crops or animals. From the early sixteenth century, the tending of natural growth was gradually extended by metaphor to the process of human development.

22. We are indebted to Nahum Chandler for this reference also; see n. 19 above.

23. Sinclair (1977:55) also notes here that early African explorers imitated the first "discoverers" of America in portraying the savage as both a beastly barbar-

ian and an innocent babe in the wilderness; it was an ambiguity that would later express itself in Kipling's popular depiction of the natives of empire as "half-devil and half-child" (see Bradley 1976:89; Brantlinger 1985:178).

24. For further discussion, see Sypher (1942:108) and Fairchild (1928:37).

25. See, for example, Dodd's "The African Prince" (1749, reprinted in several collections and in the *Lady's Poetical Magazine* of 1781), and Letitia Landon's poem of the same title (quoted by Fairchild 1928:289).

26. See especially Day and Bicknell's *The Dying Negro* (1775) and Colman's *Inkle and Yarico* (1788).

27. The phrase is from the title of Clarkson's *Essay on the Slavery and Commerce of the Human Species, Particularly the African* (1816), a translation of his Latin dissertation which was awarded first prize at the University of Cambridge in 1785.

F O U R

1. Strictly speaking, we should qualify the term "the [Southern] Tswana" every time we use it. After all, the label was itself a product of the process of ethnic group formation under the impact of colonialism. To do this, however, would make our narrative almost unreadable.

2. These accounts have focused primarily on the Tshidi-Rolong (Tshidi) polity. See, for example, J. Comaroff (1985); J.L. Comaroff (1973, 1987a); Comaroff and Comaroff (n.d.). Analyses of the Tshidi sociocultural order of later periods are to be found in J.L. Comaroff (n.d., 1982) and Comaroff and Roberts (1981). For writings on other aspects of Southern Tswana culture and society, see the bibliography in Schapera, *The Tswana*, especially the latest editions.

3. The sources used here are discussed in the references annotated in n. 2, as well, of course, as in chapter 1. We repeat that we rely mainly on the accounts of early missionaries, explorers, and travelers, many of whom will become familiar figures as we proceed. Obviously, these writings recorded events and observations whose significance for a modern understanding of Tswana society and history were not appreciated by their authors. Nonetheless, with hindsight and a different analytic perspective, they yield a fine-grained description of the Southern Tswana world in the nineteenth century. Our interpretation of this material is also informed by our own fieldwork among the Tshidi—although we are well aware that ethnographic research does not, of itself, equip anthropologists with the ability to "read" the social arrangements and cultural categories of an earlier period. (Nor can it establish which of those arrangements and categories were undergoing transformation and which were being reproduced at the time.) But, we believe, just as a historical imagination enriches ethnography, so an ethnographic sensibility may enrich historiography.

4. Note that Maggs (1976a, 1976b), who has done extensive archeological work on the Sotho-Tswana peoples, does not take issue with Legassick's reconstruction (see 1976a:287). Nor is this surprising. For all the great advances in

South African archeology over the past twenty years, little definitive new material has become available on the early social and political organization of these peoples: recall Hall's (1987:13) admission, quoted in chapter 1, that "the finer details are still a blur." In his own discussion of (precontact) Tswana social life, in fact, Maggs (1976a:276ff.) relies on the published accounts of missionaries and explorers—and on the first generation of ethnographers, most notably Schapera.

5. Willoughby ([1899]:1). For earlier comments to the same effect, see Burchell (1824:2,552f.), Lichtenstein (1973:74f.); Moffat (1842:309, 254f.), Mackenzie (1871:501f.), and especially Livingstone (1857:20–27). A parenthetic note about sources is in order here: although never a missionary among Southern Tswana, Willoughby intended his published comments on topics of ethnographic interest to apply to *all* Tswana, unless otherwise specified; in his writings, in fact, he was always careful to record regional variations in cultural practices. Willougby was well qualified to make such comparative statements, since he knew almost as much about the Tlhaping and Rolong as he did about the Ngwato, the Kwena, and the Kgatla. Not only was he an active member of a group of evangelists centered on Kuruman, but he had read the extensive accounts written by his brethren in that part of the region. For many years, too, he was head of Tiger Kloof Native Institution, situated in the heart of southern Bechuanaland.

6. See Brown (1931:285, 1926:79, 87) for evidence of nineteenth-century Tswana usages in respect of chiefship and the law. On the place of the chiefship at the apex of the polity, see, for example, Burchell (1824:2,347f.) and Barrow (1806:398f.), although Moffat (1842), Livingstone (1857), and many others also contain rich descriptions.

7. See, for example, Brown (1931:223); also Mackenzie (1871:368).

8. J. Campbell, Klaarwater, 24 July 1813 [CWM, LMS Incoming Letters (South Africa), 5-2-D]; also (1822:2,60).

9. These are our terms, of course; they are drawn from the modern anthropological lexicon. For evidence of existing structural arrangements, albeit described in different words, see, for example, J. Read, Matslakoo River, 20 May 1817 [CWM, LMS Incoming Letters (South Africa), 7-2-A]; Moffat (1842:388ff.); Livingstone (1857:17f.); Campbell (n.d., 1822:1,253ff.). Later in the century, for a variety of historical reasons, wards were grouped into sections in some chiefdoms. (For a detailed historical ethnography of the formation of wards and sections in one community, see J.L. Comaroff 1973; for more general discussion of sections, see Schapera 1938:24–28, 101ff.)

10. Wards, it seems from nineteenth-century genealogical records, might also contain matrilateral kin and affines, as well as immigrants placed in them by a chief; see J.L. Comaroff (1973; also Schapera 1952). Note too that *kgotla* appears not to have been a universal term for "ward"; some Tswana used *kgoro* ("gate"). Kinsman (1980:2) says that the Tlhaping word was *motse* (cf. Setiloane 1976:22), but Campbell (1822:2,152), an acute observer, recorded *coatlaai* (*kgotla*), and we see no reason to doubt him—especially since Livingstone (1857:17) also used *kotla*. *Kgotla*

has many other referents; among them, the chief's court, a group of agnatic kin and, in inflected form, a political council.

11. Lest it be thought that genealogical reckoning is a modern mode of representation in Africa—or purely an anthropological invention—Livingstone (1857: 17) noted its ubiquity among Tswana very early on. "Strangers," he says, were quick to recite their "genealogical trees" to him, in order to give him a sense of who they were; typically, too, they took pains to stress their closeness to the chief.

12. On sorcery (and agnation), see, for example, Campbell (1822:1,314–16); Holub (1881:1,333f.); Mackenzie (1883:236); Brown (1926:134f., 152f.). Moffat (1842) and Mackenzie (1871, 1883), among many others, give useful descriptions of agnatic conflict at different times and places.

13. In cultural perspective, of course, it does not matter what proportion of households were polygamous. The principles on which these households were built applied as well to monogamous ones, save that the latter had only one house; indeed, as far as we can tell, such families seem to have been regarded as incomplete rather than as differently structured. In the colonial period, when Tswana began to practice serial monogamy, they tended to speak of it in exactly the same way as they had done earlier of polygamy (Comaroff and Roberts 1977).

14. This is a recurrent theme in the mythology of Southern Tswana peoples: at the dawn of history, especially in early chiefly families, full siblings always acted together while half-brothers fought over position and property (see e.g., J.L. Comaroff 1973:ch.2). The documentary record makes the same point. With few exceptions, the fraternal disputes recorded in such sources as Moffat (1842), Burchell (1824), Livingstone (1857), Philip (1828), Broadbent (1865), and Mackenzie (1871, 1883)—not to mention the mission archives—were between men of different houses. Later this was to be formalized in Tswana law: the rules governing status and succession made it possible for half-brothers to contest their relative seniority; but rank *within* a house was given by sex and age, and was above negotiation (J.L. Comaroff 1978; Comaroff and Roberts 1981:ch.2).

15. The mother's brother-sister's child bond has been exhaustively covered in the literature. For a classical account, albeit written much later, see Schapera (1938). Here we are concerned only with the general nature of the bond and its broader cultural salience.

16. The passive voice here is deliberate: unlike men, who married (*nyala*), women were *taken* in marriage (*nyalwa*).

17. Elsewhere, based on an analysis of the history of Tshidi wards, we show that fraternal ties were also a basis of structural continuity: the incorporation of brothers and their descendants into larger administrative groups gave form to the polity over the long term, notwithstanding significant changes in the construction of the Southern Tswana world. Indeed, their sociopolitical hierarchy in the nineteenth century was *founded* on the complementary faces of agnation—antagonism within unity, division within continuity—born of brotherhood (see J.L. Comaroff 1973).

18. Our own ethnographic research indicates that, among those Southern Tswana who continued to cattle-link siblings in the twentieth century, bridewealth received for a woman was rarely, if ever, used for her brother's marriage. But people still spoke as if it could be, and was, put to this use.

19. Note that, in so enabling males to act in the public domain, females disabled themselves as social actors. Cattle were exchanged against rights in women, but women had no control over the values they signified. We shall return to the topic of cattle and gender again below; see also Comaroff and Comaroff (1990).

20. This section relies for its evidence on Molema (n.d., 1966), the notes of the late Professor Z.K. Matthews, and data analyzed in J.L. Comaroff (1973:ch.5). For more recent studies of Tswana marriage, see, for example, Schapera (1940, 1950, 1957, 1963); Matthews (1940); J.L. Comaroff (1980); Comaroff and Comaroff (1981); Comaroff and Roberts (1977, 1981:ch.5).

21. Those unfamiliar with the structural logic of endogamous marriage will find a basic explanation in Murphy and Kasdan (1959, 1967).

22. We have explained the structural bases of these countervailing tendencies, and their connection to marriage practices, elsewhere; for example, in Comaroff and Roberts (1981); J.L. Comaroff (1982); Comaroff and Comaroff (n.d.).

23. A few useful wordlists were included in early reports (e.g., Burchell 1824: vol.2 and Lichtenstein 1930:vol.2), and several missionaries also noted Setswana terms in passing. But systematic language texts only began to be published later in the century.

24. The earliest version of Brown's *Secwana Dictionary* known to us was issued by the LMS in South Africa in 1895; the 1931 edition, which we annotate and to which we refer frequently, is a slightly revised version of the same volume.

25. The firsthand evidence for this is very strong: see, for example, Bain (1949:55); Lichtenstein (1973:76f.); Solomon (1855:44); Campbell (1813:184, 1822:2,207–15); Moffat (1842:398f.).

26. For a sample of the voluminous evidence on clientage and non-Tswana serfdom during this period, see Lichtenstein (1973:66f.); Burchell (1824:2,346, 358, 523); Campbell (1822:1,63–64); Moffat (1842:8ff.); Mackenzie (1871: 128ff.).

27. On the social value of cattle, see, for example, Brown (1926:92f.). Campbell (1822:2,210f.) records a telling vignette about a man who, found guilty of theft, was put to death because he had no cattle with which to make restitution; his two more fortunate accomplices were spared their lives.

28. "Country" here refers to agricultural holdings—fields and cattle posts— not the bush (*naga*). The latter, as we saw earlier, was taken to be fraught with danger, and was to be avoided at any cost.

29. For an analysis of these mechanisms, see J.L. Comaroff (1975). Primary data on the negotiability of chiefly power, and its expression in public discourse, are

to be found in Solomon (1855:46); Campbell (1822,1:138, 288, 314; 2:6, 57, 154); Moffat (1842:248f., 289, 389).

30. H. Williams, Molepolole, 1894 [CWM, LMS South Africa Reports, 2–4].

31. This characterization, clearly, is ideal-typical. It is based, however, on a close reading of the evidence on the workings of Southern Tswana political economy over the long run. Historical instances are easily found for each of the situations described: see Molema (1951, 1966); J.L. Comaroff (1973); Shillington (1985).

32. See J.L. Comaroff (1973:ch.5, 6) for an analysis based on Campbell (n.d.:51, 1815:190), Mackenzie (1871:371ff., 1883:225ff.), and Moffat (1842: passim).

33. See, for example, Smith (1939:1,408) and Burchell (1824:2,347f.); but all the early missionaries comment at length on this.

34. Historical evidence suggests that the Sotho-Tswana term for "supreme being" (*modimo*) was an impersonal noun formed by adding the singular (class 3) prefix *mo* to the *-dima* stem (Moffat 1842:260–62; Smith 1950a:118). In modern Setswana, the personalized supreme being is often taken to be the singular of *badimo*, the ancestors.

35. The Catholic missions, by contrast, were later to accord the ancestors something like the status of local saints (J. Comaroff 1974).

36. In this respect, the term *modimo* contrasts interestingly with the Zulu *thixo*, which comes from "to appear."

37. For details of these rites, see, among others, Willoughby (1928:ch.3); Mackenzie (1871:ch.19); J. Comaroff (1985:ch.4).

38. This brief summary discussion of initiation rites is drawn from the detailed account provided in J. Comaroff (1985:85ff.).

39. Language (1943) recorded such an effort among the Tlhaping in the 1940's, and a version of the rite was revived among the Kgatla in postindependence Botswana (Grant 1984). We witnessed *bogwêra* ourselves among the Tshidi in the early 1970's. In chapter 7 we shall return to the struggle between the chiefs and the missions over initiation.

40. For primary evidence in support of this contention, see Moffat's (1842: 388) description of the Tshidi-Rolong capital at Pitsane.

41. Another small point: it is not clear to us why he chose to use "confederation" to describe the large Tswana polities of the eighteenth century. Aside from the conceptual problems raised by the term, there seems to be little reason not to refer to these polities as chiefdoms.

42. Wilson (1969a:176) notes, however, that it is not clear whether the chiefs benefited directly from the metal trade, the evidence on the issue being inconclusive.

43. According to Lichtenstein (1930:2,409), all Tswana knew of one an-

other, and there was frequent visiting among the royals of the different chiefdoms. However, he makes contradictory statements as to whether Tswana knew of other Bantu-speakers. In one place (1930:2,407), for example, he says that they were not familiar with the "Koossa" (Xhosa); yet, two pages later, we are told that the latter traded with the Macquini (Bakwena), the "most numerous [Tswana] tribe."

44. There are many examples of enduring alliances between Tswana chiefdoms—among them, the early nineteenth-century accord between the Tlhaping and Ratlou-Rolong, and, later, that between the Ngwaketse and Tshidi-Rolong.

45. Barrow (1801–04, 1806). For a critical response, see Lichtenstein (1973: 79); cf. also Legassick (1969b:109), who attributes the rise in warfare to intra-regional relations.

46. As Cobbing (1988:487, 490) explains, *difaqane* and *mfecane* were neologisms invented by white historians earlier in this century; they appear to have no roots in any African language, although they were obviously meant to approximate vernacular terms. While their original denotations were slightly different, the two terms have come to be used synonymously for the "[mythical] cataclysmic period of black-on-black destruction in the era of Shaka" (1988:487).

47. The rise of the Zulu state, itself a matter of considerable debate, has been explained in terms of, among other things, rising population pressure (Gluckman 1940; Omer-Cooper 1966); contact with whites (Bryant 1929); chiefly efforts to gain control over trade (Wilson 1959); the reconstruction of political culture (Walter 1969); and ecological factors (Guy 1980); see Thompson (1969b) for an overview. Cobbing's (1988) recent re-analysis of *mfecane*, to the extent that it is correct, adds yet further complication to an already vexed conundrum.

48. Cobbing (1988:492f.) claims that LMS evangelists, notably Moffat and Melville, were the "instigators and organizers" of at least one major *difaqane* battle: the hostilities at Dithakong in 1823, allegedly between the "Mantatees" (Tlokwa) and the combined forces of the Griqua, the Tlhaping, and the mission. In his re-analysis of the processes and parties involved in this "war," Cobbing suggests that the goal of the churchmen—heavily disguised in their accounts for fear of sanction by the Society—was to collect slaves for sale at the Cape. He also rejects the usual view that the Tlokwa were the aggressors, arguing that "Mantatees" was the collective name given to the (ethnically unidentified) victims of this glorified slave raid. We are not convinced. Not only is the evidence ambiguous, but this interpretation simply does not fit the pattern of historical relations—let alone the motives and machinations—among either the colonizers or the colonized at the time. It also would have us believe that there existed a baroque conspiracy among Europeans whom we know to have been bitterly antagonistic toward one another.

49. R. Hamilton, Kuruman, 25 April 1825 [CWM, LMS Incoming Letters (South Africa), 9-3-B].

50. See n. 48 above. This is the attack—or, rather, the slave raid—of 1823 that Moffat is said, by Cobbing (1988:492f.), to have organized.

F I V E

An earlier version of this chapter, with an additional section, was published in the *Journal of Historical Sociology* 1/1 (1988):6–32.

1. J. Campbell, Klaarwater, 26 July 1813 [CWM, LMS Incoming Letters (South Africa), 5-2-D]; our emphasis.

2. Such popular stories of adventure, romance, and scientific exploration sometimes borrowed directly from the mission literature. A remarkable example is Jules Verne's *The Adventures of Three Englishmen and Three Russians in South Africa.* Set in 1854, it leans heavily upon the writings of Livingstone (as well, perhaps, as those of Campbell and Moffat). Its protagonists, a team of European astronomers, follow closely the route into the interior charted by evangelical narratives. They even employ the trusty "bushman" who is said to have guided the good doctor during his travels.

3. In chapter 2 we noted the connection between the bourgeois ideology of selfhood and biography as a narrative genre; we also observed that missionary biography—an especially powerful expression of this ideology—was to become a model for the civilizing mission in Africa. For further discussion in the same spirit, see Gusdorf (1980:29), who argues that autobiography is "peculiar to Western man" and his particular consciousness of self, adding that "autobiography . . . has been of good use in [the] systematic conquest of the universe."

4. J. Campbell, Klaarwater, 26 July 1813 [CWM, LMS Incoming Letters (South Africa), 5-2-D].

5. The *John Williams*, most famous of the LMS vessels, sailed the route to the South Seas and was twice sunk and raised.

6. See, for example, Gaunt (1906:1, 15).

7. S. Broadbent, Matlwasse, 8 June 1823 [WMMS, South Africa Correspondence, 300].

8. The appeal of *The Pilgrim's Progress* as a model for the African missions may have been increased by the fact that its hero, Christian, betrayed Bunyan's own background—which was very similar to that of our Nonconformists. He was, notes James Turner (1980:91f.), a "despised itinerant manual worker excluded from landownership . . . yet . . . a householder and an artisan, descended from yeomen. . . ." (For further discussion of the social context of Bunyan and *The Pilgrim's Progress*, see Hill 1989:197ff. et passim).

9. J. Campbell, Klaarwater, 26 July 1813 [CWM, LMS Incoming Letters (South Africa), 5-2-D].

10. J. Campbell, Klaarwater, 26 July 1813 [CWM, LMS Incoming Letters (South Africa), 5-2-D].

11. Hill (1989:91) notes the well-established salience of this opposition among Puritan Dissenters in England during the time of John Bunyan (1628–88); for an-

other example, drawn from Protestant Primitivism in seventeenth-century America, see Hughes and Allen (1988:64).

12. J. Campbell, Klaarwater, 26 July 1813 [CWM, LMS Incoming Letters (South Africa), 5-2-D].

13. J. Campbell, Klaarwater, 26 July 1813 [CWM, LMS Incoming Letters (South Africa), 5-2-D].

14. Some ten years prior to this meeting, one of the first missionaries to the Tlhaping had been killed in a dispute with his local employees (du Plessis 1911: 112; see below).

15. J. Campbell, Klaarwater, 26 July 1813 [CWM, LMS Incoming Letters (South Africa), 5-2-D].

16. J. Campbell, Klaarwater, 26 July 1813 [CWM, LMS Incoming Letters (South Africa), 5-2-D].

17. J. Read, Lattakoo, 15 March 1817 [CWM, LMS Incoming Letters (South Africa), 7-1-C].

18. C. Sass, Campbell, 14 February 1823 [CWM, LMS Incoming Letters (South Africa), 9-1-A].

19. R. Moffat, Griquatown, 20 January 1825 [CWM, LMS Incoming Letters (South Africa), 9-1-C].

20. S. Broadbent, Matlwasse, 31 December 1823 [WMMS, South Africa Correspondence, 300].

21. S. Broadbent, Matlwasse, 8 June 1823 [WMMS, South Africa Correspondence, 300].

22. The phrase is taken from Mumford (1934:128).

23. J. Campbell, Klaarwater, 26 July 1813 [CWM, LMS Incoming Letters (South Africa), 5-2-D].

24. That such self-presentation was part of a coherent, ritualized strategy comes through in several of the evangelists' accounts. Witness what Campbell (1822:1,229) himself says of "Dining in Public" on his first visit to the Hurutshe capital of Kurreechane: "When dinner was put down, we extended the tent door as wide as possible, to allow as many as we could to have a view of our manner of eating. . . ."

25. For a similar encounter, see Broadbent (1865:48).

26. See, for instance, the first exchanges between the Methodists and the Seleka-Rolong; S. Broadbent, Matlwasse, 8 June 1823 [WMMS, South Africa Correspondence, 300].

27. There is not enough evidence to establish whether the Tswana attached the same elaborate symbolic significance to tobacco as did the Sotho (Murray 1975). But an elaborate material culture appears to have grown up around smoking and snuff-taking (Shaw 1974:112).

28. For a detailed account of the trade in beads between the early missionaries and the indigenous peoples of southern Africa, see Beck (1989:passim).

29. J. Archbell and T. Hodgson, Platberg, 22 October 1827 [WMMS, South Africa Correspondence (Cape), 302].

30. J. Read, Lattakoo, 15 March 1817 [CWM, LMS Incoming Letters (South Africa), 7-1-C].

31. J. Read, Lattakoo, 15 March 1817 [CWM, LMS Incoming Letters (South Africa), 7-1-C].

32. Note how spectacles serve as the key symbol of a rational-empiricist vision in Eco's *The Name of the Rose*.

33. R. Hamilton, Lattakoo, 15 May 1817 [CWM, LMS Incoming Letters (South Africa), 7-1-C].

34. J. Campbell, Klaarwater, 26 July 1813 [CWM, LMS Incoming Letters (South Africa), 5-2-D].

35. R. Moffat, Cape Town, 28 June 1817 [CWM, LMS Incoming Letters (South Africa), 7-3-A].

36. R. Moffat, Kuruman, 1 July–21 September 1824 [CWM, LMS South African Journals, 4].

37. Robert Gordon has drawn our attention to the fact that looking glasses were still being used as colonizing instruments in Papua New Guinea in the 1930's. Apparently "Australian Officers going out on patrols of first contact were specifically instructed to carry them" (personal communication).

38. For a perceptive discussion of some other African uses of mirrors, see Fernandez (1980).

39. T. Hodgson, Matlwasse, 12 January 1824 [WMMS, South Africa Correspondence, 300].

40. S. Broadbent, Matlwasse, 8 June 1823 [WMMS, South Africa Correspondence, 300].

41. J. Read, Lattakoo, 15 March 1817 [CWM, LMS Incoming Letters (South Africa), 7-1-C]. What Tswana might have meant by "God" is unclear; although the whites had already come to identify *modimo* as the vernacular term for the universal deity, their notions of their own supreme being remained implicit and impersonal. See S. Broadbent, Matlwasse, 8 June 1823 [WMMS, South Africa Correspondence, 300].

42. R. Hamilton, Kuruman, 1818–19 [CWM, South African Journals, 3].

43. J. Campbell, Klaarwater, 27 July 1813 [CWM, LMS Incoming Letters (South Africa), 5-2-D].

44. S. Broadbent, Matlwasse, 8 June 1823 [WMMS, South Africa Correspondence, 300].

45. Praise poem from the reign of Chief Lentswe of the Kgatla (1875–1924); in Schapera (1965:94).

46. R. Hamilton, Lattakoo, 15 May 1817 [CWM, LMS Incoming Letters (South Africa), 7-1-C].

47. R. Moffat, Kuruman, 17 May–26 November 1821 [CWM, LMS South African Journals, 3].

48. Dr. Waugh, London, 13 October 1817 [CWM, LMS South Africa Correspondence, 7-3-A].

49. J. Read, New Lattakoo, 5 September 1817 [CWM, LMS Incoming Letters (South Africa), 7-3-A]. Note that "New Lattakoo" was soon to become known as Kuruman. But, for a while after the establishment of the station there, the site was dubbed "*New* Lattakoo" in order to distinguish it from "(Old) Lattakoo" (Dithakong), Mothibi's earlier capital. As we shall see in chapter 6, this was part of a struggle to gain control over the context in which the evangelical encounter was to take place.

50. S. Broadbent, Matlwasse, 8 June 1823 [WMMS, South Africa Correspondence, 300].

51. S. Broadbent, Matlwasse, 31 March 1824 [WMMS, South Africa Correspondence, 300].

S I X

1. Note that we speak here of official policy only. We do not mean to imply—anywhere in this account—that those who staffed the British administration were united on such matters of policy or political action. Quite the opposite: for much of the history of the Cape Colony, government circles were riven by internal factionalism and power struggles.

2. J. Read, Lattakoo, 8 March 1817 [CWM, LMS South African Journals, 3]; the quotation from Chief Mothibi immediately below comes from the same journal entry.

3. J. Read, Lattakoo, 14 March 1817 [CWM, LMS South African Journals, 3].

4. R. Hamilton, Lattakoo, 15 May 1817 [CWM, LMS Incoming Letters (South Africa), 7-1-C].

5. J. Read, Lattakoo, 15 March 1817 [CWM, LMS Incoming Letters (South Africa), 7-1-C].

6. J. Read, Lattakoo, 15 March 1817 [CWM, LMS Incoming Letters (South Africa), 7-1-C].

7. Interestingly, the Tlhaping leaders quickly concluded that the Europeans were more demanding of material resources than they themselves were. Mothibi, in replying to Read's urgings to move his capital, claimed that Dithakong (Lattakoo)

lacked sufficient water and trees for the *missionaries'* needs, not his own, and that the Kuruman river might better serve *them* (Moffat 1842:230).

8. R. Hamilton, Lattakoo, 15 May 1817 [CWM, LMS Incoming Letters (South Africa), 7-1-C]. For an explanation of the name "New Lithako" or "New Lattakoo," soon to be known as Kuruman, see chapter 5, n. 49.

9. J. Read, New Lattakoo, 5 September 1817 [CWM, LMS Incoming Letters (South Africa), 7-2-A].

10. J. Read, New Lattakoo, 5 September 1817 [CWM, LMS Incoming Letters (South Africa), 7-2-A].

11. J. Read, New Lattakoo, 5 September 1817 [CWM, LMS Incoming Letters (South Africa), 7-2-A].

12. See Mullaney (1988) for a detailed development of this notion in a very different historical context.

13. Mrs. Hamilton, New Lattakoo, 16 February 1818 [CWM, LMS Incoming Letters (South Africa), 7-3-A].

14. R. Hamilton, New Lattakoo, 17 February 1823 [CWM, LMS Incoming Letters (South Africa), 9-1-A].

15. Water has long been recognized to have had enormous social and symbolic significance for many of the peoples of southern Africa. As Robert Gordon has reminded us, it is more than sixty years since the publication of Hoernlé's (1923) remarkable essay on "The Expression of the Social Value of Water among the Naman of South-West Africa."

16. T. Hodgson, Platberg, 31 March 1827 [WMMS, South Africa Correspondence (Cape), 302].

17. T. Hodgson, Platberg, 31 March 1827 [WMMS, South Africa Correspondence (Cape), 302]; J. Archbell, Platberg, 16 March 1828 [WMMS, South Africa Correspondence (Cape), 302]; Moffat (1842:285f.).

18. R. Moffat, Cape Town, 20 July 1824 [CWM, LMS Incoming Letters (South Africa), 9-1-A].

19. T. Hodgson, Matlwasse, 12 June 1824 [WMMS, South Africa Correspondence, 300]; see also J. Comaroff (1985:139).

20. The perceptions of the missionaries on the subject are widely documented in their letters, journals, and publications; there are literally hundreds of texts that discuss rain and rainmakers. Even as late as 1900, the Rev. Brown devoted a good part of a long dispatch from Taung to the topic; J. Brown, Taung, 1900 [CWM, LMS South Africa Reports, 3–1]. In it he admitted that rainmaking was still actively practiced among the Southern Tswana. Brown was correct: despite frequent claims by the churchmen to the contrary, the rites persisted well into the colonial period (see Schapera 1971).

21. J. Archbell, Platberg, 20 March 1832 [WMMS, South Africa Correspondence (Albany), 303].

22. J. Read, New Lattakoo, 5 September 1817 [CWM, LMS Incoming Letters (South Africa), 7-2-A].

23. J. Freeman, Kuruman, 8 December 1849 [CWM, LMS Home Odds (Freeman Deputation 1849–50), 2-4-D].

24. See S. Broadbent, Matlwasse, 8 June 1823 [WMMS, South Africa Correspondence, 300]; T. Hodgson, Matlwasse, 1 January 1824 [WMMS, South Africa Correspondence, 300].

25. S. Broadbent, Matlwasse, 8 June 1823 [WMMS, South Africa Correspondence, 300]; T. Hodgson, Matlwasse, 1 January 1824 [WMMS, South Africa Correspondence, 300]; J. Archbell and T. Hodgson, Platberg, 22 October 1827 [WMMS, South Africa Correspondence (Cape), 302]; Hodgson (1977:113, 260).

26. W.C. Willoughby, Tiger Kloof, 29 January 1914 [CWM, LMS Incoming Letters (South Africa), 76–2].

27. These references are to *Bibela E E Boitshèpō* (1952), a revised and reprinted version of Moffat's original *Secwana (Chuana) Bible*. It is annotated in our bibliography under the British and Foreign Bible Society, its publishers. For a full inventory of the various Setswana versions of the Scriptures (as well as other publications) produced at Kuruman by Moffat and his brethren, see Bradlow (1987:28f.). It is a matter of note that the use of *badimo* for "demons" has survived all revisions of the Bible.

28. It would be interesting, in this respect, to make a systematic comparison between the Nonconformists among the Tswana and the Catholics in the Belgian Congo. However, the literature on the Congo is decidedly ambiguous. Fabian (1983b, 1986), for example, argues that evangelists there played a major part in the ideological domination of native peoples through their control over education and "spontaneous processes" of language reconstruction (specifically, the production of textual translations, vocabularies, and grammars). But Yates (1980:passim), speaking of the White Fathers, notes their lack of cooperation with the language policies of the colonial state and their disinterest in literacy. Their aim, she suggests, was to Christianize without westernizing. We are grateful to our student, Ron Kassimir, for directing us to this point in an excellent essay on the topic.

29. It has been pointed out to us that *madi* might have come from Arabic, presumably via Swahili (in which *mali* denotes wealth, property, or possessions). While we cannot be sure, the evidence suggests otherwise. The word does not appear in any of the vocabularies collected by the first white visitors, some of whom seem to have searched for signs of money (see Lichtenstein 1930:2,478f.; Burchell 1824:2,583f.). Burchell, in fact, notes that the beads considered by Tlhaping as currency were referred to as *sikhaka* (1824:2,407; Lichtenstein includes the same word, but writes it as *sehacha*). What is more, some missionary reports mention the earliest Tswana dealings in cash, typically transactions with Europeans accompanied by English-Setswana translation. By the middle of the century, *madi* begins to appear increasingly in LMS and WMMS evangelical texts (wordlists, newspapers,

and, later, dictionaries). All this, taken together, points overwhelmingly to the term being an anglicism.

30. Although both examples are taken from the ruling dynasty of the Tshidi-Rolong (see J.L. Comaroff 1973), they illustrate a very general principle of naming. Some children, however, were called after senior relatives, living or dead (see Schapera 1940:213); yet others, Tswana explained to us in telling of the past, were given unappealing names so that the ancestors would not find them attractive and take them prematurely. An infant was usually named when it emerged from the birthing hut with its mother after a one or two month period of seclusion. The designation most generally used was the one chosen by members of the agnatic group, but a baby was also given a name by its matrilateral kin, by which it would be known at their homestead.

31. W.C. Willoughby, Palapye, 17 December 1894 [CWM, LMS Incoming Letters (South Africa), 51-2-C].

32. J. Campbell, Klaarwater, 26 July 1813 [CWM, LMS Incoming Letters (South Africa), 5-2-D].

33. I. Hughes, Lattakoo, 17 December 1824 [CWM, LMS South African Journals, 4].

34. S. Broadbent, Matlwasse, 31 March 1824 [WMMS, South Africa Correspondence, 300]; Moffat (1842:xv); see also the biographical sketch of Livingstone in chapter 2.

35. J. Archbell, Platberg, 7 January 1828 [WMMS, South Africa Correspondence (Cape), 302].

36. S. Broadbent, Matlwasse, 31 March 1824 [WMMS, South Africa Correspondence, 300].

37. See n. 32. Also S. Broadbent, Matlwasse, 8 June 1823 [WMMS, South Africa Correspondence, 300]; Moffat (1842:226); cf. Burchell (1824:2,582–83).

38. J. Archbell, Platberg, 7 January 1828 [WMMS, South Africa Correspondence (Cape), 302].

39. We are indebted to Debra Spitulnik for this general observation about Southern Bantu noun classes (see Spitulnik 1986). Moffat clearly grappled with the logic of differentiation among those of Setswana. He noted (1842:260–61) that the "genius of the Sechwana language warrants us to expect a correspondence between the name and the thing designated." But he was distressed by the fact that, although the word *modimo* ("supreme being") belonged to a category of personal nouns, it seemed to be used by the Tswana in an impersonal sense (1842:261).

40. J. Archbell, Platberg, 7 January 1828 [WMMS, South Africa Correspondence (Cape), 302]; Moffat (1842:xiv).

41. J. Campbell, Klaarwater, 26 July 1813 [CWM, LMS Incoming Letters (South Africa), 5-2-D]; cf. Lichtenstein (1930:2,477). Interestingly, the portrayal of Sarwa ("bushmen") as the speakers of a subhuman language continues into the present, at least in some quarters. A recent article in the *Chicago Tribune* described

this language as "a series of clickings and clatterings that sound like a handful of pebbles rolling down a marble staircase" (5 April 1987, sec. 1, p. 6).

42. J. Archbell, Platberg, 3 November 1828 [WMMS, South Africa Correspondence (Cape), 302].

43. For descriptive purposes, we distinguish between (1) *setswana* [lower case, italicized], "Tswana culture" and, when used indigenously, "Tswana life-ways"; and (2) "Setswana" [upper case, roman], the Tswana language.

44. An early biography of Moffat, *A Life's Labours in South Africa* (1872:39), compiled by his publishers, qualifies Livingstone's observations on speech styles. The "purity and harmony" of the language was preserved in the towns, it says, "by means of . . . public meetings . . . and of festivals and ceremonials"; in more isolated settlements, by contrast, Setswana was markedly less well spoken. In the absence of supportive evidence, however, it is difficult to evaluate this statement.

45. W.C. Willoughby, Palapye, 23 September 1898 [CWM, LMS Incoming Letters (South Africa), 55-2-B].

46. W.C. Willoughby, Palapye, 23 September 1898 [CWM, LMS Incoming Letters (South Africa), 55-2-B].

47. W.C. Willoughby, Palapye, 23 September 1898 [CWM, LMS Incoming Letters (South Africa), 55-2-B].

48. T. Hodgson, Platberg, 19 March 1828 [WMMS, South Africa Correspondence (Cape), 302]; J. Archbell, 20 March 1832 [WMMS, South Africa Correspondence (Albany), 303].

49. T. Hodgson, Platberg, 18 August 1829 [WMMS, South Africa Correspondence (Cape), 302]; Moffat (1842:497, 509).

50. A.J. Wookey, Vryburg, 1909 [CWM, LMS South Africa Reports, 4–2].

51. W.C. Willoughby, Palapye, 23 September 1898 [CWM, LMS Incoming Letters (South Africa), 55-2-B].

52. See also J. Archbell, Platberg, 30 March 1830 [WMMS, South Africa Correspondence (Albany), 303].

53. J. Archbell and T. Hodgson, Platberg, 30 November 1827 [WMMS, South Africa Correspondence (Cape), 302]; T. Hodgson, Platberg, 19 March 1828 [WMMS, South Africa Correspondence (Cape), 302]; Moffat (1842:480, 497).

54. R. Price, Kuruman, 12 April 1888 [CWM, LMS Incoming Letters (South Africa), 45-3-A].

55. J.T. Brown, Kuruman, 1909 [CWM, LMS South Africa Reports, 4–2].

56. The Chief was Moremi of the Tawana in Ngamiland. See E. Lloyd, Shoshong, December 1887 [CWM, LMS Incoming Letters (South Africa), 44–6-B; day of writing not given].

57. The evangelists constantly took pains to elicit admissions from the Southern Tswana that their own ways were inferior to those of Christianity (see e.g., Moffat 1842:246f.). Among other things, such admissions were regarded as a sign

that the message of civilization and universal truth was beginning to have its desired effect.

58. Note that the *Missionary Magazine and Chronicle* was a section, devoted chiefly to the concerns of the LMS, in the monthly *Evangelical Magazine and Missionary Chronicle*. Monro's essay is annotated accordingly in our bibliography.

S E V E N

1. The point has been made often in respect of African missionaries (see e.g., Beidelman 1982; or, for a particular case, Prins 1980:210 on the Paris Mission to the Lozi); although, as the "missionary imperialist" thesis correctly suggests (Dachs 1972; cf. Etherington 1978; Cope 1979), and many historical studies show (see Rotberg 1965:55f. for a striking case), the separation of church and state was not everywhere sustained in practice.

2. Of course, these were not the only "spheres" distinguished in the contemporary European worldview. As Wood (1981:66–67) reminds us, the "rigid conceptual separation of the 'economic' and the 'political' which has served *bourgeois* ideology so well" was also an integral part of "the 'fetishism' of capitalist categories."

3. LMS Directors, London, 31 January 1815 [CWM, LMS South Africa Correspondence, 6-1-A]. Recall that Somerset was averse to the presence of the Nonconformist missions in the Colony (above, chapter 1).

4. J. Freeman, Bloemfontein, 2 February 1850 [CWM, LMS Home Odds (Freeman Deputation 1849–50), 2-5-A].

5. On southern Africa, cf., among others, Schapera (1958); Etherington (1978:116); Bundy (1979:41f.); Cochrane (1987:38f.); Cuthbertson (1987); also Prins (1980) on the Lozi. Recall, too, our discussion in chapter 1 above.

6. We used a similar method, albeit in abbreviated form, in Comaroff and Comaroff (1986).

7. See, for a notable instance, Mackenzie's (1871:378) statements to the Ngwato ruler, Sekgoma. Other examples will be found below.

8. Cf. the passage in Achebe's *Things Fall Apart* in which newly arrived evangelists in West Africa enter a village and immediately ask for "the King" (1959: 153). Early missionary practice in this respect has left its mark on African historical consciousness, literary and lay alike, all over the continent.

9. J. Read, New Lattakoo, 5 September 1817 [CWM, LMS Incoming Letters (South Africa), 7-2-A].

10. R. Hamilton, Kuruman, 12 August 1820 [CWM, LMS South African Journals, 3].

11. See, for example, J. Read, Lattakoo, 1 January 1817 [CWM, LMS South African Journals, 3 (also quoted by Dachs 1972:648)]; Livingstone (1857:ch.1); Moffat (1842:284f.); Hodgson (1977:160–61).

12. Rotberg (1965:43) and Ekechi (1972:11) note much the same thing of Protestant missionaries in East and West Africa, respectively.

13. It is not surprising, therefore, that the missions were most acutely challenged by chiefs who were also famous rainmakers, perhaps the best example being Sechele of the Kwena (Livingstone 1857).

14. Cf., for example, Beidelman (1982:118) and Prins (1980:198) for similar reactions on the part of Protestant missionaries to the Kaguru and the Lozi, respectively.

15. Over the years a few of the Nonconformists began to see some virtue in reducing chiefly authority. John Mackenzie, of whom we shall say more later, was the most notable among them (Dachs 1972). Even he, however, was not unequivocal on the matter. Thus he took pains *not* to subvert the Ngwato ruler when he could have (1883:ch.9); wrote on occasion about the need to "stand by" Tswana sovereigns (e.g., J. Mackenzie, en route to Kuruman, 18 August 1876 [CWM, LMS Incoming Letters (South Africa), 38-3-C]); and often commented with regret on the erosion of their office (e.g., J. Mackenzie, Kuruman, 3 June 1878, enclosed with W. Ashton, Barkly Diamond Fields, 13 June 1878 [CWM, LMS Incoming Letters (South Africa), 39-3-B]). Note that Mackenzie is usually regarded as having been a "missionary imperialist" par excellence. On him more than anyone else is based the so-called "missionary imperialist" thesis (Dachs 1972)—according to which the evangelists allegedly called on the colonial government to break the power of chiefs, ever more so as they resisted the church (cf. also Cope 1979:3). This may have occurred among the Zulu (Etherington 1978:25f.) or the Pedi (Delius 1984:53 n.6, 1983). In the case of the Tswana, as we have said before (1986; above, chapter 1), the thesis is not so much wrong as too simple. Mackenzie's equivocations should warn us of that. So too should the fact that another notably "political" churchman, John Moffat, actively supported the chiefs where he could; see, for example, J. Moffat, Kuruman, 3 September 1878 [CWM, LMS Incoming Letters (South Africa), 39-3-C]; also Moffat (1921:207). And, if these examples are not enough to underscore the limitations of the thesis, the analysis in the present chapter should be.

16. Moffat, for example, reports that—long before the colonial government made itself felt in the interior—the presence of the LMS put an end to raiding between the Tlhaping and the Tshidi-Rolong; R. Moffat, Kuruman, 26 July 1824 [CWM, LMS South African Journals, 4].

17. For a graphic account of this struggle, see J. Ludorf, Thaba 'Nchu, 8 February 1853 [WMMS, South Africa Correspondence (Bechuana), 315]. For a full analysis of these precolonial rites, which occurred every three to five years, see J. Comaroff (1985:ch.4).

18. J. Archbell, Platberg, 27 May 1833 [WMMS, South Africa Correspondence (Albany), 303].

19. J. Archbell, Platberg, 27 May 1833 [WMMS, South Africa Correspondence (Albany), 303].

20. J. Ludorf, Thaba 'Nchu, 8 February 1853 [WMMS, South Africa Correspondence (Bechuana), 315]. In 1888 Wookey went as far as to claim that, after the death of some of the novitiates, their flesh was eaten by the others; A.J. Wookey, Molepolole, 30 October 1888 [CWM, LMS Incoming Letters (South Africa), 45-3-E]. And so cannibalism was added to the long list of perversions attributed to initiation rites.

21. J. Archbell, Platberg, 27 May 1833 [WMMS, South Africa Correspondence (Albany), 303].

22. J. Ludorf, Thaba 'Nchu, 8 February 1853 [WMMS, South Africa Correspondence (Bechuana), 315].

23. J. Archbell, Platberg, 27 May 1833 [WMMS, South Africa Correspondence (Albany), 303].

24. Native Conference of the South African District Circuit of 1907 [W.C. Willoughby Papers, Selly Oak Colleges Library (U.K.), Box 14: General Files on Children, Education and Puberty].

25. The LMS and WMMS missionaries tended to give detailed account, in their correspondence, of the social identities of their converts; see, for example, the letter from Moffat et al. included in the unsigned column entitled "Lattakoo Mission, in South Africa" in *The Missionary Magazine and Chronicle* 16:40–42 (in *The Evangelical Magazine and Chronicle* of January 1838).

26. S.M. Molema, a doctor and historian, was himself a leading member of the Methodist congregation and was heavily involved in the politics of church and chiefship during the twentieth century.

27. J. Archbell, Platberg, 27 May 1833 [WMMS, South Africa Correspondence (Albany), 303].

28. The phrase first appears in the letter referred to in n. 25.

29. Methodism among the Tshidi had its roots in the mission set up by Broadbent and Hodgson and carried on by their successors at Thaba 'Nchu, where the Rolong groupings had taken refuge during *difaqane* (chapters 4 and 5). When the Tshidi returned to their own territory, they were joined by Rev. Joseph Ludorf, of whom we shall hear more. Molema had been the first royal convert, having entered the church at Thaba 'Nchu, and became its earliest "native" leader. After conflict with the Boers broke out in 1851, and Montshiwa decided to go into exile again, Ludorf left (see below), entrusting his flock to Molema. The events described here took place once he had gone, during and after the period of exile. For accounts of this period in Tshidi history, see Matthews (1945); Molema (1951, 1966).

30. The most accessible version of the story is in a letter from Ross to the *Evangelical Magazine and Missionary Chronicle* (1858:56–57).

31. In this respect, the Nonconformists acted much like Protestant missionaries elsewhere in Africa. See, among very many examples, Eiselen (1934:69); Ekechi (1972:36f.); Beidelman (1982:25).

32. Much of Ludorf's letter (of 29 June 1863) was published in *Wesleyan Missionary Notices*, 3d ser., no. 120 (December 1863):203–07.

33. This is confirmed by several letters from Ludorf published in the *Wesleyan Missionary Notices*; see, for example, his letter of 12 October 1863 (3d ser., no. 130 [October 1864]:160, 163).

34. In a review of J. Comaroff (1985), Shillington (1987:323), who appears to read the history of Tshidi religion largely in terms of external political and material pressures, says that "1882 was hardly the moment when 'Methodism as a "state church" was formally established.'" Since he elaborates no further, and all the evidence suggests the contrary, we see no reason to revise earlier statements.

35. Two years later, interestingly, Price referred to the LMS at Molepolole as the "state church" of the Kwena [CWM, LMS Incoming Letters (South Africa), 42-3-D].

36. H. Barton, Kimberley, 12 December 1880 [Molema-Plaatje Papers (University of the Witwatersrand), Chief Montshiwa Correspondence, Ba 4].

37. See Linden (1977) for a similar analysis.

38. Molema (1951:59) reminds us that, after Chief Sechele of the Kwena was converted by Livingstone in 1848, all official functions held to be incompatible with Christianity were overseen by his younger brother, Kgosidintsi. (Sechele later became a "backslider.") Kgosidintsi, adds Ludorf (1864:161), was "a bitter enemy of the Gospel."

39. There is an enormous archival record on relations between Khama and Hepburn. For just one interesting statement on this "affair," see J. Brown, Taung, 29 February 1896 [CWM, LMS Incoming Letters (South Africa), 53-1-B]. Brown ends his letter by noting, rather acidly, that while the LMS contested the union of church and state in Britain, it was forced to "swallow it" in the South African interior.

40. See, for one example (denied, unconvincingly, by the LMS evangelists), J. Brown, Taung, 12 January 1889 [CWM, LMS Incoming Letters (South Africa), 46-1-A].

41. J.T. Brown, Kuruman, 16 June 1899, [CWM, LMS Incoming Letters (South Africa), 56-2-A].

42. For other, especially vivid, examples of missionaries caught between the church and the chiefship, see J. Brown, Taung, 12 January 1889 [CWM, LMS Incoming Letters (South Africa), 46-1-A]; R. Price, Molepolole, 29 December 1884 [CWM, LMS Incoming Letters (South Africa), 42-3-D]. A somewhat similar process occurred among the Pedi of the Eastern Transvaal, who were evangelized by the Berlin Missionary Society. When in the 1870's BMS evangelists became embroiled in conflict between the Pedi and the Boers, they managed to alienate both non-Christians and many of their own converts; see Mminele (1983); Delius (1983); Moila (1987).

43. The Great Trek, which began in 1836, is central to the political mythology and historical consciousness of white South Africans (Thompson 1985). As we said in chapter 1, it started when the European antecedents of the modern Afrikaner population, mainly small farmers, left the Cape to escape the British government, their disaffection brought to a head by the emancipation of slaves in the Colony. (Since the Trek is described in almost every history of South Africa, we do not annotate it here.)

44. As Legassick (1969a:584f.) has pointed out, Griqua dominance in the region was already on the wane. But the Tswana were in no position to notice this at the time.

45. Legassick (1969a:585f.) provides the best analysis. For a brief summary, from the perspective of the LMS, see Lovett (1899:1,591f.).

46. Philip's best known critics, among historians, are Corey (1919) and Theal (e.g., 1891:344ff.). The latter, who rather overestimated Philip's political influence, took delight in echoing Lord Charles Somerset's view of "the insidiousness of this dangerous man's character," his "disgusting evasion and perversion of the facts." Outside of church circles, the most ardent champion of the missionary has been Macmillan (1927, 1929, 1936a, 1936b, 1936c).

47. Philip's campaigns in England, and his relations with the abolitionist lobby (especially with Fowell Buxton), are well covered, if in a somewhat hagiographic fashion, in Macmillan's writings (see n. 46). For a very different interpretation, see Theal (1891:346f.).

48. The antipathy to which the attack gave rise led to, among other things, a libel suit prosecuted by one such "functionary," William Mackay. Accused by Philip of grave misconduct, Mackay was awarded substantial damages by the Cape Supreme Court. The evangelist in turn alleged that the trial, having been heard in a colonial tribunal, was not fair. In missionary and philanthropic circles, his case was sympathetically regarded: his debt was paid by subscription in England, and the LMS held him blameless (Clinton 1937:145).

49. Earlier, in 1825, he had been less sure about the absorption of the Griqua into the Colony; see, for example, Macmillan (1936c:308).

50. J. Philip, Cape Town, 12 May 1820; quoted by Macmillan (1929:39). See also Philip (1828:2,227).

51. See Legassick (1969a:586–87, also ns. 3–4) for discussion and annotation of the documentary record.

52. Insofar as such things are measurable, the Methodists probably had a slightly more coherent political identity than did the LMS, their society having taken stands on social and public issues back home. However, the WMMS was also divided by internal conflicts similar to that between Philip and Moffat (see below). Our point is that these were consistent patterns, not idiosyncratic events.

53. Nineteenth-century Griqua history was dominated by the effort of white settlers, covetous of Griqua land, to absorb the old frontier territory into the ex-

panding colonies of the interior, although the discovery of diamonds in the late 1860's was to complicate the story a great deal. Histories, both scholarly (e.g., Ross 1976) and amateur (e.g., Halford n.d.), agree on one thing: that this process of absorption was "a tragedy, *sensu strictu*" (Ross 1976:1) in that it led to the final destruction of the Griqua people.

54. J. Freeman, Mabotsa, 25 December 1849 [CWM, LMS Home Odds (Freeman Deputation 1849–50), 2-4-D].

55. The events surrounding the Sand River (1952) and Bloemfontein (1854) Conventions are fully documented in histories of South Africa; it is unnecessary either to describe or to annotate them here.

56. R. Moffat, Kuruman, 1 October 1849 [CWM, LMS Africa Odds (Philip Papers), 3-2-A]. Several of Ludorf's letters use strikingly similar phrases, many of them evocative of abolitionist rhetoric; see, for example, J. Ludorf, Motito, 16 October 1852 [WMMS, South Africa Correspondence (Bechuana), 315].

57. Although elsewhere (1857:35), in a different rhetorical mood, Livingstone is careful to point out that "Boer simply means 'farmer,' and is not synonymous with our word boor."

58. J. Freeman, Kuruman, 14 May 1849 [CWM, LMS Home Odds (Freeman Deputation 1849–50), 2-4-B].

59. See, for just a few examples, variously phrased, J. Freeman, Mabotsa, 25 December 1849 [CWM, LMS Home Odds (Freeman Deputation 1849–50), 2-4-D]; J. Freeman, Bloemfontein, 2 February 1850 [CWM, LMS Home Odds (Freeman Deputation 1849–50), 2-5-A]; Livingstone (1974:15); Ludorf (1854:194).

60. J. Ludorf, Lotlakane, 1 March 1852 [WMMS, South Africa Correspondence (Bechuana), 315].

61. Shineberg (1961:61), quoting several impeccable sources, notes that the technical limitations of early firearms—shortage of range, inaccuracy, difficulty of reloading, high rate of misfire, vulnerability to climate, and so on—persisted well into the nineteenth century. These limitations often put European soldiers at the mercy of "native" forces, especially in fighting at close quarters. Thus, she adds (1961:80), in one South African frontier war, "it took some 80,000 [British] bullets to put 25 of the enemy *hors de combat*." All this simply underscores the observation that, to the Southern Tswana, the value of guns was as much symbolic as it was practical. Firearms stood less for a brute technology of death than it did for the multifaceted powers of the Europeans. For a brief history of weaponry in nineteenth-century South Africa, see Lategan (1971:515–36).

62. G. Christie for J. Philip, Cape Town, (undated) 1849 [CWM, LMS Home Odds (Freeman Deputation 1849–50), 2-1-B].

63. J. Ludorf, Thaba 'Nchu, 8 February 1853 [WMMS, South Africa Correspondence (Bechuana), 315].

64. W. Ashton, Kuruman, 5 July 1858 [CWM, LMS Incoming Letters (South Africa), 31-1-B]. The incident to which this letter refers occurred only months af-

ter all the mission families, except the Moffats, had withdrawn from Kuruman at the prospect of a Boer attack on the station; see W. Ashton, Kuruman, 5 May 1858 [CWM, LMS Incoming Letters (South Africa), 31-1-B]. Later that year settler commandoes attacked Taung, another Tswana capital and Christian center; see W. Aston, Kuruman, 7 September 1858 [CWM, LMS Incoming Letters (South Africa), 31-1-B]. We shall discuss these attacks again in volume 2.

65. W. Ashton, Kuruman, 25 July 1858 [CWM, LMS Incoming Letters (South Africa), 31-1-B].

66. Perhaps the most eloquent description of this new colonizing process is to be found in Ludorf's long letter to William Shaw of 16 October 1852, a document we cite often (e.g., above, n. 56).

67. J. Freeman, Kuruman, 14 May 1849 [CWM, LMS Home Odds (Freeman Deputation 1849–50), 2-4-B].

68. J. Freeman, Mabotsa, 25 December 1849 [CWM, LMS Home Odds (Freeman Deputation 1849–50), 2-4-D].

69. The handwritten word is indecipherable; "give," however, seems most likely.

70. The attack on the Kwena was part of the campaign of domination by the Transvaal over the Tswana communities along its western border. For accounts of this campaign, told from the Tswana perspective, see Molema (1951:ch.8, 1966: ch.6).

71. This period of Tshidi history, including the events surrounding the recruitment of Ludorf, are most fully documented in Molema (1966), Matthews (1945), and J.L. Comaroff (1973); see also n. 29 above.

72. Ludorf's writings are fragmentary on just this point. Theal (1893:487f.) offers a version; but, apart from not specifying his sources, he was so concerned to prove the goodwill of the Boers—especially in land negotiations—that his account is hopelessly selective.

73. J. Ludorf, Motito, 16 October 1852 [WMMS, South Africa Correspondence (Bechuana), 315]. Most of the primary material for the following passage, including the extended quotation below, comes from this letter.

74. J. Ludorf, Thaba 'Nchu, 8 February 1853 [WMMS, South Africa Correspondence (Bechuana), 315].

75. In Setswana, as Ludorf's translation implies, the same word, *lobaka*, is used for both "space" and "time." This semantic elision is significant in the construction of Tswana historical consciousness (Comaroff and Comaroff 1987).

76. In the 1850's and 1860's Ludorf served not only the Seleka at Thaba 'Nchu, where his work was distinguished by its enormous energy, but also the Tshidi in exile at Moshaneng, whom he visited often.

77. Shillington (1985:ch.2) examines the discovery of diamonds, and the subsequent conflicts, from a Southern Tswana (or, more precisely, Tlhaping) perspec-

tive. He does not discuss Ludorf, however, except for one passing mention. For two important recent studies of the rise of the Kimberley diamond fields, see Worger (1987) and Turrell (1987).

78. On the implications of the "rush of traders and speculators" into Tlhaping territory, see W. Ashton, Lekhatlong, 6 July 1869 [CWM, LMS Incoming Letters (South Africa), 35-2-D].

79. See any standard South African history for an account of the relevant events. Matthews (1945:19) and Molema (1966:65f.) tell of their place in the historical consciousness of Southern Tswana.

80. It should be noted, however, that the Orange Free State did not itself take part in the Bloemhof hearings, having claimed undisputed sovereignty over Griqualand.

81. A number of missionaries noted this in their letters of the period; see, for example, R. Giddy, Colesburg, 10 June 1870 [WMMS, South Africa Correspondence (Bechuana), 316]. For a particularly striking statement, albeit written some years later, see A. Wookey, Kuruman, 23 May 1884 [CWM, LMS Incoming Letters (South Africa), 42-3-C].

82. See, again, R. Giddy, Colesburg, 10 June 1870 [WMMS, South Africa Correspondence (Bechuana), 316].

83. This is clear from Ludorf's letter to Arnot (8 November 1871), reproduced in Molema (1966:67).

84. This, too, was conveyed in a letter, written a week later (15 November) to a government personage, Sir Henry Barkly (see Molema 1966:67).

85. For an analysis of a comparable process in Zimbabwe, see Ranger (1988).

86. Of course, the fact that "the" Tswana had an ethnic identity constructed for them did not mean that they would immediately begin to act as one, let alone to submerge their internal differences. It is always a long, complicated step from the attribution of a collective identity to its invocation as the basis of political action—to ethnicity *für sich*, as it were (J.L. Comaroff 1987b).

87. See LMS Incoming Letters (South Africa) and WMMS South Africa Correspondence between 1871 and 1880. We rely heavily on this primary material for our summary of the events leading up to the uprisings of 1878 in the region.

88. I. Hughes, Griquatown, 12 June 1851 [CWM, LMS Incoming Letters (South Africa), 26-1-A].

89. J. Brown, Kuruman, 16 July 1878 [CWM, LMS Incoming Letters (South Africa), 36-3-C]. The version in the LMS archive is a newspaper cutting—without publication details given—under the title "Some Mative (sic) Difficulties."

90. A. Wookey, Kuruman, 3 September 1878 [CWM, LMS Incoming Letters (South Africa), 36-3-C].

91. J. Brown, Kuruman, 16 July 1878 [CWM, LMS Incoming Letters (South Africa), 39-3-C].

92. J. Mackenzie, Kuruman, 1 June 1878 [CWM, LMS Incoming Letters (South Africa), 39-3-B].

93. A. Wookey, Kuruman, 3 September 1878 [CWM, LMS Incoming Letters (South Africa), 36-3-C].

94. A. Wookey, Kuruman, 3 September 1878 [CWM, LMS Incoming Letters (South Africa), 36-3-C]. See also J. Mackenzie, Kuruman, 10 July 1878 [John Mackenzie Papers (University of the Witwatersrand), Correspondence no. 365].

95. See also J. Moffat, Kuruman, December 1876 [CWM, LMS Incoming Letters (South Africa), 38-3-D]. There is voluminous correspondence surrounding these events in the LMS files for 1876.

96. Mackenzie had spent most of his years with the Ngwato at Shoshong, further to the north, but had come to Kuruman before the 1878 uprising. (For biographical details, see W.D. Mackenzie 1902; Sillery 1971.) It is to be noted that the Moffat Institution had first been established at Shoshong; while there, Mackenzie had been closely involved in its development (see volume 2).

97. J. Mackenzie, Kuruman, 2 April 1879 [CWM, LMS Incoming Letters (South Africa), 40-1-B]. The second half of this letter, written to the LMS Foreign Secretary, is a catalogue of complaints against Moffat. The latter was also sent a copy by Mackenzie, which could not have made relations between them any easier.

98. The discovery of gold in the Transvaal (and elsewhere in southern Africa) occurred in stages, beginning soon after the diamond rush. While there is a large literature on the topic, the most accessible event histories are to be found in older accounts of the South African past (e.g., Bryden 1904:158f.), more recent general introductions to the subject (e.g., Denoon and Nyeko 1984:96f.), or radical efforts to rewrite it (e.g., Parsons 1983).

99. Among other things, the Transvaal had taken over Tswana territory some forty miles beyond the Keate line (Sillery 1971:41f.). To add further confusion, a land court under Andries Stockenstrom had "disproved" Waterboer's rights to Griqualand—and, therefore, the legal basis of the British annexation of the diamond fields (see e.g., Walker 1928:367).

100. Again, these processes are well covered in standard South African histories. One thing is noteworthy, though. Mackenzie does not seem to have realized that the political rationale for confederation—and for the annexation of the Transvaal—actually ran *counter* to his own plans (Sillery 1971:44f.). Where the missionary desired more direct imperial intervention, the point of unifying South Africa was to devolve *greater* control to the colonists—partly as a means by which Her Majesty's Government might reduce administrative costs. In the short run, as it happens, the confederation scheme failed.

101. J. Mackenzie, Kuruman, 18 August 1877 [CWM, LMS Incoming Letters (South Africa), 39-1-C]. On 20 April 1877 the missionary had himself asked the Governor to annex the Transvaal; W. Littleton (for Sir Bartle Frere), Cape Town, 9 May 1877 [John Mackenzie Papers (University of the Witwatersrand), Correspondence no. 334].

102. Hall (1975:passim) argues against those who have stressed Mackenzie's humanitarianism, or have made his liberalism out to be unusual for the period (e.g., Sillery 1971; Holmberg 1966). The missionary, he claims, was concerned to bring about the racial subordination of the Tswana in the interests of British imperialism; in this respect he was no different from anyone else—even capitalists like Rhodes—save that the beneficiary of his schemes were the British at home rather than settlers in the Colony. The argument, in our view, is as oversimplified as those which he (rightly) criticizes.

103. J. Mackenzie, Cape Town, 31 December 1884 [CWM, LMS Incoming Letters (South Africa), 42-3-D].

104. B. Frere, Cape Town, 13 June 1879 [CWS, LMS Incoming Letters (South Africa), 40-1-C]. Northcott (1972:657–58) mentions that in 1878 Mackenzie had pressed on Frere "the need for Commissioners to reside with native chiefs." He goes on to suggest that the governor responded immediately by offering the missionary just such a post, but that Mackenzie turned it down because, as an imperialist, he did not wish to be a servant of the colonial government.

105. J. Whitehouse (Acting Foreign Secretary of the LMS, London), 27 November 1879 (in Mackenzie 1975:134). A note on annotations here: since many of Mackenzie's papers are now published in places more accessible than the mission (or other) archives, we list the most easily available reference known to us in each case.

106. J. Mackenzie, Cape Town, 31 December 1884 [CWM, LMS Incoming Letters (South Africa), 42-3-D].

107. J. Mackenzie (to O. Lanyon), Kuruman, 24 September 1878 [John Mackenzie Papers (University of the Witwatersrand), Correspondence no. 377a].

108. The events of this period of Mackenzie's life are fully recorded by his biographers (W.D. Mackenzie 1902; Sillery 1971), as well as in his own writings (especially 1887). Here we are only concerned with their barest outline.

109. See F. Chesson (Aborigines' Protection Society), London, 18 October 1882 [John Mackenzie Papers (University of the Witwatersrand), Correspondence no. 493]. In this letter to Mackenzie, Chesson declares openly that "we should put pressure on the government in connection with the efforts of the Boers to crush" the Southern Tswana.

110. It was during this period of crisis that the "heathen" chief, Montshiwa, declared "religious freedom" and made Methodism the "state church" of his people, seeking thereby to sustain his close ties with the WMMS.

111. R. Wardlaw Thompson, Kanye, 22 February 1884 [CWM, LMS Incoming Letters (South Africa), 42-3-A].

112. See, for example, A. Wookey, Kuruman, 13 September 1884 [CWM, LMS Incoming Letters (South Africa), 42-3-D]. But, for a more equivocal reaction, see R. Wardlaw Thompson, Kuruman, 14 March 1884 [CWM, LMS Incoming Letters (South Africa), 42-3-B].

113. E. Ashley, Under-Secretary of State for the Colonies, 12 February 1884 (in Mackenzie 1975:163; Sillery 1971:82).

114. See Hansard, 3d ser., vol. 285:79, 28 February 1884 (in Sillery 1971:82).

115. Since this period in Mackenzie's life is carefully detailed in Sillery (1971:86ff.), we do not annotate it here.

116. As Sillery (1971:89) notes, Rhodes even converted Hofmeyr, leader of the Afrikaner Bond, to the idea of annexing Bechuanaland to the Cape. In fact, Rhodes and Hofmeyr, colonial capitalist and Afrikaner nationalist, sustained a mutually beneficial alliance until the Jameson Raid of 1895 (see below). It was an alliance that symbolized the potent subcontinental forces ranged against Mackenzie.

117. See, for example, R. Wardlaw Thompson, Kuruman, 14 March 1884 [CWM, LMS Incoming Letters (South Africa), 42-3-B]. Among the published commentaries, Shillington (1985:152–53) gives the best explanation for Mackenzie's difficulties.

118. The Warren Expedition is widely discussed in the historical literature; see, among many others, Holmberg (1966:112f.); Sillery (1971:121f.); Shillington (1985:170f.); Molema (1966:155). One irony, noted by Smith (1950b:101), is worthy of mention. In part, the Expedition was despatched because Rhodes failed as comprehensively as had Mackenzie to resolve the southern Bechuanaland problems—not surprisingly, given the forces at work. With the Cape Colony not interested in annexing the territory, Rhodes had himself called on the Imperial Factor in the form of British military intervention.

119. Warren had long favored an imperial policy for Griqualand and Bechuanaland that was, down to its last details, identical to Mackenzie's; see the *Diamond Fields Advertiser*, 2 May 1879.

120. R. Wardlaw Thompson, London, 4 December 1884 (in Mackenzie 1975:141–42). A passage from this letter is quoted by Sillery (1971:116).

121. The constitutional history of British Bechuanaland and the Protectorates is summarized by, among others, Sillery (1952:pt.1) and Stevens (1967:pt.2).

122. J. Brown, Kuruman, 16 December 1884 [CWM, LMS Incoming Letters (South Africa), 42-3-D].

123. Brown did not fully grasp Mackenzie's plan, which did *not* involve "Cape Colonists" annexing Tswana territory. Still, his opinion of the Tswana reaction to the alienation of their land, and his criticism of Mackenzie, echoed the view of a number of his colleagues.

124. J. Moffat (to Bower), Grahamstown, 17 July 1885 (in Mackenzie 1975:153).

125. Moffat's given reason for resigning was that no vacant mission station could be found for him. But his withdrawal spoke of deeper dissension in the LMS. For his side of the story, see J. Moffat, Molepolole, 7 April 1879 [CWM, LMS Incoming Letters (South Africa), 40-1-B].

126. As he knew, however, he had "lost caste" with other former colleagues (Moffat 1921:188). Still, his ties to the LMS were never really broken (see below).

127. The Transvaal was under British control at the time, this being after the annexation of 1877 but before the first Anglo-Boer War and the retrocession of the republic.

128. See Captain C.E. Hore's verbatim statement in the Proceedings of the Eighth Ordinary General Meeting of the Society (London, 9 June 1891), appended to a paper by the Rev. Frank Surridge. We annotate it under Surridge (1891).

129. See, for example, his letter to S. Shippard, 10 July 1889 (in Mackenzie 1975:242).

130. The more general point is that Moffat did not draw as sharp a distinction between colonialism and imperialism as did Mackenzie. In the realpolitik of the age, the connection between them was easily blurred; certainly, it was open to debate. Thus, for example, the Governorship of the Cape, a *colonial* position, was typically held by the man who was also High Commissioner, an *imperial* representative of the Crown. For those who shared Mackenzie's views, this was an unfortunate confusion of political roles and principles.

131. The minute was written by Edward Fairfield, 24 November 1892, C.0. 417/90:259 (quoted in Maylam 1980:28).

132. See *Correspondence Respecting the War between the Transvaal Republic and the Neighbouring Native Tribes*, C. 1748 (1877), Inclosure 1 in No. 1 (prepared by R. Southey), p. 2; Inclosure 2 in No. 1 (prepared by Sir Henry Barkly), p. 3. Such Colonial Office documents echo the rhetoric of the evangelists of the period; sometimes, in fact, they were influenced by missionary political discourse.

133. The protest took two forms. First, the directors of the LMS passed a resolution against the dispossession of the "rebels'" land. This was communicated to Sprigg, who replied defending the policy; see J.G. Sprigg, Cape Town, 2 November 1897 [CWM, LMS Incoming Letters (South Africa), 54-3-D]. Then, second, the Bechuanaland District Committee passed a resolution against indenture at its meeting of 14 March 1898 and published it in the *Bechuana News* of 19 March [CWM, LMS Incoming Letters (South Africa), 55-1-A]. As is shown by a leading article in the *Diamond Fields Advertiser* (1 November 1878), Sprigg had long expressed strong ideas about the positive social effects of wage labor on blacks (see also volume 2).

134. Shillington (1985:ch.9) notes how difficult it is to identify the events and actors that might be said to have constituted a "rebellion."

135. The "rebels" were in fact given a choice of indentured labor or standing trial for treason. All took the first option, "although J.S. Moffat took two to stand trial as a test case which was dismissed for lack of evidence" (Shillington 1985:240).

136. Minutes of the Meeting of the Bechuanaland District Committee, Vryburg, 14 March 1898 [CWM, LMS Incoming Letters (South Africa), 55–1 -A]. A newly-formed Women's Committee of the LMS in Cape Town had also urged the

Directorate to appoint a minister to the indentured laborers; see Mrs. Anderson and others, Cape Town, 23 November 1897 [CWM, LMS Incoming Letters (South Africa), 54-3-E].

137. See, for an early example, the editorial comment in the "General News" column of the *Diamond Fields Advertiser*, 16 April 1879.

138. Not only had the LMS intervened in the case of the Tswana "rebels," but in 1887 the WMMS complained on behalf of Montshiwa against government agents, troops, and settlers who allegedly had seized Tshidi land, raped local women, and promoted the sale of alcohol. The Methodists published their protest (WMMS 1887), appealed to the Secretary of State for the Colonies, and lobbied in London and Cape Town against further "interference" in Bechuanaland.

139. See Brown (1931:214) for a contemporary translation of *morafe* (*morahe*); this dictionary, as we noted earlier, was compiled in the late nineteenth century.

140. [Draft] Treaty between Paramount Chief Montsioa, his Sons and Councillors and the Imperial Government, Mafikeng, 22 May 1884 [Molema-Plaatje Papers (University of the Witwatersrand), Chief Montshiwa Correspondence, Ba 9].

141. This is clear from the various letter books kept by Chief Montshiwa, and housed (in 1969–70) in the Tshidi-Rolong "tribal offices" at Mafeking. Copies of his correspondence are also to be found in the Molema-Plaatje Papers (University of the Witwatersrand); see Chief Montshiwa Correspondence, file [Ba].

142. Paramount Chief, Headmen and Councillors [Tshidi-Rolong], Mafikeng, January 1903 [Molema-Plaatje Papers (University of the Witwatersrand), Chief Wessels Papers, Bb 3].

143. As we shall see in volume 2, this style of political discourse was to reappear later, when the early black South African protest movements formulated their appeals for "native rights."

BIBLIOGRAPHY

Abrams, Meyer H.
   1953   *The Mirror and the Lamp: Romantic Theory and the Critical Tradition*. New York: Oxford University Press. Reprinted, 1958; New York: Norton.

Achebe, Chinua
   1959   *Things Fall Apart*. New York: Astor-Honor Inc.
   1978   An Image of Africa. *Research in African Literatures* 9:1–15.

Adamson, Walter L.
   1980   *Hegemony and Revolution: A Study of Antonio Gramsci's Political and Cultural Theory*. Berkeley and Los Angeles: University of California Press.

Ajayi, J.F. Ade
   1965   *Christian Missions in Nigeria, 1841–1891: The Making of a New Elite*. London: Longmans.
   A Life's Labours in South Africa
   1872   *A Life's Labours in South Africa: The Story of the Life Work of Robert Moffat*. London: John Snow.

Alloula, Malek
   1986   *The Colonial Harem*. Translated by M. and W. Godzich. Minneapolis: University of Minnesota Press.

Altick, Richard D.
   1957   *The English Common Reader: A Social History of the Mass Reading Public, 1800–1900*. Chicago: University of Chicago Press.

Alverson, Hoyt
   1978   *Mind in the Heart of Darkness: Value and Self-Identity among the Tswana of Southern Africa*. New Haven and London: Yale University Press.

Anderson, Benedict
   1983   *Imagined Communities: Reflections on the Origin and Spread of Nationalism*. London: Verso.

Anderson, Perry
   1976–77   The Antinomies of Antonio Gramsci. *New Left Review* 100:5–78.

Anstey, Roger
   1968   Capitalism and Slavery: A Critique. *Economic History Review*, 1st ser., 21:307–20.

Arbuthnot, John ["a Farmer"]
   1773   *An Inquiry into the Connection between the Present Price of Provisions, and the Size of Farms. . . .* London: T. Cadell.

Arnold, Matthew
    1903   *Essays in Criticism.* 1st ser. London: Macmillan. Original edition, 1865.
Asad, Talal
    1973   Two European Images of Non-European Rule. In *Anthropology and the Colonial Encounter*, ed. T. Asad. London: Ithaca Press.
Ashton, Thomas S.
    1948   *The Industrial Revolution, 1760–1830.* London: Oxford University Press.
Austen, Ralph A., and Woodruff D. Smith
    1969   Images of Africa and British Slave-Trade Abolition: The Transition to an Imperialist Ideology, 1787–1807. *African Historical Studies* 2:69–83.
Ayala, Flavia
    1977   Victorian Science and the "Genius" of Woman. *Journal of the History of Ideas* 38:261–80.
Ayandele, Emmanuel A.
    1966   *The Missionary Impact on Modern Nigeria, 1842–1914.* London: Longmans, Green.
Babcock, Barbara A.
    1975   Mirrors, Masks, and Metafiction: Studies in Narrative Reflexivity. Ph.D. diss., University of Chicago.
Bain, Andrew G.
    1949   *Journals of Andrew Geddes Bain.* Edited by M.H. Lister. Cape Town: The Van Riebeeck Society.
Bakhtin, Mikhail M.
    1981   *The Dialogic Imagination: Four Essays.* Edited by M. Holquist. Translated by C. Emerson and M. Holquist. Austin: University of Texas Press.
Banks, (Mrs.) G. Linnaeus
    1876   *The Manchester Man.* Altrincham: John Sherrat & Son; Manchester: E.J. Morten.
Barker, Francis
    1984   *The Tremulous Private Body: Essays on Subjection.* London and New York: Methuen.
Barrow, John
    1801–04   *An Account of Travels into the Interior of Southern Africa in the Years 1797 and 1798.* 2 vols. London: Cadell & Davies.
    1806   *A Voyage to Cochinchina.* London: Cadell & Davies.
Barthes, Roland
    1967   *Elements of Semiology.* Translated by A. Lavers and C. Smith. London: Jonathan Cape.
Beck, Roger B.
    1989   Bibles and Beads: Missionaries as Traders in Southern Africa in the Early Nineteenth Century. *Journal of African History* 30:211–25.

Beidelman, Thomas O.
　1974　Social Theory and the Study of Christian Missionaries in Africa. *Africa* 44:235–49.
　1981　Contradictions between the Sacred and the Secular Life: The Church Missionary Society in Ukaguru, Tanzania, East Africa, 1876–1914. *Comparative Studies in Society and History* 23:73–95.
　1982　*Colonial Evangelism: A Socio-Historical Study of an East African Mission at the Grassroots.* Bloomington: Indiana University Press.

Behn, Aphra
　1915　*The Works of Aphra Behn.* 6 vols. Edited by M. Summers. London: W. Heinemann.

Bellah, Robert N.
　1988　Foreword. In *Illusions of Innocence: Protestant Primitivism in America, 1630–1875,* by Richard T. Hughes and C. Leonard Allen. Chicago: University of Chicago Press.

Benson, Mary
　1963　*The African Patriots: The Story of the African National Congress of South Africa.* London: Faber & Faber.
　1966　*South Africa: The Struggle for a Birthright.* Rev. ed. of *The African Patriots.* New York: Funk & Wagnalls.

Benveniste, Emile
　1971　*Problems in General Linguistics.* Translated by M.E. Meek. Florida: University of Miami Press.

Berlin, Isaiah
　1980　*Against the Current: Essays in the History of Ideas.* Edited by H. Hardy. New York: Viking Press.

Blaikie, William G.
　n.d.　*The Personal Life of David Livingstone, Chiefly from his Unpublished Journals and Correspondence in the Possession of his Family.* New York: Fleming H. Revell.

Blake, William
　1966　*Complete Writings with Variant Readings.* Edited by G. Keynes. London: Oxford University Press.

Bloch, Ernst et al.
　1980　*Aesthetics and Politics.* Translated and edited by R. Taylor. London: Verso.

Bloch, Maurice, and Jean H. Bloch
　1980　Women and the Dialectics of Nature in Eighteenth-Century French Thought. In *Nature, Culture, and Gender,* ed. C.P. MacCormack and M. Strathern. Cambridge: Cambridge University Press.

Blumenbach, Johann F.
　1969　*On the Natural Varieties of Mankind.* Translated by T. Bendyshe from the 1775/1795 editions. New York: Bergman Publishers.

Bohannan, Paul
    1964   *Africa and Africans*. New York: The Natural History Press.

Bonner, Phillip
    1983   *Kings, Commoners and Concessionaires: The Evolution and Dissolution of the Nineteenth-Century Swazi State*. Cambridge: Cambridge University Press.

Bourdieu, Pierre
    1977   *Outline of a Theory of Practice*. Translated by R. Nice. Cambridge: Cambridge University Press.
    1984   *Distinction: A Social Critique of the Judgement of Taste*. Translated by R. Nice. Cambridge: Harvard University Press.

Bourdillon, Michael F.C.
    1983   Review of *Colonial Evangelism*, by T.O. Beidelman, 1982. *Man*, n.s. 18:215.

Bowden, Witt
    1925   *Industrial Society in England Towards the End of the Eighteenth Century*. New York: Macmillan.

Bowles, William Lisle
    1813   *The Missionary; a Poem*. London: J. Murray.

Bradley, Edwin J.
    1978   Whigs and Nonconformists: Presbyterians, Congregationalists, and Baptists in English Politics, 1715–1790. Ph.D. diss., University of Southern California.

Bradley, Ian C.
    1976   *The Call to Seriousness: The Evangelical Impact on the Victorians*. New York: Macmillan.

Bradlow, Frank R.
    1987   *Printing for Africa: The Story of Robert Moffat and the Kuruman Press*. Kuruman: Kuruman Moffat Mission Trust.

Brantlinger, Patrick
    1985   Victorians and Africans: The Genealogy of the Myth of the Dark Continent. *Critical Inquiry* 12:166–203.

Breutz, Paul L.
    1956   *The Tribes of Mafeking District*. Ethnological Publication, no. 32. Pretoria: Department of Native Affairs.
    1959   *The Tribes of Vryburg District*. Ethnological Publication, no. 46. Pretoria: Department of Native Affairs.

Brigg, Arthur
    1867   Letter from Wittebergen, 20 July 1866. *Wesleyan Missionary Notices— relating to Foreign Missions*, 3d ser. 158 (25 January):28–31.

Briggs, Asa
    1959   *The Age of Improvement 1783–1867*. London: Longmans.

1960   The Language of 'Class' in Early Nineteenth Century England. In *Essays in Labour History*, ed. A. Briggs and J. Saville. London: Macmillan.

1979   *Iron Bridge to Crystal Palace: Impact and Images of the Industrial Revolution.* London: Thames & Hudson.

Briggs, John, and Ian Sellers, eds.

1973   *Victorian Nonconformity*. London: Edward Arnold.

British and Foreign Bible Society, The

1952   *Bibela E E Boitshèpō*. Reprinted from the revised edition of the *Secwana (Chuana) Bible*, 1908. London: The British and Foreign Bible Society.

Broadbent, Samuel

1865   *A Narrative of the First Introduction of Christianity amongst the Barolong Tribe of Bechuanas, South Africa*. London: Wesleyan Mission House.

Brontë, Charlotte

1969   *Jane Eyre*. Edited by J. Jack and M. Smith. London: Oxford University Press. First edition, under the pseudonym Currer Bell, 1847; London: Smith, Elder.

1981   *Shirley*. Edited by H. Rosengarten and M. Smith. London: Oxford University Press. First edition, under the pseudonym Currer Bell, 1849; London: Smith, Elder.

Brookes, Edgar H.

1974   *White Rule in South Africa: 1830–1910*. Pietermaritzburg: University of Natal Press.

Brown, J. Tom

1921   Circumcision Rites of the Becwana Tribes. *Journal of the Royal Anthropological Institute* 51:419–27.

1926   *Among the Bantu Nomads: A Record of Forty Years Spent among the Bechuana*. . . . London: Seeley Service.

1931   *Secwana Dictionary*. Tiger Kloof: London Missionary Society.

Bryant, Alfred T.

1929   *Olden Times in Zululand and Natal*. . . . London: Longmans, Green.

Bryden, Henry A.

1904   *A History of South Africa: From the First Settlement by the Dutch, 1652, to the Year 1903*. London and Edinburgh: William Sands.

Buffon, George L.L.

1791   *Natural History, General and Particular*. Translated by W. Smellie. London: A. Strahan.

Bundy, Colin

1979   *The Rise and Fall of the South African Peasantry*. London: Heinemann.

1987   Street Sociology and Pavement Politics: Aspects of Youth and Student Resistance in Cape Town, 1985. *Journal of Southern African Studies* 13:303–30.

Bunyan, John
1678   *The Pilgrim's Progress from this World.* . . . Printed for Nath. Ponder at the Peacock in the Poultrey near Cornhil.

Burchell, William J.
1822–24   *Travels in the Interior of Southern Africa.* 2 vols. London: Longman, Hurst, Rees, Orme, Brown & Green. Reprinted, 1967; Cape Town: Struik.

Burridge, Kenelm
1973   *Encountering Aborigines. A Case Study: Anthropology and the Australian Aboriginal.* New York: Pergamon Press.

Campbell, John
1813   *Travels in South Africa.* London: Black, Parry. Reprinted, 1974; Cape Town: Struik.
1822   *Travels in South Africa.* . . . *Being a Narrative of a Second Journey.* . . . 2 vols. London: Westley. Reprinted, 1967; New York and London: Johnson Reprint Corporation.
n.d.   *John Campbell Papers* Cape Town: South African Library.

Campbell, Reginald J.
1930   *Livingstone.* New York: Dodd, Mead.

Camper, Petrus
1821   *The Works of the Late Professor Camper, on the Connexion between the Science of Anatomy and the Arts of Drawing, Painting, Statuary.* . . . New ed., edited by T. Cogan. London: sold by J. Hearne.

Carlyle, Thomas
1829   Signs of the Times. *Edinburgh Review* 98:439–59. Reprinted in *Sartor Resartus and Selected Prose,* 1970; New York: Holt, Rhinehart & Winston.
1842   *On Heroes, Hero-Worship, and the Heroic in History.* New York: D. Appelton.

Cassanelli, Lee V.
1982   *The Shaping of Somali Society: Reconstructing the History of a Pastoral People, 1600–1900.* Philadelphia: University of Pennsylvania Press.

Chadwick, Owen
1966   *The Victorian Church.* Part 1. New York: Oxford University Press.

Chandler, James K.
1984   *Wordsworth's Second Nature: A Study of the Poetry and Politics.* Chicago: University of Chicago Press.

Cheal, David J.
1979   Hegemony, Ideology and Contradictory Consciousness. *The Sociological Quarterly* 20:109–17.

Chirenje, J. Mutero
1976   Church, State, and Education in Bechuanaland in the Nineteenth Century. *International Journal of African Historical Studies* 9:401–18.

Clapham, John H.
  1926 *An Economic History of Modern Britain: The Early Railway Age,*
  1820–1850. 3 vols. Cambridge: Cambridge University Press.

Clarkson, Thomas
  1816 *An Essay on the Slavery and Commerce of the Human Species, Particularly the*
  African. Georgetown: David Barrow (private publisher), J.N. Lyle (printer).
  1839 *The History of the Rise, Progress, and Accomplishment of the Abolition of the*
  African Slave Trade by the British Parliament. London: John W. Parker.

Clinton, Desmond K.
  1937 *The South African Melting Pot: A Vindication of Missionary Policy,*
  1799–1836. London: Longmans, Green.

Cobbing, Julian
  1988 The Mfecane as Alibi: Thoughts on Dithakong and Mbolompo. *Journal*
  of African History 29:487–519.

Cochrane, James R.
  1987 *Servants of Power: The Role of English-speaking Churches in South Africa,*
  1903–1930. . . . Johannesburg: Ravan Press.

Coetzee, John M.
  1988 *White Writing: On the Culture of Letters in South Africa.* New Haven: Yale
  University Press.

Cohn, Bernard S.
  1985 The Command of Language and the Language of Command. In *Subal-*
  tern Studies, vol. 4, ed. Ranagit Guha. New Delhi: Oxford University Press.

Cole, George D.H.
  1932 *A Short History of the British Working Class Movement, 1789–1925.* 3 vols.
  London: George Allen & Unwin.

Coleridge, Samuel Taylor
  1912 *The Complete Poetical Works of Samuel Taylor Coleridge.* . . . Oxford: Clarendon Press.

Collinson, Patrick
  1986 *From Iconoclasm to Iconophobia: The Cultural Impact of the Second English*
  Reformation. The Stetson Lecture, 1985. Reading: University of Reading.

Colman, George
  1788 *Inkle and Yarico: An Opera.* Dublin: H. Chamberlaine.

Comaroff, Jean
  1974 Barolong Cosmology: A Study of Religious Pluralism in a Tswana Town.
  Ph.D. diss., University of London.
  1985 *Body of Power, Spirit of Resistance: The Culture and History of a South Afri-*
  can People. Chicago: University of Chicago Press.

Comaroff, Jean, and John L. Comaroff
  1986 Christianity and Colonialism in South Africa. *American Ethnologist*
  13:1–20.

1988 Through the Looking Glass: Colonial Encounters of the First Kind. *Journal of Historical Sociology* 1:6–32.

1989 The Colonization of Consciousness in South Africa. *Economy and Society* 18:267–95.

1990 Goodly Beasts and Beastly Goods: Cattle and Commodities in a South African Context. *American Ethnologist* 17:195–216.

Comaroff, John L.

1973 Competition for Office and Political Processes among the Barolong boo Ratshidi of the South Africa–Botswana Borderland. Ph.D. diss., University of London.

1975 Talking Politics: Oratory and Authority in a Tswana Chiefdom. In *Political Language and Oratory in Traditional Society*, ed. M. Bloch. London: Academic Press.

1978 Rules and Rulers: Political Processes in a Tswana chiefdom. *Man*, n.s. 13:1–20.

1980 Bridewealth and the Control of Ambiguity in a Tswana Chiefdom. In *The Meaning of Marriage Payments*, ed. J.L. Comaroff. London and New York: Academic Press.

1982 Dialectical Systems, History and Anthropology: Units of Study and Questions of Theory. *Journal of Southern African Studies* 8:143–72.

1984 The Closed Society and its Critics: Historical Transformations in the Theory and Practice of African Ethnography. *American Ethnologist* 11:571–83.

1987a *Sui Genderis*: Feminism, Kinship Theory, and Structural "Domains." In *Gender and Kinship: Essays Toward a Unified Analysis*, ed. J. F. Collier and S. J. Yanagisako. Stanford: Stanford University Press.

1987b Of Totemism and Ethnicity: Consciousness, Practice and the Signs of Inequality. *Ethnos* 52:301–23.

1989 Images of Empire, Contests of Conscience: Models of Colonial Domination in South Africa. *American Ethnologist* 16:661–85.

n.d. *Culture, Class, and the Rise of Capitalism in an African Chiefdom*. Manuscript in preparation.

Comaroff, John L., and Jean Comaroff

1981 The Management of Marriage in a Tswana Chiefdom. In *Essays on African Marriage in Southern Africa*, ed. E. J. Krige and J. L. Comaroff. Cape Town: Juta.

1987 The Madman and the Migrant: Work and Labor in the Historical Consciousness of a South African People. *American Ethnologist* 14:191–209.

n.d. The Long and the Short of It: Time, Structure, and Practice in Social Analysis. Manuscript.

Comaroff, John L., and Simon A. Roberts

1977 Marriage and Extramarital Sexuality: The Dialectics of Legal Change amongst the Kgatla. *Journal of African Law* 21: 97–123.

1981 *Rules and Processes: The Cultural Logic of Dispute in an African Context*. Chicago: University of Chicago Press.

Cook, Mercer
  1936 Jean-Jacques Rousseau and the Negro. *Journal of Negro History*
    21:294–303.

Cooley, Charles H.
  1964 *Human Nature and the Social Order*. New York: Schocken Books.

Cooper, Frederick, and Ann Stoler
  1989 Introduction. *American Ethnologist* 16:609–21. Special number on
    "Tensions of Empire: Colonial Control and Visions of Rule."

Cope, Richard L.
  1979 Christian Missions and Independent African Chiefdoms in South Africa
    in the 19th Century. *Theoria* 52:1–23.

Corey, George E.
  1919 *The Rise of South Africa: A History of the Origin of South African Colonisa-
    tion and of its Development towards the East from the Earliest Times to 1857*. Lon-
    don: Longmans, Green.

Crabbe, George
  1855 *George Crabbe's Poetical Works*. Boston: Phillips, Sampson.

Crummey, Donald
  1972 *Priests and Politicians: Protestant and Catholic Missions in Orthodox Ethiopia,
    1830–1868*. Oxford: Clarendon Press.

Curtin, Philip D.
  1964 *The Image of Africa: British Ideas and Action, 1780–1850*. Madison: Uni-
    versity of Wisconsin Press.

Cuthbertson, Greg
  1987 The English-speaking Churches and Colonialism. In *Theology and Vio-
    lence: The South African Debate*, ed. C. Villa-Vicencio. Grand Rapids: William
    B. Eerdmans.

Cuvier, Georges
  1827–35 *The Animal Kingdom*. . . . 16 vols. London: Geo. B. Whittaker.

Dachs, Anthony J.
  1972 Missionary Imperialism: The Case of Bechuanaland. *Journal of African
    History* 13:647–58.

Dale, Robert W.
  1907 *History of English Congregationalism*. Completed and edited by A. W. W.
    Dale. London: Hodder & Stoughton.

Dalzel, Archibald
  1799 *Geschichte von Dahomy, einem Inländischen Königreich in Afrika*. Translated
    from *The History of Dahomey*, 1793. Leipzig: Schwickert.

Darnton, Robert
  1984 *The Great Cat Massacre And Other Episodes in French Cultural History*. New
    York: Basic Books.

Davenport, T. R. H.
>   1969   The Consolidation of a New Society: The Cape Colony. In *The Oxford History of South Africa*, vol. 1, ed. M. Wilson and L. M. Thompson. New York: Oxford University Press.

Davidson, Arnold I.
>   1987   Sex and the Emergence of Sexuality. *Critical Inquiry* 14:16–48.

Davies, Horton
>   1951   *Great South African Christians*. Cape Town: Geoffrey Cumberledge, Oxford University Press.
>   1961   *Worship and Theology in England: From Watts and Wesley to Maurice, 1690–1850*. Princeton: Princeton University Press.

Davis, Peter B.
>   1966   *The Problem of Slavery in Western Culture*. Ithaca: Cornell University Press.
>   1975   *The Problem of Slavery in the Age of Revolution 1770–1823*. Ithaca: Cornell University Press.

Day, Thomas, and John Bicknell
>   1775   *The Dying Negro, a Poem*. London: W. Flexny.

de Certeau, Michel
>   1984   *The Practice of Everyday Life*. Translated by S.F. Rendall. Berkeley and Los Angeles: University of California Press.
>   1988   *The Writing of History*. Translated by T. Conley. New York: Columbia University Press.

Defoe, Daniel
>   1927   *The Life and Strange Surprizing Adventures of Robinson Crusoe. . . .* 3 vols. Oxford: Basil Blackwell. First edition, 1719; London: W. Taylor.

de Gruchy, John W.
>   1979   *The Church Struggle in South Africa*. Cape Town: David Philip.

de Kiewiet, Cornelius W.
>   1936   Social and Economic Developments in Native Tribal Life. In *The Cambridge History of the British Empire*, vol. 8, *South Africa, Rhodesia and the Protectorates*, ed. A.P. Newton and E.A. Benians. Cambridge: Cambridge University Press.

de Kock, W. J. (editor-in-chief)
>   1968   *Dictionary of South African Biography*. Vol. 1. Cape Town: Nasionale Pers for the National Council for Social Research.

Delius, Peter
>   1983   *The Land Belongs to Us: The Pedi Polity, the Boers, and the British in the Nineteenth-Century Transvaal*. Johannesburg: Ravan Press.
>   1984   *The Conversion: Death Cell Conversations of 'Rooizak' and the Missionaries, Lydenburg 1875*. Johannesburg: Ravan Press.

Denoon, Donald
>   1973   *Southern Africa Since 1800*. New York and Washington: Praeger.

Denoon, Donald, and Balam Nyeko
    1984   *Southern Africa Since 1800*. 2d ed. London and New York: Longman.

de Riencourt, Amaury
    1983   *Women and Power in History*. London: Honeyglen Publishing. Originally
    published as *Sex and Power in History*, 1974; New York: D. McKay Co.

Dickens, Charles
    1908a The Niger Expedition. In *The Works of Charles Dickens*, National Edi-
    tion, vol. 35, *Miscellaneous Papers, Plays and Poems*, vol. 1. London: Chapman
    and Hall. First published in *The Examiner*, 19 August 1848.
    1908b The Noble Savage. In *The Works of Charles Dickens*, National Edition,
    vol. 34, *Reprinted Pieces*. London: Chapman and Hall. First published in
    Household Words, 11 June 1853.
    1853   *Bleak House*. London: Bradbury & Evans.
    1971   *Our Mutual Friend*. Edited by S. Gill. Harmondsworth: Penguin.
    1972   *The Mystery of Edwin Drood*. Edited by M. Cardwell. Oxford: Clarendon
    Press.

Diderot, Denis
    1972   *Supplément au Voyage de Bougainville*. Paris: Garnier-Flammarion. Origi-
    nal edition, 1773–74.

Dodd, William
    1749   The African Prince, Now in England, to Zara at his Father's Court.
    Gentleman's Magazine 19 (July): 323–25. Reprinted in *The Lady's Poetical
    Magazine* (1781), 1:287–92.

[Dodd, William]
    1847   *The Laboring Classes of England, Especially those Engaged in Agriculture and
    Manufacture; in a Series of Letters*, by an Englishman. Boston: John Putnam.

Drescher, Seymour
    1977   *Econocide: British Slavery in the Era of Abolition*. Pittsburgh: University of
    Pittsburgh Press.
    1987   *Capitalism and Antislavery: British Popular Mobilization in Comparative
    Perspective*. New York: Oxford University Press.

Dubos, René Jules
    1979   *Mirage of Health: Utopias, Progress, and Biological Change*. New York: Har-
    per Colophon.

du Plessis, Johannes
    1911   *A History of Christian Missions in South Africa*. London: Longmans,
    Green.

Durkheim, Emile
    1947   *The Elementary Forms of the Religious Life: A Study in Religious Sociology*.
    Translated by J. W. Swain. Glencoe: The Free Press.

Eagleton, Terry
    1975   *Myths of Power: A Marxist Study of the Brontës*. London: Macmillan.

Eco, Umberto
1983   *The Name of the Rose*. Translated by W. Weaver. New York: Harcourt Brace Jovanovich.

Edwards, John
1886   *Reminiscences of the Early Life and Missionary Labours of the Rev. John Edwards*. Edited by W. C. Holden. Grahamstown, South Africa: T. H. Grocott.

Eiselen, Werner M.
1934   Christianity and the Religious Life of the Bantu. In *Western Civilization and the Natives of South Africa*, ed. I. Schapera. London: Routledge & Kegan Paul.

Ekechi, F. K.
1972   *Missionary Enterprise and Rivalry in Igboland, 1857–1914*. London: Frank Cass.

Eliade, Mircea
1964   *Shamanism: Archaic Techniques of Ecstasy*. Translated by W. R. Trask. New York: Pantheon Books for the Bollingen Foundation.

Ellis, Amanda M.
1967   *Rebels and Conservatives: Dorothy and William Wordsworth and their Circle*. Bloomington and London: Indiana University Press.

Elmslie, Walter A.
1970   *Among the Wild Ngoni: Being Some Chapters in the History of the Livingstonia Mission in British Central Africa*. 3d ed. London: Frank Cass. Original edition, 1899.

Elphick, Robert
1981   Africans and the Christian Campaign in Southern Africa. In *The Frontier in History: North America and Southern Africa Compared*, ed. H. Lamar and L.M. Thompson. New Haven: Yale University Press.

Elphick, Robert, and V. C. Malherbe
1989   The Khoisan to 1828. In *The Shaping of South African Society, 1652–1840*, ed. R. Elphick and H. B. Giliomee. Middletown, Conn.: Wesleyan University Press.

Engels, Friedrich
1968   *The Condition of the Working Class in England*. Translated and edited by W. O. Henderson and W. H. Chaloner. Stanford: Stanford University Press.

Etherington, Norman
1978   *Preachers, Peasants, and Politics in Southeast Africa, 1835–1880: African Christian Communities in Natal, Pondoland, and Zululand*. London: Royal Historical Society.
1983   Missionaries and the Intellectual History of Africa: A Historical Survey. *Itinerario* 7:116–43.

Evans-Pritchard, Edward E.
1937   *Witchcraft, Oracles and Magic among the Azande*. Oxford: Clarendon Press.

1940   *The Nuer: A Description of the Modes of Livelihood and Political Institutions of a Nilotic People.* Oxford: Clarendon Press.

Fabian, Johannes
1983a   *Time and the Other: How Anthropology Makes its Object.* New York: Columbia University Press.
1983b   Missions and the Colonization of African Languages: Developments in the Former Belgian Congo. *Canadian Journal of African Studies* 17:165–87.
1986   *Language and Colonial Power: The Appropriation of Swahili in the Former Belgian Congo, 1880–1938.* Cambridge: Cambridge University Press.

Fairchild, Hoxie N.
1928   *The Noble Savage: A Study in Romantic Naturalism.* New York: Columbia University Press.

Fanon, Frantz
1967   *Black Skin, White Masks.* Translated by C. L. Markmann. New York: Grove Press.

February, Vernon
1989   'In die Koloniale Geskiedenis kan ons Tekens van Verowering Terugvind . . .' (In conversation with H. van Vuuren.) *Die Suid-Afrikaan* 24 (December): 40–42.

Femia, Joseph V.
1975   Hegemony and Consciousness in the Thought of Antonio Gramsci. *Political Studies* 23:29–48.
1981   *Gramsci's Political Thought: Hegemony, Consciousness, and the Revolutionary Process.* Oxford: Clarendon Press.

Ferguson, James
1985   The Bovine Mystique: Power, Property and Livestock in Rural Lesotho. *Man,* n.s. 20:647–74.

Ferguson, Margaret
1989   Grace Abounded. Review of *A Tinker and a Poor Man,* by Christopher Hill, 1989. *The New York Times Book Review,* 12 March, 31.

Fernandez, James W.
1980   Reflections on Looking into Mirrors. *Semiotica* 30:27–39.

Fields, Karen E.
1985   *Revival and Rebellion in Colonial Central Africa.* Princeton: Princeton University Press.

Figlio, Karl
1976   The Metaphor of Organization: An Historiographical Perspective on the Bio-Medical Sciences of the Early Nineteenth Century. *History of Science* 14:17–53.

Findlay, George G., and William W. Holdsworth
1922   *The History of the Wesleyan Methodist Missionary Society,* vol 4. London: The Epworth Press.

Fisher, Humphrey J.
   1973   Conversion Reconsidered: Some Historical Aspects of Religious Conversion in Black Africa. *Africa* 43:27–40.

Fogel, Robert W.
   1989   *Without Consent or Contract: The Rise and Fall of American Slavery.* New York and London: W.W. Norton & Co.

Fordyce, James
   1776   *The Character and Conduct of the Female Sex. . . .* London: R. Stevenson.

Fortes, Meyer, and Edward E. Evans-Pritchard, eds.
   1940   *African Political Systems.* London: Oxford University Press for the International African Institute.

Foster, John
   1974   *Class Struggle and the Industrial Revolution: Early Industrial Capitalism in Three English Towns.* London: Weidenfeld & Nicolson.

Foucault, Michel
   1973   *Madness and Civilization: A History of Insanity in the Age of Reason.* Translated by R. Howard. New York: Vintage Books.
   1975   *The Birth of the Clinic: An Archeology of Medical Perception.* Translated by A.M. Sheridan Smith. New York: Vintage Books.
   1978   *The History of Sexuality.* Translated by R. Hurley. New York: Pantheon Books.
   1979   *Discipline and Punish: The Birth of the Prison.* Translated by A. Sheridan. New York: Vintage Books.
   1980a   *Power/Knowledge: Selected Interviews and Other Writings, 1972–77.* Edited by C. Gordon; translated by C. Gordon et al. New York: Pantheon Books.
   1980b   *Herculine Barbin, Being the Recently Discovered Memoirs of a Nineteenth-Century French Hermaphrodite.* Translated by R. McDougall. New York: Pantheon Books.

Frazer, James
   1964   *The Golden Bough: A Study in Magic and Religion.* Abridged ed. New York: The New American Library. Original abridged ed., 1922.

Friedman, John B.
   1981   *The Monstrous Races in Medieval Art and Thought.* Cambridge: Harvard University Press.

Friedrich, Paul
   1979   *Language, Context, and the Imagination: Essays.* Edited by A. Dil. Stanford: Stanford University Press.

Fuller Ossoli, Sarah M.
   1855   *Woman in the Nineteenth Century.* New York: Sheldon, Lamport. Original edition, 1845.

Gates, Henry L., Jr., ed.
   1986   *"Race," Writing, and Difference.* Chicago: University of Chicago Press.

Originally published in two special issues of *Critical Inquiry*, 12/1 (1985); 13/1, (1986).

Gauguin, Paul
1985   *Noa Noa: The Tahitian Journal.* Translated by O. F. Theis. New York: Dover Publications.

Gaunt, Lewis H.
1906   *School-Mates: Pictures of School-time and Play-time in the Mission Field.* London: London Missionary Society.

Gaventa, John
1980   *Power and Powerlessness: Quiescence and Rebellion in an Appalachian Valley.* Urbana: University of Illinois Press.

Geertz, Clifford
1973   *The Interpretation of Cultures: Selected Essays.* New York: Basic Books.

Genovese, Eugene D.
1971   *In Red and Black: Marxian Explorations in Southern and Afro-American History.* New York: Pantheon Books.
1974   *Roll, Jordan, Roll: The World the Slaves Made.* New York: Pantheon Books.

George, Katherine
1958   The Civilized West Looks at Primitive Africa: 1400–1800. A Study in Ethnocentrism. *Isis* 49:62–72.

Geras, Norman
1987   Post-Marxism? *New Left Review* 163:40–82.

Gerhart, Gail M., and Thomas Karis
1977   *From Protest to Challenge: A Documentary History of African Politics in South Africa 1882–1964*, Vol. 4, *Political Profiles 1882–1964*. Edited by T. Karis and G. M. Carter. Stanford: Hoover Institution Press.

Gibbon, Edward
1797   *The History of the Decline and Fall of the Roman Empire.* 12 vols. London: Printed for W. Strahan & T. Cadell.

Giddens, Anthony
1979   *Central Problems in Social Theory: Action, Structure, and Contradiction in Social Analysis.* Berkeley and Los Angeles: University of California Press.
1987   *Social Theory and Modern Sociology.* Stanford: Stanford University Press.

Gilman, Sander L.
1985   Black Bodies, White Bodies: Toward an Iconography of Female Sexuality in Late Nineteenth Century Art, Medicine and Literature. *Critial Inquiry* 12:204–242.

Gluckman, Max
1940   The Kingdom of the Zulu. In *African Political Systems*, ed. M. Fortes and E. E. Evans-Pritchard. London: Oxford University Press for the International African Institute.

1963   *Order and Rebellion in Tribal Africa: Collected Essays*. London: Cohen & West.

Gluckman, Max, J. Clyde Mitchell, and John A. Barnes
1949   The Village Headman in British Central Africa. *Africa* 19:89–106.

Godzich, Wlad
1987   Foreword: In Quest of Modernity. In *Ideology of Adventure: Studies in Modern Consciousness, 1100–1750*, vol. 1, by Michael Nerlich. Translated by R. Crowley. Minneapolis: University of Minnesota Press.

Goody, Jack R.
1977   *The Domestication of the Savage Mind*. Cambridge: Cambridge University Press.

Gould, Stephen J.
1981   *The Mismeasure of Man*. New York: W.W. Norton & Co.
1985   *The Flamingo's Smile: Reflections in Natural History*. New York: W.W. Norton & Co.

Goveia, Elsa V.
1965   *Slave Society in the British Leeward Islands at the End of the Eighteenth Century*. New Haven: Yale University Press.

Gramsci, Antonio
1971   *Selections from the Prison Notebooks*. Edited and translated by Q. Hoare and G. Nowell Smith. New York: International Publishers.

Grant, Sandy
1984   The Revival of *Bogwera* in the Kgatleng—Tswana Culture or Rampant Tribalism? A Description of the 1982 *Bogwera*. *Botswana Notes and Records* 16:7–17.

Gray, Richard
1983   An Anthropologist on the Christian Kaguru. Review of *Colonial Evangelism*, by T. O. Beidelman, 1982. *Journal of African History* 24:405–07.

Grove, Richard
1989   Scottish Missionaries, Evangelical Discourses and the Origin of Conservation Thinking in Southern Africa 1820–1900. *Journal of Southern African Studies* 15:163–87.

Gusdorf, Georges
1980   Conditions and Limits of Autobiography. Translated by J. Olney. In *Autobiography: Essays Theoretical and Critical*, ed. J. Olney. Princeton: Princeton University Press.

Guy, Jeff
1980   Ecological Factors in the Rise of Shaka and the Zulu Kingdom. In *Economy and Society in Pre-Industrial South Africa*, ed. S. Marks and A. Atmore. London: Longman.
1983   *The Heretic: A Study of the Life of John William Colenso, 1814–1883*. Johannesburg: Ravan Press.

Haldon, Charles
  1912   Foreign Missions and English Literature. *The East and the West*
  10:246–61.

Halévy, Elie
  1924   *A History of the English People.* Vol. 1, *In 1815.* Translated by E. I. Watkin
  and D. A. Barker. New York: Harcourt, Brace.
  1971   *The Birth of Methodism in England.* Translated and edited by B. Semmel.
  Chicago: University of Chicago Press.

Haley, Bruce
  1978   *The Healthy Body and Victorian Culture.* Cambridge: Harvard University
  Press.

Halford, Samuel J.
  n.d.   *The Griquas of Griqualand: A Historical Narrative of the Griqua People. Their
  Rise, Progress, and Decline.* Cape Town: Juta.

Hall, Charles
  1805   *The Effects of Civilization on the People in European States.* London: for the
  author and sold by T. Ostell & C. Chappel. Reprinted, 1965; New York: A.M.
  Kelley.

Hall, Kenneth O.
  1975   Humanitarianism and Racial Subordination: John Mackenzie and the
  Transformation of Tswana Society. *The International Journal of African Historical Studies* 8:97–110.

Hall, Martin
  1987   *The Changing Past: Farmers, Kings and Traders in Southern Africa,
  200–1860.* Cape Town: David Philip.

Hall, Stuart
  1986   Gramsci's Relevance for the Study of Race and Ethnicity. *Journal of
  Communication Inquiries* 10:5–27.
  1988   The Toad in the Garden: Thatcherism among the Theorists. In *Marxism
  and the Interpretation of Culture,* ed. C. Nelson and L. Grossberg. Urbana and
  Chicago: University of Illinois Press.

Hallden, Erik
  1968   *The Culture Policy of the Basel Mission in the Cameroons, 1886–1905.*
  Lund: Berlingska Boktryckeriet.

Halpern, Jack
  1965   *South Africa's Hostages: Basutoland, Bechuanaland and Swaziland.* Harmondsworth: Penguin.

Hammond, Dorothy, and Alta Jablow
  1977   *The Myth of Africa.* New York: The Library of Social Science. Originally
  published as *The Africa that Never Was,* 1970.

Hammond, John L., and Barbara Hammond
  1928   *The Town Labourer, 1760–1832: The New Civilization.* New York: Longmans, Green.

Hanks, William F.
1989 Text and Textuality. *Annual Review of Anthropology* 18:95–127.

Hannerz, Ulf
1983 Tools of Identity and Imagination. In *Identity: Personal and Socio-Cultural: A Symposium*, ed. A. Jacobson-Widding. Atlantic Highlands, N.J.: Humanities Press.

Harlow, Barbara
1986 Introduction. In *The Colonial Harem*, by Malek Alloula. Minneapolis: University of Minnesota Press.

Harlow, Vincent T.
1936 The British Occupations, 1795–1806. In *The Cambridge History of the British Empire*, vol. 8, *South Africa, Rhodesia and the Protectorates*, ed. A. P. Newton and E. A. Benians. Cambridge: Cambridge University Press.

Harries, Patrick
1988 The Roots of Ethnicity: Discourse and the Politics of Language Construction in South-East Africa. *African Affairs* 87, no. 346:25–52.

Harris, William C.
1838 *Narrative of an Expedition into Southern Africa, during the Years 1836, and 1837.* . . . Bombay: The American Mission Press. Reprinted, 1967; New York: Arno Press.

Hattersley, Alan F.
1952 The Missionary in South African History. *Theoria* 4:86–88.

Hazlitt, William
1815 The Round Table (no. 19). *The Examiner* 402 (10 September):586–87.

Headlam, Cecil
1936 The Failure of Confederation, 1871–1881. In *The Cambridge History of the British Empire*, vol. 8, *South Africa, Rhodesia and the Protectorates*, ed. A. P. Newton and E. A. Benians. Cambridge: Cambridge University Press.

Hebdige, Dick
1979 *Subculture: The Meaning of Style*. New York: Methuen.
1988 *Hiding in the Light: On Images and Things*. London and New York: Routledge (Comedia Books).

Heidegger, Martin
1977 *The Question Concerning Technology, and Other Essays*. Translated by W. Lovitt. New York: Harper & Row.

Heise, David R.
1967 Prefatory Findings in the Sociology of Missions. *Journal for the Scientific Study of Religion* 6:49–58.

Hill, Christopher
1969 *Reformation to Industrial Revolution*. The Pelican Economic History of Britain, vol. 2, 1530–1780. Harmondsworth: Penguin.

1989   *A Tinker and a Poor Man: John Bunyan and His Church, 1628–1688*. New York: Alfred A. Knopf.

Hirschman, Albert O.
1977   *The Passions and the Interests: Political Arguments for Capitalism before its Triumph*. Princeton: Princeton University Press.

Hobsbawm, Eric J.
1957   Methodism and the Threat of Revolution in Britain. *History Today* 7:115–24.
1962   *The Age of Revolution, 1789–1848*. New York: New American Library (Mentor Book).
1964   *Labouring Men: Studies in the History of Labour*. London: Weidenfeld & Nicolson.

Hodgen, Margaret T.
1964   *Early Anthropology in the Sixteenth and Seventeenth Centuries*. Philadelphia: University of Pennsylvania Press.

Hodgson, Thomas L.
1977   *The Journals of the Rev. T. L. Hodgson: Missionary to the Seleka-Rolong and the Griquas, 1821–1831*. Edited by R. L. Cope. Johannesburg: Witwatersrand University Press for the African Studies Institute.

Hoernlé, Winifred
1923   The Expression of the Social Value of Water among the Naman of South-West Africa. *South African Journal of Science* 20:514–26. Reprinted 1985 in W. Hoernlé, *The Social Organization of the Nama and Other Essays*. Edited by P. Carstens. Johannesburg: Witwatersrand University Press.

Holbrook, Martin L.
1882   *Parturition without Pain: A Code of Directions for Escaping from the Primal Curse*. New York: Fowler & Wells.

Holmberg, Ake
1966   *African Tribes and European Agencies: Colonialism and Humanitarianism in British South and East Africa, 1870–1895*. Göteborg: Scandinavian University Books.

Holt, Thomas C.
1982   "An Empire over the Mind": Emancipation, Race, and Ideology in the British West Indies and the American South. In *Region, Race, and Reconstruction*, ed. J. M. Kousser and J. M. McPherson. New York: Oxford University Press.

Holub, Emil
1881   *Seven Years in South Africa: Travels, Researches, and Hunting Adventures, between the Diamond-Fields and the Zambesi (1872–79)*. 2 vols. Translated by E. E. Frewer. Boston: Houghton Mifflin.

Hook, Andrew, and Judith Hook
1974   Introduction. In *Shirley*, by Charlotte Brontë. Harmondsworth: Penguin.

Hope, Marjorie, and James Young
    1981   *The South African Churches in a Revolutionary Situation*. Maryknoll, N.Y.:
    Orbis Books.

Horton, Robin
    1967   African Traditional Thought and Western Science. *Africa* 37:50–71,
    155–87.
    1971   African Conversion. *Africa* 41:85–108.
    1975   On the Rationality of Conversion. *Africa* 45:219–35, 372–99.

Houghton, Walter E.
    1957   *The Victorian Frame of Mind, 1830–1870*. New Haven and London: Yale
    University Press for Wellesley College.

Hughes, Richard T., and C. Leonard Allen
    1988   *Illusions of Innocence: Protestant Primitivism in America, 1630–1875*. Chi-
    cago: University of Chicago Press.

Hume, David
    1854   *The Philosophical Works*. 4 vols. Edinburgh: Adam & Charles Black; Bos-
    ton: Little, Brown.

Hutchinson, Bertram
    1957   Some Social Consequences of Nineteenth Century Mission Activity
    among the South African Bantu. *Africa* 27:160–77.

Inskeep, Raymond R.
    1969   The Archeological Background. In *The Oxford History of South Africa*,
    vol. 1, ed. M. Wilson and L. M. Thompson. London: Oxford University
    Press.
    1979   *The Peopling of Southern Africa*. New York: Barnes & Noble.

Jameson, Fredric
    1981   *The Political Unconscious: Narrative as a Socially Symbolic Act*. Ithaca: Cor-
    nell University Press.
    1984   The Politics of Theory: Ideological Positions in the Postmodernism De-
    bate. *New German Critique* 33:53–65. Reprinted 1987 in *Interpretive Social
    Science: A Second Look*, ed. P. Rabinow and W. M. Sullivan. Berkeley and Los
    Angeles: University of California Press.

Jeal, Tim
    1973   *Livingstone*. New York: G. P. Putnam's Sons.

Johnston, Harry H.
    n.d.   *David Livingstone*. London: Charles H. Kelly.

Jones, Gareth Stedman
    1983   *Languages of Class: Studies in English Working Class History, 1832–1982*.
    Cambridge: Cambridge University Press.

Jordanova, Ludmilla J.
    1980   Natural Facts: A Historical Perspective on Science and Sexuality. In *Na-*

ture, Culture, and Gender, ed. C. P. MacCormack and M. Strathern. Cambridge: Cambridge University Press.

1981   The History of the Family. In *Women in Society: Interdisciplinary Essays*, The Cambridge Women's Studies Group. London: Virago Press.

Junod, Henri A.
1927   *The Life of a South African Tribe*. 2 vols. 2d ed. London: Macmillan.

Kapferer, Bruce
1988   The Anthropologist as Hero: Three Exponents of Post-Modernist Anthropology. *Critique of Anthropology* 8:77–104.

Kelly, John
1982   Mongol Conquest and Zulu Terror: An Analysis of Cultural Change. M.A. diss., Dept. of Anthropology, University of Chicago.

Kenrick, William
1753   *The Whole Duty of Woman. By a Lady. Written at the Desire of a Noble Lord*. London: Printed for R. Baldwin.

Keppler, Carl F.
1972   *The Literature of the Second Self*. Tucson: University of Arizona Press.

Kinsman, Margaret
1980   Notes on the Southern Tswana Social Formation. Paper read to the Africa Seminar, University of Cape Town, 1980.

1983   'Beasts of Burden': The Subordination of Southern Tswana Women, ca. 1800–1840. *Journal of Southern African Studies* 10:39–54.

Knorr, Klaus E.
1944   *British Colonial Theories, 1570–1850*. Toronto: University of Toronto Press.

Kolben, Peter
1731   *The Present State of the Cape of Good Hope*. 2 vols. Translated from the German by Mr. Medley. London: W. Innys.

Kraditor, Aileen S.
1972   American Radical Historians on their Heritage. *Past and Present* 56:136–53.

Kuper, Hilda
1946   *The Uniform of Colour*. Johannesburg: Witwatersrand University Press.

Laclau, Ernesto, and Chantal Mouffe
1985   *Hegemony and Socialist Strategy: Towards a Radical Democratic Politics*. Translated by W. Moore and P. Cammack. London: Verso.

Lacquer, Thomas
1986   Orgasm, Generation, and the Politics of Reproductive Biology. *Representations* 14:1–41.

Laitin, David D.
1986   *Hegemony and Culture: Politics and Religious Change among the Yoruba*. Chicago: University of Chicago Press.

Language, F. J.
  1943   Die Bogwêra van die Tlhaping. *Tydskrif vir Wetenskap en Kuns*
  4:110–34.

Larrain, Jorge
  1979   *The Concept of Ideology*. Athens: University of Georgia Press.
  1983   *Marxism and Ideology*. London: Macmillan.

Lategan, Felix V.
  1971   Fire-Arms, Historical. In *Standard Encyclopaedia of Southern Africa*, vol 4.
  Cape Town: Nasou Ltd.

Leach, Edmund R.
  1954   *Political Systems of Highland Burma*. London: Bell.

Leach, Graham
  1986   *South Africa: No Easy Path to Peace*. London: Routledge & Kegan Paul.

Lears, T. J. Jackson
  1985   The Concept of Cultural Hegemony: Problems and Possibilities. *American Historical Review* 9:567–93.

Lecky, William E.H.
  1892   *A History of England in the Eighteenth Century*, vol. 3. New York:
  D. Appleton.

Legassick, Martin C.
  1969a   The Griqua, the Sotho-Tswana and the Missionaries, 1700–1840:
  The Politics of a Frontier Zone. Ph.D. diss., University of California, Los
  Angeles.
  1969b   The Sotho-Tswana Peoples before 1800. In *African Societies in Southern Africa*, ed. L. M. Thompson. London: Heinemann Educational Books.
  1989   The Northern Frontier to c. 1840: The Rise and Decline of the Griqua
  People. In *The Shaping of South African Society, 1652–1840*, ed. R. Elphick
  and H. B. Giliomee. Middletown, Conn.: Wesleyan University Press.

Lepsius, Richard
  1855   *Standard Alphabet for Reducing Unwritten Languages and Foreign Graphic Systems to a Uniform Orthography in European Letters*. London: Seeleys. New
  version of the second, revised edition (1863), edited by J. A. Kemp, 1981;
  Amsterdam: Benjamins.

Lévi-Strauss, Claude
  1966   *The Savage Mind*. London: Weidenfeld & Nicolson.
  1976   *Structural Anthropology*, vol. 2. Translated by M. Layton. New York:
  Basic Books.

Lichtenstein, Henry [W. H. C.]
  1928–30   *Travels in Southern Africa in the Years 1803, 1804, 1805 and 1806*.
  2 vols. Translated from the 1812–15 edition by A. Plumptre. Cape Town:
  The Van Riebeeck Society.
  1973   *Foundation of the Cape* (1811) and *About the Bechuanas* (1807). Translated
  and edited by O. H. Spohr. Cape Town: A. A. Balkema.

Lichtheim, George
  1967   *The Concept of Ideology, and Other Essays.* New York: Random House.

Lichtman, Richard
  1975   Marx's Theory of Ideology. *Socialist Revolution* 5 (no. 23):45–77.

Linden, Ian
  1977   *Church and Revolution in Rwanda.* Manchester: Manchester University Press.

Lindley, Augustus F.
  1873   *Adamantia: The Truth about the South African Diamond Fields.* London: W.H. & L. Collingridge.

Livingstone, David
  1857   *Missionary Travels and Researches in South Africa. . . .* London: Murray.
  1960   *Livingstone's Private Journals, 1851–1853.* Edited by I. Schapera. Berkeley and Los Angeles: University of California Press.
  1974   *David Livingstone: South African Papers, 1849–1853.* Edited by I. Schapera. Cape Town: The Van Riebeeck Society.

Lloyd, Christopher
  1970   *Mr. Barrow of the Admiralty: A Life of Sir John Barrow, 1764–1848.* London: Collins.

London Missionary Society
  1838   *The Missionary Magazine and Chronicle* 16 (January).

Long, Edward
  1774   *The History of Jamaica; or, General Survey of the Ancient and Modern State of that Island. . . .* 3 vols. London: T. Lowndes.

Lorimer, Douglas A.
  1978   *Colour, Class and the Victorians.* New York: Holmes & Meier.

Lovejoy, Arthur O.
  1923   The Supposed Primitivism of Rousseau's Discourse on Inequality. *Modern Philology* 21:165–86.

Lovell, Reginald I.
  1934   *The Struggle for South Africa, 1875–1899: A Study in Economic Imperialism.* New York: Macmillan.

Lovett, Richard
  1899   *The History of the London Missionary Society, 1795–1895.* 2 vols. London: Henry Frowde.

Ludorf, Joseph D. M.
  1854   Extract of a Letter from the Rev. Joseph Ludorf, Thaba 'Nchu (17 August 1854). *Wesleyan Missionary Notices—relating to Foreign Missions*, 3d ser., no. 12 (December 1854):194.
  1863   Extract of a Letter from Moshaning (29 June 1863). *Wesleyan Missionary Notices—relating to Foreign Missions*, 3d ser., no. 120 (December 1863):203–07.

1864 Letter from Thaba 'Nchu (26 September 1864). *Wesleyan Missionary Notices—relating to Foreign Missions*, 3d ser., no. 130 (October 1864):160–63.

Lukes, Steven
1974 *Power: A Radical View*. London: Macmillan.

Lye, William F.
1969 The Distribution of the Sotho Peoples after the Difaqane. In *African Societies in Southern Africa*, ed. L. M. Thompson. London: Heinemann Educational Books.

Lye, William F., and Colin Murray
1980 *Transformations on the Highveld: The Tswana and Southern Sotho*. Cape Town and London: David Philip.

Mackenzie, John
1871 *Ten Years North of the Orange River: A Story of Everyday Life and Work among the South African Tribes*. Edinburgh: Edmonston & Douglas.
1883 *Day Dawn in Dark Places: A Story of Wanderings and Work in Bechwanaland*. London: Cassell. Reprinted, 1969; New York: Negro Universities Press.
1887 *Austral Africa: Losing It or Ruling It*. 2 vols. London: Sampson Low, Marston, Searle & Rivington.
1975 *Papers of John Mackenzie*. Edited by A. J. Dachs. Johannesburg: Witwatersrand University Press for the African Studies Institute.

Mackenzie, William D.
1902 *John Mackenzie: South African Missionary and Statesman*. New York: A. C. Armstrong & Son.

Macmillan, William M.
1927 *The Cape Colour Question: A Historical Survey*. London: Faber & Gwyer.
1929 *Bantu, Boer, and Briton: The Making of the South African Native Problem*. London: Faber & Gwyer.
1936a Political Development, 1822–1834. In *The Cambridge History of the British Empire*, vol. 8, *South Africa, Rhodesia and the Protectorates*, ed. A. P. Newton and E. A. Benians. Cambridge: Cambridge University Press.
1936b The Problem of the Coloured People, 1792–1842. In *The Cambridge History of the British Empire*, vol. 8, *South Africa, Rhodesia and the Protectorates*, ed. A. P. Newton and E. A. Benians. Cambridge: Cambridge University Press.
1936c The Frontier and the Kaffir Wars, 1792–1836. In *The Cambridge History of the British Empire*, vol. 8, *South Africa, Rhodesia and the Protectorates*, ed. A. P. Newton and E.A. Benians. Cambridge: Cambridge University Press.

Macquart, Louis C.H.
1799 *Dictionnaire de la Conservation de l'Homme ou d'Hygiène et d'Éducation Physique et Morale*. 2 vols. Paris: Bidault.

Maggs, Tim M.
1976a *Iron Age Communities of the Southern Highveld*. Occasional Publications of the Natal Museum, no.2. Pietermaritzburg: Council of the Natal Museum.

1976b   Iron Age Patterns and Sotho History on the Southern Highveld: South Africa. *World Archaeology* 7:318–32.

1980   The Iron Age South of the Zambezi. In *Southern African Prehistory and Paleoenvironments*, ed. R. G. Klein. Rotterdam and Boston: A. A. Balkema.

Majeke, Nosipho

1952   *The Role of the Missionaries in Conquest.* Johannesburg: Society of Young Africa.

Malinowski, Bronislaw

1954   *Magic, Science and Religion and Other Essays.* Garden City, N.Y.: Doubleday.

Mann, Michael

1986   *The Sources of Social Power.* Vol. 1, *A History of Power from the Beginning to A.D. 1760.* Cambridge: Cambridge University Press.

Mantoux, Paul

1928   *The Industrial Revolution in the Eighteenth Century: An Outline of the Beginnings of the Modern Factory System in England.* Translated by M. Vernon. London: Jonathan Cape.

Marais, Johannes S.

1944   *Maynier and the First Boer Republic.* Cape Town: Maskew Miller.

Markham, Clements R.

1895   *Major James Rennell and the Rise of Modern English Geography.* London: Cassell.

Marks, Shula

1972   Khoisan Resistance to the Dutch in the Seventeenth and Eighteenth Centuries. *Journal of African History* 13:55–80.

1978   Natal, the Zulu Royal Family and the Ideology of Segregation. *Journal of Southern African Studies* 4:172–94.

1989   Cultures of Subordination and Subversion. *Social History* 14:225–31.

Marrat, Jabez

1894   *Missionary Veterans in South Africa: Biographical Sketches of the Revs. B. Shaw, T. L. Hodgson, and J. Edwards.* London: Charles H. Kelly.

Marx, Karl

1955   Contribution to the Critique of Hegel's Philosophy of Right [Introduction]. In *On Religion*, by K. Marx and F. Engels. 2d imp. Moscow: Foreign Languages Publishing House.

1963   *The Eighteenth Brumaire of Louis Bonaparte.* New York: International Publishers.

1967   *Capital: A Critique of Political Economy.* 3 vols. Edited by F. Engels; translated from the third German edition by S. Moore and E. Aveling. New York: International Publishers.

Marx, Karl, and Friedrich Engels

1968   *Manifesto of the Communist Party.* In *Selected Works*, by K. Marx and F. Engels. New York: International Publishers.

1970   *The German Ideology*. Edited, with an Introduction by C. J. Arthur. New York: International Publishers.

Mason, Peter
1987   Notes on Cormorant Fishing: Europe and its Others. *Ibero-Amerikanisches Archiv*, n.f. 13:147–74.

Mathur, Dinesh C.
1971   *Naturalistic Philosophies of Experience*. St. Louis: Warren H. Green.

Matthews, Zachariah K.
1940   Marriage Customs among the Barolong. *Africa* 13:1–24.
1945   A Short History of the Tshidi Barolong. *Fort Hare Papers* 1:9–28.
n.d.   Fieldwork Reports. Botswana National Archives.

Mauss, Marcel
1966   *The Gift*. Translated by I. Cunnison. London: Cohen & West.

Maylam, Paul R.
1980   *Rhodes, the Tswana, and the British: Colonialism, Collaboration, and Conflict in the Bechuanaland Protectorate, 1885–1899*. Westport and London: Greenwood Press.

Mbiti, John S.
1969   *African Religion and Philosophy*. London: Heinemann.

McClintock, Anne
1987   "Azikwelwa" (We Will Not Ride): Politics and Value in Black South African Poetry. *Critical Inquiry* 13:597–623.

Mears, W. Gordon A.
n.d.   The Bechuana Mission or the Advance of Christianity into the Transvaal and the Orange Free State. *Methodist Missionaries*, no. 4. Rondebosch, Cape Town: The Methodist Missionary Department.
1955   *Methodist Torchbearers*. Rondebosch, Cape Town: The Methodist Missionary Department.
1970   *Wesleyan Baralong Mission in Trans-Orangia, 1821–1884*. Pamphlet reprint. Cape Town: Struik.

Mentzel, Otto F.
1921–25   *A Complete and Authentic Geographical and Topographical Description of the . . . African Cape of Good Hope. . . .* 2 parts. Translated from the 1785–87 original two-volume German edition by H.J. Mandelbrote. Cape Town: The Van Riebeeck Society.

Merriman, Nathaniel J.
1957   *The Cape Journals of Archdeacon N.J. Merriman, 1848–1855*. Edited by D. H. Varley and H. M. Matthew. Cape Town: The Van Riebeeck Society.

Mill, John S.
1929   *Principles of Political Economy with Some of their Applications to Social Philosophy*. New imp. of the 1909 edition, edited by W. J. Ashley. London and New York: Longmans, Green.

1982   *Collected Works of John Stuart Mill*. Vol. 6, *Essays on England, Ireland, and the Empire*. Edited by J. M. Robson. London: Routledge & Kegan Paul; Toronto: University of Toronto Press.

Milton, John

1667   *Paradise Lost: A Poem Written in Ten Books*. London: P. Parker.

Mitchell, W. J. Thomas

1986   *Iconology: Image, Text, Ideology*. Chicago: University of Chicago Press.

Miyoshi, Masao

1969   *The Divided Self: A Perspective on the Literature of the Victorians*. New York: New York University Press.

Mminele, S. P. P.

1983   The Berlin Lutheran Missionary Enterprise at Botŝabelo, 1865–1955. M.A. diss., University of the North (Sovenga).

Moffat, John S.

1886   *The Lives of Robert and Mary Moffat*. New York: A.C. Armstrong & Son.

n.d.   *Our Relations to the Native Races*. Published as part of a pamphlet with *Secular and Sacred: An Address*, by the Rev. S. J. Helm. Cape Town: n.p.

Moffat, Robert

1842   *Missionary Labours and Scenes in Southern Africa*. London: Snow. Reprinted, 1969; New York: Johnson Reprint Corporation.

Moffat, Robert U.

1921   *John Smith Moffat C.M.G., Missionary: A Memoir*. London: John Murray.

Moila, Moeahabo P.

1987   Toward an Anthropologically Informed Theology: The Kingdom of God Theology, Christian Presence, and Conflict in Pedi Society. Ph.D. diss., Lutheran School of Theology, Chicago.

Molema, Silas M.

1920   *The Bantu, Past and Present*. Edinburgh: Green.

1951   *Chief Moroka: His Life, His Times, His Country and His People*. Cape Town: Methodist Publishing House.

1966   *Montshiwa, 1815–1896: Barolong Chief and Patriot*. Cape Town: Struik.

n.d.   Research Notes and Personal Papers. Held by the Molema family and the University of the Witwatersrand, Johannesburg.

Monro, John

1837   Pretences of a Bechuana Woman to Immediate Communion with the Divine Being. *Evangelical Magazine and Missionary Chronicle*, n.s. 15:396–97.

Montgomery, James

1860   *Poems of James Montgomery*. London: Routledge, Warne & Routledge.

The Monthly Review

1790   Review of *Proceedings of the Association for Promoting the Discovery of the Interior Parts of Africa* 2:60–68.

Moodie, John W. D.
  1835   *Ten Years in South Africa*. 2 vols. London: R. Bentley.

Moore, Edward
  1744   *Fables for the Female Sex*. London: Printed by J. Lister for T. Davies.

Moore, Thomas
  1718   *Mangora, King of the Timbusians. Or, The Faithful Couple: A Tragedy*. London: W. Harvey.

Moorhouse, Geoffrey
  1973   *The Missionaries*. Philadelphia: J.B. Lippincott.

Mphahlele, Ezekiel
  1959   *Down Second Avenue*. London: Faber & Faber.
  1962   *The African Image*. London: Faber & Faber.

Mullaney, Steven
  1988   *The Place of the Stage: License, Play, and Power in Renaissance England*. Chicago: University of Chicago Press.

Muller, C. F. J.
  1969   The Period of the Great Trek, 1834–1854. In *Five Hundred Years: A History of South Africa*, ed. C. F. J. Muller. Pretoria: Academica.

Müller, F. Max
  1891   *The Science of Language*, vol. 1. New York: Charles Scribner's Sons.

Mumford, Lewis
  1934   *Technics and Civilization*. New York: Harcourt, Brace.

Murphree, Marshall W.
  1969   *Christianity and the Shona*. London: Athlone Press.

Murphy, Robert F., and Lionel Kasdan
  1959   The Structure of Parallel Cousin Marriage. *American Anthropologist* 61:17–29.
  1967   Agnation and Endogamy: Some Further Considerations. *Southwestern Journal of Anthropology* 23:1–14.

Murray, Colin
  1975   Sex, Smoking and the Shades. In *Religion and Social Change in Southern Africa*, ed. M. G. Whisson and M. West. Cape Town: David Philip.

Neill, Stephen
  1964   *A History of Christian Missions*. Harmondsworth: Penguin.
  1966   *Colonialism and Christian Missions*. London: Lutterworth Press.

Nerlich, Michael
  1987   *Ideology of Adventure: Studies in Modern Consciousness, 1100–1750*. 2 vols. Translated by R. Crowley. Minneapolis: University of Minnesota Press.

Nesbitt, Alexander, ed.
  n.d.   *Glass*. London: Printed for the Committee of Council on Education by Chapman & Hall.

Newton, Arthur P., and Ernest A. Benians, eds.
　1936　*The Cambridge History of the British Empire*, vol. 8, *South Africa, Rhodesia and the Protectorates*. Cambridge: Cambridge University Press.

Norris, Robert
　1968　*Memoirs of the Reign of Bossa Ahadee, King of Dahomey. . . .* Facsimile of the 1789 edition. London: Frank Cass.

Northcott, William C.
　1961　*Robert Moffat: Pioneer in Africa, 1817–1870.* London: Lutterworth Press.
　1969　Introduction. In *Missionary Labours and Scenes in Southern Africa*, by Robert Moffat. Reprint edition. New York and London: Johnson Reprint Corporation.
　1972　John Mackenzie and Southern Africa. *History Today* 22:656–63.

Obelkevich, James
　1976　*Religion and Rural Society: South Lindsey, 1825–1875.* Oxford: Clarendon Press.

Okihiro, Gary Y.
　1976　Hunters, Herders, Cultivators, and Traders: Interaction and Change in the Kgalagadi, Nineteenth Century. Ph.D. diss., University of California, Los Angeles.

Omer-Cooper, John D.
　1966　*The Zulu Aftermath: A Nineteenth Century Revolution in Bantu Africa.* London: Longmans.

Oosthuizen, P. J.
　1973　*Nkosi, Sikelel' iAfrika.* In *Standard Encyclopaedia of Southern Africa*, vol. 8, ed. D. J. Potgieter. Cape Town: Nasou.

Opie, Amelia A.
　1802　*Poems.* London: For T. N. Longman & O. Rees by Taylor & Wilks.
　1826　*The Black Man's Lament.* London: Harvey & Darton.

Ortner, Sherry B.
　1984　Theory in Anthropology since the Sixties. *Comparative Studies in Society and History* 26:126–66.

Park, Mungo
　1799　*Travels in the Interior Districts of Africa, Performed under the Direction and Patronage of the African Association, in the Years 1795, 1796, and 1797.* London: W. Bulmer.
　1816　*Travels in the Interior Districts of Africa: Performed in the Years 1795, 1796, and 1797. With an Account of a Subsequent Mission to that Country in 1805.* 2 vols. London: John Murray.
　1860　*Travels in the Interior of Africa.* Edinburgh: Adam & Charles Black.

Parsons, Neil Q.
　1983　*A New History of Southern Africa.* New York: Holmes & Meier.

Pauw, Berthold A.

    1960   *Religion in a Tswana Chiefdom*. London: Oxford University Press for the International African Institute.

Peel, John D. Y.

    1968   *Aladura: A Religious Movement among the Yoruba*. London: Oxford University Press for the International African Institute.

    1977   Conversion and Tradition in Two African Societies—Ijebu and Buganda. *Past and Present* 76:108–41.

Peires, Jeffrey B.

    1981   *The House of Phalo: A History of the Xhosa People in the Days of Their Independence*. Johannesburg: Ravan Press.

    1989   The British and the Cape, 1814–1834. In *The Shaping of South African Society, 1652–1840*, ed. R. Elphick and H.B. Giliomee. Middletown, Conn.: Wesleyan University Press.

Philip, John

    1828   *Researches in South Africa; Illustrating the Civil, Moral, and Religious Condition of the Native Tribes*. 2 vols. London: James Duncan. Reprinted, 1969; New York: Negro Universities Press.

Plaatje, Solomon T.

    n.d.   *Native Life in South Africa*. New York: The Crisis.

Post, Ken

    1978   *Arise Ye Starvelings: The Jamaican Labour Rebellion of 1838 and Its Aftermath*. The Hague: Martinus Nijhoff.

    1986   Can One Have an Historical Anthropology? Some Reactions to Taussig and Chevalier. *Social Analysis* 19:78–84.

Pratt, Mary L.

    1985   Scratches on the Face of the Country; or, What Mr. Barrow Saw in the Land of the Bushmen. *Critical Inquiry* 12:119–43.

Prins, Gwyn

    1980   *The Hidden Hippopotamus: Reappraisal in African History: The Early Colonial Experience in Western Zambia*. Cambridge and New York: Cambridge University Press.

Purkis, John A.

    1970   *A Preface to Wordsworth*. London: Longman.

Rabinow, Paul, and William M. Sullivan

    1987   The Interpretive Turn: A Second Look. In *Interpretive Social Science: A Second Look*, ed. P. Rabinow and W.M. Sullivan. Berkeley and Los Angeles: University of California Press.

Ranger, Terence O.

    1975   *Dance and Society in Eastern Africa, 1890–1970: The Beni Ngoma*. Berkeley and Los Angeles: University of California Press.

1986 Religious Movements and Politics in Sub-Saharan Africa. *African Studies Review* 29:1–69.

1987 Taking Hold of the Land: Holy Places and Pilgrimages in Twentieth-Century Zimbabwe. *Past and Present* 117:158–94.

1988 Missionaries, Migrants and the Manyika: The Invention of Ethnicity in Zimbabwe. In *The Creation of Tribalism in Southern Africa: Studies in the Political Economy of an Ideology*, ed. L. Vail. Berkeley and Los Angeles: University of California Press.

Ransford, Oliver

1978 *David Livingstone: The Dark Interior*. New York: St. Martin's Press.

Rau, William E.

1979 Chewa Religion and the Ngoni Conquest. In *Guardians of the Land: Essays on Central African Territorial Cults*, ed. M.J. Schoffeleers. Gwelo, Zimbabwe: Mambo Press.

Read, James

1850 Report on the Bechuana Mission. *Evangelical Magazine and Missionary Chronicle* 28:445–47.

Reed, John R.

1975 *Victorian Conventions*. Athens: Ohio University Press.

Reiter, Rayna [Rapp]

1975 Men and Women in the South of France: Public and Private Domains. In *Toward an Anthropology of Women*, ed. R. R. Reiter. New York: Monthly Review Press.

Rey, Charles F.

1988 *Monarch of all I Survey: Bechuanaland Diaries, 1929–1937*. Edited by N. Parsons and M. Crowder. Gaborone, Botswana: The Botswana Society; New York: Lilian Barber Press; London: James Currey.

Reyburn, H. A.

1933 The Missionary as Rain Maker. *The Critic* 1:146–53.

Reyneke, J. L.

1972 Towery by die Bakgatla-baKgafela. In *Etnografiese Studies in Suidelike Afrika*, ed. J. F. Eloff and R. D. Coertze. Pretoria: Van Schaik.

Richards, Audrey I.

1935 A Modern Movement of Witch-Finders. *Africa* 8:448–61..

[Roberts, John S.]

n.d. *The Life and Explorations of Dr. Livingstone. . . .* London and Newcastle on Tyne: Adam & Co.

Romano, Carlin

1983 But Was He A Marxist? Review of *Approaches to Gramsci*, ed. A. S. Sassoon, 1982. *Village Voice*, 29 March, 41.

Roscoe, William

1787–88 *The Wrongs of Africa, a Poem*. London: Printed for R. Faulder.

Ross, Andrew
  1986   *John Philip (1775–1851): Missions, Race and Politics in South Africa.*
  Aberdeen: Aberdeen University Press.

Ross, Robert
  1976   *Adam Kok's Griquas: A Study in the Development of Stratification in South Africa.* Cambridge and New York: Cambridge University Press.

Ross, William
  1858   Letter. *Evangelical Magazine and Missionary Chronicle* 36:56–57.

Rotberg, Robert I.
  1965   *Christian Missionaries and the Creation of Northern Rhodesia, 1880–1924.* Princeton: Princeton University Press.

Rowbotham, Sheila
  1976   *Hidden From History: Rediscovering Women in History from the 17th Century to the Present.* New York: Vintage Books.

Russell, Bertrand
  1961   *History of Western Philosophy and its Connection with Political and Social Circumstances from the Earliest Times to the Present Day.* London: George Allen & Unwin. Original edition, 1946.

Rybczynski, Witold
  1986   *Home: A Short History of an Idea.* New York: Viking Penguin.

Rzepka, Charles J.
  1986   *The Self as Mind: Vision and Identity in Wordsworth, Coleridge, and Keats.* Cambridge and London: Harvard University Press.

Sacks, Karen
  1975   Engels Revisited: Women, the Organization of Production and Private Property. In *Toward an Anthropology of Women*, ed. R. R. Reiter. New York: Monthly Review Press.

Sahlins, Marshall D.
  1976   *Culture and Practical Reason.* Chicago: University of Chicago Press.
  1981   *Historical Metaphors and Mythical Realities: Structure in the Early History of the Sandwich Islands Kingdom.* Ann Arbor: University of Michigan Press.
  n.d.   Social Science, Or the Tragic Western Sense of Human Imperfection. Manuscript.

Said, Edward W.
  1978   *Orientalism.* New York: Pantheon Books.

Samarin, William J.
  1984   The Linguistic World of Field Colonialism. *Language in Society* 13:435–53.

Sandilands, Alexander
  1953   *Introduction to Tswana.* Tiger Kloof: London Missionary Society.

Sansom, Basil
  1974   Traditional Rulers and their Realms. In *The Bantu-Speaking Peoples of*

Southern Africa, ed. W. D. Hammond-Tooke. London: Routledge & Kegan Paul.

Schapera, Isaac

1933   *The Early Cape Hottentots, Described in the Writings of Olfert Dapper (1668), Willem ten Rhyne (1686), and Johannes Gulielmus de Grevenbroek (1695)*. Original texts and translations by I. Schapera and B. Farrington. Cape Town: The Van Riebeeck Society.

1935   The Social Structure of the Tswana Ward. *Bantu Studies* 9:203–24.

1938   *A Handbook of Tswana Law and Custom*. London: Oxford University Press for the International African Institute. 2d ed., 1955.

1940   *Married Life in an African Tribe*. London: Faber & Faber.

1943   *Native Land Tenure in the Bechuanaland Protectorate*. Alice, South Africa: Lovedale Press.

1950   Kinship and Marriage among the Tswana. In *African Systems of Kinship and Marriage*, ed. A. R. Radcliffe-Brown and D. Forde. London: Oxford University Press for the International African Institute.

1952   *The Ethnic Composition of Tswana Tribes*. London: London School of Economics and Political Science.

1953   *The Tswana*. London: International African Institute. Rev. ed., 1976.

1957   Marriage of Near Kin among the Tswana. *Africa* 27:139–59.

1958   Christianity and the Tswana. *Journal of the Royal Anthropological Institute* 88:1–9.

1963   Agnatic Marriage in Tswana Royal Families. In *Studies in Kinship and Marriage*, ed. I. Schapera. London: Royal Anthropological Institute.

1965   *Praise-Poems of Tswana Chiefs*. London: Clarendon Press.

1970   *Tribal Innovators: Tswana Chiefs and Social Change, 1795–1940*. London: Athlone Press.

1971   *Rainmaking Rites of Tswana Tribes*. Leiden: Afrika-Studiecentrum.

Schnorrenberg, Barbara B., with Jean E. Hunter

1979   The Eighteenth-Century Englishwomen. In *The Women of England: From Anglo-Saxon Times to the Present*, ed. B. Kanner. Hamden, Conn.: Archon Books.

Seaver, George

1957   *David Livingstone: His Life and Letters*. New York: Harper Brothers; London: Lutterworth Press.

Setiloane, Gabriel M.

1976   *The Image of God among the Sotho-Tswana*. Rotterdam: A.A. Balkema.

Shapiro, Judith

1981   Ideologies of Catholic Missionary Practice in a Postcolonial Era. *Comparative Studies in Society and History* 23:130–49.

Shaw, Margaret

1974   Material Culture. In *The Bantu-speaking Peoples of Southern Africa*, ed. W. D. Hammond-Tooke. London: Routledge & Kegan Paul.

Shelley, Percy Bysshe
    1882   *The Poetical Works of Percy Bysshe Shelley*. 4 vols. Edited by H. B. Forman. Reissue, with the notes of Mary Wollstonecraft Shelley. London: Reeves & Turner.

Shillington, Kevin
    1985   *The Colonisation of the Southern Tswana, 1870–1900*. Johannesburg: Ravan Press.
    1987   Culture, not History. Review of *Body of Power, Spirit of Resistance*, by Jean Comaroff, 1985. *Journal of African History* 28:321–23.

Shineberg, Dorothy
    1971   Guns and Men in Melanesia. *Journal of Pacific History* 6:61–82.

Silitshena, Robson M.K.
    1979   Chiefly Authority and the Organization of Space in Botswana: Towards an Exploration of Nucleated Settlements among the Tswana. *Botswana Notes and Records* 11:55–67.
    1983   *Intra-rural Migration and Settlement Changes in Botswana*. Leiden: Afrika-Studiecentrum.

Sillery, Anthony
    1952   *The Bechuanaland Protectorate*. Cape Town and New York: Oxford University Press.
    1971   *John Mackenzie of Bechuanaland, 1835–1899: A Study in Humanitarian Imperialism*. Cape Town: A.A. Balkema.

Simon, Edith
    1966   *The Reformation*. New York: Time-Life Books.

Sinclair, Andrew
    1977   *The Savage: A History of Misunderstanding*. London: Weidenfeld & Nicolson.

Smith, Adam
    1937   *An Inquiry into the Nature and Causes of the Wealth of Nations*. Edited by E. Cannan. New York: The Modern Library. Original edition, 1776.
    1976   *The Theory of Moral Sentiments*. Indianapolis: Liberty Classics. Original edition, 1759.

Smith, Andrew
    1939   *The Diary of Dr. Andrew Smith, 1834–1836*. 2 vols. Edited by P. R. Kirby. Cape Town: The Van Riebeeck Society.

Smith, Edwin W.
    1925   *Robert Moffat, One of God's Gardeners*. London: Church Missionary Society.
    1950a   The Idea of God among South African Tribes. In *African Ideas of God: A Symposium*, ed. E. W. Smith. London: Edinburgh House Press.
    1950b   *The Blessed Missionaries*. London: Oxford University Press.

Smith, Sydney
   1808   Publications Respecting Indian Missions. *Edinburgh Review* 12 (April–July): 151–81.
   1809   Review of "Strictures on two Critiques in the Edinburgh Review, on the Subject of Methodism and Missions," by John Styles. *Edinburgh Review* 14 (April–July): 40–50.

Smith-Rosenberg, Carroll, and Charles Rosenberg
   1973   The Female Animal: Medical and Biological Views of Woman and her Role in Nineteenth-century America. *Journal of American History* 40:323–56.

Solomon, Edward S.
   1855   *Two Lectures on the Native Tribes of the Interior.* Cape Town: Saul Solomon.

South African Students' Organization [SASO]
   1978a   Resolution on Black Theology. Resolution no. 57 taken at General Students' Council, 1971. Reprinted in *African Perspectives on South Africa: A Collection of Speeches, Articles and Documents*, ed. H. W. van der Merwe, N. C. J. Charton, D. A. Kotzé, and A. Magnusson. Stanford: Hoover Institution Press; Cape Town: David Philip; London: Rex Collings.
   1978b   Policy Manifesto. Reprinted in *African Perspectives on South Africa: A Collection of Speeches, Articles and Documents*, ed. H. W. van der Merwe, N. C. J. Charton, D. A. Kotzé, and A. Magnusson. Stanford: Hoover Institution Press; Cape Town: David Philip; London: Rex Collings.
   1978c   *Understanding SASO.* Introductory paper to a "Formation School," Edendale, 1971. Reprinted in *African Perspectives on South Africa: A Collection of Speeches, Articles and Documents*, ed. H. W. van der Merwe, N. C. J. Charton, D. A. Kotzé, and A. Magnusson. Stanford: Hoover Institution Press; Cape Town: David Philip; London: Rex Collings.

Southey, Robert
   1809   Periodical Accounts, Relative to the Baptist Missionary Society, &c. *Quarterly Review* 1 (February–May):193–226.
   1815   *The Minor Poems of Robert Southey.* London: Longman, Hurst, Rees, Orme, & Brown.

Spain, David H.
   1984   Review of *Colonial Evangelism*, by T.O. Beidelman, 1982. *American Anthropologist* 86:205–07.

Spicker, Stuart F., ed.
   1970   *The Philosophy of the Body: Rejections of Cartesian Dualism.* Chicago: Quadrangle Books.

Spitulnik, Debra A.
   1986   Semantic Structuring and Infrastructuring: Nominal Class Struggle in ChiBemba. M.A. diss., Department of Anthropology, University of Chicago.

Spivak, Gayatri C.
1985   Three Women's Texts and a Critique of Imperialism. *Critical Inquiry*
12:243–61.

Stedman, John Gabriel
1988   *Narrative of a Five Years' Expedition against the Revolted Negroes of Surinam. . . .* Edited from the 1790 manuscript by R. and S. Price. Baltimore: The
Johns Hopkins University Press.

Steedman, Andrew
1835   *Wanderings and Adventures in the Interior of Southern Africa.* 2 vols. London: Longman.

Stevens, Richard P.
1967   *Lesotho, Botswana, and Swaziland: The Former High Commission Territories
in Southern Africa.* London: Pall Mall Press.

Stocking, George W.
1987   *Victorian Anthropology.* New York: The Free Press; London: Collier
Macmillan.

Stoler, Ann
1985   Perceptions of Protest: Defining the Dangerous in Colonial Sumatra.
American Ethnologist 12:642–58.

Stow, George W.
1905   *The Native Races of South Africa.* London: Swan Sonnenschein.

Strayer, Robert
1976   Mission History in Africa: New Perspectives on an Encounter. *The African Studies Review* 19:1–15.

Streak, Michael
1974   *The Afrikaner as Viewed by the English, 1795–1854.* Cape Town: Struik.

Street, Brian V.
1975   *The Savage in Literature: Representations of 'Primitive' Society in English
Fiction, 1858–1920.* London and Boston: Routledge & Kegan Paul.

Sundkler, Bengt G. M.
1961   *Bantu Prophets in South Africa.* 2d ed. London: Oxford University Press
for the International African Institute.

Surridge, Frank H.
1891   Paper on Matabeleland and Mashonaland (with discussion). *Journal of
the Royal Colonial Institute* 22:450–76.

Sypher, Wylie
1942   *Guinea's Captive Kings: British Anti-Slavery Literature of the XVIIIth Century.* Chapel Hill: University of North Carolina Press.

Tambiah, Stanley J.
1968   The Magical Power of Words. *Man*, n.s. 3:175–208.

Taussig, Michael
1984   Culture of Terror—Space of Death: Roger Casement's Putumayo Re-

port and the Explanation of Torture. *Comparative Studies in Society and History* 26:467–97.

1987   *Shamanism, Colonialism, and the Wild Man: A Study in Terror and Healing.* Chicago: University of Chicago Press.

Tawney, Richard H.

1926   *Religion and the Rise of Capitalism.* London: J. Murray.

1978   *History and Society: Essays.* Edited by J. M. Winter. London and Boston: Routledge & Paul.

Tennyson, Alfred Lord

1859   *Idylls of the King.* London: E. Moxon.

Theal, George M.

1891   *History of South Africa (1795–1834).* London: Swan Sonnenschein.

1893   *History of South Africa (1834–1854).* London: Swan Sonnenschein.

1900   *History of South Africa: The Republics and Native Territories From 1854 to 1872.* London: Swan Sonnenschein.

1902   *The Progress of South Africa in the Century.* The Nineteenth Century Series. London and Edinburgh: W. & R. Chambers Ltd.; Toronto and Philadelphia: Linscott.

1910   *The Yellow and Dark-Skinned People of Africa South of the Zambesi: A Description of the Bushmen, the Hottentots, and Particularly of the Bantu. . . .* London: Swan Sonnenschein.

Thomas, Antoine L.

1773   *Essay on the Character, Manners, and Genius of Women of Different Ages.* Translated from the French of M. Thomas by Mr. Russell. London: Printed for G. Robinson.

Thomas, Keith V.

1984   *Man and the Natural World: Changing Attitudes in England, 1500–1800.* Harmondsworth: Penguin.

Thomas, Thomas M.

1873   *Eleven Years in Central South Africa. . . .* London: John Snow.

Thomis, Malcolm I.

1974   *The Town Labourer and the Industrial Revolution.* London: B.T. Batsford.

Thompson, Edward P.

1963   *The Making of the English Working Class.* London: Gollancz.

1967   Time, Work-discipline and Industrial Capitalism. *Past and Present* 38:56–97.

1975   *Whigs and Hunters: The Origins of the Black Act.* London: Allen Lane.

1978   *The Poverty of Theory and Other Essays.* New York: Monthly Review Press.

Thompson, Leonard M.

1969a   Co-operation and Conflict: The High Veld. In *The Oxford History of South Africa*, vol. 1, ed. M. Wilson and L.M. Thompson. London: Oxford University Press.

1969b   Co-operation and Conflict: The Zulu Kingdom and Natal. In *The Ox-*

ford History of South Africa, vol. 1, ed. M. Wilson and L.M. Thompson. London: Oxford University Press.

1985   *The Political Mythology of Apartheid*. New Haven: Yale University Press.

Thorne, John
1867   Letter. *Wesleyan Missionary Notices—relating to Foreign Missions*, 3d ser., no. 168 (December 1867):184–85.

Thorpe, William A.
1935   *English Glass*. London: A. & C. Black.

Tilly, Louise A., and Joan W. Scott
1978   *Women, Work, and Family*. New York: Holt, Rinehart & Winston.

Tlou, Thomas
1970   Khama: Great Reformer and Innovator. *Botswana Notes and Records* 3:98–105.
1973   The Batawana of Northwestern Botswana and Christian Missionaries, 1877–1906. *Transafrican Journal of History* 3:112–28.
1974   The Nature of Batswana States: Towards a Theory of Batswana Traditional Government—the Batawana case. *Botswana Notes and Records* 6:57–75.

Toynbee, Arnold
1969   *Toynbee's Industrial Revolution*. Reprint of *Lectures on the Industrial Revolution in England, Popular Addresses, Notes and Other Fragments*, 1884. New York: Augustus M. Kelley.

Trapido, Stanley
1980   'The Friends of the Natives': Merchants, Peasants and the Political and Ideological Structure of Liberalism in the Cape, 1854–1910. In *Economy and Society in Pre-Industrial South Africa*, ed. S. Marks and A. Atmore. London: Longman.

Trexler, Richard C.
1984   We Think, They Act: Clerical Readings of Missionary Theatre in 16th Century Spain. In *Understanding Popular Culture*, ed. S. Kaplan. Berlin: Mouton.

Troeltsch, Ernst
1912   *Protestantism and Progress: The Significance of Protestantism for the Rise of the Modern World*. Translated by W. Montgomery. New York: G.P. Putnam's Sons.
1949   *The Social Teaching of the Christian Churches*. 2 vols. Translated by O. Wyon. London: George Allen & Unwin.

Turner, James
1980   Bunyan's Sense of Place. In *The Pilgrim's Progress: Critical and Historical Views*, ed. V. Newey. Liverpool: Liverpool University Press.

Turner, Terence S.
1980   The Social Skin. In *Not Work Alone*, ed. J. Cherfas and R. Lewin. London: Temple Smith.

Turner, Victor W.
    1967   *The Forest of Symbols: Aspects of Ndembu Ritual.* Ithaca and London: Cornell University Press.
Turrell, Robert V.
    1987   *Capital and Labour on the Kimberley Diamond Fields, 1871–1890.* Cambridge and New York: Cambridge University Press.
Vaughan, Robert
    1862   *English Nonconformity.* London: Jackson, Walford, & Hodder.
Verne, Jules
    1876   *The Adventures of Three Englishmen and Three Russians in South Africa.* Translated by E. E. Frewer. London: Sampson Low, Marston, Searle, & Rivington. Original edition, 1872.
Voloshinov, Valentin N.
    1973   *Marxism and the Philosophy of Language.* Translated by L. Matejka and I. R. Titunik. New York: Seminar Press.
Walker, Eric A.
    1928   *A History of South Africa.* London: Longmans, Green.
Walshe, Peter
    1971   *The Rise of African Nationalism in South Africa: The African National Congress, 1912–1952.* Berkeley and Los Angeles: University of California Press.
Walter, Eugene V.
    1969   *Terror and Resistance: A Study of Political Violence.* . . . New York: Oxford University Press.
Walzer, Michael
    1985   *Exodus and Revolution.* New York: Basic Books.
Ward, Thomas H., ed.
    1885   *Men of the Reign: A Biographical Dictionary of Eminent Persons of British and Colonial Birth who have Died During the Reign of Queen Victoria.* London and New York: George Routledge & Sons.
Warner, Wellman J.
    1930   *The Wesleyan Movement in the Industrial Revolution.* London and New York: Longmans, Green.
Warren, Max A. C.
    1965   *The Missionary Movement from Britain in Modern History.* London: SCM Press.
Warton, Joseph
    1811   *The Poetical Works of Joseph Warton.* Collated by T. Park. In *The Works of the British Poets*, vol. 25, ed. T. Park. London: J. Sharpe.
Watts, Michael R.
    1978   *The Dissenters.* Vol. 1, *From the Reformation to the French Revolution.* Oxford: Clarendon Press.

Weber, Max
1958   *The Protestant Ethic and the Spirit of Capitalism*. Translated by T. Parsons. New York: Charles Scribner.

Welbourn, Frederick B.
1961   *East African Rebels: A Study of Some Independent Churches*. London: SCM Press.
1965   *East African Christian*. London: Oxford University Press.

Wesley, John
1835   *The Works of Rev. John Wesley*. 7 vols. New York: Eaton & Mains.

Wesleyan Methodist Missionary Society
1887   *Affairs of Bechuanaland: A Letter to the Right Honourable The Secretary of State for the Colonies, from the Wesleyan Missionary Committee Concerning the Complaints of the Chief Montsioa, of Mafeking*. Pamphlet. London: Wesleyan Mission House.

West, Cornel
1982   *Prophesy Deliverance!: An Afro-American Revolutionary Christianity*. Philadelphia: Westminster Press.

Westphal, E. O. J.
1963   The Linguistic Prehistory of South Africa. *Africa* 33: 237–65.

Wheeler, Anna, and William Thompson
1825   *An Appeal of One-Half of the Human Race, Women, Against the Pretensions of the Other Half, Men, to Retain Them in Political and Thence in Civil and Domestic Slavery*. London: Longman, Hurst, Rees, Orme, Brown & Green.

White, Charles
1799   *An Account of the Regular Gradation in Man, and in Different Animals and Vegetables; and From the Former to the Latter. . . .* London: Printed for C. Dilly.

Whitefield, George
1772   *The Works of the Reverend George Whitefield, M.A.*, vol. 5. London: Printed for Edward & Charles Dilly.

Whiteside, J.
1906   *History of the Wesleyan Methodist Church of South Africa*. London: Elliot Stock; Cape Town: Juta.

Wickham, W. A.
1912   Robinson Crusoe and Christian Missions. *The East and the West: A Quarterly Review for the Study of Missionary Problems* 10:168–87.

Wilberforce, William
1807   *A Letter on the Abolition of the Slave Trade; Addressed to the Freeholders and Other Inhabitants of Yorkshire*. London: Printed for T. Cadell, W. Davies, & J. Hatchard.

Willan, Brian
1984   *Sol Plaatje: South African Nationalist, 1876–1932*. Berkeley and Los Angeles: University of California Press.

Williams, Eric E.
1961   *Capitalism and Slavery*. New York: Russell & Russell.

Williams, Raymond
1973   *The Country and the City*. London: Chatto & Windus.
1976   *Keywords: A Vocabulary of Culture and Society*. London: Oxford University Press.
1977   *Marxism and Literature*. London: Oxford University Press.

Willoughby, William C.
[1899]   *Native Life on the Transvaal Border*. London: Simpkin, Marshall, Hamilton, Kent.
1912   *Tiger Kloof: The London Missionary Society's Native Institution in South Africa*. London: London Missionary Society.
1923   *Race Problems in the New Africa*. Oxford: Clarendon Press.
1928   *The Soul of the Bantu: A Sympathetic Study of the Magico-religious Practices and Beliefs of the Bantu Tribes of Africa*. New York: Doubleday.
1932   *Nature-Worship and Taboo: Further Studies in "The Soul of the Bantu"*. Hartford: The Hartford Seminary Press.

Wilson, Monica
1952   *Keiskammahoek Rural Survey*. Vol. 3, *Social Structure*. Pietermaritzburg: Shuter & Shooter.
1959   *Divine Kings and the 'Breath of Men'*. Cambridge: Cambridge University Press.
1969a   The Sotho, Venda, and Tsonga. In *The Oxford History of South Africa*, vol. 1, ed. M. Wilson and L. M. Thompson. London: Oxford University Press.
1969b   Co-operation and Conflict: The Eastern Cape Frontier. In *The Oxford History of South Africa*, vol. 1, ed. M. Wilson and L. M. Thompson. London: Oxford University Press.
1976   *Missionaries: Conquerors or Servants of God?* Address given at the opening of the South African Missionary Museum. Lovedale: South African Missionary Museum.

Wilson, Monica, and Leonard M. Thompson
1969   Preface. In *The Oxford History of South Africa*, vol. 1, ed. M. Wilson and L. M. Thompson. London: Oxford University Press.

Winnifrith, Tom
1973   *The Brontës and their Background: Romance and Reality*. London: Macmillan.

Wollstonecraft, Mary
1967   *A Vindication of the Rights of Woman; With Strictures on Political and Moral Subjects*. Edited by C. W. Hagelman, Jr. New York: W.W. Norton & Company. Original edition, 1792.

Wonderly, William L., and Eugene A. Nida
1963   Linguistics and Christian Missions. *Anthropological Linguistics* 5:104–44.

Wood, Ellen M.
1981   The Separation of the Economic and the Political in Capitalism. *New Left Review* 127:66–95.

Wordsworth, William
1948   *A Guide through the District of the Lakes in the North of England, with a Description of the Scenery, &c. for the Use of Tourists and Residents.* Facsimile of the 5th ed., 1835. Malvern: The Tantivy Press.
1954   *The Poetical Works of William Wordsworth.* 5 vols. 2d ed. Edited by E. de Selincourt and H. Darbishire. London: Oxford University Press.

Worger, William H.
1987   *South Africa's City of Diamonds: Mine Workers and Monopoly Capitalism in Kimberley, 1867–1895.* New Haven and London: Yale University Press.

Worsley, Peter M.
1968   *The Trumpet Shall Sound: A Study of 'Cargo' Cults in Melanesia.* New York: Schocken Books.

Wright, Marcia
1971   *German Missions in Tanganyika, 1891–1941: Lutherans and Moravians in the Southern Highlands.* Oxford: Clarendon Press.

Wrong, Dennis H.
1979   *Power: Its Forms, Bases and Uses.* Oxford: Basil Blackwell; New York: Harper & Row.

Yates, Barbara A.
1980   The Origins of Language Policy in Zaire. *Journal of Modern African Studies* 18:257–79.

Zulu, Lawrence
1972   Nineteenth Century Missionaries: Their Significance for Black South Africa. In *Essays on Black Theology*, ed. M. Motlhabi. Johannesburg: University Christian Movement.

INDEX

Alienation, and salvation, 67
Alken, Henry, 73–74
Alliances, Tswana
  between chiefdoms, 164–65,
  and matrilaterality, 134–37, 140
  with missionaries, 184
Alloula, Malek, 188
Althusser, Louis, 35
Altick, Richard D., 63
Alverson, Hayt, 141, 226
Ancestors (Tswana), 153–155,
  338 n.30
  and chiefship, 155
  in male agnatic politics, 154
  misunderstood by missionaries, 154
  royal, 158
Anderson, Benedict, 52, 63, 76, 87,
  322 n.37
Androcentrism
  biologization of, 105–8
  in bourgeois ideology and practice,
  61, 69
  in Tswana ideology and practice,
  137, 240
  see also Eurocentrism; Gender
Anglican Church, 44, 47, 124, 258
  and evangelicals, 79
Anglo-Boer War, First (1880–1901),
  296, 351 n.127
Anstey, Roger, 120
Anthropology, 23
  and colonial encounters, xiii, 9–11
  as a critical project, 11, 16
  critiques of, 10, 15–16
  historical, 6, 10, 30, 37, 38–39
  and historiography, 9–10, 17
  and postmodernism, 15–16,
  316 n.12 (*see also* Postmodernism)
Antislavery ideology, 45, 79–80, 92–
  93, 118–25
  and Africa, 120–25
  centrality to bourgeois hegemony,
  120
  and evangelical Protestantism, 118–
  22
  and free trade, 80, 119–21

and imperialism, 116, 125
  Quaker roots of, 119
  see also Noble savage
Apartheid, 28
  antecedents (pre-20th century), 12,
  117, 223, 307
  political mythology of, 40
Arbuthnot, John, 71
Archbell, James, 85, 211, 245, 260
Architecture, 12
  and domination, 206
  of mission stations, 33
  precolonial Tswana, and female
  bodily symbolism, 133
  schoolroom as model for chapel, 233
  and utilitarianism, 65
  see also Discipline; Gender; Space
Arnold, Matthew, 60, 320 n.20
Asad, Talal, 86
Asthon, William, 55, 56, 75, 276
Austen, Ralph, 88, 118, 122
Autobiography, 172
Ayala, Flavia, 107
Ayandele, Emmanuel A., 7, 259

Babcock, Barbara, 187
Bain, Andrew G., 127, 133
Banks, G. Linnaeus, 320 n.21
Banks, Sir Joseph, 324 n.8
Bantustans. *see* "Ethnic Homelands"
Baptism, 238–39
  contrasted with circumcision and
  initiation, 259
Baptists, 51–52
Barbin, Herculine, 106
Barker, Francis, 62, 63
Barkly, Sir Henry, 282, 347 n.84
Barnes, John A., 127
Barolong boo Rapulana (Rapulana),
  40, 165
Barolong boo Ratlou (Ratlou), 40, 165
Barolong boo Ratshidi (Tshidi), 1, 36,
  40,165, 264, 279–80, 352
Barolong boo Seleka (Seleka), 40, 165,
  181, 209, 236, 280